THE PHONOLOGY OF THE WORLD'S LANGUAGES

Series Editor: Jacques Durand, University of Salford

The Lexical Phonology of Slovak

THE PHONOLOGY OF THE WORLD'S LANGUAGES

The phonology of most languages has until now been available only in a fragmented way, through unpublished theses, or articles scattered in more or less accessible journals. Each volume in this series will offer an extensive treatment of the phonology of one language within a modern theoretical perspective, and will provide comprehensive references to recent and more classical studies of the language. The following will normally be included: an introduction situating the language geographically and typologically, an overview of the theoretical assumptions made by the author, a description of the segmental system and of the rules or parameters characterizing the language, an outline of syllable structure and domains above the syllable, a discussion of lexical and postlexical phonology, an account of stress and prominence, and, if space allows, some overview of the intonational structure of the language.

While it is assumed that every volume will be cast in a modern non-linear framework, there will be scope for a diversity of approach which reflects variations between languages and in the methodologies and theoretical preoccupations of the individual authors.

Forthcoming titles:

The Phonology of Dutch
Geert Booij

The Phonology and Morphology of Tamil
Prathima Christdas

The Phonology of Danish
Hans Basbøll

The Phonology of German
Richard Wiese

THE
LEXICAL
PHONOLOGY
OF
SLOVAK

—

Jerzy Rubach

CLARENDON PRESS · OXFORD
1993

Oxford University Press, Walton Street, Oxford OX2 6DP

Oxford New York Toronto
Delhi Bombay Calcutta Madras Karachi
Kuala Lumpur Singapore Hong Kong Tokyo
Nairobi Dar es Salaam Cape Town
Melbourne Auckland Madrid

and associated companies in
Berlin Ibadan

Oxford is a trade mark of Oxford University Press

Published in the United States
by Oxford University Press Inc., New York

British Library Cataloguing in Publication Data
Data available

Library of Congress Cataloging in Publication Data
The lexical phonology of Slovak / Jerzy Rubach.
(The Phonology of the world's languages)
Includes bibliographical references and index.
1. Slovak language—Phonology. 2. Lexical phonology. 3. Slovak
language—Grammar, Generative. I. Title. II. Series.
PG5240.R8 1993 491.8'715—dc20 92–38746
ISBN 0–19–824000–7

Typeset by Graphicraft Typesetters Ltd, Hong Kong
Printed in Great Britain
on acid-free paper by
Biddles Ltd., Guildford and King's Lynn

To my son, Paweł

EDITORIAL PREFACE

Jerzy Rubach's *The Lexical Phonology of Slovak* will be the first thorough analysis of Slovak to become available to the community of linguists and would be a welcome addition to any series on modern phonology. It is therefore particularly fitting that it should appear as the first volume in this series, *The Phonology of the World's Languages*.

The aim of the series is to offer extensive treatments of the world's languages within a modern theoretical perspective. The reader may recall that the heyday of structuralist and of early generative phonology saw the publication of a large number of monographs on the phonology of individual languages. Thus in the late sixties, under the influence of the work of Morris Halle and Noam Chomsky—embodied in their monumental *The Sound Pattern of English*—many authors offered generative analyses of familiar and less familiar languages. One could cite, for example, Harris on Spanish, Kuroda on Yawelmani, McCawley on Japanese, and Schane on French. In recent years phonologists seem to have been less keen to provide comprehensive overviews of individual languages, except in pedagogical publications. Part of the reason has been rapid change in methods of phonological modelling and a preference for work testing delimited aspects of theory (for example, feature structure, vowel harmony, syllable structure, or stress) on individual languages. As a result, the information that we have about many languages is rather old, or is scattered in journals which are not always easily accessible. It would seem particularly useful to have, once again, thorough descriptions of some of the world's languages which make use of the concepts shared by phonologists working within modern theoretical frameworks.

The series can be characterized as 'generative' and 'non-linear' in approach. It is intended that authors of books in the series will espouse the ideal of explicitness which lies at the root of the generative tradition, and that they will also make use of some of the concepts of the non-linear tradition, in particular in the analysis of syllable structure and stress systems, and in extending the scope of distinctive features beyond individual segments. Volumes in the series will not, however, be theoretically monolithic. Diversity will be encouraged, and authors will undoubtedly pursue slightly different orientations within the guidelines set for them. This first monograph, for example, makes extensive use of the Lexical Phonology model, which organizes phonological derivations into morphologically based strata. Nevertheless, the reader will find that *The Lexical Phonology of Slovak* offers a full account of segmental structure and syllable structure, and is not solely concerned with the interaction between phonology and morphology. Within a few years, the volumes in this series will be indispensable reference works for the general linguist and the language specialist alike.

JACQUES DURAND

December 1992

PREFACE

This book is a study of Slovak phonology within a framework of the recent theories offered by the generative perspective on language. In particular, it is a study carried out in the paradigm of Lexical Phonology, which has been enriched by insights coming from a non-linear outlook on phonological representation.

Part I provides background information about the theoretical framework (Chapter 1), segmental structure (Chapter 2), and morphology viewed from the perspective of the needs of phonological analysis (Chapter 3). Part II, which forms the core of this book, is a study of cyclic rules as well as of the relations which hold inside and between various levels of phonological representation (Chapters 4–7). Part III (Chapters 8 and 9) is devoted to investigating the properties of non-cyclic (postcyclic and postlexical) rules.

This is the first book-length description of Slovak in generative terms. The literature published hitherto includes only a few articles and shorter studies, which do not go beyond discussing some selected problems of Slovak phonology. With the exception of one article (Kenstowicz and Rubach 1987), they are all couched in the outdated framework of the classic generative phonology of the 1960s and the early 1970s. Against this background the literature on Polish (not to mention English) looks enormous. It includes at least thirteen books and doctoral dissertations as well as a hundred or so articles and monographic studies.

My enchantment with Slovak in the past few years would not have resulted in this book if I had not been able to spend a research period of twelve months at the University of Bielefeld in the Federal Republic of Germany. My research there was made possible by a fellowship offered to me by the Alexander von Humboldt Foundation, whose assistance and support I hereby gratefully acknowledge. I would like to thank the Department of Linguistics at the University of Iowa where the final stages in the preparation of the manuscript were carried out. I also thank the Department of Linguistics at the University of Washington where I worked on the revisions suggested by the reviewers. I am indebted to my Slovak consultants, whose help and encouragement have brought my work to fruition: L'ubomir D'urovič, Peter Durčo, Marek Miňo, as well as many others, some of whom I only know from correspondence: Ábel Král', Martin Votruba, Emília Nemcová, Slavomír Ondrejovič, Štefan Baláž, Ignác Čapek, Louise Hammer, and Jozef Lieskovský. I thank the many respondents who answered my questionnaires distributed to them by my Slovak colleagues.

This book has profited from the discussion and advice of Geert E. Booij, Greg Dogil, Jacques Durand, Dafydd Gibbon, Michael Kenstowicz, Paul Kiparsky, Catherine O. Ringen, and Andrew Spencer. Needless to say, the responsibility for the content of this book and whatever errors it may contain is solely mine.

JERZY RUBACH

CONTENTS

7. SYLLABLE STRUCTURE 211

III. NON-CYCLIC RULES

8. POSTCYCLIC RULES 255

9. POSTLEXICAL RULES 277

10. CONCLUSION 289

LIST OF TABLES

ABBREVIATIONS AND SYMBOLS

acc.	accusative	R	root node
Adj.	adjective	sg.	singular
Adv.	adverb	SL	supralaryngeal node
C	consonant	*SPE*	*The Sound Pattern of English*
C_0	zero or more consonants		by N. Chomsky and M. Halle
COR	coronal node		(1968)
dat.	dative	SSA	Syllable Structure Algorithm
DI	derived imperfective	SSC	Strict Cyclicity Constraint
dimin.	diminutive	SSG	Sonority Sequencing
DOR	dorsal node		Generalization
EM	extrametrical	TB	tongue-body node
fem.	feminine	UR	underlying representation
gen.	genitive	V	verb *or* vowel
ger.	gerund	voc.	vocative
imper.	imperative	WFR	word-formation rule
indic.	indicative	α	variable ranging over + and −
inf.	infinitive		(showing agreement in these
instr.	instrumental		values)
IPA	International Phonetic	μ	mora
	Alphabet	σ	syllable node (also N″)
L	laryngeal node *or* liquid	∅	zero
loc.	locative	~	is in free variation with
m	*mot* (i.e. a phonological word)	#	word boundary
masc.	masculine	*	unsyllabified or extrasyllabic
N	noun *or* syllable nucleus		(e.g. *C = extrasyllabic
N′	rhyme node		consonant, *L = extrasyllabic
N″	syllable node (also σ)		liquid, *r = extrasyllabic r); *also*
nom.	nominative		used to signal an incorrect or
OCP	Obligatory Contour Principle		non-existent form
part.	participle	// //	underlying representation
perf.	perfective	/ /	intermediate representation
pl.	plural	[ ]	phonetic representation *or*
PL	place node		distinctive feature
pres.	present		

a	IPA [a]	e	lax mid front unrounded vowel
á	long a (IPA [aː])		(IPA [ɛ])
ä	front low vowel (IPA [æ])	é	long e (IPA [ɛː])
ǽ	long ä (IPA [æː])	γ	voiced velar fricative
c	alveolar voiceless affricate	ɦ	voiced laryngeal
č	postalveolar voiceless affricate	i	IPA [i]
ḍ	non-anterior voiced coronal stop	í	long i (IPA [iː])
d′	prepalatal voiced stop	i̯	front glide

í   long l
l′ prepalatal lateral
n′ prepalatal nasal
o   lax mid back rounded vowel
    (IPA [ɔ])
ó   long o (IPA [ɔː])
ŕ   long r
š   postalveolar voiceless fricative
ṭ   non-anterior voiceless coronal stop
t′ prepalatal voiceless stop
u   IPA [u]

ú   long u (IPA [uː])
ü   front rounded vowel (IPA [y])
ų   back glide
ɤ   mid back unrounded vowel
v   labiodental voiced fricative
ʋ   labiodental approximant (sonorant)
ž   postalveolar voiced fricative
ʒ   alveolar voiced affricate
ǯ   postalveolar voiced affricate
′   palatalization

PART I

Background

1

THEORETICAL BACKGROUND

1.1. AIMS OF THE BOOK

The aim of this book is twofold: descriptive and theoretical. On the one hand, we intend to provide a fairly complete description of Slovak phonology in generative terms. On the other hand, we would like to investigate how the recent developments in phonological theory can contribute to such a description. Thus, on the theoretical side Slovak is used as a testing ground for confirming or disconfirming the validity of various concepts in the most recent theories, such as Lexical Phonology, Three-Dimensional Phonology, Prosodic Phonology, and Autosegmental Phonology. It is shown how these theories can be combined together in a coherent analysis of a large body of data.

Lexical Phonology is a theory about the organization of grammar. It investigates primarily how the problem of the interaction of morphology and phonology is reflected in the organization of phonological rules. It assigns more structure to phonology than has traditionally been assumed. Phonological rules are of different types: cyclic, postcyclic, and postlexical, with each type exhibiting characteristic properties of its own.

Three-dimensional, prosodic, and autosegmental phonologies, which can be grouped together under the term 'non-linear phonology', are theories about the structure of phonological representation. Thus, they are complementary to Lexical Phonology. These theories illuminate the phonology of Slovak by providing a framework in which allegedly unrelated segmental representations, such as those for long vowels and diphthongs, can be shown to exhibit a common denominator at higher levels of phonological structure. Conversely, problems such as the existence of vowels which play no role in prosodic representations can also be clarified.

As a description of Slovak this book is intended to serve as a source of reference for future studies that, it is hoped, will arise out of the interest that this book may generate. Therefore, much emphasis has been laid on providing extensive data. On the one hand, they have been drawn from the standard grammars, which, with the exception of some three short books, are all written in Slovak and hence are largely inaccessible to researchers not familiar with this language. On the other hand, the data come from my work with Slovak consultants, which has clarified a number of gaps or even contradictions in the standard grammars.

1.2. LEXICAL PHONOLOGY

Lexical Phonology as a theory dates back formally to 1982, the year of the publication of Kiparsky's 'From Cyclic to Lexical Phonology', although its roots go back much earlier. On the one hand, it owes much to *The Sound Pattern of English* (Chomsky and Halle 1968, *SPE* hereafter). It was in *SPE* that generative phonology as a theory was fully spelled out and that the notion of the phonological cycle first introduced by Chomsky, Halle, and Lukoff (1956) came to fruition. On the other hand, Lexical Phonology grew out of opposition to *SPE*, and in particular to the lack of constraints on the abstractness of underlying representations. Of special importance here are the influential articles by Kiparsky (1968, 1973), Mascaró's (1976) dissertation, and Halle's (1978) contribution. The concept of derived environment that Halle (1978) called the most significant phonological discovery of the 1970s comes from Kiparsky's work. Mascaró (1976) combined the concept of the cycle with the concept of derived environment rules. Halle (1978), revising Mascaró's ideas, formulated the Strict Cyclicity Constraint, which in its spirit, though not in its wording, has survived till today. The incentive for Lexical Phonology came also from morphological studies, in particular from Chomsky's (1970) claim that word-formation takes place in the lexicon and Siegel's (1974) assertion that morphological derivation is stratal, that is, different word-formation rules apply at different levels.

Lexical Phonology is a theory of the organization of the phonological component of the grammar, which is viewed as structured in more complex ways than was assumed in *SPE*. Recognition is given to the fact that different phonological rules may have a different status. Some rules, it is claimed, apply in the lexicon and hence are called lexical rules. They are opposed to postlexical rules which apply after syntax. Chomsky's (1970) Lexicalist Hypothesis lies at the heart of this division of rules. Lexical Phonology is an extreme embodiment of Chomsky's claim. It is extreme since, first, not only derivational but also inflectional morphology is assumed to be carried out in the lexicon; and, second, phonological rules (more exactly: lexical rules) also apply in the lexicon (Pesetsky 1979). This view implies that the relation between morphology and phonology must be much closer than hitherto assumed. How close this relation is is a matter of debate. The classic Lexical Phonology model of Kiparsky (1982) assumes that word-formation rules (WFRs hereafter) are interspersed with lexical rules in the sense that lexical rules as a class reapply after every step in a word-forming morphological derivation. In the work immediately preceding the birth of Lexical Phonology, such as Rubach (1981, 1984), this link is regarded as indirect: WFRs apply as traditionally believed, that is, before phonology. The link between morphology and phonology is provided by the Bracketing Convention, which assigns brackets [ ] at morpheme boundaries. Phonological derivation is then organized according to the order in which the brackets have been assigned: from the innermost to the outermost constituents. Such a view predicts that the order of morphological operations need not in all cases correspond to the order of phonological operations that are called cycles. For example, the Bracketing Convention leaves the option of either first assigning the brackets to the root and all the suffixes and only then to the stem plus prefixes, or the other way round. Given this view it is possible that WFRs may derive prefix-plus-root structures before deriving root-plus-suffix structures and yet phonological rules may apply in the root-plus-suffix cycles before applying in the prefix-plus-stem cycles. Polish requires precisely this type of relation between morphology and phonology (cf. Rubach 1981, 1984). The special status of prefixes becomes clear when we realize that in most cases they derive historically from prepositions, hence they are, as it were, word-level affixes from the phonological (but not morphological) point of view.

Within the framework of Lexical Phonology, Halle (1987) and Halle and Vergnaud (1987) have recently advocated that the traditional relation between morphology and phonology should be adhered to. The former wholly precedes the latter but some affixes are marked as cyclic and some as non-cyclic. The order in which morphological operations are carried out is therefore not essential, as non-cyclic affixes will not be processed in the cyclic phonological component anyway. In this way one can counter the objections raised by critics of Lexical Phonology such as Sproat (1985), Aronoff and Sridhar (1987), and others, who point to certain paradoxes concerning the order of affixation in morphology. However, many of these paradoxes (some of which were noted originally in Pesetsky 1979) yield to alternative interpretations which make use of the non-isomorphic nature of concepts such as the morphological word versus the phonological word (cf., for example, Booij and Rubach 1984, more recently Booij and Lieber 1989). The essence of this proposal is that some affixes may have the status of phonological words and consequently they may form separate domains for the application of cyclic rules.

We do not wish to engage in the debate about the exact nature of the relationship between morphology and phonology. Let us note, however, that if all WFRs can be assumed to apply in the cyclic stratum/component (as is the case in Slovak and Polish), then morphological paradoxes referring to the order of affixation do not arise. To put it differently: if there is only one stratum/component in which word-formation is carried out, then problems such as 'a Class 2 (stratum 2) affix precedes a Class 1 (stratum 1) affix' are not encountered.[1] It seems possible, therefore, to maintain the

---

[1] That affix-ordering in English cannot be solved by postulating two or more strata in which word-formation takes place has been convincingly demonstrated by Fabb (1988).

classic assumption that WFRs and cyclic rules are interspersed and apply in tandem (Pesetsky 1979, Kiparsky 1982). In what follows we shall revise this model by assuming with Booij and Rubach (1987) that the universal model contains a postcyclic lexical component. We shall also stipulate that the model should make available to us only one cyclic stratum/component and that only this stratum/component can interact with WFRs.

WFRs interact with a subset of phonological rules that are called cyclic. The term 'cyclic' is used here in the sense that phonological rules as a class reapply after every step in a word-forming derivation starting with the root cycle (the first cycle). For example, the structure Root + Suffix 1 is an input to the cyclic rules in the same way as the subsequently created structure Root + Suffix 1 + Suffix 2. This mode of interaction between morphology and phonology implies that cases should exist in which the correct application of a WFR is conditioned by the prior application of a cyclic phonological rule. That is, the morphology in cycle 2 may refer to the phonological information provided in cycle 1. Indeed, precisely such instances of the dependence of morphology on phonology have been uncovered.

The best-known case is Siegel's (1974) example concerning deverbal nominalizations formed by adding the suffix -al in English. This suffix is added to verbs with final stress such as *deny—deni+al, propose—propos+al*, but not **promis+al*. The -al can be added correctly in cycle 2 if the verbs are assigned stress on the root cycle, that is, on the first cycle of the derivation.

A similar example from Dutch was discussed by Booij and Rubach (1984). Denominal adjectives are formed by adding either the suffix -isch or the suffix -ief. However, the former is added only if the base noun ends in a stressed syllable (*ie* stands for [i]):

(1) *a.* psychologie 'psychology'—psycholog+isch

　　hysterie 'hysteria'—hyster+isch

　b. agressie 'aggression'—agress+ief

　　inventie 'invention'—invent+ief

Thus, we might just as well assume that English fits into the universal model without additional stipulations, in that all WFRs apply in the cyclic stratum/component only. (I therefore abandon the suggestion of Booij and Rubach (1987) that English exceptionally permits postcyclic word-formation.) What remains as a problem and needs to be investigated is how to account for the arguably different phonological behaviour of Class 1 and Class 2 affixes. However, given the array of devices made available by the current theory, such as phonological words, cyclic/postcyclic affixes, and extrametricality, problems of this type are likely to be apparent rather than real (see e.g. Booij and Rubach 1984).

The final vowel in (1*a*) is stressed in the first cycle. This enables the adjective-forming WFR to attach the required suffix in the second cycle. The final stressed vowel of the nominal base is then deleted before the vowel of the suffix. The stress rule applies anew in the second cycle. It is therefore a classic instance of a cyclic rule.

Not all phonological rules that apply in the lexicon are cyclic. Some rules must 'wait' until the whole word has been derived. Final Devoicing in German is one such case. The rule devoices obstruents at the end of the syllable and syllable structure is assigned cyclically (cf. Rubach 1990). A word such as *Hund* 'dog' surfaces with a voiceless consonant: [hunt]. If Final Devoicing were permitted to apply cyclically, then the predicted result would be that all morpheme-final obstruents should be voiceless. This prediction follows from the fact that on the root cycle the morpheme-final consonant is automatically syllable-final as no other phonological material has yet been added. On the other hand, if Final Devoicing is postcyclic, then the prediction is different. The CV Rule (see 1.3) that (re)syllabifies the sequence $(VC)_\sigma (V)_\sigma$ into $(V)_\sigma (CV)_\sigma$ can take effect, making Final Devoicing inapplicable. The CV Rule applies to consonants which stand immediately before a vowel; hence it does not affect the consonant of the preceding morpheme if the next morpheme itself begins with a consonant. The facts of German require that Final Devoicing must be postcyclic. Taking *Hund* 'dog', *Hund+lein* (dimin.), and *Hund+e* (pl.) as examples, we show this in (2), where (2*a*) is the incorrect derivation[2] and (2*b*) is the correct one. We conclude that final Devoicing cannot be a cyclic rule. Yet it must be lexical since it applies before rules that refer to morphological information and that are consequently lexical (cf. Rubach 1990). To summarize, there are two kinds of lexical rules: cyclic and postcyclic. The former interact with WFRs while the latter apply to fully derived words and are thus word-level rules.

The distinction of two classes of rules—cyclic and postcyclic—does not yet give a full picture of phonological derivation, since some rules can evidently belong to neither of these classes. Typical here are the rules that apply across word boundaries. They cannot be lexical for the simple reason that concatenations of words are derived by the syntax and do not exist in the lexicon. That is, words and lexicalized phrases are in the lexicon, but sentences are not. There must therefore be yet a third class of phonological rules: postlexical rules.

Polish Surface Palatalization is a classic example of a postlexical rule

---

[2] Note that the Strict Cyclicity Constraint that we present below cannot block the application of Final Devoicing on the first cycle since syllable-structure assignment, which is free to apply on all cycles, provides a derived environment for Final Devoicing. While the issue whether syllabification can create derived environments has been regarded as controversial (Kiparsky 1985), it is generally assumed that it can, but only for the rules that crucially mention syllable structure in their structural descriptions (Clements and Keyser 1983).

(2) *a.* Cycle 1

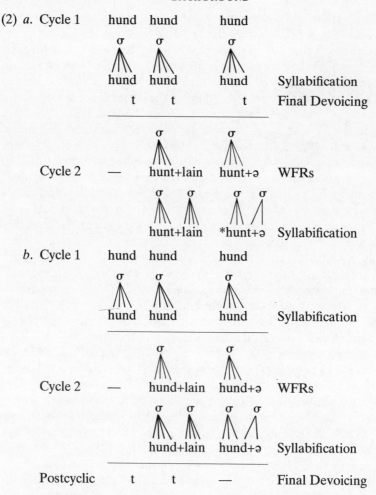

(cf. Rubach 1984). It palatalizes consonants in an allophonic manner before *i* and *j* both inside words and across word boundaries. Note that at the melodic tier, to which the rule is sensitive, *i* and *j* are non-distinct (see 1.3 below).

(3) Surface Palatalization $\quad$ [+cons] $\rightarrow \begin{bmatrix} +\text{high} \\ -\text{back} \end{bmatrix} / \_\_ \begin{bmatrix} +\text{high} \\ -\text{back} \end{bmatrix}$

Examples are given in (4); *cz* and *sz* denote the sounds [č] and [š], respectively. (Here and below we use a simplified transcription system that is different from the IPA symbols in some cases. The correspondences are given in the List of abbreviations and symbols at the beginning of the book, and for convenience the contrasts are summarized again in Table 1, p. 31 below.)

(4) *a.* [p']: pisać 'write', skup inwentarza 'purchase of livestock'
b. [č']: Chile, gracz indyjski 'Indian player'
c. [s']: sinolog 'sinologist', spis imienny 'name list'
d. [š']: Chicago, wasz idealizm 'your idealism'

The question may be asked whether postlexical and postcyclic (lexical) rules could not be conflated. Notice that any such attempt would of necessity have to go in the direction of reclassifying all postcyclic rules as postlexical and not the other way round, since unquestionably sentence phonology cannot be assigned in the lexicon. However, eliminating postcyclic rules is not possible. We mentioned earlier that German Final Devoicing had to be postcyclic and lexical since it applied before rules that referred to morphological information. This reason may not be convincing because it is theory-internal. Indeed, as we explain later, reference to morphological information is a diagnostic feature of lexical rules (Mohanan 1986). Fortunately, independent evidence exists to document the need for distinguishing between postcyclic and postlexical rules. Polish provides a relevant example.

In addition to rule (3) Polish has Retraction, a rule that changes /i/ into the back vowel [ɨ] after hard coronals:[3]

(5) Retraction $\quad i \rightarrow ɨ /$ $\begin{bmatrix} +\text{coron} \\ +\text{back} \end{bmatrix}$ —

Retraction cannot be cyclic since it must be ordered after postcyclic rules (see Rubach 1984). As an additional reason we might mention the fact that Retraction applies morpheme-internally and, as we explain below, structure-changing applications such as those effected by Retraction are prohibited morpheme-internally if a rule is cyclic. Retraction applies inside morphemes to 'nativize' borrowings. Some of them have already been established with the [ɨ] pronunciation as the only variant. These may be interpreted as having an underlying //ɨ//. However, more recent borrowings show variation which may be explained only as due to Retraction. That is, when entering Polish, borrowings may be exceptions to Retraction but they soon become assimilated and yield to the rule. The [ɨ] variants are unambiguously judged as 'nativized'.

(6) maksim+um [s'i] ~ [sɨ] 'maximum'
reżim [ž'i] ~ [žɨ] 'regime'
rizott+o [r'i] ~ [rɨ] 'risotto'

---

[3] The term 'hard' means a [+back] consonant, that is, a consonant that is not prepalatal. In Polish, as in Russian, all consonants are phonetically either [+back] or [−back].

Incidentally, it may be observed that the very fact that Retraction may have exceptions bans it from the class of postlexical rules, since, as we explain below, only lexical rules may have exceptions (Mohanan 1986).

In order to give the reader a better grasp of the data we add that Retraction accounts also for phonological alternations. One such example is the verbalizing suffix *i*. It appears phonetically either as [i] in (7*a*) or as [i̵], spelled *y*, in (7*b*). Note: -*ć*, a prepalatal affricate, is an infinitive ending.

(7) *a.*   traf 'well-aimed shot'—traf+i+ć [traf′+i+ć] 'to aim'
        skup 'purchase'—skup+i+ć [skup′+i+ć] 'to purchase'
  b.   partacz[-č] 'bungler'—partacz+y+ć [partač+i̵+ć] 'to bungle'
        kurz [-š] (owing to Final Devoicing) 'dust'—kurz+y+ć [kuž+i̵+ć]
        'to dust'
  c.   krok 'step'—krocz+y+ć [kroč+i̵+ć] 'to step'
        strach [-x] 'fright'—strasz+y+ć [straš+i̵+ć] 'to frighten'

There is no doubt that //i// is the underlying representation and [i̵] is derived by Retraction. This is documented most clearly by (7*c*), where the underlying velars //k, x// are changed into postalveolars [č, š] by 1st Velar Palatalization, a rule that applies before the front vowels /i, e/ (cf. Rubach 1984). It should be noted that [č, š] are phonetically hard, hence they trigger Retraction.

Observe now that Surface Palatalization (3) and Retraction (5) perform mutually incompatible operations. If both rules belong to the same (postlexical) component, then there is no way in which they can be ordered. In (8) we look at the derivation of *partacz+y+ć* //partač+i+ć// 'bungle' and *gracz indyjski* 'Indian player', underlying //grač in-//, phonetic [grač′ in]. Neither the order in (8*a*) nor that in (8*b*) gives the correct result:

(8) *a.*   partač+i+ć   grač in-
        partač+i+ć   *grač in-   Retraction
        —   —   Surface Palatalization
  b.   partač+i+ć   grač in-
        *partač′+i+ć   grač′ in-   Surface Palatalization
        —   —   Retraction

No such problems arise if Retraction is postcyclic and Surface Palatalization postlexical. On the contrary, an explanation is readily available. Retraction applies in the lexicon, where words such as *partacz+y+ć* 'bungle' exist but phrases such as *gracz indyjski* 'Indian player' do not. The variation noted in (6) is explained by making the recent borrowings exceptions to Retraction. The marking for exceptionality tends to be lost in the process of the accommodation of borrowings. In (9) we repeat the derivation from (8) and add one for *režim* 'regime'; (9*b*) is the conservative pronunciation, the innovating form is given in (9*c*).

(9) *a.* partač+i+ć   *b.* režim   *c.* režim   *Postcyclic*
       partač+i+ć   (exception)   režïm   Retraction
<hr>
                                                 d. grač in-   *Postlexical*
       —   rež'im   —   grač' in-   Surf. Pal.

We conclude that it is necessary to distinguish between lexical postcyclic rules and postlexical rules. Our discussion is summarized in (10), which presents the model of Lexical Phonology with the modifications suggested by Booij and Rubach (1987).

(10)

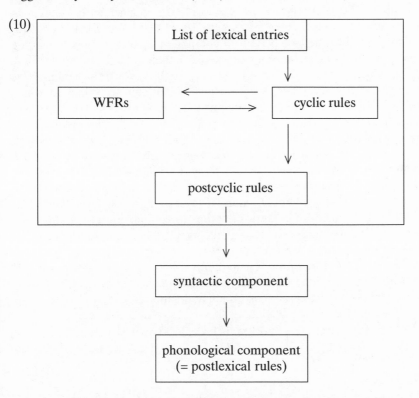

This model identifies three components in which phonological rules apply: cyclic, postcyclic, and postlexical. It does not preclude the possibility that each of these components may be structured further, but the assumption is that further structuring is not available universally. Rather, it requires motivation on a language-specific basis.

Essential properties of the model in (10) are the following. First, universally there are only two components (strata) in the lexicon. Second, one of these components is cyclic and the other postcyclic. Third, it is only the cyclic component that is permitted to interact with word-formation rules. We may add that with regard to the postlexical component it has been suggested that more structure may be necessary. Kaisse (1985) interprets the distinction between syntactically conditioned and purely phonologically conditioned rules of external sandhi as the distinction between two postlexical strata (P-1 and P-2, respectively).

Summing up, the model in (10) represents the core structure of Lexical Phonology in the sense that it is available at no cost. Extensions of this model need to be argued for. It may be noted at this point that for the purposes of Slovak (as well as Polish; see Rubach 1984) no such extensions are necessary.

A difference of opinions has emerged with regard to the status of lexical and postlexical rules. Mohanan (1982, 1986) and Kiparsky (1985) assume that rules do not belong to components. Rather, they constitute a module with particular rules marked for their domain of application, such as stratum 1, 2, etc. Thus, rules may apply in several domains. This contrasts with a classic view of Lexical Phonology according to which rules are assigned to strata (components in terms of (10)) and each stratum forms a 'miniphonology' (Kiparsky 1982). The classic view is more restrictive than the modular interpretation and it leads to interesting predictions that we spell out below. We wish merely to note that very few well-documented cases have been discovered to support the claim that one rule may apply in more than one stratum/component. Vedic accentuation is one such well-documented example (Halle and Mohanan 1985). This means that Kiparsky's (1982) position has to be relaxed to the extent that under exceptional circumstances a rule may be interpreted as being applicable in more than one stratum.

Given that rules belong to components, the further generalization (11) about the organization of phonology can be made: a set of rules belonging to one component forms a block (Booij and Rubach 1987).

(11)

cyclic lexical rules	postcyclic lexical rules	postlexical rules
1.	1. rule X	1. rule Z
2.	2.	2.
•	•	•
•	•	•
•	•	•
rule W	rule Y	

Ordering is a stipulation that exists in all versions of Lexical Phonology (such as Mohanan 1982, 1986) and, for that matter, in practically all versions of generative phonology, beginning with Halle (1959). The suggestion made by Booij and Rubach (1987) is that additional mileage for the theory can be gained from the independently motivated ordering relationships between rules. In particular, predictions can be made regarding the membership of a rule in one of the three components, which entails predicting the behaviour of a rule in a given language. More specifically, suppose that rule A is ordered before rule W in (11). It is then predicted that A must be cyclic since rules form disjoint blocks. Given its status, A will show the properties of cyclic rules such as: it must apply in the domain of a word, it must obey the Strict Cyclicity Constraint (see below), it may refer to morphological information, etc. Needless to say, any rule which is ordered before A must behave in the same way. Conversely, rule B ordered after rule X in (11) cannot be cyclic. All rules ordered between X and Y are word-level postcyclic rules, whereas all rules ordered after Z are predictably postlexical. These predictions are suspended with respect to a rule C which, like Vedic accentuation, happens to be precisely one of those exceptional rules that may apply in more than one component. Then, ordering relationships established on the basis of rule C do not tell us anything about the status of other rules in the grammar.

Yet another organizational principle of Lexical Phonology needs to be mentioned. It is assumed that the traditional boundaries do not play any role in phonology. They have been replaced by cyclic brackets which coincide with morpheme junctures. This is not merely a technicality. The superiority of such a view has been motivated by Kiparsky (1982), Mohanan (1982, 1986), Kaisse and Shaw (1985), and others. Brackets are available in one component (stratum) only. At the end of the component they are erased by the Bracket Erasure Convention. This predicts, for example, that postlexical rules cannot be conditioned by the internal structure of words. While we accept bracket erasure, we shall use pluses rather than brackets in this book and we shall keep the pluses till the final stages of derivation. We believe this will enhance the clarity of exposition.

Lexical and postlexical rules exhibit different properties. There is a general consensus among researchers that the following diagnostic properties characterize lexical rules (for further details, see 6.8 and 8.1 below):

(12) (i) Lexical rules apply cyclically;
    (ii) Their application is subject to the Strict Cyclicity Constraint;
    (iii) They apply in the domain of a word;
    (iv) They enter into structure-preserving derivations;
    (v) They may refer to lexical information which basically includes the following three types:
        (a) morphological information;
        (b) subdivision of the vocabulary according to lexical classes;
        (c) exceptionality.

Cyclic rules display all five types of properties, or a subset thereof, whereas postcyclic rules are restricted to the diagnostics (iii), (iv), and (v). Slovak bears testimony to the fact that these diagnostic properties are a correct characterization of lexical rules. We make this point in Chapter 6. In Chapters 8 and 9 we investigate in some detail the properties of postcyclic rules as opposed to postlexical rules. Thus, the relevant evidence from Slovak will come later. At this stage we shall only explain what is meant by each of the criteria in (12) on the basis of theoretically constructed examples or examples from languages which have already been investigated in a way that is relevant to our purposes. We begin with the diagnostics given last in (12) since they are either self-explanatory or simple to explain.

The fact that lexical rules may refer to lexical information (Mohanan 1982) fits well into the theory since the relevant part of phonology is carried out in the lexicon. The criterion of exceptionality is self-explanatory. We have seen one postcyclic rule which has exceptions (Retraction in (5)). Classic cyclic rules of English such as Trisyllabic Shortening exhibit the same property; compare *divin+ity* vs. *obes+ity*, which is an exception.

A subdivision of the vocabulary into lexical classes may be reflected in the statement of lexical rules. These classes are either purely lexical or morphologically oriented. The distinction of native versus non-native layers of the vocabulary illustrates the former and the verb classes of Slovak (see (1*a*) in 3.1.1) the latter type of class. That the lexical feature [native] can play a role is demonstrated by Velar Softening in English. This rule changes *k* into *s* but only in the Romance stratum of the vocabulary; compare: *electric—electric+ity* vs. *keen, kill, monarch+ism, stick+y, black+ish*.

The use of morphological information is clear as a criterion. For example, the celebrated rule of Vowel Deletion ($V \rightarrow \emptyset / - V$), which exists in all Slavic languages, applies only to verbs. Similarly, the so-called Second Velar Palatalization is restricted to apply before some case endings only. In Polish the rule affects //k, g//, which are turned into [c, ʒ] in nouns, pronouns, and adjectives in the nom. pl. and the dat./loc. sg. (cf. Rubach 1984). In Slovak the rule turns //k, x// into [c, s] but it operates only in nouns and only in the nom. pl. (see 4.3). It should also be noted that we do not assume with Aronoff (1976) that allomorphy rules precede all phonological rules. Consequently, rules of an allomorphy type are permitted to apply in both the cyclic and the postcyclic components. (As shown in (10) above, the postcyclic component is in the lexicon and hence it is different from the postlexical component, in which allomorphy rules are not found.)

Structure preservation, mentioned in (12(iv)), incorporates the idea that the output of lexical derivation is 'phonemic' and not 'allophonic'. That is, the types of segments created in lexical derivations correspond to the types of segments that exist in the underlying representation. Thus, for example, English Aspiration cannot be a lexical rule because aspirated consonants are not underlying segments. It is generally assumed that lexical *rules* are structure-preserving. This, however, seems to be too strong a claim. We believe that it is more appropriate to talk about lexical *derivations* as being structure-preserving. Such an assumption makes it permissible for a particular rule to generate outputs that are not necessarily phonemic, while it still preserves the insight that the output of the lexicon is phonemic and, consequently, rules such as Aspiration are predictably postlexical. Polish illustrates precisely this type of situation (Andrew Spencer, personal communication).

A cyclic rule of Coronal Palatalization produces palatalized dento-alveolars such as /t'/ and /s'/.[4] These are phonemic, as /t', s'/ are underlying segments in Polish. However, in the case of the liquid //r// the change into /r'/ is not phonemic. The intermediate stage /r'/ is subsequently turned either back into [r] or into the fricative [ž], both of which are phonemic changes. The reason for such a roundabout way of deriving [ž] is that some /r'/s depalatalize to [r]. At the same time [ž] is derived not only by Coronal Palatalization but also by other palatalization rules, notably, by 1st Velar Palatalization. In the latter case the underlying source of the surface [ž] is //g// and not //r//. If Coronal Palatalization changed //r// into [ž] in one step, there would be no way of determining which žs should depalatalize to [r] since, first, only the žs from //r// depalatalize, and, second, the žs from //r// and the žs from //g// occur in the same context (see Rubach 1984). In sum, Coronal Palatalization must derive /r'/ and not /ž/. The /r'/ is not an underlying segment and hence the rule is not structure-preserving for liquids (but it is structure-preserving for obstruents). However, the derivation is structure-preserving because a later lexical rule turns /r'/ into [ž] or [r], which are underlying segments.

Returning to (12), the assumption in (12(iii)) that lexical rules apply in the domain of a word must be relaxed slightly to permit the so-called 'small phrases' to be derived in the lexicon, if they are lexicalized. This point is illustrated clearly in Rubach (1985). Briefly, Polish has a rule that accounts for e–∅ alternations by determining the circumstances under which *e* appears phonetically. This rule, known as Yer Vocalization, is cyclic, and yet it applies to small phrases. However, such phrases must be treated as lexicalized for independent reasons. They are idiomatic from the semantic point of view and they display a stress pattern that is typical for words. Below we give an example of *e* vocalizing inside a word in (13*a*) and in the preposition of a phrase in (13*b*). The *e* predictably does

---

[4] Later spell-out rules turn /t', s', .../ into prepalatals, whereby stops become affricates. (The analysis is entirely parallel to that found in Slovak; see Chapter 4.) Thus, the effects of Coronal Palatalization are distinct from the effects of Surface Palatalization (see Rubach 1984).

not vocalize if the same phrase is not used idiomatically and hence is not lexicalized, as in (13c):

(13) *a.* krew 'blood'—krw+i (gen. sg.)
 b. we krwi 'in blood' (in one's nature)
 c. w krwi 'in the blood'

The contrast between (13*b*) and (13*c*) is accounted for by assuming that (13*b*) but not (13*c*) is available in the lexicon. The vocalization rule is lexical for independent reasons (cf. Rubach 1985 and 1984).

We shall now discuss the principle in (12(ii)): the Strict Cyclicity Constraint (SCC hereafter). It is one of the most important principles in Lexical Phonology. It captures the insights developed by Kiparsky over a period of several years (cf. Kiparsky 1968, 1973). The essence of the SCC is that cyclic rules apply in derived environments. An environment is described as derived if either (i) or (ii) is satisfied:

(14) Derived environment:
 (i) a structure arises owing to a morphological operation (addition of an affix); such environments are said to be derived morphologically;
 (ii) a structure arises as a result of applying a phonological rule at an earlier stage in the same cycle; such environments are said to be derived phonologically.

Given that cyclic rules are subject to the SCC, which restricts their application to derived environments, a number of important predictions follow. They have been investigated for Polish by Rubach (1984). Below we review briefly a few examples.

Polish Coronal Palatalization is a cyclic rule (t, s, . . . → t′, s′ / — front vowels; see n. 4). This follows from its ordering before other cyclic rules. A prediction is made that words such as *serwis* 'service' do not undergo the rule, that is, the //s// remains unpalatalized, even though it stands before a front vowel. This prediction is correct: the phonetic form is [serv′ iš]. The explanation here is that the sequence /se/ is wholly contained within one morpheme, hence the environment is not derived and the SCC blocks Coronal Palatalization. A further prediction is that the final *s* of *serwis* should palatalize if a front vowel suffix is appended. This is exactly what happens: *serwis+ie* //servis+e// (loc. sg.) and *serwis+ik* //servis+ik// (dimin.) surface as [serv′iś+e] and [serv′iś+ik], respectively. Coronal Palatalization applies since the final *s* is in a derived environment: the front vowel that follows *s* has been derived morphologically through suffixation.

More generally, we can conclude that a morphologically derived environment is one that arises across morpheme boundaries. This, however, is a certain simplification. Structures which are wholly contained within affixes also count as derived. The reason for this is that affixes, unlike roots, are not listed in the lexicon. Rather, they appear as part of the WFRs. That is, it is only lexical roots that are morphologically underived. Could we therefore assume that derived environment application can be simply explained as a ban on applying cyclic rules to roots? This is not correct, since environments may also be derived phonologically (clause (14(ii)) above). Again Polish provides a clear example of such a situation. The earlier-mentioned rule of 1st Velar Palatalization changes velars into postalveolars:

(15) 1st Velar Pal. (Polish)   k, g, x → č, ǯ, š / — front vowels

Some examples are given in (16):

(16) *a.* bok 'side'—bocz+ek [boč+ek] (dimin.)
 b. mózg 'brain'—móżdż+ek [mužǯ+ek] (dimin.)
 c. dach //dax// 'roof'—dasz+ek [daš+ek] (dimin.)
 d. Bóg 'God'—Boż+e [bož+e] (voc. sg.)
  drąg //drong// 'pole'—drąż+ek /dronž+ek/ (dimin.)

The change in (16*d*) is unexpected. Evidently, //g// is turned into [ž] here and not into [ǯ]. The generalization is that this change occurs if //g// is preceded by a sonorant, hence the contrast between (16*b*) and (16*d*). An attempt to build this generalization into rule (15) is either simply impossible (if the rule is expressed formally in terms of features) or at best would result in rather a baroque statement. The solution is to posit Spirantization:

(17) Spirantization   ǯ → ž / [+sonor] —

Again, because of ordering both 1st Velar Palatalization and Spirantization are cyclic. This prediction is confirmed by descriptive evidence, as neither 1st Velar Palatalization nor Spirantization can apply in underived environments: *poker* 'poker', *brydż* [briǯ] 'bridge'. (Note that /ǯ/ appears after a sonorant, hence the environment of Spirantization is met.) How do we derive the structures in (16*d*)? Let us look at the vocative form *Boż+e* 'God':

(18) bog+e
  boǯ+e   1st Velar Palatalization
  bož+e   Spirantization

This /ž/, unlike the underlying //ǯ// in *brydż* 'bridge', is subject to Spirantization, even though both the environment (the preceding sonorant) and the input /ǯ/ are wholly contained within the root morpheme. The application of Spirantization is made possible by the fact that the /ǯ/ is derived from //g// earlier in the same cycle. That is, it arises because of the

application of 1st Velar Palatalization, thereby illustrating clause (14(ii))
of the derived environment definition.

The decision to separate 1st Velar Palatalization from Spirantization
finds striking confirmation in the accommodation of borrowings. Newly
borrowed or unfamiliar words such as *parking* 'car park' and *dyftong*
'diphthong' appear either with [ǯ] or with [ž] before front vowels:
parkindž+ek ~ parkinž+ek (dimin.), *dyftondž+ek ~ dyftonž+ek* (dimin.).
The forms with [ǯ], spelled *dż*, are outputs of 1st Velar Palatalization but
remain exceptions to Spirantization before ultimately ceding to it. If 1st
Velar Palatalization changed underlying //g// into [ž] in one step, then the
forms with [ǯ] after sonorants could not be generated at all. Spirantization
is thus confirmed as a rule. Recall now that Spirantization is cyclic and
that it applies in phonologically (not morphologically) derived environments. This illuminates the importance of (14(ii)) as separate from (14(i)).
It also shows that the predictions made by (14) are non-trivial.

As already mentioned, the SCC restricts cyclic rules to derived environments. In recent years it has been demonstrated that such a restriction
is correct only for the rules that change structure, that is, the rules that
transform one segment into another, thereby producing contrasts. Rules
such as stress, syllabification, and context-free redundancy rules that fill in
unspecified values of segments (see 2.3.1) add structure, that is, they enrich
rather than alter the existing representations. It is generally believed
that such rules are not subject to Strict Cyclicity. Drawing upon the work
by Mascaró (1976), Halle (1978), Kiparsky (1982), and particularly Halle
and Mohanan (1985), we can now state the SCC as follows:

(19) The Strict Cyclicity Constraint (SCC):
      Cyclic rules cannot effect contrastive changes in environments not
      derived in their cycle.

Let us clarify: a contrastive change is one that derives an allomorph which
enters into a phonological opposition with another allomorph of a given
morpheme. Thus, in a language that contrasts palatalized and non-
palatalized consonants, palatalization rules effect contrastive changes.

The restriction to the current cycle in (19) is important. It means that
changes performed on earlier cycles do not count as derived environment.
The essence of this statement is that only the changes that are feeding
(i.e. that provide inputs) with respect to a given rule create derived
environments. We shall illustrate the operation of the SCC in Part II of
this book.

We now return to the diagnostic properties in (12) and explain the
concept of cyclic application. This concept is independent of the SCC. It
is motivated by three types of evidence: (i) availability of derivational
information, (ii) ordering paradoxes, and (iii) descriptive predictions.

The first type of evidence comes from *SPE*. The classic examples here are words such as *compEnsation* vs. *condEnsation* (capital letters mark the relevant vowels). *SPE* observes that the reason why the *e* in *compensation* reduces to schwa but the one in *condensation* does not is to be sought in the derivational history of these words. The first word comes from *compEnsate*, where the *e* is unstressed, while the second word comes from *condEnse*, where the *e* bears stress. This derivational information is available if the words are derived cyclically, that is, if we look at the verb cycle before deriving the noun in the next cycle.

Ordering paradoxes arise if two rules X and Y are required to apply in the order 'X before Y' in one derivation but 'Y before X' in another derivation. A classic example comes from Halle (1963). We do not wish to defend the particular statements in Halle's analysis of almost thirty years ago. Our purpose is to explain what an ordering paradox is, especially since Slovak displays such paradoxes (see Chapter 6).

Halle (1963) formulates a rule of palatalization for Russian which derives, amongst others, [š] from //s// before a sequence of a non-round vowel followed by a round vowel. Schematically:

$$V \qquad V$$
(20) s → š / — [–round] [+round]

Russian also has Vowel Deletion, a rule that applies in all Slavic languages:

(21) V → ∅ / — V

The verb *pišu* 'I write' (an *a*-stem verb) does not require that the rules should apply cyclically. It suffices that rule (20) be ordered before (21):

(22) p′is+a+o+u
     p′iš+a+o+u   Rule (20)
     p′iš+o+u   Rule (21)
     p′iš+u   Rule (21)

However, for the derivation of *brošu* 'I throw' (an *i*-stem verb) this ordering yields an incorrect output:

(23) bros′+i+i+u
     —   Rule (20)
     bros′+i+u   Rule (21)
     *bros′+u   Rule (21)

We obtain [s′] instead of the correct [š]. It seems that the correct output can be derived if we reverse the order so that (21) can precede (20). This, however, is false too, as both *i*s will be deleted and the sequence of vowels required by (20) will not arise. The correct result can be derived if (20) applies after the first but before the second application of (21). Thus, (21) needs to be ordered in two different places: we have an ordering paradox.

Halle points out that this paradox is resolved if we assume that the rules
apply cyclically. Relevant here are cycles 3 and 4 (see (24)).

(24)	[[p′is+a+o]+u]	[[bros′+i+i]+u]	
Cycle 3	p′is+a+o	bros′+i+i	
	p′iš+a+o	—	Rule (20)
	p′iš+o	bros′+i	Rule (21)
Cycle 4	p′iš+o+u	bros′+i+u	
	—	broš+i+u	Rule (20)
	p′iš+u	broš+u	Rule (21)

A third type of evidence for cyclic application comes from the
contradictory effects that a rule may have depending on whether it is
applied cyclically or non-cyclically. We shall use here a theoretical example and delay the presentation of real cases till Chapters 6 and 8 (see
the Rhythmic Law and Glide Shortening). Assume that there is a rule
which shortens vowels after a long vowel (length is marked by an accent):

(25) $\acute{V} \rightarrow V / \acute{V}C_0 —$

This rule yields different outputs, depending on how it is applied. We take
a hypothetical string of vowels and apply the rule cyclically in (26a) and
non-cyclically in (26b).

(26)	a.	$\acute{V}C_0 + \acute{V}C_0 + \acute{V}C_0$	
Cycle 2		$\acute{V}C_0 + \acute{V}C_0$	
		$\acute{V}C_0 + VC_0$	Rule (25)
	b.	$\acute{V}C_0 + \acute{V}C_0 + \acute{V}C_0$	
Cycle 2		$\acute{V}C_0 + VC_0 + VC_0$	Rule (25)
Cycle 3		$\acute{V}C_0 + VC_0 + \acute{V}C_0$	
		—	Rule (25)

In (26a) the final vowel remains long while in (26b) it shortens. The
cycle has empirical consequences that must not be overlooked or
underestimated.

Given that the cycle plays a role in derivation (a claim that we shall
substantiate in this book), Lexical Phonology is an admirably suitable
framework in which to express such insights. Notice that the cycle need
not be stipulated as a special device. It follows naturally from the Lexical
Phonology model since WFRs and cyclic phonological rules interact with
one another, in the sense that only a sequence of no more than two
morphemes is available for derivation at a time.

1.3. REPRESENTATIONS

We have presented Lexical Phonology as a theory relating to the organization of the grammar. In this section we introduce two other theories: the skeletal theory and the syllabic theory. They both refer to the nature of phonological representations.

Halle and Vergnaud (1980) proposed that phonological representations should be viewed as three-dimensional. They are composed of three independent tiers: the melody, called also the segmental tier; the skeleton; and the syllabic structure. The essence of this proposal is that tiers may be largely independent of each other, in that sequences of units at one tier need not correspond linearly to sequences of units at another tier. Representations constructed in this way are known as non-linear. Let us look at some examples which are relevant for the purposes of this book.

A long vowel is construed as a single melody unit linked to two X slots where the X slots encode the old concept of segmentation. Thus, a long vowel counts as two segments. Diphthongs also count as two segments. They are different from long vowels in that each X slot is linked to a different melody segment. Diphthongs should be kept distinct from sequences of vowels that may have the same melodic representation. The desired distinction is achieved by referring to syllable structure, in particular to the syllable nucleus. A diphthong is dominated by one N (that is, nucleus), while a sequence of vowels carries N over each vowel because each vowel is a separate syllable (27).

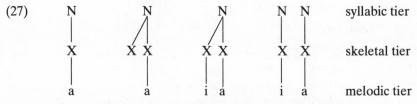

(27)   N   N   N   N N   syllabic tier

        X   X X   X X   X X   skeletal tier

        a   a   i a   i a   melodic tier

short vowel long vowel diphthong vowel sequence

In order to count the number of syllables we look at the syllabic tier, to see how many segments there are we look at the skeletal tier, and to determine the feature composition of segments we look at the melodic tier. The latter represents articulatory gestures. Long [aː] is therefore simply an [a] at this tier since the positioning of the organs of speech is constant during the whole articulation. In Chapter 2 we shall explain that the melodic tier comprises sets of phonetic features which are attached to articulatory nodes. The representations in (27), which use simple transcription symbols, are thus abbreviations for these sets of features.

Given three-tiered representations it is no longer necessary to use the feature [syllabic]. This is an important step forward, since [syllabic] has always stood out amongst the traditional phonetic features because it has

never been possible to define it along the same lines as other features such
as [labial] or [nasal], that is by evoking an articulatory correlate. That
syllabicity is a matter of structure (positioning in a sequence of segments)
rather than of articulation is best documented by the fact that consonants
may be syllabic only in certain environments. Thus, in *little* the first *l* is
non-syllabic whereas the second *l* is syllabic. This fact is captured precisely by transferring syllabic relations from the feature tier (the melody)
to a separate syllable-structure tier.

A further advantageous consequence of three-dimensional representations is the possibility of expressing a relation between vowels and glides.
The contrast between, for example, /i/ and /j/ can now be conveniently
viewed as a contrast of constituency within a syllable. The /i/ carries a
nucleus while the /j/ does not, that is, /j/ is either part of the onset or part
of the coda. At the melodic tier both are represented by the same set of
features that we abbreviate in (28) as [i]. (Recall that sigma stands for a
syllable node, V for any vowel.)

(28)

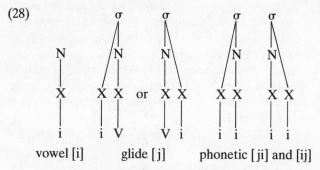

vowel [i]   glide [j]   phonetic [ji] and [ij]

To summarize, the significance of distinguishing a skeleton as a separate
tier of representation consists in the fact that, first, length, and more
generally segmental relations, can now be expressed independently of the
melodic representation (compare [a] and [aː] in (27) above) and, second,
syllable structure can be built on Xs rather than directly on melodic
segments (feature complexes). There is substantial evidence in favour of
this new perspective on phonological representation.

The representation of length and segmentation at the skeletal tier has
drawn much support from studies of compensatory lengthening (cf., for
example, Sezer and Wetzels 1986). Briefly, compensatory lengthening
can now be characterized as a deletion of a melodic segment and a
reassociation of the floating X slot with a neighbouring vowel. That is, the
melodic segment is deleted but the X slot remains intact. The freed X slot
can therefore be linked to a vowel. With its original X slot plus now the
added one the vowel is interpreted as long. The concept of compensating
for a deleted segment is thus given a formal expression.

Transferring syllable organization from the phonetic segments (the 'melody' in the new terms) to the skeleton is motivated in a variety of ways. Syllable templates which express the canonical structure of the syllable are constructed on the skeleton. We can thus state facts such as 'the maximum onset may consist of no more than two segments'. We express this by referring to two X slots before the nucleus. Also, we can define formally the well-known concept of heavy cluster, which includes either a complex nucleus or a simple nucleus followed by a consonant. The two have a common representation at the rhyme, a syllable constituent that groups the nucleus and the coda. The rhyme is branching (that is, it has two X slots) in both instances. Heavy clusters play an important role in determining the location of stress in, for example, English (*SPE*).

Another argument in favour of the mediation of the skeleton between the melody and the syllable comes from the possibility of a unified treatment of long vowels and diphthongs. These are different at the melodic tier (see (27) above) but identical at the interface between the skeleton and the nucleus, as in both instances the nucleus is composed of two X slots. For example, Kenstowicz and Rubach (1987) have demonstrated that the possibility of finding a common denominator for long vowels and diphthongs plays a crucial role in the statement of shortening and lengthening rules in Slovak. This point will be developed further in Chapter 6.

With the skeleton as a separate tier of representation we expect that it should be possible for a language to have a skeletal slot that lacks a melodic representation (a floating X slot) and vice versa: a melodic segment that lacks a skeletal slot (a floating melody). Indeed, it has been found in the literature that both of these situations exist. For example, Clements and Keyser (1983) claim that in Turkish, lexical roots may end in a floating X slot. Similarly, Anderson (1982) interprets French schwa as a skeletal slot without an associated vocalic melody. And conversely, floating matrices, that is melodic segments without an X slot, have been postulated as a representation of the so-called 'yers', Slavic vowels that alternate with zero (Kenstowicz and Rubach 1987, Rubach 1986; see Chapter 5).

Finally, skeletal representations have been motivated on morphological grounds. There is abundant literature on this subject, starting with McCarthy (1979). The primary evidence is drawn from the root morphology of Semitic languages and from reduplication.

Recent work on skeletal representation goes in the direction of reinterpreting X-slot representations in terms of moras. This approach has been articulated particularly clearly by Hayes (1989). Slovak does not support such a reinterpretation. We consider this problem briefly in Chapter 5.

Our discussion so far has centred on the skeletal tier. In the remainder of this section we shall introduce some basic concepts of syllabic representation. Central to the understanding of the syllable is the notion of sonority hierarchy.

Ever since Whitney (1865) and Jespersen (1904), linguists have observed that segments differ in their sonority (cf. Clements 1985 for an excellent historical review of this problem). At one end of the scale we have vowels (more precisely: low vowels) as the most sonorous segments. At the other end we have obstruents, stops specifically, which are least sonorous. The syllable is typically constructed according to the relative sonority of its constituents. Vowels, as most sonorous, are in the centre. The sonority of segments decreases as we move to the syllable margins: the onset in one direction and the coda in the other. This regularity has become known in the generative literature as the Sonority Sequencing Generalization (Selkirk 1984). It can be worded as follows:

(29) Sonority Sequencing Generalization (SSG):
      The sonority of segments must decrease towards the edges of the syllable in accordance with the following scale:
      nucleus—liquids—nasals—fricatives—stops.

Thus, English *trust* is a well-formed syllable since the sonority scale is observed both to the left and to the right of the nucleus. Needless to say, not all classes of segments enumerated in (29) must be present; it is sufficient that the order in which segments occur be in accordance with (29).

The SSG can be overridden by language-specific constraints. For example, in Polish no sequential relations hold between fricatives and stops, that is, fricatives and stops can occur in either order (Rubach and Booij 1990*a*). On the other hand, language-specific constraints may introduce further conditions that sharpen the SSG. For instance, in English, syllable onsets may not contain stops followed by nasals. Thus, *pm-, *tn-, etc. are ill-formed.

In the typical case syllable structure is not present in the underlying representation. It is assigned by rules. We shall follow Levin (1985) in assuming that the syllable is characterized as a projection of the primitive category N (that is, nucleus). The node N" is the syllable node (abbreviated often as the sigma sign σ). It may but does not have to contain an onset, hence the X slot in the CV Rule in (30) is optional (Levin 1985). Syllable structure is assigned by a set of rules that we shall call the Syllable Structure Algorithm (SSA hereafter). It includes two universal rules, shown in (30). The CV Rule is endowed with the power to resyllabify strings, thereby expressing the universal generalization that VCV is always syllabified as V-CV and never VC-V. (Any divergence from this pattern must be effected by language-specific resyllabification.)

In addition to the universal rules in (30), the SSA normally also contains an Onset Rule that attaches the prenuclear Xs to N", and a Coda

(30) SSA   N-Placement

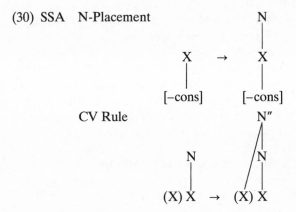

Rule that erects a rhyme node represented as N' between the N and the N". English *trip* is therefore syllabified as shown in (31).

(31)

The Onset Rule and the Coda Rule are typically language-specific. Some languages may lack them altogether. Others may impose constraints on the membership of segments in the onset and in the coda as regards both the type of segments that are permitted and the number of segments.

The task of the SSA is to organize Xs into syllables. In the course of syllabifying strings the SSA consults the melody to check whether neither the SSG nor language-specific constraints (if any) are violated. If syllabifying a given segment would lead to such a violation, then the segment (more exactly: the consonant) is not syllabified. Such unsyllabified consonants are referred to as extrasyllabic. Different languages deal with extrasyllabic consonants in different ways. In some languages they are deleted. In others they receive a nucleus node, that is, they become syllabic. In yet another class of language extrasyllabic consonants are tolerated. We shall give examples of the latter two types of situations in English and Polish.

In English *l* is syllabic in *simple* and *simpleton* [sɪmpltən] but not in *simply*, *pill*, and *salt*. Similarly, *m* and *n* are syllabic in *spasm* and *button* but not in *mummy* and *man*. In surface terms the rule seems to be as follows:

(32) $[+\text{sonor}] \rightarrow [+\text{syllabic}] / C — \begin{cases} \# \\ C \end{cases}$

This statement is inadequate in several different ways. It fails to answer some basic questions: (i) why do sonorants and not other consonants become syllabic? (ii) why should a word boundary and a consonant function in exactly the same way, even though one refers to grammatical structure and the other constitutes a truly phonological context? (iii) why does the *m* of *film* not become syllabic? To counter the last objection we would have to require that the consonant on the left in the environment of (32) should be an obstruent, but this is hardly an explanation of the facts since such a restriction is entirely arbitrary.

A much more insightful way of handling these facts is to look at syllable structure. In all the instances in which the sonorant becomes syllabic it is extrasyllabic at an earlier stage of derivation, a result that follows from the SSG. Sonorant syllabification is now stated in (33), where the asterisk means 'extrasyllabic'. We use a simplified representation by omitting the X tier.

(33) Sonorant Syllabification

$$\sigma \\ | \\ {}^*C \rightarrow C$$

The derivation of *simple, simpleton,* and *simply* is given in (34). Sonorant Syllabification is a phonological rule and not a subrule of the SSA. This statement is motivated by the fact, amongst others, that the resolution of extrasyllabic consonants by making them syllabic is language-specific. In Polish, as we explain below, such a resolution does not take place. After Sonorant Syllabification in (34) the SSA recurs and the CV Rule acts in its capacity as a resyllabification rule. The recurrence of the SSA after

(34) sɪmpl   sɪmpltən   sɪmplɪ

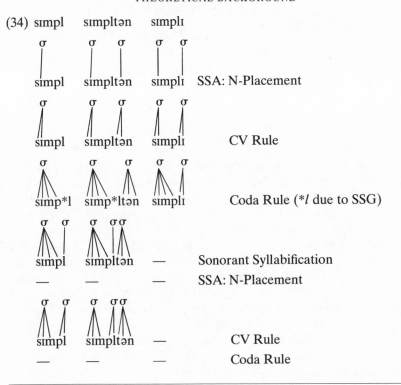

SSA: N-Placement

CV Rule

Coda Rule (*l due to SSG)

Sonorant Syllabification

SSA: N-Placement

CV Rule

Coda Rule

every phonological (and word-formation) rule is a universal property of a syllable structure algorithm. As shown by Itô (1986) and Rubach and Booij (1990a), syllabification is continuous, that is, it reapplies after each rule throughout the whole derivation: in the cyclic, postcyclic, and post-lexical components.

Extrasyllabic consonants also arise in Polish. For example, the r in rtęć [rteńć] 'mercury' cannot be syllabified since the SSG would be violated: the sonorant would be further from the nucleus than the obstruent. The extrasyllabic r does not become syllabic. Neither does it delete. In order to be pronounced it must be licensed prosodically (Itô 1986), that is, it must be made a constituent of prosodic structure. This effect is achieved by postulating a rule of adjunction. Rubach and Booij (1990b) claim that extrasyllabic consonants are adjoined not to the syllable but to the phonological word node abbreviated as m (for mot = phonological word). The node mot is erected at the end of the cyclic derivation and it groups all the syllables of the word, as shown in (35). Other types of adjunction are also possible: for example, in some languages extrasyllabic consonants are attached to the syllable node (cf. Steriade 1982).

The concept of extrametricality requires some explanation. Hayes

(35)

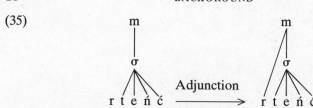

(1982) suggests that a segment or a whole syllable can undergo a rule that makes it extrametrical (EM hereafter), that is, invisible to rules of syllable structure. The assignment of extrametricality is subject to an important restriction: extrametricality is possible only at edges of constituents (syllables, words, etc.), that is, at the beginning or at the end but not in the middle of a constituent. This restriction is known as the Peripherality Condition. Its effect is an automatic erasure of extrametricality if the segment or a syllable stops being constituent-final, for example under suffixation.

To see how extrametricality works, let us look at the following simple example. In English, syllables closed by a consonant attract stress. Thus, *erupt* has final stress while *marry* does not. For the purposes of this rule the final syllable in *edit* counts as open, that is, it does not attract stress. To put it differently, *edit* behaves like *marry* and both contrast with *erupt*. The relevant distinction can be made by assuming that the last consonant is extrametrical. Then, *edit* has the structure $edi(t)_{EM}$ and hence is parallel to *marry*. Naturally, final extrametricality applies to *erupt* as well but in this instance the result is different: *t* becomes extrametrical while *p* does not since *p* is not the last consonant: $erup(t)_{EM}$. Thus, the final syllable is closed and, consequently, it attracts stress, exactly as required.

As mentioned earlier, extrametricality is erased by the Peripherality Condition when the extrametrical material stops being at an edge of a constituent. Thus, for instance, the *l* in *royal+ty* is extrametrical on cycle 1: $roya(l)_{EM}$. When *-ty* is added on cycle 2, the extrametricality of *l* is auto-matically erased. Suppose, however, that we derive the word *royal* itself, that is, there is no cycle 2 and hence the Peripherality Condition is not applicable. Then, extrametricality is erased by convention at the end of the component (here, the cyclic component).

Finally, it should be noted that extrametricality is defined on the skeleton—that is, skeletal slots are made invisible. This has the desired effect for the SSA since syllable structure is constructed on the skeleton. The melodic portion of the representation remains visible and hence it is open to the operation of rules that are defined on the melodic tier only.

With the theoretical background presented in this chapter we are now in a position to analyse the structure of Slovak. The next two chapters introduce the basic facts in the area of phonology and morphology.

2

SLOVAK PHONOLOGY: BACKGROUND

In this chapter we give background information about Slovak phonology. After a general introduction in sections 2.1 and 2.2, we discuss the inventory of underlying segments in section 2.3, and then present an informal summary of the most important phonological rules. These rules are discussed in detail in later chapters, but it is necessary to introduce them briefly now since they form a closely knit system and a discussion of any one of them relies to a large extent on a knowledge of them all.

2.1. THE SLOVAK LANGUAGE

Slovak is a West Slavic language spoken by approximately five million people in Slovakia, a country which occupies about one-third of the territory of the former Czech and Slovak Federal Republic. Its nearest relatives are the other West Slavic languages: Czech, Polish, and Sorbian. The closest relationship is to Czech, with which Slovak is practically mutually intelligible. Although the history of Slovakia goes back more than one thousand years, the written language was first codified in 1787 by Anton Bernolák in the study entitled *Dissertatio philologica critica de letris Slavorum* (cf. Stanislav 1977). The first comprehensive grammar of Slovak is Ľudovít Štúr's *Nauka reči slovenskej* (1846).

There are three groups of dialects in Modern Slovak: West Slovak, Central Slovak, and East Slovak. One distinctive feature of these dialects is the treatment of length. According to Stanislav (1977), East Slovak, spoken in the region bordering Poland, has lost vowel length, which makes it similar to Polish. West Slovak, on the other hand, has long vowels but, like Czech, it does not have the shortening rule known as the Rhythmic Law which is characteristic for Central Slovak. It is Central Slovak that is the source of the literary language described by linguists and it is this variety of educated Slovak that we present in this book.

There are a number of grammars and other studies of Slovak which provide a very good description of the data: Letz (1950), Pauliny (1968), Isačenko (1968), Dvonč *et al.* (1966), Dvončová *et al.* (1969), Ďurovič (1973, 1975), Kráľ (1988), Sabol (1989), to mention just a few. On the other hand, the generative literature on Slovak phonology is surprisingly modest. It includes three longer articles: Isačenko (1966), Kenstowicz and Kisseberth (1979, a chapter based on Kenstowicz 1972), Kenstowicz and

Rubach (1987), and a few shorter articles and notes: Browne (1970, 1971), Birnbaum (1981). Horecký's (1975) 'Generatívny opis fonologického systému spisovej slovenčiny' (Generative Description of the Phonological System of Literary Slovak) does not go beyond a discussion of distinctive features. Anderson's (1974) discussion of the Rhythmic Law in one chapter is based on Browne (1970).

2.2. ORTHOGRAPHY AND TRANSCRIPTION SYMBOLS

Slovak orthography is largely phonemic and unambiguous. An accent over a vowel or a liquid denotes length: *í, ý, ú, é, ó, á, ĺ, ŕ.* The letters *i* and *y* (*í* and *ý* for long vowels) are two orthographic ways of expressing the sound [i]. The *y* is used for [i] to mean that the preceding sound is not palatalized. On this point Slovak is different from Polish, in which the letter *i* denotes the sound [i] and the letter *y* stands for the back vowel [ɨ]. In the fourteenth century Slovak lost this distinction still preserved in Polish (Stanislav 1977). The umlaut over the *ä* marks a front vowel [æ].[1] For typographic convenience we shall transcribe [æ] as [ä], that is, exactly as it is spelled. The letter sequences *ie, ia,* and *iu* are normally the way of writing the diphthongs [ie, ia, iu]. However, they sometimes denote vowel sequences. Attention will be drawn whenever the latter is the case. The letter *ô* refers unambiguously to the rising diphthong [uo].

In the system of consonants the following orthoepic correspondences should be noted:

ch: a voiceless velar fricative [x]
h: a voiced laryngeal fricative [ɦ]
c, dz: voiceless and voiced affricates [ts, dz]
č, dž: voiceless and voiced postalveolar affricates [tʃ, dʒ]
š, ž: voiceless and voiced postalveolar fricatives [ʃ, ʒ]
ť, ď, ľ, ň: prepalatal non-continuants [ṱ, ḓ, ḻ, ɲ]. However, before *i* and *e* the diacritics are not written. This causes ambiguity morpheme-internally, where both soft and hard non-continuants may appear before *i* and *e*. We shall provide transcriptions whenever the distinction is relevant.

Further divergences between the spelling and pronunciation are due to phonological rules, notably Voice Assimilation and *v*-Gliding. Slovak requires that sequences of obstruents agree as to voicing. The rule is regressive. Thus, *podpis* 'signature' is pronounced [potpis] and *kosba* 'reaping' [kozba]. In addition, obstruents are devoiced word-finally:

---

[1] The vowel [æ], spelled *ä*, is pronounced in what Kráľ (1988) and Sabol (1989) describe as 'higher style' (careful educated speech). In other styles it coalesces with the vowel *e*.

TABLE 1. *Correspondences between symbols used in the text and those of the IPA*

Our symbol	IPA symbol	Description
í, ú	iː, uː	long high tense vowels
e, o	ɛ, ɔ	mid lax vowels
é, ó	ɛː, ɔː	long mid lax vowels
á	aː	long low back vowel
ä	æ	front low vowel
š, ž	ʃ, ʒ	postalveolar fricatives
c, ʒ	ts, dz	alveolar affricates
č, ǯ	tʃ, dʒ	postalveolar affricates
t', d'	ṭ, ḍ	prepalatal stops
l', n'	ḷ, ɲ	prepalatal lateral and nasal
v	ʋ	labiodental approximant (sonorant)

rozkaz 'order' [roskas]. The letter *v* denotes a labiodental approximant in syllable onsets and the glide [u̯] in syllable codas: *voda* [voda] 'water' vs. *šev* [šeu̯] 'seam'. These differences will be marked in the transcription whenever they are relevant.

For typographic reasons we shall simplify the transcription and depart from the standards of the IPA. We summarize these departures in Table 1. Let us make note of two formal problems. First, at the underlying level /t', d', l', n'/ are assumed to be [–back, +anter], that is, soft alveolars. They are spelled out as [–back, –anter, +high] by a rule that we discuss in Chapter 4. Second, we shall follow the convention of enclosing underlying segments in double slashes, intermediate representations in single slashes, and phonetic transcriptions in square brackets.

2.3. UNDERLYING INVENTORY

2.3.1. Consonants

Most contrasts in the class of consonants are obvious and need not be exemplified here. For instance, Horecký (1975: 11) provides a number of 'minimal pairs' such as *kosa* 'scythe'—*koza* 'goat'. We shall therefore limit our discussion to the cases which might in principle be unclear. These reduce in fact to the phonemic status of prepalatals and velars.

One of the diachronic developments in the history of Slovak is the rise of prepalatals and of some velars which did not exist in Proto-Slavic. Their origin can be traced to the operation of various deletion rules which affected front vowels and glides. The net result is that prepalatals contrast with the corresponding alveolars in contexts which can no longer be conceived of as predictable:

(1) ni*t* 'rivet'—ni*t'* 'thread'; *d*at' 'give'—*d*'atel' 'woodpecker'; plá*n* 'plan'— plá*ň* 'plain'; *l*úh 'lye'—*l*'ud 'people'

We conclude that prepalatals are underlying segments in Modern Slovak.

With regard to the velars, Slovak is known to have undergone the change from [g] to [ɦ] in the thirteenth century (Pauliny 1963: 172). Polish did not undergo such a change. The correspondences are as follows:

(2) | Polish | Slovak | Gloss |
|--------|--------|-----------|
| gad | had | 'reptile' |
| grom | hrom | 'thunder' |
| noga | noha | 'leg' |
| Bóg | Boh | 'God' |

Pauliny (1963) points out that the rule later stopped being operative. This can be established on the basis of the accommodation of borrowings. Early loanwords, such as Hungarian *Waag* (a name), were taken over with *h*: *Wah*; later ones, such as German *Grund*, with *g*: *grunt* 'ground'. Today there is no doubt that *g*, *h*, and *ch* //x// are independent underlying segments. Compare:

(3) groš 'penny'—hroch 'hippopotamus'—chrobák 'cockchafer'

We shall claim, however that the voiced laryngeal fricative [ɦ] is not an underlying segment. It is derived by rule from the underlying voiced velar fricative //ɣ// (see the discussion in 9.3).

In representing segments we shall avail ourselves of the advances that have been made in the recent work on phonetic features. Ever since Jakobson *et al.* (1952) it has been known that segments are better thought of as bundles of features. This theory was developed in great detail in *SPE*, which, however, did not differentiate between the status of various features and claimed that every segment must be specified for every feature, regardless of whether the feature is contrastive or not. Recent work has shown that neither of these assumptions can be maintained. On the one hand, features seem to have more structure than has hitherto been assumed, and, on the other hand, full specification of every segment for all features no longer appears to be desirable.

Clements (1985, 1988), Sagey (1986), and others have shown that features must be organized in a hierarchical fashion. They are all grouped under the general node known as the Root Node, which is further linked to the skeletal X slot. Below the Root Node features are organized according to articulators and the articulators are marked as nodes. In the theory of Clements (1988) the structure of articulator nodes is as shown in (4). (Note that TONGUE BODY corresponds to VOCALIC in Clements's later work, for example Clements 1991.)

(4)

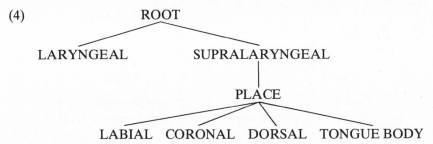

Nodes act like single-valued features in that they are either activated and then they are marked as present, or they are not activated and then they are absent. In other words, nodes act in a non-binary fashion. This means that one cannot refer to the absence of a node as a defining property of a natural class. For instance, in the *SPE* theory it was possible to refer to labials and dorsals (that is, velars) by specifying them as a class of [−coron] segments. Given (4), such a step is not possible. We can refer only to the presence of labials, coronals, and dorsals (as well as tongue-body segments: see below) separately or to all of them simultaneously. In the latter case we specify that a given rule affects the place node. There is some debate on whether this way of viewing natural classes is correct (cf., for instance, Dogil and Luschützky 1990). Christdas (1988) argues that CORONAL and LABIAL should be features and not nodes, which would permit us to use these properties with a minus value in defining natural classes. (Recall that features, unlike nodes, are binary.) Slovak provides partial support for Christdas's position.

In Slovak back /a/ and front /ä/ are two different phonemes (underlying segments). They contrast after labial consonants (Isačenko 1966):

(5) past+a 'paste'—päst' 'fist'
    mas+a 'mass'—mäs+o 'meat'
    vad+a 'defect'—hoväd+o 'beast'

There is also an alternation between [ä] and [a]. A relevant example here is the suffix for young creatures -*ä* (for a detailed discussion, see 5.6):

(6) *a.* holub 'pigeon'—holúb+ä
        chlap 'man'—chláp+ä
    b. hus 'goose'—hús+a
        det+i 'children'—diet'+a

Whether [ä] or [a] is underlying can easily be determined by looking at the examples where palatalization rules could potentially apply. Before front vowels Slovak palatalizes /t, d, n, l/ to [t', d', n', l'] by Coronal

Palatalization and /k, g, x/ to [č, ʒ, š] by First Velar Palatalization. (These rules are introduced later in this chapter.) The suffix -ä/a induces both types of palatalization:

(7) a. had 'reptile'—hád'+a
       pan 'man'—páň+a
    b. vlk 'wolf'—vĺč+a
       vnuk 'grandchild'—vnúč+a

We conclude that //ä // is the underlying representation of the suffix. The fact that //ä // surfaces as [a] in (6b) and (7) must therefore be accounted for by a rule. At this stage the rule could be stated as applying simply after coronals. Informally:

(8) ä → a / CORONAL —

This rule can be expressed in terms of nodes given in (4). We say that it applies if the CORONAL node is activated. That such a statement is in fact untenable, however, can be deduced from the alternations between [ä] and the diphthong [ia] which occur in the lengthening environments. In these environments ä, e, o diphthongize to ia, ie, ô [uo] and i, u, a lengthen to í, ú, á (see section 2.5 below). Relevant here is the contrast between the underlying //a // and //ä //:

(9) a. lan+o 'string'—lán (gen. pl.)
       hoväd+o 'beast'—hoviad (gen. pl.)
    b. val+i+t' 'fall'—vál'+a+t' (derived imperfective, henceforth DI)
       väz 'link' (N)—viaz+a+t' 'bind' (DI)

The presence of //ä // is often disguised by rule (8):

(10) a. žab+a 'frog'—žiab (gen. pl.)
     b. čl' ap+nú+t' 'make a noise'—čliap+a+t' (DI)

That //ä // is underlying is shown by the occurrence of ia in the lengthening environments of the gen. pl. and the derived imperfective. The //ä // in the words on the left in (10) surfaces as [a] because of rule (8).

The crucial evidence to determine whether the reference to CORONAL in (8) is sufficient can be obtained by looking at the context of velars. A relevant example here is the word o+kad+i+t' 'to incense'. In the derived imperfective it surfaces with ia: o+kiadz+a+t'. Thus, //ä // is underlying in the root kad //käd//. To derive the surface [a] in the perfective form o+kad+i+t' rule (8) must be amended to apply not only after coronals but also after velars. Given the node structure in (4), this cannot be done since there is no way of grouping these two classes of segments to the exclusion of labials. One way of solving the dilemma is to assume with Christdas (1988) that [labial] is not a node but a feature; hence it is binary and [−labial] provides the desirable natural class.

Before we restate rule (8) formally it is necessary to see where features fit in the tree given in (4). This in itself is subject to much debate. For example, Sagey (1986) assumes that the vowel features [back], [high], and [low] are grouped under the node DORSAL, while Clements (1988) places them under the added node TONGUE BODY. The feature [contin] has been assumed to hang off the ROOT node by Sagey (1986) and off the SUPRALARYNGEAL node by Clements (1988). Clements (1988) introduces the features [vocoid] and [approximant] and drops the more traditional features [consonantal] and [lateral]. Slovak does not provide any evidence to resolve these problems. For the purposes of this study I assume the node and feature hierarchy in (12). It is based on Clements (1988), with the aforementioned modification that [labial] is a feature and not a node. Also, I keep the traditional features [consonantal] and [lateral]. A convention is assumed that nodes are written in capital letters while features appear in square brackets. The abbreviations used in (12) and in subsequent parts of this book are summarized in (11).

(11) *Nodes*   *Features*
     R = ROOT   [lat] or [later] = [lateral]
     L = LARYNGEAL   [cons] = [consonantal]
     SL = SUPRALARYNGEAL   [nas] = [nasal]
     PL = PLACE   [cont] or [contin] = [continuant]
     COR = CORONAL   [son] or [sonor] = [sonorant]
     DOR = DORSAL   [lab]= [labial]
     TB = TONGUE BODY   [distr] or [distrib] = [distributed]
                                      [anter] = [anterior]

The features [s.g.] = [spread glottis] and [c.g.] = [constricted glottis] are added for completeness in (12). They do not function distinctively in Slovak.

(12)

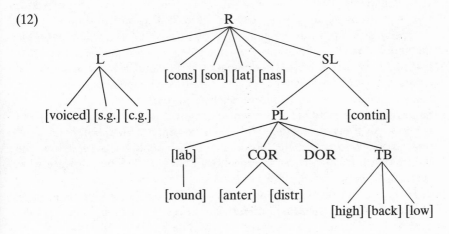

We can now state rule (8) formally. It backs the front low vowel //ä// after the segments that are [–lab], as shown in (13).

(13) *ä*-Backing

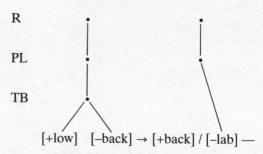

Following Czaykowska-Higgins (1988), nodes which are activated are marked with a dot and a convention is adopted that irrelevant intermediate nodes are omitted, hence SL is not marked in (13).

The advantage of viewing the traditional *SPE* features as a geometrically structured system of nodes and features is apparent particularly in the statement of assimilation rules. Such rules can now be easily conceived of as spreading features from one 'segment' to another or as linking and de-linking (that is, deleting) nodes in the neighbouring 'segments'. These types of operation will be illustrated by our analysis of Slovak in this book.

In addition to feature hierarchies such as those in (12) recent work in phonology has centred on determining to what extent underlying or intermediate derivational representations need to be specified. The debate about this problem is known in the literature as the discussion of the theory of underspecification. It was initiated in works by Kiparsky (1982) and Archangeli (1984), and it has led to the emergence of two different variants of the theory: radical underspecification (notably, Archangeli and Pulleyblank (forthcoming)) and contrastive underspecification (Steriade 1987, Clements 1988). The two theories differ in the extent to which representations need to be specified. The radical variant does not permit the specification of both the plus and the minus value of a given feature in the underlying representation. Only one value may be specified. The other is supplied by the so-called complement and default rules, which may be either universal or language-specific. Contrastive underspecification, on the other hand, does not impose such requirements on representations. Segments are specified to the extent that is necessary in order to bring out contrasts in a given language. We shall not engage in the debate about underspecification. For the purposes of this book we shall adopt the theory of contrastive underspecification. Below we briefly illustrate what is meant by underspecification.

Two facts can be assumed as certain: phonetic representations must be ultimately fully specified and underlying representations must not be fully specified. The extent to which they need to be underspecified is largely an open question. Below we look at two examples which support the theory of underspecification.

Kiparsky (1982, 1985) draws attention to the fact that voicing of sonorants is a universally predictable property. This redundancy may therefore be extracted from underlying representations and stated in the form of a rule: [+sonor] → [+voiced]. Not only does such a statement capture an important generalization but it also simplifies phonological rules. Given a language such as Polish or Slovak which requires that clusters of obstruents must be uniformly voiced or voiceless, the rule of Voice Assimilation need not specify the input as restricted to obstruents. This is true if the rule applies at the stage where the redundancy supplying [+voiced] to sonorants has not taken effect yet. Voice Assimilation can then be viewed as a natural process of linking which determines the feature composition of the laryngeal node of one segment on the basis of the content of the laryngeal node of another segment.

In a slightly different way one can argue for the need of underspecification on the basis of prepalatal consonants in Slovak. Universal considerations do not come into play here, but language-specific ones do. In phonetic terms [t', d', n', l'] are [−back, −anter, +high]. Do they need to be specified for all these features at the underlying level? Hardly. The relevant contrast with [t, d, n, l] can be made by specifying them as [−back]. The remaining features [−anter, +high] can be supplied by a redundancy rule. (This rule is formulated in (18) in Chapter 4.) The advantages of such an interpretation extend beyond the underlying representation. Three in particular should be named. First, as we mentioned earlier, Slovak has a palatalization rule which turns /t, d, n, l/ into [t', d', n', l'] before front vowels (see Coronal Palatalization in (29) below). The statement of palatalization can be considerably simplified if the features [−anter, +high] can be added later by a redundancy rule. Palatalization merely adds the feature [−back]. Second, supplying [−back] need not be conceived of as an addition of a feature. Rather, what happens is that [−back] is spread onto the consonant from the following vowel, which permits us to view palatalization as a natural assimilation process (see rule (17) in Chapter 4). If palatalization were to supply [−anter, +high] in addition to [−back], then it could not be a spreading rule since it takes effect not only before the [+high] *i* but also before *e* and *ä*, which are [−high]. Third, in some contexts both underlying and derived palatals must be depalatalized, that is, turned into [t, d, n, l]. The statement of depalatalization can again be considerably simplified if the underlying and the derived *t'*, *d'*, *n'*, *l'* carry only [−back] as the distinctive feature (see section 8.3).

In Table 2 we give an inventory of underlying consonants in Slovak. Dots specify nodes, plus and minus signs refer to features. All members of the inventory are [+consonantal]. Affricates are specified as complex segments, that is, segments that are [−contin] in the first phase and

TABLE 2. *Underlying consonants of Slovak*

	Labials					Dento-alveolars								Postalveolars[a]					Prepalatals				Velars			
	p	b	f	v	m	t	d	s	z	c	ʒ	n	l	r	š	ž	č	ǯ	t'	d'	n'	l'	k	g	x	ɣ
COR						•	•	•	•	•	•	•	•	•	•	•	•	•	•	•	•	•				
anter						+	+	+	+	+	+	+	+	-	-	-	-	-	-	-	-	-				
DOR																			•	•	•	•	•	•	•	•
TB back																			-	-	-	-	+	+	+	+
L voice	-	+	-	+	•	-	+	-	+	-	+	•	•	•	-	+	-	+	-	+	•	•	-	+	-	+
Other features																										
lab	+	+	+	+	+																					
nas					+							+									+					
cont	-	-	+	+		-	-	+	+	?	?			-	+	+	?	?					-	-	+	+
sonor	-	-	-	+	+	-	-	-	-	-	-	+	+	+	-	-	-	-	-	-	+	+	-	-	-	-
lat													+									+				

[a] By contrast with Polish, [r] and [l] are phonetically postalveolar in Slovak (cf. Kráľ 1988). However, for reasons that we give in 4.5, *l* is underlyingly [+anter].

[+contin] in the second. The combination [-/+contin] is denoted in the table by a question mark. Note that /v/ is a sonorant in Slovak in both the underlying and the phonetic representation. The features not specified in the table are supplied by redundancy rules. For example, all segments under the node DORSAL are [-sonor].

2.3.2. Syllable nuclei

Slovak displays an opposition of length in vowels and liquids. In addition, it has three rising diphthongs [ie, ia, uo]. The fourth diphthong [iu] has a highly limited distribution. It will be discussed in Chapter 6. Recall that acute accents denote length.

(14) i u í ú (iu)
　　 e o é ó ie uo
　　 ä a á ia
　　 l r ĺ ŕ

We note that there is a gap in the system of long vowels: a front low ä́ does not exist. Further, the mid vowels e and o are lax [ɛ, ɔ]. Attention should be drawn to the fact that the distribution of length is not accompanied by any distinction in terms of quality (Sabol 1989: 37). The segments in (14) are contrastive. In (15) we adduce some examples demonstrating that the contrasts cannot be attributed to context. Liquids, both short and long, are syllabic. Most examples are taken from Horecký (1975):

(15) krik 'shout'—krík 'bush'
　　 kur+a 'chicken'—kúr+a 'cure'
　　 leno 'but'—lén+o 'feud'
　　 mol 'mole'—mól+o 'pier'
　　 rad 'row'—grád 'degree'
　　 čln 'boat'—tĺk 'pestle'
　　 krčm+a 'inn'—kŕč 'cramp'

In the framework of three-dimensional phonology the opposition of length is expressed at the skeletal tier as the opposition of one versus two slots dominating a single melody. That is, short and long vowels have the same representation at the melodic tier. In this way the system of underlying vowels is reduced to six: see (16). Redundancy rules fill in the missing values and supply non-contrastive features such as [round] and [tense].

Whether diphthongs are underlying or not is a debatable matter and we postpone this discussion till Chapter 6. For the moment let us concentrate merely on phonetic facts. In Central Slovak a phonetic distinction is made

(16) Underlying vowels[2]

	i	u	e	o	ä	a
TONGUE BODY	•	•	•	•	•	•
back	−	+	−	+	−	+
high	+	+	−	−		
low					+	+

---

between diphthongs and glide–vowel sequences on the one hand, and vowel sequences on the other (cf. Jakobson 1931, Král' 1988). Isačenko (1968) gives the following minimal pairs:

(17) *a.* Diphthong   *Glide–vowel sequence*
       ziabnut' 'freeze'   zjavit' 'appear'
       obiehat' 'run around'   objektiv 'objective'

     b. Diphthong   *Vowel sequence*
       kúria 'they smoke'   kúria 'curia'
       pária 'they steam'   pária 'pariah'

It should be noted, however, that the phonetic distinctions in (17*a*) are limited to a very small group of words. The contrasts in (17*b*), on the other hand, are quite common. It is this dialect that is assumed as standard in all grammars of Slovak and in the pronouncing dictionary (Král' 1988) which we shall use as the basic source of data for the purposes of this book. However, attention should be drawn to the fact that there are dialects of Slovak which treat the contrasts in (17) differently. These dialects are generally described as substandard. Král' (1988) gives the following classification of what he calls 'mistaken' pronunciations:

(18) Standard [i̯e, i̯a, i̯u] are rendered as:
    a. glide-plus-vowel sequences [je, ja, ju]:[3]
        čierny 'black' [či̯erni] → [čjerni]
        poriadok 'order' [pori̯adok] → [porjadok]
        paniu 'lady' (acc. sg.) [pan'i̯u] → [pan'ju]
    b. vowel sequences [ie, ia, iu]:
        [čierni], [poriadok], [pan'iu]

---

[2] The glide [j] is interpreted in this book as derivable from the vowel melody //i // by rules of syllable structure. The other glide, [u̯], has a very limited distribution. It occurs only as part of the diphthong *o* [uo] or as a realization of //v// in syllable coda. We assume that it is derived by rules in all instances.

[3] Birnbaum (1981) reports that in a language game based on the insertion of the consonant [p] plus an adjacent vowel his two consultants did not distinguish between the rising diphthongs and the sequences of [j] plus a vowel. He proposes a rule that resyllabifies the onglide of a rising diphthong into the syllable onset. It is not clear whether or not his consultants were speakers of dialect (18*a*).

c. long vowels with neither a glide nor an *i* preceding, that is [é, á, ú]:
[čérni], [porádok], [pan'ú]

d. glide plus long vowel [jé, já, jú]:
[čjérni], [porjádok], [pan'jú]

In sum, these dialects exhibit either a diphthong loss (18c–d) or syllabic restructuring of the onglide: as an onset in (18a) or as a vowel in (18b).

Similar variation is found with the diphthong ô [u̯o]. (For accuracy the onglide is represented here as [u̯]; elsewhere in the text we ignore this detail and represent the diphthong [u̯o] as [uo].) Standard Central Slovak draws a clear distinction between the diphthong [u̯o] and the sequence [vo] containing a labiodental approximant followed by a vowel: *dôvod* [du̯ ovot] 'proof'. According to Kráľ (1988), substandard dialects render [u̯o] as one or other of the following:

(19) a. standard [u̯o, vo] are neutralized to [vo]: *dôvod* [dvovot] 'proof'
    b. or they are neutralized to [u̯o]: *dvor* [du̯or] 'yard'
    c. the diphthong [u̯o] is monophthongized either as a long vowel or as a short vowel: *môžem* [móžem] 'I can', *pôjdem* [pojd'em] 'I go'

It is not clear from Kráľ's data whether the dialects in (19a–b) have in their systems the sounds [u̯] and [v], respectively. In what follows we shall limit our discussion to the standard dialect.

2.4. STRESS

The dialects of Western and Central Slovak are similar to Czech in that they exhibit initial stress. In Eastern Slovak, as in Polish,[4] main stress falls on the penult (Stanislav 1977).

In addition to the main stress, polysyllabic words may receive secondary stresses. According to Letz (1950), secondary stresses form an alternating pattern starting from the main stress. They have a rhythmic function. The examples in (20) are taken from Letz (1950). Note that *ie* is a diphthong.

(20) a. ûčiteľ 'teacher', záhradník 'gardener', vysoký 'high'
        (stress: 1 2 / 1 2 / 1 2)

    zostava 'set', stolica 'capital', silnejší 'stronger'
    (stress: 1 2 / 1 2 / 1 2)

    b. nepoveziem 'I won't carry', nepovezieme 'we won't carry'
    (stress: 1 2 / 1 2)

    c. najpochopiteľnejšieho 'most obvious' (masc. gen. sg.)
    (stress: 1 2 2 2)

---

[4] In Polish the main stress is penultimate. Rhythmic secondary stresses are assigned from the beginning of the word and exhibit an alternating pattern, exactly like the words in (20); see Rubach and Booij (1985).

Král' (1988) confirms that there may be a chain of secondary stresses, as in (21*a*), but he does not mark final rhythmic stresses (21*b*) and permits lapses of either one or two syllables between rhythmic stresses (21*c*).

(21) *a.* odpočúvat' 'listen in'
$\overset{1}{}\;\overset{2}{}$

    b. predpokladajú 'they presume', parazitický 'parasitic'

    c. najneočakávanejší ~ najneočakávanejší 'most unexpected'

In compounds the main stress of the second constituent (the one on the right) is weakened to a secondary stress. Note that some compounds are built by adding the linking phoneme *o*.

(22) veľk+o+dušný 'generous', dobr+o+voľný 'optional',

    devätnást+ročný 'nineteen-year' (Letz 1950),

    pol+o+vodič 'semiconductor', poľn+o+hospodár 'farmer'

I shall not attempt to provide a formal analysis of stress in Slovak since, on the one hand, the data are incomplete and, on the other hand, stress rules do not, as far as I know, interact with any rules of segmental phonology.

2.5. MAJOR RULES OF SLOVAK PHONOLOGY

Slovak phonology is close-knit in the sense that phonological rules interact to a relatively high degree. While this makes a phonological system interesting, it also makes the task of its presentation rather difficult. To facilitate this task we summarize all the major rules briefly below. The rules are stated informally but reference is made to the sections of the book in which they are discussed in detail from both the formal and the descriptive points of view.

Yer Vocalization (see 5.3)

Slovak has 'fleeting' vowels *e* and *o* which are known as 'yers'. (The name is sometimes spelled 'jers' in accordance with the Slavic tradition.) These vowels alternate with zero. Phonetically they are indistinguishable from the non-alternating *e* and *o*. Also, the distribution of the yers *e*, *o* and the 'regular' vowels *e*, *o* is not predictable. The yers must therefore be made distinct in the underlying representation from the corresponding *e*, *o*. How this distinction is expressed is a matter of debate and we postpone the solution of this problem till Chapter 5. For the moment we assume that the relevant distinction is somehow made. To distinguish typographically the yers *e*, *o* from the regular vowels *e*, *o* we represent the former as capital *E*, *O* and the latter simply as *e*, *o*. It is a generalization that the yers surface phonetically (as [e] and [o], respectively) if another yer follows in the next syllable:

(23) Yer Vocalization $\left\{ \begin{matrix} E \\ O \end{matrix} \right\} \to \left\{ \begin{matrix} e \\ o \end{matrix} \right\} / - C_0$ yer

In all other environments yers delete context-freely. (We shall assume that they are stray-erased, that is, they delete by the convention known as Stray Erasure (Steriade 1982) because they are not linked to higher levels of representation: the skeleton and the syllable structure; see Chapter 5.) We hasten to add that, following the recognized tradition in the generative phonology of Slavic, the so-called zero endings, that is endings with no overt vowel phonetically, are interpreted as yers. Thus, a word such as *krídl+o* 'wing' has a yer between the *d* and the *l*. The yer surfaces as [e] in the gen. pl. *krídel* //krídEl+V//, where V is an unspecified yer of the gen. pl. The root yer also surfaces before the diminutive suffix //Ec//, which itself contains a yer: *krídel+c+e* //krídEl+Ec+e//. As already mentioned, unvocalized yers are deleted.

Vowel Lengthening (see 6.1.1.3 and 6.2.3)

The presence of a yer in the following syllable induces Vowel Lengthening, for example *bab+a* 'old woman' (-*a* is the fem. nom. sg. ending)—*báb* //bab+V//, gen. pl.

(24) Vowel Lengthening $V \to \acute{V} / - C_0$ yer

Diphthongization (see 6.3)

Mid vowels //e, o// and the front low vowel //ä// are diphthongized to [ie, uo, ia] when lengthened, for example *žen+a* 'woman'—*žien* //žen+V//, gen. pl.

(25) Diphthongization $\{\acute{e}, \acute{\ddot{a}}, \acute{o}\} \to \{ie, ia, uo\}$

Rhythmic Law (see 6.1.2.2 and 6.2.3)

Long vowels shorten if they are preceded by a long vowel. For example, the dat. pl. ending of feminine nouns has a long vowel. It appears phonetically in words such as *bab+ám* 'old woman' (dat. pl.). However, in *lúk+a* 'meadow'—*lúk+am* (dat. pl.) the *a* is short.

(26) Rhythmic Law $\acute{V} \rightarrow V / \acute{V} C_0$ —

From the point of view of the Rhythmic Law no distinction is made between long vowels and diphthongs. The latter may both trigger and undergo the rule; compare *nes+iem* 'I carry' and *môž+em* 'I can'. The shortened diphthongs *ie, ia, ô* [uo] appear phonetically as single vowels [e, a, o].

Glide Shortening (see 8.2)

Long non-high vowels shorten if they follow a glide. For example, we have just said that the dat. pl. ending of feminine nouns is *-ám*. The ending appears with a short *a* after *j*: *zmij+am* 'viper'.

(27) Glide Shortening $\acute{V} \rightarrow V / j$ —
                           [–high]

First Velar Palatalization (see 4.2)

Velars //k, g, x, ɣ// become postalveolars [č, ӡ, š, ž] before front vowels and glides. Note that stops become affricates, for example *bok* 'side'—*boč+i+t'* 'keep away'.

(28) 1st Velar Palatalization   {k, g, x, ɣ} → {č, ӡ, š, ž} / — {i, j, e, ä}

Coronal Palatalization (see 4.5)

Coronal non-continuants //t, d, n, l// change into prepalatal [t', d', n', l'] before front vowels and *j*. (Note that, before *j*, stops undergo a further change into affricates; see below.) This is shown by examples such as *let* 'flight'—*let+ie+t'* [t'] 'fly'—*let+ím* [t'] 'I fly'.

(29) Coronal Palatalization   {t, d, n, l} → {t', d', n', l'} / — {i, j, e, ä}

Iotation (see 4.6)

Dento-alveolar obstruents //t, d, s, z// change into [c, ӡ, š, ž] before *j*. The fricatives become postalveolar while the stops become alveolar affricates. If the stops are preceded by *s* or *z*, then they change into prepalatals while the preceding *s* or *z* surfaces as a postalveolar spirant.

(30) Iotation $\left\{\begin{matrix} t, d, s, z \\ st, zd \end{matrix}\right\} \rightarrow \left\{\begin{matrix} c, ӡ, š, ž \\ št' \quad žd' \end{matrix}\right\} / — j$

For example: *prat+a+t'* 'hide'—*prac+em* 'I hide'. The /j/ that triggers Iotation is not visible on the surface since it is deleted after consonants (see (24) in Chapter 8).

Vowel Deletion (see 3.1.3)

This is a general rule of Slavic originally discovered by Jakobson (1948). It simplifies vowel clusters in verbs:

(31) Vowel Deletion $V \rightarrow \emptyset / — V]_{VERB}$

Thus, in our preceding example *prac+em* 'I hide' there is a single vowel on the surface. A representation at an earlier derivational stage has a vocalic sequence /prat+a+ém/, where *-a* is a verbalizing suffix and *-ém* is an inflectional ending.

3

MORPHOLOGY

In this chapter we introduce the basic facts of Slovak descriptive morphology. Our intention is to prepare the ground for the discussion of cyclic phonological rules in the subsequent chapters of this book. Consequently, the presentation of the facts is not complete and we concentrate primarily on inflection. Our aim is to establish the underlying representations of the most important morphemes and to state basic allomorphy rules.

3.1. VERB MORPHOLOGY

Below we review the structure of the verb. We start with the presentation of verbal stems and then proceed to the analysis of inflectional forms.

3.1.1. Verb stems

Typologically there are two classes of verbs: inherent verbs and derived verbs. The characteristic feature of the former is that they are monosyllabic and end in consonants, hence we call them C-verbs. Derived verbs, on the other hand, are formed by adding verbalizing suffixes to nominal or adjectival bases, or directly to roots. We list some examples below.

(1) *a.* C-verbs:
    Class 1, ending in an obstruent: nes+ú 'they carry', klad+ú 'they put'
    Class 2, ending in a sonorant: pij+ú 'they drink', žuj+ú 'they chew'
  b. *i*-verbs   čist+ý 'clean'—čist+i+t' 'to clean'
                  hniezd+o 'nest'—hniezd+i+t' 'to nest'
  c. *e*-verbs   let 'flight'—let+e+l 'he flew'
                  vid 'sight'—vid+e+l 'he saw'
  d. *ä*-verbs   krik 'shout' (N)—krič+a+t' 'to shout'
                  beh 'running'—bež+a+t' 'to run'
  e. *a*-verbs   vlád+a (-*a* is an inflectional ending) 'government'
                  —vlád+a+t' 'to govern'
                  rehot 'laughter'—rehot+a+t' 'laugh'
  f. *aj*-verbs   chov 'breeding'—chov+aj+ú 'they breed'
                  hr+a 'play' (N)—hr+aj+ú 'they play'

g. ej-verbs   rozum 'mind'—rozum+ej+ú 'they understand'
               drah+ý 'expensive'—draž+ej+ú 'they become expensive'
h. ova-verbs   obed 'dinner'—obed+ova+t' 'dine'
               mil+ý 'dear'—mil+ova+t' 'love'

A striking fact about the verbalizing suffixes *ä* and *a* in (1*d, e*) is that the vowel always surfaces as [a]. Why do we posit then an underlying //ä//? This step is justified on both phonological and morphological grounds. Phonologically the verbs in //ä// contrast with those in //a// in that they show effects of palatalization. Thus, 1st Velar Palatalization changes the //k// of *krik* 'shout' (N) into the [č] of *krič+a+t'* 'to shout'. The morphological contrast between the *ä-* and the *a*-stems is seen, for example, in the gerund, where the former take the allomorph *-iac* and the latter the allomorph *-úc: krič+iac* 'shouting', *vlád+uc* 'governing'. The fact that phonetically //ä// and //a// are represented identically as [a] is easily accounted for by the rule of *ä*-Backing which turns /ä/ into [a] after non-labial consonants (see rule (13) in Chapter 2).

3.1.2. Infinitive

The infinitive is formed by adding the morpheme //t'// to the verb stem, for example *rehot+a* 'laugh'—*rehot+a+t'* 'to laugh'. The infinitive suffix triggers three allomorphy rules, two of which we discuss immediately below. (The third rule is discussed in 3.1.9.)

The root-final consonant of C-verbs changes in accordance with the following pattern:

(2) t → s: plet+ú 'they weave'—plies+t'
     d → z (further to [s] by Voice Assimilation): ved+ú 'they lead'—
        vies+t'
     h → z (further to [s] by Voice Assimilation): strieh+ol 'he guarded'—
        striez+t'
     k → c: riek+ol 'he said'—riec+t'[1]

The allomorphy rule in (2) is uninteresting in the sense that it does not interact with any other rules except Voice Assimilation. A better insight into the phonology of Slovak can be obtained by looking at the rule of *e*-Lengthening. Isačenko (1966: 196) points out that the vowel *e* is lengthened in the infinitive:

(3) *e*-Lengthening   e → é / — t']$_{INF}$.

---

[1] In the verb *moh+ol* 'he could' the *h* changes into /ʒ/ and further into [c] by Voice Assimilation: *môc+t'*. This is a reflex of the fact that historically the *h* comes from /g/ in this instance.

Thus, the infinitive of the *e*-verbs given in (1c) is *let+ie+t'* 'fly' and *vid+ie+t'* 'see'. (Recall that long *é* is further diphthongized to *ie* by rule (25) from Chapter 2.)

Rule (3) also affects *ej*-verbs, hence the infinitives of the examples in (1g) are *rozum+ie+t'* 'understand' and *draž+ie+t'* 'become expensive'. These verbs are made inputs to *e*-Lengthening since Slovak, like other Slavic languages, has a rule that deletes *j* before consonants (cf. Isačenko 1966: 195):

(4) Postvocalic *j*-Deletion $j \to \emptyset / — C$

The operation of this rule will be illustrated further in 3.1.3 and 3.1.12.

The examples in (5) indicate that *e*-Lengthening and Postvocalic *j*-Deletion interact not only with each other but also with the Rhythmic Law. Note that *-y* is the inflectional ending of the adjectives.

(5) múdr+y 'clever'—múdr+ej+ú 'they become clever'—múdr+ie+t' 'to become clever'
   príkr+y 'hard'—príkr+ej+ú 'they become hard'—príkr+ie+t' 'to become hard'

The verbs are derived from adjectives by adding the suffix *-ej*, as shown on the surface in the 3rd pl. indicative. The infinitive form is as follows:

(6) prikr+ie+t' 'harden': príkr+ej+t'
   príkr+e+t'   Postvocalic *j*-Deletion (4)
   —   Rhythmic Law (2/26)
   príkr+é+t'   *e*-Lengthening (3)
   príkr+ie+t'   Diphthongization (2/25)

Note: the number to the left of the slash refers to the chapter, the number to the right denotes a rule. Thus, 2/26 means rule (26) in Chapter 2. The chapter number is omitted if we quote a rule from the current chapter.

It is crucial in (6) that the rules apply in the order as given. Notice that the Rhythmic Law does not take effect since at the relevant stage the *e* is still short. The fact that the *e* is short in the underlying representation is not motivated merely by the desire to explain the violations of the Rhythmic Law in (6). The primary motivation comes from the observation that the *e* is short in other conjugational forms such as the 3rd pl. indicative *rozum+ej+ú* 'they understand', the passive participle *rozum+e+n+ý* 'understood', or the past participle *rozum+e+l* 'understood'.

3.1.3. Imperative

The imperative is manifested on the surface in four different ways (we look at the 2nd sg.):

(7) *a.* as the vowel *i*, but only in a restricted class of cases (see Chapter 7), for example, *tr+ú* 'they rub'—*tr+i*

 b. as a zero: *čuj+ú* 'they feel'—*čuj*, *rozum+ej+ú* 'they understand'—*rozum+ej*

 c. as a reflex of palatalization with no overt vowel on the surface, for example as a reflex of Coronal Palatalization in C-verbs: *klad+ú* 'they put'—*klad'*

 d. as a truncation of the verbalizing morpheme: *kos+i+t'* 'mow'—*kos*, *kop+a+t'* 'dig'—*kop*

The fact given in (7*d*), truncation, indicates that the imperative morpheme is a vowel. The surface forms are then derived by Vowel Deletion, a well-known rule of Slavic phonology that was originally discovered by Jakobson (1948):

(8) Vowel Deletion $V \rightarrow \emptyset \, / — V]_{VERB}$

Vowel Deletion will be motivated further in subsequent sections of this chapter.

The facts of palatalization mentioned in (7*c*) suggest that the imperative vowel must be front. At first glance it seems to be /i/, as indeed found on the surface in (7*a*). However, the appearance of [i] in phonetic representation is restricted to a certain class of verbs that we shall discuss in 7.2. The examples in (7*b–d*) indicate that normally the *i* is not found phonetically. It is therefore a deletable *i*, the type of vowel that we called a yer (see 2.5). Recall that yers delete whenever they are not followed by a yer. This is exactly the situation in the imperative. A derivation of our examples in (7*c–d*) is now as follows. The yer is represented as a capital letter.

(9) klad+I   kos+i+I

 —   kos+I   Vowel Deletion (8)

 klad'+I —   Coronal Palatalization (2/29)

 klad'   kos   Yer Deletion

While the imperative yer fulfils an important phonological function for the data in (7*c–d*) and in derivation (9), it seems to be superfluous for the examples in (7*b*). This is only apparent. The data in (7) exemplify the 2nd sg. of the imperative. The person ending here is zero. However, in the 1st pl. and the 2nd pl. the person endings are *-me* and *-te*, respectively. The yer is necessary to block the rule of Postvocalic *j*-Deletion. Below we derive the infinitive and the 1st pl. imperative forms of the C-verb //čuj// 'feel':

(10) čuj+t' čuj+I+me

 ču+t'   —   Postvocalic *j*-Deletion (4)

 —   čuj+me   Yer Deletion

C-verbs ending in /ij/ undergo an allomorphy rule in the imperative that deletes the /j/:

(11) Allomorphy j-Deletion $j \rightarrow \emptyset / i - I]_{IMPER.}$

Thus, we have the alternations shown in (12), where the infinitive is subject to Postvocalic j-Deletion, the 3rd pl. shows the surface [j], and the imperative is derived by rule (11).

(12) *Infinitive*   *3rd pl. indic.*   *Imper.: 2nd sg., 1st pl., 2nd pl.*
     pi+t' 'drink'   pij+ú   pi, pi+me, pi+te
     ši+t' 'sew'   šij+ú   ši, ši+me, ši+te
     kry+t' [kri+t'] 'hide' kryj+ú   kry, kry+me, kry+te

The deletion of the /j/ in the imperative is conditioned phonologically in the sense that the preceding vowel must be *i*, hence the imperative of, for example, *žu+t'* //žuj+t'// 'chew' is *žuj* and not **žu*. Neither can the rule be generalized to other morphological forms, that is, beyond the imperative. This is shown by the fact that the gen. pl. of *zmij+a* 'viper' is *zmij+í*. We shall return to the analysis of the imperative in Chapter 7.

3.1.4. Past participle

The past participle is formed by adding the suffix *l* to the verb stem, hence it is also known as the *l*-form:

(13) *a.* čist+i+t' 'clean'—čist+i+l 'cleaned'
        rehot+a+t' 'laugh'—rehot+a+l 'laughed'
    b. chov+a+t' 'breed' (compare chov+aj+ú 'they breed')—chov+a+l
        'bred'
        pi+t' 'drink' (compare pij+ú 'they drink')—pi+l 'drunk'

It is evident from the comparison with the 3rd pl. indicative that the verbs in (13b) undergo Postvocalic j-Deletion not only in the infinitive but also in the *l*-form. The past participle is followed by a gender ending which is zero for the masc. sg., *-a* for the fem. sg., *-o* for the neuter sg., and *-i* for the pl. (all genders). Taking the fem. sg. as an example we obtain the following structure for the participle 'cleaned':

(14) adjective   verbalizing suffix   past participle   gender
     čist   +   i   +   l   +   a

It may be asked whether the masc. sg. gender ending is not a yer vowel which is simply not seen on the surface (that is, it is deleted) since the environment of Yer Vocalization (2/23) is not met. This is the situation in Polish. In Slovak there is little evidence to substantiate the interpretation of the masc. sg. as a yer. The only word which would require this interpretation is the verb *ist'* 'go'. In the preterite it exhibits vowel–zero alternations that are typically accounted for by postulating a sequence of yers in the underlying representation:

(15) šie+l 'he went'—š+l+a 'she went'—š+l+o 'it went'

This alternation can be derived by Yer Vocalization if the verb root has a yer and the masc. sg. ending is also a yer: //šI+l+U//, where the capital letters denote yers: front and back, respectively. We may note, however, that the verb *ist'* requires suppletive forms in any case. Thus, for example, the present tense 3rd sg. is *id+e* 'he goes', which cannot be related phonologically to the infinitive or to the past participle. In fact, these two forms themselves cannot be related either. We shall therefore assume that the inflected forms of *ist'* are all instances of suppletion. This makes it unnecessary to interpret the masc. sg. ending as a yer. Rather, it is simply zero.

The past participle is used in the preterite and in the past perfect tense. In the 1st and 2nd persons of the preterite the auxiliary verb *byt'* appears in the present tense. In the past perfect, *byt'* is in the *l*-form and it is preceded by the present-tense forms of *byt'* in the 1st and 2nd persons. The pronouns may, but need not, appear:

(16) (ja) som čist+i+l 'I cleaned'
    (on) čist+i+l 'he cleaned'
    (ja) som bol čist+i+l 'I had cleaned'
    (on) bol čist+i+l 'he had cleaned'

3.1.5. Perfect participle

The perfect participle is formed by adding the suffix //vš// to the verb stem. This suffix is in turn followed by the gender endings of the adjectival conjugation. For example, in the nom. sg. we have *-í* in the masculine, *-ia* in the feminine, and *-ie* in the neuter forms:[2]

(17) *a.* čist+i+t' 'clean'—čist+i+vš+í 'having cleaned'
    kup+ova+t' 'buy'—kup+ova+vš+í 'having bought'
    b. rozum+ie+t' 'understand'—rozum+ej+ú 'they understand'—
    rozum+e+vš+í 'having understood'
    pi+t' 'drink'—pij+ú 'they drink'—na+pi+vš+í 'having drunk'

The forms of (17*b*) illustrate the operation of Postvocalic *j*-Deletion (4). Recall that the infinitive *ie* is an effect of *e*-Lengthening (3) and Diphthongization (2/25). We should add that the perfect participle suffix carries

---

[2] We argue in Chapter 6 that the endings are long vowels and not diphthongs. The phonetic [ia] and [ie] are derived by Diphthongization.

an arbitrary restriction: it does not attach to Class 1 verbs, that is, to the
C-verbs that end in an obstruent (see (1a) above).

3.1.6. Passive participle

The passive participle has the following structure: verb stem + passive
participle + inflectional ending of the adjectival declension. Isačenko
(1966) points out that there are three suffixes of the passive participle: -t,
-en, and -n. Their distribution is predictable from the structure of the verb
stem. The suffix -t is added to Class 2 C-verbs, that is to those C-verbs that
end in a sonorant, for example pij+ú 'they drink'—pi+t+ý 'drunk' (the j is
deleted by Postvocalic j-Deletion). The suffix -en attaches to Class 1 C-
verbs, that is, to those C-verbs that end in an obstruent. It also attaches to
i-stems. Thus nes+ú 'they carry' and pros+i+t' 'ask' have the participles
nes+en+ý 'carried' and pros+en+ý 'asked', respectively. The latter shows
the operation of Jakobson's Vowel Deletion (8):

(18) pros+i+en   i is a verbalizing morpheme: compare pros+b+a 'request'
      pros+en   Vowel Deletion

Incidentally, note that in Slovak, by contrast with other Slavic languages
such as Czech, Polish, or Sorbian, the configuration i+en does not trigger
Iotation: compare Slovak pros+en- and Czech proš+en- (we discuss
Iotation in 4.6).

The third allomorph of the passive participle -n occurs elsewhere. In
(19) we give some examples. On the left we list that form of the verb
which shows what type of verb stem we are dealing with:

(19) a. pís+a+t' 'write'—pís+a+n+ý 'written'
          mil+ova+t' 'love'—mil+ova+n+ý 'loved'
      b. rozum+ej+ú 'they understand'—rozum+e+n+ý 'understood'
          čít+aj+ú 'they read'—čít+a+n+ý 'read'

Evidently, the verbs in (19) take -n and not -en. Had the latter been
appended, the verbs in (19a) would have undergone Vowel Deletion, like
pros+en+ý in (18) above. On the other hand, the verbs in (19b) would
have kept their j, that is they would not have been subject to Postvocalic
j-Deletion. We sum up the distribution of the passive participle suffixes
in (20):

(20) Passive Participle $\emptyset \rightarrow$ $\begin{cases} \text{t / [+sonor]}_{\text{C-VERB}} \, \text{—} \\ \text{en /]}_{\{\text{C-VERB, i-VERB}\}} \, \text{—} \\ \text{n / elsewhere} \end{cases}$

3.1.7. Gerund and present participle

The gerund has two allomorphs: *-iac* and *-úc*. Their distribution is as follows:

(21) Gerund $\emptyset \rightarrow$ $\begin{cases} \text{iac / [V, –back] —} \\ \text{úc / elsewhere} \end{cases}$

That is, verb stems that end in the front vowels *-i*, *-e*, and *-ä* take the *-iac* allomorph, and all other verbs take *-úc*. For example:

(22) *a.* pros+i+t' 'ask'—pros+iac 'asking'
     vid+ie+t' 'see'—vid+iac 'seeing'
     krič+a+t' 'shout'—krič+iac 'shouting'
  b. nies+t' 'carry'—nes+ú 'they carry'—nes+úc 'carrying'
     čít+a+t' 'read'—čít+aj+ú 'they read'—čít+aj+úc 'reading'
     rozum+ie+t' 'understand'—rozum+ej+ú 'they understand'—
     rozum+ej+úc 'understanding'

The present participle is homophonous with the gerund and the distribution of the allomorphs is identical. In morphological terms the present participle differs from the gerund because it requires the addition of the adjectival inflectional endings. Thus, *pros+iac* 'asking' is the gerund and *pros+iac+i* 'asking' (masc. nom. sg.) is the present participle. In phonological terms the gerund and the present participle are similar in that the allomorph *-iac* is an exception to the Rhythmic Law: *chvál+i+t'* 'praise' —*chvál+iac*—*chvál+iac+i*. However, they are different with regard to the behaviour of the allomorph *-úc*. The gerund *-úc* undergoes the Rhythmic Law while the present participle *-úc* does not: *rýp+a+t'* 'dig'—*rýp+uc*— *rýp+úc+i*.

The gerund and the present participle present a problem from the point of view of phonology. They trigger 1st Velar Palatalization (2/28) even when their allomorph has a back vowel:

(23) piec+t' 'bake'—piek+l+a 'she baked'—peč+úc, peč+úc+i
    striez+t' 'guard'—strieh+l+a 'she guarded'—strež+úc, strež+úc+i

The words in (23) require explanation. The infinitives have the consonants *c* or *z* as a result of the allomorphy rule summarized in (2) above. The underlying segments here are //k, fi//. The diphthong *ie* in the infinitive and in the past tense is due to Closed Syllable Lengthening, rule (28) in Chapter 6. Consequently, the underlying representations of the verb stems in (23) are //pek// and //strefi//, respectively. What needs to be accounted for is the palatalization in the gerund/present participle //pek+úc// and //strefi+úc//. To resolve this dilemma we shall avail ourselves of the solution proposed by Isačenko (1966).

Slovak, like other Slavic languages, has a stem extension allomorphy rule that adds the vowel *i* after front-vowel stems and the vowel *e* in the remaining types of verbs. These vowels are seen on the surface in the present tense. We shall discuss them in the following section. In anticipation of this discussion let us state the distribution of the extension vowels:

(24) Extension $\emptyset \rightarrow \begin{Bmatrix} \text{í} / [\text{V}, -\text{back}] \\ \text{é} / \text{elsewhere} \end{Bmatrix}$ —]PRESENT, GER., PRES. PART.

The extension vowels are not found on the surface in the gerund/present participle since these morphemes are represented by vowel suffixes and hence Vowel Deletion takes effect. The derivations of *peč+úc* 'baking' and *strež+úc* 'guarding' are now as follows:

(25) pek+úc   strefi+úc
     pek+éúc   strefi+éúc   Extension (24)
     peč+éúc   strež+éúc   1st Velar Palatalization (2/28)
     peč+úc   strež+úc   Vowel Deletion (8)

We now proceed to the discussion of the present tense, where the extension vowels are found in surface representations.

3.1.8. Present tense

A comparison of various types of verbs such as *nesiem* 'I carry' vs. *prosím* 'I ask' permits us to establish the system of the present-tense endings. Dvonč *et al.* (1966: 464) give the following list:

(26)   *Singular* *Plural*
     1st person -m   -me
     2nd person -š   -te
     3rd person zero   -ú/u, -ia/a

We take these to be the underlying representations of the endings, with one modification. In the 3rd pl. it is necessary to recognize two and not four allomorphs, as the short variants -*u* and -*a* are predictable from the Rhythmic Law. Further generalizations in phonological terms are not possible. The endings -*ú* and -*ia* cannot be derived from a common representation by any *sensu stricto* phonological rule. Their distribution is governed by an allomorphy rule that is sensitive to the type of the verb stem:

(27) *a.* pros+i+t' 'ask'—pros+iac 'asking'—pros+ia 'they ask'
       vid+ie+t' 'see'—vid+iac 'seeing'—vid+ia 'they see'
       krič+a+t' 'shout' (*ä*-verb)—krič+iac 'shouting'—krič+ia 'they shout'

b. nies+t' 'carry'—nes+úc 'carrying'—nes+ú 'they carry'
pi+t' 'drink'—pij+úc 'drinking'—pij+ú 'they drink'
čít+a+t' 'read'—čít+aj+úc 'reading'—čít+aj+ú 'they read'
rozum+ie+t' 'understand'—rozum+ej+úc 'understanding'—
rozum+ej+ú 'they understand'

Clearly the distribution of the 3rd pl. allomorphs is the same as that of the gerund/present participle:

(28) 3rd pl. present $\emptyset \rightarrow \begin{Bmatrix} \text{ia} / [\text{V}, -\text{back}] \\ \text{ú} / \text{elsewhere} \end{Bmatrix}$ —

The present tense triggers the application of Extension, a rule that we stated in (24) above. The vowel *í* is inserted after front-vowel stems and *é* occurs elsewhere. Compare the forms of the 1st sg. present in (29) below. On the left we list the verb form that shows the type of the stem. On the right we give the 1st sg. The spelling corresponds roughly to the phonetic representation. In slashes we posit the structures derived by Extension. They are subject to Vowel Deletion (8) and Diphthongization (2/25):

(29) *a.* pros+i+t' 'ask'—pros+í+m /pros+i+ím/ 'I ask'
vid+e+l 'he saw'—vid+í+m /vid+e+ím/ 'I see'
krič+a+t' 'shout'—krič+í+m /krik+ä+ím/ 'I shout'
b. nes+úc 'carrying'—nes+iem /nes+ém/ 'I carry'
ber+úc 'taking'—ber+iem /ber+ém/ 'I take'
piek+l+a 'she baked', peč+úc 'baking'—peč+iem /pek+ém/
'I bake'

The 3rd pl. present of the C-verbs exhibits the same peculiarity as the gerund/present participle, that is, velars are palatalized even though the ending is -*ú*: *peč+ú* 'they bake', *strež+ú* 'they guard'. Given Extension (24), this is not unexpected. The underlying representation //pek+ú// is augmented by introducing *é*: /pek+éú/. The derivation proceeds in exactly the same way as was the case with *peč+úc* in (25) above.

Verbs with the verbalizing morphemes -*ej* and -*aj* exhibit a different type of conjugational pattern. Below we give two examples which we present in the same way as the words in (29), that is, verb-type form, 1st sg. form, and the representation after Extension:

(30) rozum+ej+úc 'understanding'—rozum+ie+m /rozum+ej+ém/
'I understand'
chov+aj+úc 'breeding'—chov+á+m /xov+aj+ém/ 'I breed'

Isačenko (1966: 191) proposes that the verbalizing suffix and the extension vowel are contracted into a long vowel: *ej+é → é* and *aj+é → á*. Let us observe that the *ej*-stems are different from the *aj*-stems in that they are exceptions to the Rhythmic Law. Consequently, we have two rules of coalescence rather than one:

(31) *ej*-Coalescence   ej + é → é

(32) *aj*-Coalescence   aj + é → á

The difference between these rules comes to light when we look at long-vowel stems. Thus, the 1st sg. forms of *múdr+ej+úc* 'becoming clever' and *čít+aj+úc* 'reading' are *múdr+ie+m* and *čít+a+m*. That is, the second but not the first form is subject to the Rhythmic Law. We propose to account for this fact by ordering *aj*-Coalescence before and *ej*-Coalescence after the Rhythmic Law. The derivations of our examples are then as shown in (33).

(33) múdr+ej+m   čít+aj+m
      múdr+ej+ém   čít+aj+ém   Extension (24)
      —   čít+á+m   *aj*-Coalescence (32)
      —   čít+a+m   Rhythmic Law (2/26)
      múdr+é+m   —   *ej*-Coalescence (31)
      múdr+ie+m   —   Diphthongization (2/25)

The coalescence rules apply in all the persons of the present-tense conjugation except the 3rd pl. Thus, we have *rozum+ej+ú* 'they understand' and *chov+aj+ú* 'they breed' with the verbalizing suffixes *-ej* and *-aj* surfacing phonetically. There is nothing unusual about this fact. Notice that it is only the 3rd pl. ending that has a vowel suffix. Recall now that Slovak has Vowel Deletion (8). It must therefore be the case that the extension vowel is deleted prior to the application of the coalescence rules (31) and (32). Notice that we cannot simply assume that the extension vowel is not inserted in the 3rd pl. This is made clear by the fact that C-verbs such as *piec+ť* 'bake', underlying //pek//, undergo 1st Velar Palatalization in the 3rd pl. The palatalization is due to the extension vowel, and the representation of *peč+ú* 'they bake' is /pek+éú/ at the relevant stage. We now predict that the gerund/present participle forms should not undergo coalescence either, since they also are represented by a vocalic suffix. This is borne out. In the gerund our examples are *rozum+ej+úc* 'understanding' and *chov+aj+úc* 'breeding'. In (34) we look at sample derivations of the verbs 'understand' and 'bake' in the 1st sg. and the 3rd pl. These derivations establish the ordering relationships between rules: Extension, 1st Velar Palatalization, Vowel Deletion, and *ej*-Coalescence.

3.1.9. *n*-Verbs

We have now prepared the ground for a discussion of more complex verb classes. In this section we look at *n*-verbs. In the following two sections we consider partially irregular verbs.

(34) *a.* rozum+ej+m rozum+ej+ú
   rozum+ej+ém rozum+ej+éú Extension (24)
   —   rozum+ej+ú Vowel Deletion (8)
   rozum+é+m —   *ej*-Coalescence (31)
   rozum+ie+m —   Diphthongization (2/25)
  b. pek+m   pek+ú
   pek+ém   pek+éú Extension (24)
   peč+ém   peč+éú 1st Velar Palatalization (2/28)
   —   peč+ú Vowel Deletion (8)
   peč+iem —   Diphthongization (2/25)

The verbalizing morpheme *n* has a perfective meaning (completed action). It is added to adjectives, nouns, and roots in order to derive verbs such as those shown in (35). Note that *ý* is an inflectional ending of the adjective.

(35) *a.* slab+ý 'weak'—slab+nú+t' 'become weak'
   chud+ý 'slim'—chud+nú+t' 'become slim'
   zámok 'lock'—zamk+nú+t' 'to lock'
   pad (compare u+pad+ok 'fall' (N))—pad+nú+t' 'fall'
  b. to+nú+t' 'drown'—to+pi+t' sa 'get drowned'
   vi+nú+t' 'bend'—o+vi+t' 'bend around', o+víj+a+t' (DI)
   ply+nú+t' 'swim'—plýv+a+t' (DI)

The question is whether the verbalizing suffix is *-n* or *-nú*, as seems to be prompted by the infinitive form. We begin by clarifying that, regardless of how we further interpret the verbalizing suffix, the length of *u* in *-nú* is not a property of the underlying representation. In all forms other than the infinitive, the *u* is short, for example *pad+nu+vš+í* 'having fallen', *pad+nu+t+ý* 'fallen'. Isačenko (1966) suggests that the *u* is lengthened by a rule that is sensitive to the presence of the infinitive suffix:

(36) *u*-Lengthening u → ú / — t']$_{INF.}$

This rule is similar to *e*-Lengthening which we discussed in 3.1.2. However, it is different from it in two important respects. First, it applies before and not after Postvocalic *j*-Deletion, since the *j* blocks *u*-Lengthening in verbs such as *žu+t'* //žuj+t'// 'chew': compare *žuj+e* 'he chews'. Second, *u*-Lengthening precedes rather than follows the Rhythmic Law. This is shown by the fact that the lengthened *u* shortens in accordance with the Rhythmic Law, for instance *vlád+nu+t'* 'rule', *roz+hliad+nu+t'* 'look around'.

 With the conclusion that the length of the *ú* in *-nú* is derived by rule, we now restate our initial question: is the verbalizing morpheme *-n* or *-nu*? There are two arguments, one morphological and one phonological, that can be presented in favour of the former possibility:

(i) With respect to the selection of the passive participle allomorph the words in (35) behave like C-verbs. That is, they select -*t*, which, we may recall, is added to C-verbs that end in a sonorant: compare *pi+t'* 'drink' (*pij+ú* 'they drink')—*pi+t+ý* 'drunk' and *pad+nú+t'* 'fall'—*pad+nu+t+ý* 'fallen'. This indicates that the *u* is not present in the underlying representation to which Passive Allomorphy (20) applies. The *u* must therefore be inserted by a later rule. We return to this matter below.

(ii) Verb stems that end in a back vowel trigger the rule of *j*-Insertion. The inserted *j* shortens the vowel (see Glide Shortening in 8.2). Thus, the *a*-stems *rehot+a+t'* 'laugh' and *sten+a+t'* 'groan' appear as *rehoc+em* 'I laugh' and *sten+em* 'I groan' in the present tense. The extension vowel //é// is [e] rather than [ie]. Against this background we observe that the verbs in the *n*-class do not shorten the extension vowel: compare *to+nú+t'* 'drown'—*to+n+iem* 'I drown'.[3] Consequently, the back vowel *u* cannot be present in the conjugation, since otherwise *j*-Insertion and hence Glide Shortening would have taken effect.

We conclude that the verbs in (35) are C-verbs that end in -*n*. We must now account for the occurrence of *u* in these verbs. The generalization is straightforward: *u* is inserted before a consonantal suffix.

(37) *u*-Insertion $\emptyset \rightarrow u / n — C]_{n\text{-VERB}}$

Below we give the underlying representation as well as some conjugational forms of two examples from (35):

(38) *a.* stem //pad+n//: pad+nú+t' //pad+n+t'// 'fall', pad+nu+vš+í
    //pad+n+vš+í// 'having fallen', pad+nu+t+ý //pad+n+t+í// 'fallen'
 b. stem //to+n//: to+nú+t' //to+n+t'// 'drown', to+nu+vš+í
    //to+n+vš+í// 'having drowned', u+to+nu+t+ý //u+to+n+t+í//
    'drowned', to+nu+l //to+n+l// 'he drowned'

In the case of the infinitive, the *u* inserted by (37) is further lengthened by rule (36).

Allomorphy *u*-Insertion (37) interacts with another rule that deletes unsyllabified *n* (hence the morpheme -*n*) before the past-tense suffix -*l*. Compare the past feminine forms of the following verbs:[4]

(39) *a.* pad+nú+t' 'fall'—pad+l+a //pad+n+l+a// 'she fell'
    slab+nú+t' 'become weak'—slab+l+a //slab+n+l+a// 'she became weak'
 b. to+nú+t' 'drown'—to+nu+l+a //to+n+l+a// 'she drowned'
    vi+nú+t' 'bend'—vi+nu+l+a //vij+n+l+a// 'she bent'

---

[3] The relevant examples are in (35*b*), since the words in (35*a*) are subject to an independent shortening rule; see CC-Shortening in (43) below.

[4] We quote the verbs in the feminine rather than in the masculine form since the latter involves additional complications: at a later stage the vowel *o* is inserted before the lateral; see the discussion in Chapter 7.

The morpheme *n* is deleted if the verb root ends in a consonant:

(40) *n*-Deletion n → ∅ / C — l

We sum up our discussion by looking at the derivation of *pad+nú+t'* 'fall', *pad+l+a* 'she fell', and *to+nu+l+a* 'she drowned'. We look at cycle 3 only:

(41) pad+n+t' pad+n+l to+n+l
— pad+l — *n*-Deletion (40)
pad+nu+t' — to+nu+l *u*-Insertion (37)
pad+nú+t' — — *u*-Lengthening (36)

The order of the allomorphy rules is as given: *n*-Deletion bleeds (i.e. pre-empts the application of) *u*-Insertion.

Finally, it may be observed that certain *n*-verbs as well as non-syllabic (vowelless) verbs induce the shortening of the extension vowel:

(42) *a.* pad+nú+t' 'fall'—pad+n+em 'I fall'
slab+nú+t' 'become weak'—slab+n+em 'I become weak'
b. žn+uc 'mowing'—žn+em 'I mow'
tn+úc 'cutting'—tn+em 'I cut'

We discuss the non-syllabic verbs of (42*b*) in section 5.6. For the present, let us merely observe that they, like the verbs in (42*a*), induce shortening which is triggered by an onset cluster of a consonant followed by a nasal:

(43) CC-Shortening é → e / C N —

If there is no cluster or if the second member of the cluster is not a nasal, the shortening does not take place: compare *to+n+iem* 'I drown', *tr+iem* 'I rub'. The last example highlights the same problem as that of the *n*-verbs discussed in this section: are we dealing with a C-stem verb or with a vowel verb? We discuss this further in the following section.

3.1.10. *Triet'* verbs

In a small class of verbs such as *triet'* 'rub', *mriet'* 'die', *driet'* 'work hard', *priet'* 'quarrel', *vriet'* 'boil', and a few others[5] we find the following pattern of conjugational forms:

(44) trie+t' 'rub', tre+l 'he rubbed', na+tre+vš+í 'having rubbed', tre+t+ý 'rubbed', tr+iem 'I rub', tr+ú 'they rub', tr+úc 'rubbing'

---

[5] All of these verbs except *mlie+t'* 'grind' have prevocalic *r*. It is questionable whether *mliet'* should belong to the *triet'* class of verbs since it shows unpredictable irregularity in the present tense; compare *tr+iem* 'I rub' vs. *mel+iem* 'I grind': the appearance of *e* in *mliet'* is unexpected.

The question is whether *trie+t'* belongs to vowel-stem verbs and hence has the representation //tre// or whether it belongs to C-verbs and consequently has the representation //tr//. Observe that the representation //trie// or rather //tré//, where [ie] comes from Diphthongization, is implausible. The *ie* appears only in the infinitive and can thus be accounted for by *e*-Lengthening (3). (Note that the *ie* in *tr+iem* 'I rub' is an extension vowel.) In sum, we must choose between //tre// and //tr// as the underlying representations. If we assume //tr//, then Slovak must have an allomorphy rule that inserts *e* before suffixes that begin with a consonant:

(45) *e*-Insertion $\emptyset \rightarrow e / r - C]_{\text{VERB}}$

The representations of the infinitive and the past participle are then //tr+t'// and //tr+l//. The former is subject to *e*-Insertion and *e*-Lengthening, the latter only to *e*-Insertion: *trie+t'*, *tre+l*. We shall argue that the correct representation of this verb is indeed //tr//[6] and hence *e*-Insertion must be recognized as a rule of Slovak.

Four types of argument can be adduced in favour of //tr// as the underlying representation. These arguments come to light when we compare *trie+t'* with *vid+ie+t'* 'see', an *e*-stem verb (see (1c) above):

(46) *a.* tr+iem 'I rub'—vid+ím 'I see'
      b. tr+ú 'they rub'—vid+ia 'they see'
      c. tr+úc 'rubbing'—vid+iac 'seeing'
      d. tre+t+ý 'rubbed'—vid+en+ý 'seen'

Evidently, the two verbs behave differently with respect to the selection of the extension vowel in (46*a*), the 3rd pl. present ending in (46*b*), the gerund allomorph in (46*c*), and the passive participle allomorph in (46*d*). With respect to the allomorph distribution rules *trie+t'* behaves like a C-verb ending in a sonorant, such as *to+nú+t'* //to+n+t'// 'drown' or *pi+t'* //pij+t'// 'drink'. Compare the following with the forms of *trie+t'* in (46):

(47) to+n+iem 'I drown', pij+ú 'they drink', pij+úc 'drinking', pi+t+ý //pij+t+í// 'drunk' (the *j* is deleted by rule (4))

We conclude that *trie+t'* is a C-verb and its proper representation is //tr//.[7]

---

[6] In fact all *triet'* verbs have a yer between the two consonants of the root. The presence of the yer manifests itself as a triggering effect for Yer Vocalization in the prefix: compare *z+viezt'* 'deliver' vs. *zo+triet'* 'rub out' (see Chapter 5).

[7] Slovak has eight irregular verbs that are similar to the *triet'* verbs. These verbs include words such as *bra+t'* 'take' and *hna+t'* 'chase'. The irregularity consists in the fact, amongst others, that the present-tense stem has *e* between the consonants of the root: *ber+iem* 'I take', *žen+iem* 'I chase'. This *e* is in fact a yer, since it triggers Yer Vocalization in the prefix, for example *zo+bra+t'* 'take together'. However, the yer of the root in *ber+iem* 'I take' cannot be derived by Yer Vocalization, since it is not followed by a yer; see Chapter 5.

3.1.11. *Siat'* verbs

The last class of partially irregular verbs is composed of a few members such as *siat'* 'sow', *viat'* 'blow', *liat'* 'pour', *smiat' sa* 'laugh', *hriat'* 'heat', and some others. The irregularity consists here in an exchange of *ia* and *ej* in various conjugational forms:

(48)   *ia*: sia+t' 'sow', sia+l 'he sowed', za+sia+t+y 'sown', za+sia+vš+i
                  'having sown'
       ej: sej+em 'I sow', sej+ú 'they sow', sej+úc 'sowing'

As is evident from the examples in (48), *ia* appears before consonantal and *ej* before vocalic suffixes. We must therefore choose between the following two allomorphy rules:[8]

(49)   *a.* ia → ej / — V
       b. ej → ia / — C   or rather:
             ej → ǎ / — C
             (since *ia* can be derived by Diphthongization)

Notice that the selection of the appropriate allomorphy rule is tantamount to the selection of the appropriate verb stem. In particular, the question is whether *siat'* verbs are vowel-stem verbs and hence end in //ǎ// (surface [ia] by Diphthongization) or whether they are C-stem verbs and hence end in *-j*. To resolve this dilemma we apply the by-now familiar tests involving the selection of the competing allomorphs of the extension vowel in (50*a*), the 3rd pl. present ending in (50*b*), the gerund suffix in (50*c*), and the passive participle suffix in (50*d*). We compare *siat'* 'sow' with the C-verb *pit'* 'drink' that ends in //j// and with the *ä*-verb *krič+a+t'* 'shout' (see (1*d*) in 3.1.1):

(50)   *a.* sej+em   pij+em[9]   krič+ím
       b. sej+ú   pij+ú   krič+ia
       c. sej+úc   pij+úc   krič+iac
       d. za+sia+t+y   pi+t+ý   za+krič+a+n+ý

There is no doubt that *siat'* behaves like *pit'*. We conclude that *siat'* is a C-verb whose underlying representation is //sej//. Consequently, the

---

[8] A third possibility would be to assume that the verb root is //sej// and that there is a rule inserting *a* before consonants. A further rule would then effect a coalescence: /ej+a/ → [ǎ]. An interpretation along these lines is proposed by Isačenko (1966), who assumes, however, that the *a* is underlying and not epenthetic. This step is undesirable since, as we demonstrate in (50), *siat'* verbs should be analysed as C-stem rather than vowel-stem verbs. The proposal to insert the *a* and then coalesce it with *ej* avoids this difficulty but it is more complex than the two suggestions made in (49). This is presumably what happened historically, but such considerations have no place in synchronic analysis.

[9] Observe that the extension vowel is short in *sej+em* 'I sow' and *pij+em* 'I drink'. This is due to the rule of Glide Shortening (2/27).

correct allomorphy rule is (49*b*) and not (49*a*). Notice further that (49*b*) must apply before the Rhythmic Law as the root vowel causes the shortening of the inflectional ending in *za+sia+t+y* 'sown'; compare the long *ý* in *pi+t+ý* 'drunk'.

3.1.12. Derived imperfectives

Slovak, like other Slavic languages, has a productive system of deriving imperfective verbs. They are deverbal formations that arise through suffixation and express incomplete or frequentative actions. In Slovak, derived imperfectives are particularly complex since, on the one hand, the number of imperfective suffixes is large (larger than in Polish) and, on the other hand, there is much variation, that is, the same verb may have several different imperfective forms.

Descriptive grammars such as Dvonč *et al.* (1966) list as many as six imperfective suffixes: *-a*, *-ova*, *-áva*, *-iava*, *-ieva*, and *-úva*,[10] and claim that, with the exception of *-iava* (a variant of *-áva*), their distribution is unpredictable. While this claim may be true with respect to morphology, it is not true with respect to phonology. That is, it seems difficult to establish why a given verb takes, for example, *-a* rather than *-ova* as an imperfective suffix or why with some verbs both *-a* and *-ova* occur. However, as we shall show, the phonological shape of the suffix—for example, why it is *-áva* and not *-ova* or *-a*—is largely predictable, or even completely predictable if we ignore two small classes of verbs that undergo lexically governed allomorphy rules. We claim that there are only two imperfective suffixes: *-aj* and *-ova*, and all the remaining suffixes are derivable from a combination of these two.

We begin with the observation that the suffix *-a* is in fact underlying //aj//. This is shown most clearly by the fact that *-a* alternates with *-aj* in predictable ways:

(51) o+vlád+nu+t' 'command' (perf.)—o+vlád+a+t' 'command' (DI),
        o+vlád+a+m 'I command', o+vlád+aj+ú 'they command',
        o+vlád+aj (imper.)
      po+núk+nu+t' 'offer' (perf.)—po+núk+a+t' 'offer' (DI),
        po+núk+a+m 'I offer', po+núk+aj+ú 'they offer', po+núk+aj
        (imper.)

The forms given first in each example are perfective verbs containing the perfectivizing suffix *-n*. Recall that the *u* of *-nu* is derived by *u*-Insertion

---

[10] Kochik (1971) believes that the imperfective suffix is *-v* and that imperfectivization involves a change of the verb class: assignment to the *a*-verbs. Our solution diverges radically from this proposal.

(37). The imperfective forms following the dashes in (51) lack the perfective -*n*. We can assume that either this suffix is deleted before the imperfective -*a* and we thereby avoid a contradiction (a perfective suffix followed by an imperfective suffix), or that the imperfective suffix -*a* is added to roots rather than to the perfective form with -*n*. Whichever the solution, it is clear that -*a* is independent of -*nu*.

The suffix -*a* appears phonetically either as [a] or as [aj]. The distribution of the variants is fully predictable: [a] occurs before consonants whereas [aj] appears before vowels and word-finally. Recall that Slovak has Postvocalic *j*-Deletion (4) that deletes *j* before consonants, hence the [a] variant. We conclude that the underlying representation of the -*a/aj* suffix is //aj//.

Let us investigate further the behaviour of -*aj*. Consider the following words:

(52) dvih+nú+t' 'raise'—dvíh+a+t'
    val+i+t' 'destroy'—vál'+a+t'
    vy+dur+i+t' 'chase away'—vy+dúr+a+t'
    na+prav+i+t' 'repair'—na+práv+a+t'

The forms on the right are imperfectives derived from the verbs on the left. The imperfective suffix -*aj* appears as *a* because of Postvocalic *j*-Deletion: compare *dvíh+a+t'* 'raise'—*dvíh+aj+ú* 'they raise'. A striking fact about the imperfective forms is that the syllable nucleus is lengthened. Slovak therefore has the rule which we state informally as follows:[11]

(53) *aj*-Lengthening $V \rightarrow \acute{V} / — aj]_{DI}$

It is clear from the comparison of *dvih+nu+t'* 'raise'—*dvíh+a+t'* and *val+i+t'*—*vál'+a+t'* that the lengthening takes place before -*aj*[12] and not, for instance, before the configuration *i+aj*, as the latter example might suggest. In *dvíh+a+t'* the structure is //dvih+aj+t'//. Even clearer evidence for this view is provided by the fact that C-verbs undergo *aj*-Lengthening, for example *uži+t'* 'use'—*užij+ú* 'they use'—*užív+a+t'* (DI; for the alternation *j ~ v* see below). We conclude from this discussion that *i*-verbs in (52) must lose their stem vowel before *aj*-Lengthening applies. The desired result is obtained by ordering *aj*-Lengthening (53) after Vowel Deletion (8).

A different effect again of the -*aj* suffix comes to light when we consider the following verbs:

---

[11] The intervening consonants have no influence on rules of lengthening and shortening since, as we explain in Chapter 6, these rules are stated at the interface of the skeleton and the syllable tier.

[12] *aj*-Lengthening has some exceptions, particularly in the class of C-verbs, for example *pri+peč+ú* 'they burn'—*pri+pek+a+t'* (DI), *pad+nú+t'* 'fall'—*pad+a+t'* (DI). Some verbs show variation: *za+plet+ú* 'they weave together'—*za+plet+a+t'* or *za+pliet+a+t'* (DI). The latter variant is regular: the root *e* lengthens to *é* and diphthongizes to *ie*.

(54) lom+i+t' 'break'—lám+a+t'
do+sol+i+t' 'add salt'—do+sál'+a+t'
umor+i+t' 'tire'—umár+a+t'
zvon+i+t' 'ring'—vy+zváň+a+t'
rob+i+t' 'do'—vy+ráb+a+t'

The addition of -*aj* triggers the rule of *o*-Lowering:

(55) *o*-Lowering $o \rightarrow a \, / — C \, aj]_{DI}$

This rule is ordered after Vowel Deletion since only then do the relevant syllables become adjacent.

Finally, as pointed out originally by Flier (1972) in his analysis of Russian, -*aj* induces the backing of the glide:

(56) Glide Backing $j \rightarrow [+back] \, / — aj]_{DI}$

Rule (56) changes /j/ into the back glide /u̯/, which is further spelled out as a labiodental sonorant [*v*] (see Chapter 8). This is illustrated by the following examples:[13]

(57) u+my+t' 'wash'—u+myj+ú 'they wash'—u+mýv+a+t'
po+ču+t' 'feel'—po+čuj+ú 'they feel'—po+čúv+a+t'
zo+ši+t' 'sew together'—zo+šij+ú 'they sew together'—zo+šív+a+t'

Unlike the previous two rules, Glide Backing is ordered before Vowel Deletion (8). This ordering is supported by the fact that verb stems ending in vowels systematically do not undergo Glide Backing:

(58) na+kroj+i+t' 'cut'—na+kráj+a+t'
na+poj+i+t' 'make to drink'—na+páj+a+t'
vy+doj+i+t' 'milk'—vy+dáj+a+t'

We summarize our discussion by presenting in (59) the derivation of the first example from each of (54), (57), and (58).

(59)
lom+i+aj+t'	u+mij+aj+t'	na+kroj+i+aj+t'	
—	u+miu̯+aj+t'	—	Glide Backing (56)
lom+aj+t'	—	na+kroj+aj+t'	Vowel Deletion (8)
lóm+aj+t'	u+míu̯+aj+t'	na+krój+aj+t'	*aj*-Lengthening (53)
lám+aj+t'	—	na+kráj+aj+t'	*o*-Lowering (55)
lám+a+t'	u+míu̯+a+t'	na+kráj+a+t'	Postvocalic *j*-Deletion (4)

---

[13] There are at least three exceptions to be noted: *bi+t'* 'beat'—*bij+at'*, *pi+t'* 'drink'—*pij+a+t'*, *roz+vi+t'* sa 'develop'—*roz+vij+at'* sa. These exceptions could not be accounted for by assuming with Isačenko (1966) that the stems are //bi// rather than //bij//, etc., and by claiming further that *j* is inserted intervocalically after Glide Backing has applied. The explanation would be false, as in some other //Cij// verbs Glide Backing applies as predicted: see *zo+ši+t'* 'sew together' in (57) as well as *uži+t'* 'use'—*užív+a+t'* mentioned earlier.

Notice, incidentally, that *o*-Lowering must precede Diphthongization ($\acute{o} \rightarrow uo$) so that the latter is blocked as required.

The imperfective suffix *-ova* contrasts with *-aj* in that it causes shortening rather than lengthening:[14]

(60) od+pís+a+t' (*a*-stem) 'write back'—od+pis+ova+t'
    z+níž+i+t' 'lower'—z+niž+ova+t'
    o+chrán+i+t' 'protect'—o+chraň+ova+t'
    kúp+i+t' 'buy'—kup+ova+t'

The respective rule is stated informally as follows:

(61) *ova*-Shortening $\acute{V} \rightarrow V / —$ ova]$_{DI}$

Rule (61) applies after Vowel Deletion (8), as only then are the relevant syllables adjacent.

A further difference between *-aj* and *-ova* is the fact that the former but not the latter triggers *o*-Lowering. This is best shown by examples that admit both forms of derived imperfectives:

(62) zaclon+i+t' 'cover'—zacláň+a+t' *vs.* zacloň+ova+t'
    vy+stroj+i+t' 'adorn'—vy+stráj+a+t' *vs.* vy+stroj+ova+t'

To summarize, there are two imperfective suffixes: *-aj* and *-ova*. These suffixes are independent of each other in the sense that they should not be derived from a common source by allomorphy rules. The implausibility of such a step lies not only in the fact that they have a very different phonological make-up. The primary reason is a different phonological behaviour:

   (i) *-aj* causes lengthening whereas *-ova* causes shortening;
  (ii) *-aj* triggers *o*-Lowering while *-ova* does not;
 (iii) *-aj* induces Glide Backing but *-ova* does not (at least, there are no relevant examples).

We shall now consider the remaining imperfective suffixes and show that they are in fact derivable from combinations of the existing suffixes *-aj* and *-ova* by phonological rules plus two allomorphy rules.

In the class of *-áva* and *-ieva* imperfectives a careful distinction must be drawn between alleged examples that are, as it were, *faux amis*, and the real cases. Consider the words set out in (63). For clarity of exposition we have isolated *-áva* in the imperfective verbs on the right as if it were one morpheme (the traditional view: cf. Dvonč *et al.* 1966: 418). However, as we show below, it is in fact a combination of morphemes.

---

[14] Attention should be drawn to the fact that the imperfective *-ova* is homophonous with the verbalizing suffix *-ova*. The latter is used to turn nouns into verbs and has no imperfectivizing function. Consequently, it does not induce shortening, for example *betón* 'concrete'—*betón+ova+t'* 'lay concrete', *chlór*—*chlór+ova+t'* 'chlorinate'.

(63) *Infinitive*   *3rd pl.*   *DI infinitive*
  a. vy+čerp+a+t' 'run out'   vy+čerp+aj+ú   vy+čerp+áva+t'
     po+žehn+a+t' 'say farewell'   po+žehn+aj+ú   po+žehn+áva+t'
     roz+mot+a+t' 'unwind'   roz+mot+aj+ú   roz+mot+áva+t'
  b. voň+a+t' 'smell'   voň+aj+ú   von+iava+t'
     požič+a+t' 'borrow'   požič+aj+ú   požič+iava+t'
  c. klam+a+t' 'deceive'   klam+ú   klam+áva+t'
     pre+sek+nú+t' 'cut through'   pre+sek+n+ú   pre+sek+áva+t'
  d. s+kop+a+t' 'kick'   s+kop+ú   s+kop+áva+t'
     v+bod+nú+t' 'cut into'   v+bod+n+ú   v+bod+áva+t'

The first guess at the morphemic structure of *-áva* is that the suffix is composed of double *-aj*, that is, the suffix is actually *-aj+aj*. This view is supported by two facts. First, the *v* of *-áva* can then be derived by Glide Backing (56). Second, there is indeed firm evidence that the suffix *-aj* may attach multiply in order to stress the frequentative meaning of the verb:

(64) *Infinitive*   *3rd pl.*   *DI inf.*   *Double DI inf.*
     vy+ši+t' 'sew on'   vy+šij+ú   vy+šív+a+t'   vy+šív+av+a+t'
     na+da+t' 'scold'   na+daj+ú   na+dáv+a+t'   na+dáv+av+a+t'
     za+rob+i+t' 'earn'   za+rob+ia   za+ráb+a+t'   za+ráb+av+a+t'

There is no doubt that the words on the far right in (64) are formed by adding a second *-aj* and not just *-a*; compare the imperative *vy+šív+av+aj* 'sew on'. A sample derivation of the double imperfective for 'sew on' is given in (65). We assume that the verb is derived cyclically, that is, phonological rules as a class are reapplied after adding a new morpheme, and we begin with cycle 3. It should be noted that *aj*-Lengthening is blocked on cycle 5 by the Strict Cyclicity Constraint since both the input and the environment are wholly contained in the previous cycle (see (19) in Chapter 1).

We conclude from this discussion that, first, an imperfective suffix may be added more than once, and, second, the [*v*] in derived imperfectives is derived from //j// by Glide Backing. Now we return to the verbs in (63*a*).

There are two crucial differences between the data in (63*a*) and (64):

(i) The suffix *-áva*, that is, //aj+aj//, does not cause the lengthening of the preceding vowel. Thus, *vy+čerp+áv+a+t'* 'run out' contrasts with *vy+šív+av+a+t'* 'sew on', since in the latter the stem vowel *i* has been lengthened while in the former the stem vowel *e* has not. This fact has consequences for the *-av* suffix itself. In *vy+čerp+áv+a+t'* //vi+čerp+aj+aj+t'// the first *-aj* (*-av* after Glide Backing) is long since the Rhythmic Law is inapplicable. On the other hand, the first *-aj* in *vy+šív+av+a+t'* //vi+šij+aj+aj+t'// is short as predicted by the Rhythmic Law.

(65) Cycle 3   vi+šij+aj
                vi+šiu̯+aj   Glide Backing (56)
                vi+šíu̯+aj   aj-Lengthening (53)
                —   Rhythmic Law (2/26)
                —   Postvocalic j-Deletion (4)

      Cycle 4   vi+šíu̯+aj+aj
                 vi+šíu̯+au̯+aj   Glide Backing
                 vi+šíu̯+áu̯+aj   aj-Lengthening
                 vi+šíu̯+au̯+aj   Rhythmic Law
                 —   Postvocalic j-Deletion

      Cycle 5   vi+šíu̯+au̯+aj+t'
                 —   Glide Backing
                 (BLOCKED)   aj-Lengthening
                 —   Rhythmic Law
                 vi+šíu̯+au̯+a+t'   Postvocalic j-Deletion

      Postcyclic vi+šív+av+a+t' Glide Strengthening (8/21)

(ii) The suffix -áva, that is //aj+aj//, induces o-Lowering of verbs such as those in (64) but not those in (63a). Thus, za+rob+i+t' 'earn'— za+ráb+av+a+t' contrasts with roz+mot+a+t' 'unwind'—roz+mot+áv+a+t'.

In sum, from the point of view of phonological behaviour we have two different sequences of //aj+aj//: that in (63a) and that in (64). How can this be explained? The answer lies in morphemic structure. Notice that the first -aj in (63a) is not an imperfective suffix but a verbalizing morpheme. It is only the second -aj that carries the function of imperfectivization. On the other hand, the sequence //aj+aj// in (64) is genuinely a sequence of two imperfective suffixes. This fact comes to light when we look at the 3rd pl. form, for example vy+šij+ú 'they sew on'. Clearly, the stem is //šij// and the verb in question belongs to the class of C-stems. The 3rd pl. form in (63a) contrasts with that in (64) since the suffix -aj appears on the surface, even though the verb has not undergone imperfectivization: vy+čerp+aj+ú 'they run out'. The -aj is therefore a verbalizing and not an imperfective suffix. Consequently, the rules of aj-Lengthening and o-Lowering are inapplicable. The verbs in (63a) constitute faux amis, that is, they look like double imperfectives but in fact are not. The morphological structure of these verbs is [[[Root] aj]$_{VERB}$ aj]$_{DI}$.

An explanation along the same lines is also available for the verbs in (63b). Like the examples in (63a), they show neither lengthening of the root vowel nor lowering of o: požič+iav+a+t' 'borrow' (DI), von+iav+a+t' 'smell' (DI). Their underlying representations are identical to those of the verbs in (63a):

$$[[[[požič] aj]_{VERB} aj]_{DI} t']_{INF.} \quad and \quad [[[[von'] aj]_{VERB} aj]_{DI} t']_{INF.}$$

The difference between these verbs and those in (63a) lies in the fact that the stems end in a 'soft' consonant. This consonant triggers the rule of Fronting (see 6.5) that turns /á/ into /ǻ/. The long front /ǻ/ is subject to Diphthongization, which derives [ia]. In sum, the verbs in (63b) are also instances of *faux amis*: it is only the second but not the first -*aj* that is an imperfective suffix.

The verbs in (63c–d) present a much more complex problem. From the point of view of phonological behaviour, the surface -*áva* (we deliberately do not indicate its morphological structure) is entirely parallel to the -*áva* found in (63a–b), that is, //aj+aj//. It neither induces lengthening of the root vowel nor triggers *o*-Lowering: *klam+áva+t'* 'lie', *s+kop+áva+t'* 'kick'. However, at this point the parallel ends. The verbs in (63c–d) are different from those in (63a–b) because they are not instances of *aj*-stems. A comparison of the infinitive with the 3rd pl. form shows that we are dealing here with *a*- and *n*-stems: *klam+at'* 'lie'—*klam+ú* //klam+a+ú//, *pre+sek+nú+t'* 'cut across'—*pre+sek+n+ú* //pre+sek+n+ú//. In the first example the *a* is deleted by Vowel Deletion (8); in the second example the perfective -*n* is found on the surface. (The long *u* is the result of rules (37) and (36).) Consequently, the -*áva* in the imperfective forms is indeed a sequence of two imperfective suffixes and not a sequence of a verbalizing suffix plus an imperfective suffix.[15] If we now go along the lines of the analysis proposed for the verbs in (64), that is, postulate a double imperfective //aj+aj//, then we cannot account for the phonological effects of the -*áva* in (63c–d). In particular, we cannot explain why both *aj*-Lengthening and *o*-Lowering fail to apply.

Fortunately, a different account of these facts is available. Recall our claim that there are two imperfective suffixes: -*ova* and -*aj*. It is only the latter that triggers lengthening and the lowering of *o*. The former actually shortens the root vowel by rule (61). The desired result is achieved if we postulate that the -*áva* in (63c–d) is composed of //ova+aj// rather than of //aj+aj//. The derivation of *s+kop+áv+a+t'* 'kick' and *v+bod+áv+a+t'* 'cut into' is then as shown in (66) (beginning with the -*ova* cycle).

We conclude that, in spite of the surface similarity between the -*áva* in (64) and in (63c–d), we have here two different underlying representations of the suffix sequences: //aj+aj// in the former and //ova+aj// in the latter. We also conclude that the four imperfective suffixes given by

---

[15] Recall that the perfective suffix -*n* is dropped before the imperfective -*aj*—or rather, as pointed out earlier, the imperfective form of these verbs is formed directly from the verb root.

(66)

Cycle 4	z+kop+a+ova	v+bod+ova	
	z+kop+ova	—	Vowel Deletion (8)
	—	—	*aj*-Lengthening (53)
	— ·	—	*o*-Lowering (55)
	—	—	Postvocalic *j*-Deletion (4)

Cycle 5	z+kop+ova+aj	v+bod+ova+aj	
	z+kop+ov+aj	v+bod+ov+aj	Vowel Deletion
	z+kop+óv+aj	v+bod+óv+aj	*aj*-Lengthening
	z+kop+áv+aj	v+bod+áv+aj	*o*-Lowering
	—	—	Postvocalic *j*-Deletion

Cycle 6	z+kop+áv+aj+t'	v+bod+áv+aj+t'	
	z+kop+áv+a+t'	v+bod+áv+a+t'	only Postvocalic *j*-Deletion is applicable

Dvonč *et al.* (1966), that is: *-a*, *-ova*, *-áva*, and *-iava*, can be reduced to two, //aj// and //ova//, plus combinations thereof.

Against this background let us look at *-ieva*, a fifth suffix in the list given by Dvonč *et al.* (1966). Consider the data presented in (67).

(67)

	Infinitive	*3rd pl.*	*DI infinitive*
a.	o+star+ie+t' 'become old'	o+star+ej+ú	o+star+ieva+t'
	o+t'až+ie+t' 'become heavy'	o+t'až+ej+ú	o+t'až+ieva+t'
	do+rozum+ie+t' 'come to terms'	do+rozum+ej+ú	do+rozum+ieva+t'
b.	vy+modl+i+t' 'pray'	vy+modl+ia	vy+modl+ieva+t'
	vy+chod+i+t' 'go out'	vy+chod+ia	vy+chod+ieva+t'
	vy+jasn+i+t' 'explain'	vy+jasn+ia	vy+jasn+ieva+t'
c.	sídl+i+t' 'settle'	sídl+ia[16]	sídl+ieva+t'
	chvál+i+t' 'praise'	chvál+ia	chvál+ieva+t'
	súd+i+t' 'judge'	súd+ia	súd+ieva+t'

Even a cursory inspection of (67*a*) shows that these are instances of *faux amis*. As demonstrated by the 3rd pl. present tense, we have here *ej*-stem verbs.[17] The DI forms are instances of simple imperfectivization: //o+star+ej// → /o+star+ej+aj/ with the rules of Glide Backing, *aj*-Lengthening, Postvocalic *j*-Deletion, and Diphthongization deriving the

---

[16] Recall that the 3rd pl. ending *-ia* is an exception to the Rhythmic Law.

[17] The diphthong *ie* in the infinitive is derived from //ej// by Postvocalic *j*-Deletion (4), *e*-Lengthening (3), and Diphthongization (2/25).

surface form *o+star+iev+a+t'* 'become old'. By far the majority of *-ieva* imperfectives belong to the class of *ej*-verbs.

Unfortunately, the verbs in (67*b*–*c*), a clear minority, cannot be discarded as *faux amis*. These verbs belong to the class of *i*-stems and the surface *-ieva* cannot be obtained by any of the rules that we have introduced so far. Transferring the strategy used in the analysis of *-áva* to the analysis of *-ieva*, we can assume that we are dealing with a double imperfective, hence *-ieva* is either //aj+aj// or //ova+aj//. We still need an allomorphy rule that would change a back vowel into *e*. Of the two viable representations //ova+aj// seems to be more likely, since the vowel *o* and the desired output *e* agree in height. As mentioned earlier, the true instances of *-ieva* come from the class of *i*-stems. The verbalizing *i* can be put to work and the respective allomorphy rule is then stated as follows:

(68) *ieva*-Allomorphy   i+ova → i+eva

Some kind of lexical marking is unavoidable in connection with (68). The point is that *-ieva* imperfectives are exceptional with *i*-stem verbs. Normally, *i*-stems take *-aj* or *-ova* and the verbalizing *i* is deleted by Vowel Deletion:

(69) z+voln+i+t' 'slow down'—z+válň+a+t' //z+voln+i+aj+t'//
      z+níž+i+t' 'lower'—z+niž+ova+t' //z+n'iž+i+ova+t'//

We propose that the marking of the *-ieva* imperfectives should be encoded in the lexicon as an exception feature *vis-à-vis* Vowel Deletion. With this assumption things start falling into place. The *i* vowel blocks correctly the application of *ova*-Shortening (61) in (67*c*): *sídl+iev+at'* 'settle'. One can also explain why the diphthong *ie* of *-ieva* does not undergo the Rhythmic Law. Anticipating somewhat the discussion in Chapter 6, we may observe here that Slovak has an independently motivated rule of Contraction which turns sequences of *i* plus a vowel into a diphthong. For reasons that have nothing to do with the analysis of *-ieva*, Contraction is ordered after the Rhythmic Law. The relevant part of the verb *sídl+iev+a+t'* 'settle' is now derived as follows:

(70) sídl+i+ova
      sídl+i+eva   *ieva*-Allomorphy
      —   Rhythmic Law
      sídl+ieva   Contraction: i+e → ie (diphthong)

The last imperfective suffix mentioned by Dvonč *et al.* (1966) is *-úva*. It is characterized as a 'learned style' equivalent of *-áva* (p. 419). Thus, we have the following free variants:

(71) perfective: z+hrab+a+t' 'fork together'—z+hrab+ú (3rd pl.), hence
      an *a*-stem
      imperfective: z+hrab+áv+a+t' ~ z+hrab+úv+a+t'

An analysis prompts itself. Recall that -*áv+a* has been interpreted as the sequence //ova+aj//. The suffix -*úv+a* is also //ova+aj//. The presence of *aj* explains why -*úv+a* has a long vowel (*aj*-Lengthening). The variant with *u* is then derived by an allomorphy rule, *ova → uva*, which applies in a learned style. This analysis is convincingly confirmed by verbs such as *kúp+i+t'* 'buy'—*kup+úv+a+t'* and *pís+a+t'* 'write'—*vy+pis+úv+a+t'*. Notice that the root vowel is shortened in the -*úva* form. Given our assumptions, this is a predictable effect. An illustration of cycles 4 and 5 in the derivation of the imperfective for 'write' is given in (72).

(72) Cycle 4   *vi+pís+a+ova*
             vi+pís+ova   Vowel Deletion (8)
             vi+pís+ova   *ova*-Shortening (61)
             —   *aj*-Lengthening (53)

     Cycle 5   *vi+pis+ova+aj*
             vi+pis+ov+aj   Vowel Deletion
             —   *ova*-Shortening
             vi+pis+uv+aj   *ov → uv* stylistic allomorphy
             vi+pis+úv+aj   *aj*-Lengthening

On the infinitive cycle (cycle 6) the *j* is deleted by Postvocalic *j*-Deletion.

We close this section by looking at all possible imperfective forms of the verb *o+beh+nú+t'* 'run around', a C-stem with the perfective suffix -*n*:

(73) o+bieh+a+t' //o+befi+aj+t'//
     o+beh+ova+t' //o+befi+ova+t'//
     o+beh+áv+a+t' and o+beh+úv+a+t' //o+befi+ova+aj+t'//

All these forms can be derived by the system of rules that we have developed so far. We need only draw attention here to the fact that the lengthened *é* (an effect of *aj*-Lengthening) appears phonetically as [ie] owing to Diphthongization.

In summary, Slovak has two rather than six imperfective suffixes. They are -*aj* and -*ova*. All the remaining suffixes are derived from these two by rules.

3.2. DECLENSION

Slovak is an inflecting language. Nouns, adjectives, pronouns, and numerals exhibit declension in the singular and the plural. There are six cases: nominative, genitive, dative, accusative, locative, and instrumental. A seventh case, the vocative, is obsolete. It has survived only in a small class of masculine nouns such as *človek* 'man'—*člověč+e* (voc. sg.). The endings of the vocative are -*e* and -*u*. For most nouns the vocative has been replaced by the nominative.

In the following sections we shall look at the declension paradigms of adjectives and nouns, since they, unlike pronouns and numerals, constitute an open system. We shall list all the major paradigms, bypassing those which are clearly irregular and refer to a highly restricted class of morphemes, or sometimes to a single morpheme (for example, the declension of *pani* 'lady' in Dvonč *et al.* 1966). Our presentation is biased in the sense that we concentrate on those aspects of declension that may be of interest from the point of view of phonology. We begin with a general characterization of declension parameters.

3.2.1. Overview

A fairly complex system of allomorphy that arises both in the structure of the inflectional endings and in the phonological shape of the stems is governed by ten parameters or factors: number, gender, [animate], [personal], morphological class, softness of the final consonant, diphthong–vowel distinction, palatalization, length, and vowel–zero alternations in the stem. In what follows we shall briefly indicate which of these parameters should be regarded as constituent factors in word-formation and which are merely manifestations of phonological rules.

3.2.1.1. *Number*

Disregarding for the present such well-known phenomena as *pluralia tantum*, limitation to the singular number in the case of uncountable nouns, and the like, a statement can be made that nouns and adjectives exhibit distinct declension paradigms in the singular and in the plural. The Old Slavic dual number has survived only in a few instances, such as the alternative nom. and gen. pl. of *ok+o* 'eye' and *uch+o* 'ear', given second in each of the following pairs: *ok+á/oč+i, uch+á/uš+i* and *ôk/oč+ú, úch/uš+ú*. It also appears in the declension of *dva* 'two', *oba* 'both', and one or two other words.

3.2.1.2. *Gender*

There are three genders: masculine, feminine, and neuter. Assignment to a given gender is morphological in the case of adjectives and lexical in the case of nouns. That is, in nouns the gender is arbitrary. Stems and suffixes must be encoded with their specification for gender. This is best illustrated by such an extreme case as the gender changes in the noun *chlap* 'man' when it undergoes suffixation. One would expect that the gender should stay constant since in this instance we have a classic example of what might be termed 'natural gender'. If we set aside lexicalization,[18] the gender fluctuation is as follows:

(74) *a.* masculine: chlap, chlap+ec (dimin.), chlap+ík (dimin.), chlap+ák (dimin.)

feminine: chlap+in+a (dimin.; -*a* is an inflectional ending)

neuter: chlap+isk+o (augmentative; -*o* is an inflectional ending), chláp+ä 'young man'

b. complex suffixation:

$[[[chlap]_{masc.} \check{c}]_{masc.} a]_{neuter}$

$[[[[chlap]_{masc.} \check{c}]_{masc.} isk]_{neuter} o]_{nom. sg.}$

The *č* in (74*b*) is a palatalized version of the suffix -*ec*, where the *c* has been turned into *č* by Affricate Palatalization (see 4.4) and the *e*, which is a yer, has been deleted (see Chapter 5). Clearly, Slovak adheres to the Righthand Head Rule (Williams 1981) in the sense that the rightmost morpheme determines the gender of the whole word except the inflectional ending, which itself is governed by gender.

Gender is an important parameter in declension. It appears in its full form in all paradigms with the exception of the plural of adjectives, where the relevant distinction is between masculine and non-masculine adjectives. That is, feminine and neuter adjectives fall together. A special feature of the masculine declension of nouns is that the stem must end in a consonant, even if it is a borrowing. Masculine nouns that end in a vowel are either indeclinable, for example *kakadu* 'cockatoo', *boa* 'boa', or receive a partly adjectival declension, for instance *Verdi*, *Goethe*.

3.2.1.3. *The feature [animate]*

This semantic feature plays a role in the declension of masculine nouns and adjectives. For example, [+animate] nouns have the ending -*ovi* while [–animate] nouns have the ending -*e* in the loc. sg.: *chlap+ovi* 'man' vs. *dub+e* 'oak'. With [+animate] nouns, adjectives, and pronouns the ending of the accusative (both singular and plural) is always the same as the ending of the genitive: *kapitán+a* 'captain', *kapitán+ov* (pl.), *pekn+ého* 'beautiful', *pekn+ých* (pl.). On the other hand, [–animate] nouns and adjectives have the same form in the nominative and in the accusative: *med* 'honey', *med+y* (pl.), *pekn+ý* 'beautiful', *pekn+é* (pl.).

3.2.1.4. *The feature [personal]*

This feature permits us to draw fine distinctions within the class of [+animate] nouns and in the declension of adjectives. Consequently, like

---

[18] The augmentative form in -*isk+o* that we list below sometimes tends to lose its augmentative meaning. The noun reverts then to the 'natural gender', which is masculine.

[animate], it plays a role only in the masculine paradigm. Nouns referring to people take *-i*, *-ovia*, or *-ia* as the nom. pl. ending, while [–personal] nouns take *-y* or *-e*:

(75) *a.* kapitán+i 'captains', syn+ovia 'sons', učitel+ia 'teachers'
       b. dub+y 'oaks', stroj+e 'clothes'

Adjectives, whose gender must always agree with that of the nouns, take *-í* in the nom. pl. when the governing noun is [+personal] and *-é* when it is [–personal]: *pekn+í, pekn+é* 'beautiful'.

The distinction of [animate] and [personal] as two separate parameters becomes particularly clear when we consider alternative plural forms of nouns denoting animals: *baran+i* [-n'+i] ~ *baran+y* [-n+i] 'rams', *sokol+i* [-l'+i] ~ *sokol+y* [-l+i] 'falcons'. The first form in each pair has the [+personal] palatalizing *-i* suffix, the second has a non-palatalizing *-y* which is characteristic for non-personal nouns. Unsurprisingly, the first form appears only when animal names are used as descriptions of people, whereas the second form is the unmarked case. Two exceptions must be noted with regard to this observation: *vlc+i* ~ *vlk+y* 'wolves' and *vtác+i* ~ *vták+y* 'birds' are in a genuine free variation, that is, personification is not at play here.[19] This irregularity goes back to the time when [personal] was not a consideration in declension. The only relevant parameter was [animate].

3.2.1.5. *Morphological class*

Not all facts about declension in Slovak can be derived from lexical and semantic features that are, as it were, independent of the declension paradigms themselves. For nouns, but generally not for adjectives, it becomes necessary to distinguish arbitrary morphological classes (usually not more than two). This step is well supported when more than one inflectional ending is different for some nouns and this difference cannot be determined from the otherwise available parameters. For example, *syn* 'son' has a zero ending in the nom. sg. and *-a* in the gen./acc. sg., while *hrdin+a* 'hero' has *-a* in the nom. sg. and *-u* in the gen./acc. sg. These facts are arbitrary, because in other respects the two nouns have identical properties: both are masculine and personal, and both also end in *-n*.[20] We must simply conclude that they belong to two different morphological classes. On the other hand, when a given noun or morpheme diverges

---

[19] Descriptions of Slovak such as Dvonč *et al.* (1966) quote yet a third noun: *ps+i ~ ps+y* 'dogs'. However, the difference here is purely orthographic as *s* does not undergo palatalization in Slovak and *-i/y* are both realized phonetically as [i]. Note: the forms *vlc+i* and *vtác+i* are derived by 2nd Velar Palatalization, which we discuss in 4.3.

[20] The nature of the stem-final consonant is an essential factor in declension. Hence, it is important for our present purpose that both nouns should end in the same consonant, as this factor cannot then be at play; see the discussion of [soft] below.

from the general pattern in one case only, we may assume that this property is encoded in the lexicon as a fact about this particular noun. That is, rather than carrying a lexical specification [class X], it carries the specification, for example, '-*i* in the gen. pl.' A real instance where this procedure is applicable is the word *lož+e* 'bed'. It is entirely parallel to soft-stem nouns such as *líc+e* 'face' except for the gen. pl.: *lož+í* vs. *líc*. Only a handful of words are like *lož+e* and take -*í* in the gen. pl.

3.2.1.6. *The feature [soft]*

The selection of an appropriate inflectional ending may depend on the nature of the stem-final consonant. In particular, a distinction is drawn between the so-called soft and hard stems. Soft stems terminate in palatal or formerly palatalized segments: [t', d', n', l', j] which are prepalatal, [c, ʒ] which are alveolar, and [š, ž, č, ǯ] which are postalveolar. The latter two classes of consonants used to be palatalized, that is [–back], in Middle Slovak but no longer are: they have 'hardened' in the course of history and today they are not soft in the phonetic sense.

A phonological problem arises at this point. Should we treat all 'soft' consonants as phonologically [–back] or should we rather operate with a diacritic feature [soft]? Depending on how this question is answered, we can regard softness as either a phonological or a lexical property. This problem will be discussed in 6.5. For the moment let us use [soft] as a cover feature without making a commitment as to the nature of this property.

In the case of nouns, soft stems select a subset of endings that is unpredictably different from that of hard stems. For example, *koč* 'carriage' (masc.) takes -*i* in the loc. sg. and -*e* in the nom./acc. pl., while *med* 'honey', which is otherwise parallel to *koč*, takes -*e* and -*y* in the same cases:

(76) loc. sg.: koč+i, med+e
    nom./acc. pl.: koč+e, med+y

The remaining differences are summarized in (77):

(77) feminine:
        gen. sg.: ulic+e 'street', os+y 'wasp'
        dat./loc. sg.: ulic+i, os+e
        nom./acc. pl.: ulic+e, os+y
    neuter:
        nom./acc. sg.: vrec+e 'bag', blat+o 'mud'
        loc. sg.: vrec+i, blat+e

The system of inflectional endings can be simplified if we assume that the distinct phonological representations of the endings are derived by rule.

Thus, if the underlying representation of the loc. sg. in (76) is //e//, as in *med+e* 'honey', then the variant *-i* of *koč+i* 'carriage' can be interpreted to come from raising: *e → i* / SOFT —. Such statements have the status of allomorphy rules. Observe that the raising is not a phonological generalization, since the nom./acc. pl. in (76) is an exact mirror image of the loc. sg.: *-e* appears with soft stems and *-y* [i] with hard stems. The feature [soft] is thus quasi-phonological. It triggers allomorphy rules but also, as we point out below, phonological rules. The latter situation obtains in the case of adjectives where a sweeping generalization can be made by postulating a rule of Fronting (see 6.5).

3.2.1.7. *Diphthong–vowel distinction*

The distinction between diphthongs and vowels is the first of the four declension parameters that we interpret in purely or almost purely phonological terms. The latter reservation is made for a couple of nouns that behave like soft stems, even though they do not end in one of the 'soft' consonants (see 6.5).

A superficial glance at the feminine dat. pl. of words such as *kos+ám* 'scythe' and *ulic+iam* 'street' or the neuter nom. pl. *blat+á* 'mud' and *vrec+ia* 'bag' may suggest that here, as in (76) and (77), we have phonologically unpredictable alternations between vowels and diphthongs in the endings. This impression is incorrect. We demonstrate in 6.5 that the distribution of diphthongs and vowels is entirely predictable from the rule of Fronting. The only restriction is that the relevant vowels must be long. The //á// fronted to /ǽ/ is further subject to Diphthongization which derives surface [ia].

3.2.1.8. *Palatalization*

The endings which contain surface front vowels [i, e] sometimes trigger palatalization and sometimes do not. For example, the *-e* of the fem. loc. sg. in nouns induces Coronal Palatalization, but the *-é* of the non-masculine nom. sg. in adjectives does not: *žen+e* [n′] 'wife' vs. *pekn+é* [n] 'beautiful'. Similarly, the *-i* of the nom. pl. in masculine personal nouns is palatalizing but the *-í* of the nom. pl. in masculine personal adjectives is not: *kapitán+i* [n′] 'captains' vs. *pekn+í* [n] 'beautiful'. Proposals such as restricting palatalization to [+personal] stems are untenable in view of the fact that palatalization rules apply productively in all kinds of lexical categories (including verbs) and are essential in derivational morphology (see Chapter 4).

In the case of the fem. loc. sg. *-e* there is one additional peculiarity. The *e* is palatalizing with respect to Coronal Palatalization but non-palatalizing with respect to 1st Velar Palatalization: *malin+e* [n′] 'raspberry' vs.

Amerik+e 'America' (*k* not *č*). The adjectival paradigm stands out in that all the inflectional endings are non-palatalizing. Evidently, palatalization in declension is a complex matter: should we opt for a phonological solution and posit back vowels in all instances of non-palatalizing front vowels, or should we rather resort to positing diacritics? We discuss this problem in 6.6.

3.2.1.9. *Length*

Even a cursory look at declension paradigms reveals the existence of what seems to be a fairly complex system of length relations between the stems and the inflectional endings. Let us look at the fem. dat. pl. of nouns and masc. nom. sg. of adjectives:

(78) *a.* vran+ám 'crow'—dám+am 'lady'—zmij+am 'viper'
   b. cudz+í 'foreign'—súc+i 'wise'—kohút+í 'cock' (Adj.)
   c. rád 'glad' (masc.)—rad+á (fem.), sám 'alone' (masc.)—sam+á (fem.)

At first glance these data seem to be full of contradictions. One would want to assume that the length relations in (78*a*) are explicable in terms of the Rhythmic Law: shortening after a long vowel. However, this is immediately contradicted by the third word in (78*a*), *zmij+am* 'viper', where the ending shortens after a short stem vowel. Similarly, the contrast *cudz+i* 'foreign' vs. *súc+i* 'wise' in (78*b*) follows from the Rhythmic Law, but how is it then possible for the long *í* to survive in *kohút+í* 'cock' (Adj.), the third word in (78*b*)? Finally, the root vowels of the adjectives in (78*c*) seem to shorten before long vowels of the endings, which contradicts our understanding of the Rhythmic Law.

These contradictions are only apparent. They merely indicate that length relations in Slovak are governed not by one but by several independent rules. These rules reflect phonological and morphological generalizations, since, as we show in Chapter 6, they are not limited either to the adjectival or to the nominal declension. Rather, they cut across the whole morphological system. The shortening in (78*a*) is explicable in terms of the Rhythmic Law and Glide Shortening. The alleged violation of the Rhythmic Law in (78*b*) yields to a straightforward explanation as a result of Contraction. We shall postpone the discussion of these issues till Chapters 6 and 8. For the moment let us merely introduce the problem unveiled by the data in (78*c*). The masculine adjectives *rád* 'glad' and *sám* 'alone' are the so-called short forms which lack an inflectional ending,[21] or rather have a zero as an inflectional ending. The stem vowel is short in

---

[21] In Slovak, by contrast with Russian, the short form of adjectives occurs only with a small class of words.

the feminine forms *rad+á, sam+á*. Undoubtedly, we are dealing with the lengthening of the stem vowel before the zero ending in (78c), and not with some shortening rule. Recall that Vowel Lengthening (2/24) operates before yers. These in turn become vocalized and surface phonetically if they are followed by a yer in the next syllable (see Yer Vocalization 2/23). Otherwise they delete context-freely. The lengthening in (78c) becomes clear if we assume that zero endings are in fact yers. It is also understandable why these yers never vocalize: as inflectional morphemes they are the final morpheme of the word and hence they are never followed by a suffix containing a yer. The environment of Yer Vocalization is thus never met. This analysis finds additional support in the vowel–zero alternations to which we now turn.

3.2.1.10. *Vowel–zero alternations*

In declension, but not necessarily in other contexts, vowel–zero alternations in the stems are correlated to the presence of zero versus vocalic suffixes. Zero inflectional endings trigger the surfacing of the yers in the stem (see Chapter 5). Vocalic suffixes, that is suffixes which have vowels in the phonetic representation, inhibit the surfacing of the yers. As mentioned in the previous section, these alternations are readily explicable in terms of Yer Vocalization and Yer Deletion (in fact, Stray Erasure: see Chapter 5). We only need to assume that zero endings are themselves yers. Such an assumption explains the operation of not only Yer Vocalization but also Vowel Lengthening, as both rules require a yer as their environment. That these rules are independent and converge with regard to the environment is shown on the one hand by the fact that vocalized yers may themselves undergo lengthening and that lengthening applies to all kinds of vowels. On the other hand, Yer Vocalization and Vowel Lengthening may take different paths in the sense that a given word may be an input to one but an exception to the other rule. The relevant examples here are *dlž+en* 'indebted' and *pes* 'dog'. Both are instances of yer stems, which is demonstrated by the fact that the vowels are mobile: compare *dlž+n+á* (fem. nom. sg.), *ps+a* (gen. sg.). Yer Vocalization in *dlž+en* and *pes* takes place before an inflectional yer ending: the nom. sg. of adjectives (short form) and the nom. sg. of nouns. Yet the vocalized yers do not lengthen. In the regular cases Yer Vocalization and Vowel Lengthening go hand in hand. Compare:

(79) koniec (masc. nom. sg.) 'end'—konc+a (gen. sg.)
    šeliem (fem. gen. pl.) 'beast'—šelm+a (nom. sg.)
    mydiel (neuter gen. pl.) 'soap'—mydl+o (nom. sg.)

We postpone a detailed analysis of these alternations till Chapter 5. At this point let us merely observe that Yer Vocalization and Vowel Lengthening support the interpretation of zero inflectional suffixes as yers. The inflectional yer does not trigger palatalization, hence it must be a back vowel, let us say //U//, where the capitalization denotes the property of being a yer. We summarize our discussion by providing a sample derivation of *koniec* 'end' (nom. sg.) in (80).

(80) konEc+U
    konec+U   Yer Vocalization (2/23)
    konéc+U   Vowel Lengthening (2/24)
    koniec+U   Diphthongization (2/25)
    koniec   Yer Deletion (that is, Stray Erasure)

In the next two sections we adduce all the basic paradigms for adjectives and nouns. (We omit irregular paradigms that characterize a highly restricted number of words.) These paradigms are meant as reference for discussion in subsequent chapters of this book. Most paradigms are given in two versions, *a* and *b*. The tables marked as *a* contain words which exemplify the underlying representation of inflectional suffixes most clearly. However, even in these tables there is much redundant information. The information which is crucial to establishing the underlying representations appears in italics to enhance the clarity of exposition. Tables marked as *b* contain only redundant information, where the term 'redundant' should be understood to mean 'derivable by phonological rules'. The distinction between what we consider to be relevant or redundant should be clear from the discussion of the declension parameters in the preceding sections. The presentation of paradigms is summarized by providing tables with the underlying representations of the inflectional endings.

3.2.2. Adjectives

We begin with adjectives since their structure is much simpler than that of nouns. Our example is taken from the standard reference books such as Dvonč *et al.* (1966) and Letz (1950): *pekn+ý* 'beautiful'.

There are a number of morphological generalizations which follow from Table 3*a*, such as the equivalence of certain cases and the overlap in inflectional endings, particularly between the masculine and the neuter genders. We shall not state these generalizations here, but shall merely indicate the dependency relations between various lexical parameters. Setting aside number, which is obvious from the table, they can be summarized as shown in (81).

Attention should be drawn to the masc. nom. sg. The full form has the ending -*ý* (Table 3*a*), while the short form has a yer (see 3.2.1.9; note the lengthening). It should also be pointed out that all inflectional suffixes are non-palatalizing (see 6.6). A summary of the endings is given in Table

TABLE 3a. *Adjective declension: basic pattern*

SINGULAR

	Masculine	Feminine	Neuter
nom.	*pekn+ý*	*pekn+á*	*pekn+é*
gen.	*pekn+ého*	*pekn+ej*	pekn+ého
dat.	*pekn+ému*	pekn+ej	pekn+ému
acc.	pekn+ého [+animate]	*pekn+ú*	pekn+é
	pekn+ý [−animate]		
loc.	*pekn+om*	pekn+ej	pekn+om
instr.	*pekn+ým*	*pekn+ou*	pekn+ým

PLURAL

	Masculine personal	Non-virile
nom.	*pekn+í*	*pekn+é*
gen.	*pekn+ých*	pekn+ých
dat.	*pekn+ým*	pekn+ým
acc.	pekn+ých	pekn+é
loc.	pekn+ých	pekn+ých
instr.	*pekn+ými*	pekn+ými

(81)

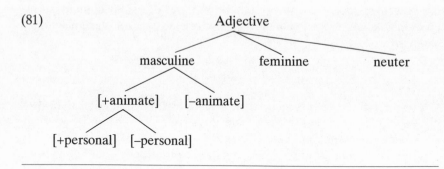

4. In the masc. nom. sg., //í// is the ending of the full form and the yer //U// the ending of the short form.

In Table 3b we present the data whose allomorphy can be accounted for by phonological rules. We limit the presentation to the masculine and the feminine genders. The word *stál+y* 'constant' illustrates the application of the Rhythmic Law (2/26), *cudz+í* 'foreign' shows the operation of Fronting (see 6.5), *súc+i* 'wise' combines both of these rules, and *had+í* 'reptilian' exemplifies Contraction (see 6.4). Attention should be drawn to

TABLE 3b. *Adjective declension: derivable pattern*

Masculine

Singular				
nom.	stál+y	súc+i	had+í	cudz+í
gen.	stál+eho	súc+eho	had+ieho	cudz+ieho
dat.	stál+emu	súc+emu	had+iemu	cudz+iemu
acc.	stál+eho	súc+eho	had+ieho	cudz+ieho
instr.	stál+ym	súc+im	had+ím	cudz+ím
Plural				
nom.	stál+y	súc+i	had+í	cudz+í
gen.	stál+ych	súc+ich	had+ích	cudz+ích
dat.	stál+ym	súc+im	had+ím	cudz+ím
acc.	stál+ych	súc+ich	had+ích	cudz+ích
loc.	stál+ych	súc+ich	had+ích	cudz+ích
instr.	stál+ymi	súc+imi	had+ími	cudz+ími

Feminine

Singular				
nom.	stál+a	súc+a	cudz+ia	had+ia
gen.	stál+ej	súc+ej	cudz+ej	had+ej
dat.	stál+ej	súc+ej	cudz+ej	had+ej
acc.	stál+u	súc+u	cudz+iu	had+iu
instr.	stál+ou	súc+ou	cudz+ou	had'+ou
Plural				
nom.	stál+e	súc+e	cudz+ie	had+ie

(other cases same as masc.)

TABLE 4. *Underlying representation of inflectional endings of adjectives*

	Masculine	Feminine	Neuter
Singular			
nom.	-í, -U	-á	-é
gen.	-éfio	-ej	-éfio
dat.	-ému	-ej	-ému
acc.	-éfio, -í	-ú	-é
loc.	-om	-ej	-om
instr.	-ím	-om	-ím

	Masc. personal	Non-virile
Plural		
nom.	-í	-é
gen.	-íx	-íx
dat.	-ím	-ím
acc.	-íx	-é
loc.	-íx	-íx
instr.	-ími	-ími

the fact that the alternations induced by soft stems of adjectives are fully predictable in terms of phonological rules and do not call for allomorphy statements. Nouns are different in this respect.

3.2.3. Nouns

We begin by introducing masculine nouns, which have the most complex system of inflection. Feminine and neuter nouns are presented in later sections. In what follows we shall not indicate cross-gender morphological redundancies since they can easily be deduced from the tables.

3.2.3.1. *Masculine*

Table 5 gives the basic paradigms. Our examples are the words *pilot* 'pilot', *gazd+a* 'farmer', *ded+o* 'grandpa', *med* 'honey', and *koniec* 'end'. Morphological generalizations, such as 'the accusative equals the genitive in [+animate] nouns' and 'the accusative equals the nominative in [−animate] nouns', were discussed in 3.2.2 and they can be read from the table. Let us therefore focus on the underlying representation of the inflectional endings wherever it is not obvious. The nom. sg. is either a yer or the vowels -*a* and -*o*. The yer is motivated by the operation of Yer

TABLE 5. *Declension of masculine nouns*

Singular					
nom.	pilot	*gazd+a*	*ded+o*	med	*koniec*
gen.	*pilot+a*	*gazd+u*	ded+a	med+u	konc+a
dat.	*pilot+ovi*	gazd+ovi	ded+ovi	*med+u*	konc+u
acc.	pilot+a	gazd+u	ded+a	med	koniec
loc.	pilot+ovi	gazd+ovi	ded+ovi	*med+e* [d']	*konc+i*
instr.	*pilot+om*	gazd+om	ded+om	med+om	konc+om
Plural					
nom.	*pilot+i* [t']	*gazd+ovia*	ded+ovia	*med+y*	*konc+e*
gen.	*pilot+ov*	gazd+ov	ded+ov	med+ov	konc+ov
dat.	*pilot+om*	gazd+om	ded+om	med+om	konc+om
acc.	pilot+ov	gazd+ov	ded+ov	med+y	konc+e
loc.	pilot+och	gazd+och	ded+och	med+och	konc+och
instr.	*pilot+mi*	*gazd+ami*	*ded+mi*	med+mi	konc+ami

Vocalization (2/23) and Vowel Lengthening (2/24) in *koniec*. The vowel -*o*, as in *ded+o*, appears only with a small number of stems. It could thus be generated from -*a* by a lexically governed allomorphy rule.

The gen. sg. has two endings, -*a* and -*u*. Their distribution is lexically governed with [–animate] nouns. In the class of personal nouns the generalization is that those stems which have a zero ending (that is, a yer) in the nom. sg. take -*a*, the others take -*u*; compare *pilot+a* and *gazd+u*. This generalization has nothing to do with the structure of the stem itself: for example, both *pilot* and *ded+o* end in a dental stop, yet they receive different endings in the gen. sg. We must therefore resort to postulating morphological classes, where *pilot* is Class 1 while *gazd+a* and *ded+o* are Class 2.

The dat. sg. illustrates the operation of [animate] as a parameter. Animate nouns take -*ovi* whereas inanimate nouns take -*u*.

The loc. sg. reveals -*ovi* as the ending of animate nouns and -*e* as well as -*i* as the endings of inanimate nouns. The -*i* is non-palatalizing, since *konc+i* does not undergo Affricate Palatalization (see 4.4). In the same class of nouns the nom. pl. has a non-palatalizing -*y* with hard stems and a non-palatalizing -*e* with soft stems: compare *med+y* and *konc+e*. Thus, [soft] plays a role in the class of inanimate nouns.

The nom. pl. endings in the class of personal nouns include -*i*, -*ovia*, and -*ia* (not mentioned in Table 5; an example is *učiteľ* 'teacher'— *učiteľ+ia*). Their distribution is lexically governed to a large extent and it does not correspond to the morphological classes that we distinguished while discussing the nom. sg. and the gen. sg. Thus, *syn* 'son' is Class 1, like *pilot*, but it takes -*ovia* in the nom. pl. like Class 2 words such as

TABLE 6. *Nouns: masculine inflectional endings*

	Singular	Plural
nom.	-U, -a	-i, -ová, -ắ, -y, -*e*
gen.	-a, -u	-o*v*
dat.	-o*v*i, -u	-om
acc.	-a, -u, -U	-o*v*, -y, -*e*
loc.	-o*v*i, -e, -y	-ox
instr.	-om	-ami

gazd+a and *ded+o*. On the other hand, *poet+a* 'poet' is Class 2 and yet it takes *-i* in the nom. pl.: *poet+i*. Further, we may note that *-ia* can be derived from //ắ// via Diphthongization (2/25). As expected, it causes palatalization: compare *brat* 'brother'—*brat+ia* [t'].

The instr. pl. *-ami/mi* is a case of allomorphy. In some instances the distribution must be governed lexically. The phonology can only help in the sense that *-ami* appears typically with stems that end in a cluster (cf. Dvonč *et al.* 1966: 84).

In Table 6 we list the underlying representations of the inflectional endings. A non-palatalizing *-i* is represented as *-y*, a non-palatalizing *-e* appears in italics. Notice that with the exception of the nom. pl. //-ắ// all the endings are short. The Rhythmic Law does not operate as there are no relevant examples. The effects of Yer Vocalization and Vowel Lengthening have already been discussed. Presenting more data in a *b* version of Table 6 is therefore superfluous.

The parameters at play in the masculine declension can be summarized as shown in (82).

(82)

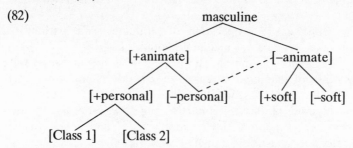

The broken line indicates that nouns denoting animals join the inanimate class in the plural. That is, in the singular they have the same pattern as *pilot*, and in the plural they follow *med* if they end in a hard consonant and *koniec* if they end in a soft consonant. It should be noted that, as shown in (82), [soft] is a subordinate parameter with respect to [animate]. This means that in cases of conflict it is [animate] that determines what

TABLE 7*a*. *Declension of feminine nouns: basic pattern*

Singular					
nom.	vod+a	Demeter	ulic+a	dlaň	noc
gen.	vod+y	Demetr+y	ulic+e	dlan+e	noc+i
dat.	vod+e [d']	Demetr+e	ulic+i	dlan+i	noc+i
acc.	vod+u	Demetr+u	ulic+u	dlaň	noc
loc.	vod+e	Demetr+e	ulic+i	dlan+i	noc+i
instr.	vod+ou	Demetr+ou	ulic+ou	dlaň+ou	noc+ou
Plural					
nom.	vod+y	Demetr+y	ulic+e	dlan+e	noc+i
gen.	vôd	Demetier	ulíc	dlan+í	noc+í
dat.	vod+ám	Demetr+ám	ulic+iam	dlan+iam	noc+iam
acc.	vod+y	Demetr+y	ulic+e	dlan+e	noc+i
loc.	vod+ách	Demetr+ách	ulic+iach	dlan+iach	noc+iach
instr.	vod+ami	Demetr+ami	ulic+ami	dlaň+ami	noc+ami

type of paradigm is appropriate. Thus, *otec* 'father' follows the paradigm of *pilot* rather than that of *koniec*.

3.2.3.2. *Feminine*

The basic paradigms of the feminine declension are illustrated in Table 7*a* by the following examples: *vod+a* 'water', *Demeter* (name), *ulic+a* 'street', *dlaň* 'palm', and *noc* 'night' (for details see Dvonč *et al.* 1966). Morphological generalizations concerning homophonous endings, such as 'the nominative equals the accusative', have been discussed before and are evident from the table. Therefore we shall limit our discussion to the allomorphy of the endings and their distribution.

The nom. sg. has two endings: -*a* and a yer. The latter is illustrated by vowel–zero alternations in *Demeter*[22] (an effect of Yer Vocalization before the inflectional yer and Yer Deletion elsewhere). The distribution of the two endings is governed by arbitrary morphological class: *vod+a* and *ulic+a* are Class 1, while *Demeter*, *dlaň*, and *noc* are Class 2.

The gen. sg. shows the operation of [soft] as a parameter. Hard stems take -*y*, soft stems take -*e*: *vod+y*, *ulic+e* (we discuss *noc+i* later). The -*e* is non-palatalizing since Affricate Palatalization is inapplicable ($c \rightarrow \check{c}$ before front vowels; see 4.4). The same distinction is well illustrated in the dat./loc. sg.: hard stems palatalize before -*e*, soft stems take -*i* (equivalent to -*y*: no Affricate Palatalization). If we set aside *noc+i* for the moment,

---

[22] The underlying representation of *Demeter* is //demetEr//, where the capital letter denotes a yer.

then [soft] determines the distribution of the nom. pl. endings: -*y* after hard stems and a non-palatalizing -*e* after soft stems.

The allomorphy in the dat./loc. pl. yields to a straightforward explanation. The long *á* undergoes Fronting when it appears after soft stems (see 6.5). The fronted *ä́* is subsequently diphthongized to [ia].

The gen. pl. has two allomorphs: a yer and a non-palatalizing -*í* (that is, equivalent to -*ý*). Their distribution parallels the distribution of -*u* vs. zero in the acc. sg. Hard stems as well as words in the *ulic*+*a* class take the yer (in the acc. sg. the same words take -*u*). The yer is motivated from two sources: Yer Vocalization in *Demeter* and Vowel Lengthening in this word as well as in *ulíc* and *vôd*. Recall that the lengthened /é, ó/ diphthongize to [ie, uo], hence the alternations.

Returning to the distribution of the yer and the non-palatalizing -*í* in the gen. pl., notice that two independent parameters are at play: morphological class and [soft]. The ending -*í* is assigned to stems that are [Class 2, +soft], the yer appears elsewhere.[23] That these parameters are independent can be seen from the way in which they combine:

(83)   [Class 1, –soft]: vod+a
       [Class 1, +soft]: ulic+a
       [Class 2, –soft]: Demeter
       [Class 2, +soft]: dlaň, noc

The relationships between the parameters are not hierarchical but horizontal. This is a point of difference between the masculine and the feminine nouns:

(84)   feminine

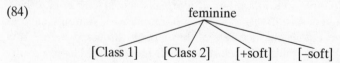

     [Class 1]   [Class 2]   [+soft]   [–soft]

The paradigm for *noc* seems to stand out in this system. The word is clearly Class 2 since it takes a zero (that is, a yer) ending in the nom. sg. and -*í* in the gen. pl. Thus, it behaves like *dlaň*, with which it shares the property of being [+soft]. The distinction between *dlaň* and *noc* is seen in the gen. sg./nom. pl.: *dlan*+*e* vs. *noc*+*i*. Should we regard this as a reason to assign *noc* to a separate class, Class 3? Probably not. The point is that, apart from a couple of lexical exceptions, the assignment of soft stems to the *noc* paradigm is predictable from the stem-final consonant. As observed by Dvonč *et al.* (1966), only the soft stems in //c, t'// take this paradigm regularly (for further discussion, see Fronting in 6.5). Dvonč *et al.* (1966: 110) point out that the *noc* paradigm is unproductive and its members tend to cross over to the *dlaň* pattern. In sum, the paradigm for

---

[23] There are a few words which take the gen. pl. -*í* in spite of their membership of Class 1, for example *šij*+*a* 'neck'—*šij*+*í*.

TABLE 7*b*. *Declension of feminine nouns: derivable pattern*

Singular			
nom.	dám+a	obyčaj	garáž
gen.	dám+y	obyčaj+e	garáž+e
dat.	dám+e	obyčaj+i	garáž+i
acc.	dám+u	obyčaj	garáž
loc.	dám+e	obyčaj+i	garáž+i
instr.	dám+ou	obyčaj+ou	garáž+ou
Plural			
nom.	dám+y	obyčaj+e	garáž+e
gen.	dám	obyčaj+í	garáž+i
dat.	dám+am	obyčaj+am	garáž+am
acc.	dám+y	obyčaj+e	garáž+e
loc.	dám+ach	obyčaj+ach	garáž+ach
instr.	dám+ami	obyčaj+ami	garáž+ami

TABLE 8. *Nouns: feminine inflectional endings*

	Singular	Plural
nom.	-a, -U	-y, -*e*
gen.	-y, -*e*	-U, -ý
dat.	-e, -y	-ám
acc.	-u, -U	-y, -*e*
loc.	-e, -y	-áx
instr.	-o*v*	-ami

noc is a subset of that for *dlaň*. It requires an allomorphy rule that turns the -*e* of *dlan+e* into the -*i* of *noc+i*.

We are now in a position to give a complete list of the feminine inflectional endings in Table 8. As in Table 6 above, -y stands for a non-palatalizing -*i* and the -*e* in italics is a non-palatalizing equivalent to //-e//.

In Table 7*b* we present examples of words that can be fully derived by means of the existing phonological rules: the Rhythmic Law (2/26) and Glide Shortening (2/27). The glosses are as follows: *dám+a* 'lady', *obyčaj* 'custom', *garáž* 'garage'.

3.2.3.3. *Neuter*

Compared to the masculine and the feminine paradigms, the system of neuter declension is relatively simple. Our examples are the words *blat+o* 'mud', *múze+um* 'museum', *plec+e* 'shoulder', and *čít+a+n+i+e* 'reading'

TABLE 9. *Declension of neuter nouns*

Singular				
nom.	*blat+o*	*múze+um*	*plec+e*	čítan+ie
gen.	*blat+a*	múze+a	plec+a	čítan+ia
dat.	*blat+u*	múze+u	plec+u	čítan+iu
acc.	blat+o	múze+um	plec+e	čítan+ie
loc.	*blat+e* [t']	*múze+u*	*plec+i*	čítan+í
instr.	*blat+om*	múze+om	plec+om	*čítan+ím*

Plural				
nom.	*blat+á*	múze+á	plec+ia	čítan+ia
gen.	*blát*	*múze+í*	pliec	čítan+í
dat.	*blat+ám*	múze+ám	plec+iam	čítan+iam
acc.	blat+á	múze+á	plec+ia	čítan+ia
loc.	*blat+ách*	múze+ách	plec+iach	čítan+iach
instr.	*blat+ami*	múze+ami	plec+ami	čítan+iami

(deverbal noun). The traditional paradigms for these words are given in Table 9. It may be observed in passing that the nominative equals the accusative with regard to the selection of the ending. To establish the underlying representations of the endings, we first look at the paradigms for *blat+o* and *plec+e*. Some differences are only apparent, others are substantial.

The alternations between *á* and *ia* in the nom./dat./loc. pl. can be easily accounted for by Fronting: *á* → *ä* after a soft consonant (see 6.5). Then, Diphthongization takes effect and derives surface [ia]. The nom. and the loc. sg. are problematic. There is no way of deriving the *-e* of *plec+e* from the *-o* of *blat+o* by means of some general phonological rule such as Fronting. This is clearly demonstrated by the fact that in the instr. sg. we have *-om* and not *-em* in the same word: *plec+e* (nom. sg.) vs. *plec+om* (instr. sg.). We may note further that the *-i* of the loc. sg. is non-palatalizing with respect to Affricate Palatalization (see 4.4) while the corresponding *-e* in *blat+e* does trigger Coronal Palatalization. In sum, there is no obvious way in which *blat+o* and *plec+e* can be assumed to have the same suffixes in the nom. and the loc. sg.

With regard to the *čítan+ie* paradigm it may be noted that, with the exception of the instr. sg. (which requires an allomorphy rule), all the variations in the inflectional endings are explicable in terms of Contraction, a rule that coalesces two vowels into a diphthong (see 6.4). Thus, *čítan+ie* does not constitute a separate paradigm.

The remaining paradigm in Table 9, that for *múze+um*, does not represent any cross-lexical regularity. It characterizes a group of borrowings such as *indivídu+um* 'strange creature', *štúdi+o* 'studio', *rádi+o*

TABLE 10. *Nouns: neuter inflectional endings*

	Singular	Plural
nom.	-o, -*e*	-á
gen.	-a	-U
dat.	-u	-ám
acc.	-o, -*e*	-á
loc.	-e, -y	-áx
instr.	-om	-ami

'radio', *kaka+o* 'cocoa', and a few others. The nom. sg. endings are different with different words. The loc. sg. *-u* of *múze+u* is also found in a class of native words whose stem ends in a velar, for instance *ok+o* 'eye'— *ok+u*. The gen. pl. *-í* of *múze+í* occurs regularly with stems that end in a vowel and exceptionally with some two or three non-vocalic soft stems: *pol+í* //l'// 'field', *oj+í* 'shaft'. In sum, the paradigm represented by *múze+um* is not consistent in the sense that it is subject to a few independent lexically governed allomorphy rules.

One further point needs to be explained. In the case of stems that end in a consonant the gen. pl. ending is a yer. The arguments are the same as in the masculine and the feminine declensions. The yer explains why vowels lengthen (with *é* diphthongizing to *ie*): *blát, pliec*. It also accounts for vowel–zero alternations in stems which contain a yer, for example *mydl+o* 'soap' (nom. sg.)—*mydiel* (gen. pl.): Yer Vocalization, Vowel Lengthening, and Diphthongization.

We summarize our discussion by showing the parameters in (85) and listing the underlying representations of the inflectional endings in Table 10.

(85)   neuter

                         [+soft]   [−soft]

Compared to the masculine and the feminine, (85) is a simple representation. The inflectional endings in Table 10 are also simpler since they involve less allomorphy. As previously, -y stands for a non-palatalizing *-i*, the *e* in italics is a non-palatalizing equivalent to //-e//, and the capital letter stands for a yer.

Instead of compiling a *b* equivalent of Table 9, that is, a table with rule-governed allomorphy, we shall merely look at one case: the nom. pl.

(86) blat+á 'muds', plec+ia 'shoulders', stád+a 'flocks', oj+a 'shafts', per+ia 'feathers' (collective), prút+ia 'twigs' (collective), štúdi+a 'studios'

This is a rather spectacular set of examples. It seems to be full of contradictions: the nom. pl. is a long vowel, a diphthong, or a short vowel; the opposition short–long/diphthong is correlated with the length of the stem in some but not in other examples; etc. It is the task of this book to provide a systematic account for variation of the type exhibited in (86) and thereby to demonstrate how phonological generalizations enable us to make sense of surface phonetic facts. The data in (86) are analysed in detail in Chapter 6.

3.3. DERIVATIONAL MORPHOLOGY

We shall limit our presentation to the phonological aspects of derivational morphology. In particular, we shall concentrate on establishing the underlying representation of some more difficult suffixes which will often be referred to in subsequent chapters of this book.

The scope of the discussion could be characterized as follows. Among derivational suffixes three classes of cases can be distinguished. First, there are suffixes such as -*ot*, which nominalizes adjectives, for example *slep+ý* 'blind'—*slep+ot+a* 'blindness'. Such suffixes are uninteresting since, on the one hand, their underlying representation is obvious and, on the other hand, they do not trigger any phonological rules. The second class of cases includes suffixes which trigger phonological rules but whose underlying representation is entirely clear. Here belong morphemes such as the comparative -*š*, which causes shortening, and the feminine -*ic+a*, which induces palatalization: *biel+y* 'white'—*bel+š+í* 'whiter', *vlk* 'wolf'—*vlč+ic+a* 'she-wolf'. Suffixes of this type will not be discussed either. Rather, we shall concentrate on a third class of suffixes. These are morphemes that trigger phonological rules and exhibit surface allomorphy which makes it unclear how they should be represented at the underlying level. The relevant cases are the suffixes that contain yers.

In order to determine the underlying representation we shall apply nine diagnostic tests. Quite obviously, not all suffixes can be tested against all these nine criteria since sometimes the relevant contexts are missing. Also, even with very high standards, it is hardly necessary to provide evidence for a given representation from as many as nine independent sources. That in some cases such overwhelming evidence can be adduced is interesting and, given that the representations under consideration contain 'abstract' vowels (yers), our presentation can be regarded as a contribution to the classic discussion of abstractness in phonology.

With a system of tightly interacting rules such as those of Slovak, it becomes impossible to clarify the details of each rule or representation in a succinct way. Therefore we shall simply assume certain interpretations. They will be discussed in detail in subsequent chapters of this book. At this point we merely wish to collect the relevant facts and indicate in what part of this study they are elaborated further.

A piece of direct evidence for the presence of yers in a suffix is the occurrence of vowel–zero alternations. In the case of Slovak, yers are the movable vowels *e* and *o*. Consequently, if a suffix exhibits surface allomorphs, one with *e* or *o* and the other without either of these vowels, then it is a yer suffix. The remaining tests for discovering whether a suffix contains a yer are indirect. They all derive from observing whether or not a given phonological rule applies. Thus, if a yer of the stem vocalizes before a certain suffix, then this suffix itself must have a yer. This follows from the fact that Yer Vocalization (2/23) applies in the environment of a following yer (for details, see Chapter 5). A third argument for diagnosing a yer in the suffix is the application of Coronal Palatalization (2/29), which turns, among others, hard *l* into soft *l'* before front vowels.[24] First Velar Palatalization (2/28) is the fourth source of evidence. This rule palatalizes /k, g, x, ɦ/ to [č, ʒ, š, ž] before front vowels (see 4.2). A fifth argument is entirely parallel: Affricate Palatalization turns /c, ʒ/ into [č, ʒ] in a palatalizing environment (see 4.4). The application of a palatalization rule (regardless of what type) before a suffix that consists of consonants alone indicates that these consonants are preceded by a front yer in the underlying representation. The yer triggers palatalization and is subsequently deleted by Yer Deletion, or rather Stray Erasure (see Chapter 5). A sixth argument is the operation of Vowel Lengthening (2/24), a rule that lengthens vowels before a yer in the next syllable (see 6.1.1.3). A seventh diagnostic rule is Yer Hiatus, which inserts /j/ between a vowel and a yer (see 5.7). Argument number eight is the familiar Postvocalic *j*-Deletion, rule (4) of this chapter. Recall that *j* is deleted before a consonant. If we find a suffix that blocks Postvocalic *j*-Deletion in spite of the fact that in surface terms it begins with a consonant, then this indicates that the consonant must be preceded by a yer which blocks the deletion of /j/. The ninth and final argument is constructed along exactly the same lines. As we show in 5.6, Slovak has a rule of Nasal Deletion that truncates *m* and *n* before a consonant across a morpheme boundary. If this rule fails to apply before what seems to be a purely consonantal suffix, then we conclude that the suffix has in fact a yer before the consonant in the underlying representation. The yer blocks the deletion of *j*.

With this background we proceed to the discussion of the particular suffixes. Yers are represented as capital letters.

The adjectivizing suffix //En//

(i) Direct proof for an underlying yer: *e* alternates with zero in *-en/n*: *dlh* 'debt'—*dlž+en* (Adj. short form)—*dlž+n+ý* (Adj. full form, see 3.2.2).

---

[24] In many cases the effect of Coronal Palatalization cannot be seen on the surface since it is undone by Depalatalization (see 8.3).

(ii) *En* triggers Yer Vocalization, for example the stem *krídl* of *krídl+o* 'wing' appears as [krídel] before *En*: *krídel+n+ý* 'wing' (Adj.). The underlying representation of the stem is //krídEl+En-//.

(iii) First Velar Palatalization applies before the adjectivizing *-n*: *mliek+o* 'milk'—*mlieč+n+y* //mliek+En-//.[25]

(iv) We also find reflexes of Affricate Palatalization: *ulic+a* 'street'— *ulič+n+ý* (Adj.), underlying //ulic+En-//.

(v) Vowel Lengthening is seen to apply in instances such as *hor+a* 'forest'—*hôr+n+y* (Adj.), underlying //fior+En-//.[26]

(vi) Yer Hiatus inserts /j/ in words such as *misi+a* 'mission'—*misi+jn+ý* (Adj.), underlying //misi+En-//.

(vii) On the other hand, Postvocalic *j*-Deletion is blocked in *báj* 'myth'—*báj+n+y* 'fantastic', underlying //báj+En-//.

(viii) Likewise, Nasal Deletion does not apply to words such as *nájom* 'lease'—*nájom+n+y* (Adj.), underlying //najOm+En-//, and to *pričín+a* 'reason'—*pričín+n+y* (Adj.), underlying //pričín+En-//.

The adjectivizing suffix // Isk //

(i) *Isk* triggers Yer Vocalization. Compare *jáger* 'hunter'—*jágr+a* (gen. sg.): *e*–zero alternation, hence underlying //jágEr//. The yer vocalizes in the adjective *jáger+sk+ý*. The underlying representation of the adjectival stem must therefore be //jágEr+Isk-//.

(ii) First Velar Palatalization applies as predicted: *súdruh* 'comrade'— *súdruž+sk+ý* 'friendly', underlying //súdrufi+Isk-//. Notice that we have not given direct evidence for the yer of *Isk*, that is, an example in which the yer of the suffix would surface phonetically. No such examples are available since *Isk* is always followed by a vocalic ending and never by a yer. Consequently, the environment of Yer Vocalization for the suffix itself is never met. This leads to some non-uniqueness. It is not possible to establish whether the yer of the suffix is *I* or *E*. We only know that it must be a front yer since it triggers palatalization.

(iii) *Isk* acts as an environment for Vowel Lengthening (but see n. 26), for example *občan* 'citizen'— *občian+sk+y* (Adj.), underlying //občän+Isk-//.

---

[25] The word *vin+en*, a short form of *vin+n+ý* 'guilty', is an exception to Coronal Palatalization since the root *n* remains hard. The other short adjectival form that potentially could be an exception to Coronal Palatalization—the word *hoden* 'worthy' with hard [d] —can be regarded as regular, because palatalization is cyclic (see Chapter 4) and the historical morpheme boundary in *hoden* has been lost, that is, we have an instance of complete lexicalization.

[26] Attention should be drawn to the fact that rather few words undergo Vowel Lengthening before *En* as well as before *Isk* and *IstEv*, which we discuss below. In most instances Vowel Lengthening does not apply before these suffixes.

(iv) Yer Hiatus inserts /j/ between the vowel of the stem and the yer of the suffix: *Ázi+a* 'Asia'—*ázij+sk+ý* 'Asian', underlying //ázi+Isk-//.

(v) The yer of *Isk* blocks Postvocalic *j*-Deletion in, for example, *zlodej* 'thief'—*zlodej+sk+ý* (Adj.), underlying //zlodej+Isk-//.

(vi) By the same token Nasal Deletion is also inapplicable, for instance *zeman* 'country squire'—*zemian+sk+y* (Adj.), underlying //zemän+Isk-//.

The abstract nominalizing suffix // IstEv//

(i) There is direct evidence for the second yer in this suffix since we have an *e*–zero alternation in, for example, *šialen+ý* 'mad'—*šialen+stvo* 'madness'—*šialen+stiev* (gen. pl.). The *E* of //IstEv// surfaces via Yer Vocalization before the yer *U* of the gen. pl. The rules of Vowel Lengthening and Diphthongization derive the surface *ie*. The underlying representation of the gen. pl. form is //šialen+IstEv+U//. In sum, the evidence for the second yer in *IstEv* is quite clear. However, the peculiar fact is that the first yer never surfaces phonetically. This is a predictable result under the version of the Strict Cyclicity Constraint that forbids cyclic rules (here Yer Vocalization) to apply morpheme-internally not only in roots but also in affixes. While this version of Strict Cyclicity would produce the required result for *IstEv* (the only such case), it would also prohibit, this time incorrectly, a number of generalizations that could otherwise be made about affixes (palatalization, diphthongization, etc.). It thus seems preferable to accept the less restrictive version of Strict Cyclicity that blocks cyclic rules from applying to roots but not to affixes. The consequence for *IstEv* is that the first yer must be marked as an exception to Yer Vocalization. However, its existence is not put into question. It is motivated by a number of disparate phonological facts that we list below.

(ii) *IstEv* triggers Yer Vocalization, for example *vojn+a* 'war'— *vojen+stv+o* 'things pertaining to war', underlying //vojEn+IstEv-//.

(iii) First Velar Palatalization is applicable, exactly as was the case with *Isk*: *súdruh* 'comrade'—*súdruž+stv+o* 'comradeship'.

(iv) Effects of Vowel Lengthening can also be observed (but see n. 26): *občan* 'citizen'—*občian+stv+o* 'citizenship', underlying //občän+IstEv+o//.

(v) Postvocalic *j*-Deletion is blocked: *papagáj* 'parrot'—*papagáj+stv+o* 'imitating', underlying //papagáj+IstEv+o//.

(vi) Neither can Nasal Deletion apply: *Slavian* 'Slav'—*Slavian+stv+o* 'Slavic studies', underlying //slavian+IstEv+o//.

The nominalizing suffix // Eb//

(i) Direct evidence for the yer comes from vowel–zero alternations in the suffix itself: *pros+i+ť* 'ask'—*pros+b+a* 'request'—*pros+ieb* (gen. pl.).

The yer of *Eb* vocalizes before the gen. pl. yer. Vowel Lengthening and Diphthongization complete the derivation. The underlying representation of the gen. pl. form is //pros+Eb+U//.[27]

(ii) *Eb* triggers Coronal Palatalization, for instance *strel+a* 'shot'— *strel'+b+a* 'shooting', underlying //strel+Eb+a //.

(iii) First Velar Palatalization is also applicable: *druh* 'friend'— *druž+b+a* 'friendship'.

(iv) On the other hand, Postvocalic *j*-Deletion is blocked correctly: *sej+ú* 'they sow'—*sej+b+a* 'sowing', underlying //sej+Eb+a //.

(v) Neither does Nasal Deletion take effect: *žen+i+t'* 'marry'—*žen+b+a* 'getting married'.

The diminutive suffixes // Ek// and //Ok//

We begin by observing that these two diminutive suffixes are homophonous with the suffixes that derive the feminine gender in agentive nouns. We note further that the distribution of *Ek* and *Ok* is not predictable. This is shown by the fact, amongst others, that some stems can take both suffixes, for example *jam+a* 'hole'—*jam+k+a* (dimin.)—*jam+iek ~ jam+ôk* (gen. pl.). This lack of predictability is not particularly disturbing. Slovak, like other Slavic languages, has a rich system of diminutive suffixes which unquestionably cannot be derived from a single underlying representation. For example, dictionaries list as many as thirteen different diminutive forms for the word *mam+a* 'mother'. Here we illustrate just a few of them: *mam+k+a* (single dimin.), *mam+ul'+k+a* (double dimin.), *mam+úl+ik* (double dimin.), *mam+ič+k+a* (double dimin.), *mam+uš+en+k+a* (triple dimin.), *mam+uš+in+k+a* (triple dimin.), *mam+ul+ien+k+a* (triple dimin.).

The evidence for the yers in *Ek* and *Ok* is the following:

(i) The vowel of the suffix alternates with zero, as predicted by Yer Vocalization and Yer Deletion/Stray Erasure:

(87) perník 'honey-cake'—perníč+ek (dimin.)—perníč+k+a (gen. sg.)
      sandál 'sandal'—sandál+ok (dimin.)—sandál+k+a (gen. sg.)

(ii) The yer of the diminutive suffix triggers Yer Vocalization in the stem:

(88) krídl+o 'wing'—krídel (gen. pl.)—krídel+k+o (dimin.)—krídel+iek
      (gen. pl.)
      jadr+o 'nucleus'—jadier (gen. pl.)—jadier+k+o (dimin.)—jadier+ok
      (gen. pl.)

---

[27] The suffix //Eb// does not trigger Vowel Lengthening: see Chapter 6, n. 7.

Recall that the zero inflectional endings are yers, hence Yer Vocalization applies in the masc. nom. sg. and in the fem./neuter gen. pl. The vocalized yers lengthen and diphthongize if they have not been shortened by the Rhythmic Law.

(iii) The diminutive suffixes trigger Vowel Lengthening. The results are visible in *jadier+k+o* 'nucleus' (dimin.) in (88) since in the other words in (87) and (88) the Rhythmic Law has undone the effects of Vowel Lengthening. We add one more example: *list* 'letter'—*líst+ok*.

(iv) The *Ek* diminutive triggers 1st Velar Palatalization: *potok* 'stream' —*potôč+ek* (dimin.).

(v) Affricate Palatalization also applies: *ulic+a* 'street'—*ulič+k+a* (dimin.)—*ulič+iek* (gen. pl.)

(vi) Yer Hiatus inserts /j/: *misi+a* 'mission'—*misi+jk+a* (dimin.)— *misi+jok* (gen. pl.)

(vii) On the other hand, Postvocalic *j*-Deletion is blocked as desired: *oj+e* 'shaft'—*oj+k+o* (dimin.)—*oj+ok* (gen. pl.)

(viii) Neither can Nasal Deletion apply: *altán* 'summer house'— *altán+k+a* (dimin.)—*altán+ok* (gen. pl.).

In connection with *Ek* we should point out that Slovak exhibits a partial irregularity, since in some words *E* is backed to *O* after /š, ž/ and in a few instances also after the corresponding affricate. The backing rule applies to lexically specified items:

(89) kožuch 'sheepskin coat'—kožúš+ok (dimin.)
    sneh 'snow'—sniež+ok (dimin.)
    chud+ák 'poor person'—chud+áč+ok (alongside the regular
      chud+áč+ek)

We also note that the originally composite suffix //Ok+Ek//, a double diminutive, seems to have developed into a morphologically non-transparent suffix //očOk//, where the first vowel is probably no longer a yer. The peculiarity of this suffix is that it never causes the lengthening of the preceding vowel, a fact that can be readily explained if indeed the first suffixal vowel is not a yer. The second vowel of //očOk// has not lost its yer status since, first, it lengthens the *o*, thus the suffix appears invariably as /ôčOk/, and, second, it alternates with zero. The *č* of /ôčOk/ indicates that the yer used to be front but has now changed into *o* because of the rule of backing that we mentioned earlier. We exemplify //očOk// in (90):

(90) žab+a 'frog'—žab+ôčk+a (dimin.)—žab+ôčok (gen. pl.)
    hrud+a 'piece'—hrud+ôčk+a (dimin.)—hrud+ôčok (gen. pl.)

That certain originally composite suffixes may grow together and become fossilized is not implausible. This is what seems to have happened to //ičEk//, an original sequence of //ik+Ek//, for example *hlav+a* 'head'—

hlav+ičk+a (dimin.)—*hlav+ičiek* (gen. pl.). The form with *-ik* alone is not available: **hlav+ik+a* does not exist. The same is true of the examples in (90). Forms with a single //Ok// are not on record. In order to derive a simple diminutive the alternative suffix //Ek// must be added: *žab+k+a* 'frog' (dimin.)—*žab+iek* (gen. pl.) and not **žab+ok*.

The diminutive and the nominal suffix //Ec//

Let us clarify at the outset that the diminutive *Ec* is homophonous with the nominalizing suffix *Ec*. Both behave in the same way, with the exception of the fact that the nominalizing suffix causes vowel shortening rather than lengthening. We shall give separate examples for each suffix only in (i) below.

(i) Direct evidence for the yer is available from vowel–zero alternations:

(91) Nominalizing: kúp+i+t' 'buy'—kup+ec 'merchant'—kup+c+a
      (gen. sg.)
     star+ý 'old'—star+ec 'old man'—star+c+a (gen. sg.)
    Diminutive: jazer+o 'lake'—jazier+c+e (dimin.)—jazier+ec
      (gen. pl.)
     per+o 'feather'—pier+c+e (dimin.)—pier+ec (gen. pl.)

(ii) It should immediately be noted that the diminutives in (91) exhibit yet another property which is characteristic for yer suffixes: they trigger Vowel Lengthening (Diphthongization derives surface *ie*).

(iii) The presence of *Ec* is the reason why Yer Vocalization makes the yers surface in stems such as *krídl+o* 'wing' (compare the gen. pl. *krídel*) —*krídel+c+e* (dimin.).

(iv) The nominal *Ec* provides examples for Yer Hiatus that inserts /j/: *Ázi+a* 'Asia'—*Ázi+jec* 'Asian'—*Ázi+jc+a* (gen. sg.).

(v) Words such as *drak+o+bij+c+a* 'dragon killer' show that *Ec* blocks Postvocalic *j*-Deletion. The example just mentioned is a compound derived from the verb *bi+t'* 'beat', whose root is //bij//: compare *bij+ú* 'they beat'.

(vi) Also, Nasal Deletion is blocked: *vier+o+lom+c+a* 'traitor', a compound containing the verb *lom+i+t'* 'break'.

The analysis of derivational suffixes brings us to the end of this chapter. By providing a number of descriptive facts about Slovak we have prepared the ground for the theoretical discussion that ensues in the following chapters.

PART II

Cyclic Rules

4

PALATALIZATION:
DERIVED-ENVIRONMENT RULES

In this chapter we look at derived-environment rules. Characteristically, these rules apply at morpheme boundaries but not morpheme-internally, a fact that assigns them to the class of cyclic rules. From the descriptive point of view this chapter deals with palatalization and the associated problems. Theoretical interest lies not only in the cyclicity of the rules but also in the statement of palatalization, particularly because in most cases palatalization is not phonetic. That is, rules do not produce segments that are [–back] phonetically. Yet, we uphold Clements's (1988) claim that palatalization is conceived of as spreading. We begin with an overview of the problems that are analysed in detail in subsequent sections of this chapter.

4.1. OVERVIEW

Below we present a typology of changes that are effected by palatalization rules. We add that all rules except Iotation apply before front vowels and glides. Iotation is limited to the environment of *j*.

(1) *a.* 1st Velar Palatalization: k, g, x, ɣ → č, ž, š, ž (postalveolars)
  b. 2nd Velar Palatalization: k, x → c, s (alveolars)
  c. Affricate Palatalization: c, ʒ → č, ǯ (postalveolars)
  d. Iotation: s, z, t, d → š, ž, c, ʒ (postalveolars/alveolars)
  e. Coronal Palatalization: t, d, n, l → t′, d′, n′, l′ (prepalatals)

Two general observations emerge from the typology in (1). First, with the exception of (1*e*), palatalization refers to changes in the place of articulation within the class of 'hard' consonants. The outputs are the consonants that used to be phonetically [–back] in Old Slovak but have 'hardened' since then. Second, again with the exception of (1*e*), stops are turned into affricates.

The first observation indicates that it is pointless to regard palatalization as the spreading of [–back]. In fact, we show in 4.2 and 4.4 that at least 1st Velar and Affricate Palatalization cannot spread [–back] since their outputs would incorrectly fall together with the outputs of Coronal

Palatalization/Iotation that behave differently towards the rule of Dentalization. If spreading [–back] is a false step, which feature is it that should
spread? The answer can be deduced from Clements's (1976, 1988) treatment of front vowels as coronal segments (see also Itô and Mester 1989).

Clements (1988) assumes that front vowels are [+coronal]. This feature
appears independently in consonants and vowels. In the latter case it
replaces the earlier feature [back]. However, for ease of reference we
shall keep the feature [back] and Clements's earlier node TONGUE
BODY. To achieve the required spreading effect for the rules in (1a–d),
we shall assume that prior to the application of these rules front vowels
are redundantly specified as non-anterior coronals.[1] We follow the convention of leaving out irrelevant nodes. Recall that R stands for ROOT
node, PL for PLACE, COR for CORONAL, and TB for TONGUE
BODY.

(2) CORONAL Specification

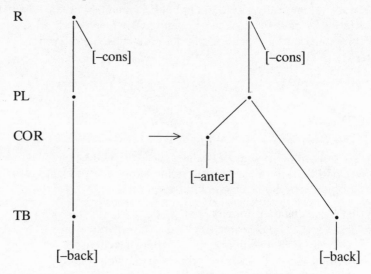

The output of (2) now defines the typology of spreading given in (1):

the spreading of COR [–anter] in (1a): 1st Velar Palatalization;
the spreading of [–anter] in (1c): Affricate Palatalization;
the spreading of [–back] in (1e): Coronal Palatalization.

---

[1] Given our use of terms, where for the purposes of contrast at the underlying level
CORONAL refers only to consonants and [back] denotes vowels (that is, Clements's
[coronal] with Vocoid Place Features), the specification of vowels as CORONAL (and
further as non-anterior) is non-distinctive. In Clements's terms rule (2) would assign the
node CORONAL to vowels in the sense CORONAL at the CONSONANT PLACE
NODE.

With regard to the second observation, that stops become affricates, we propose that Slovak should have the rule given in (3). Recall that SL stands for the SUPRALARYNGEAL NODE.

(3) Affrication

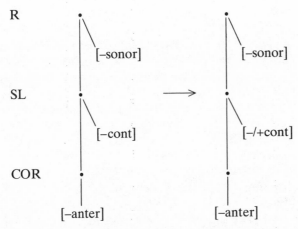

In the diagram we have assumed that non-anterior coronal (that is, postalveolar) stops undergo Affrication. This fits the facts of 1st Velar Palatalization very well. However, on the one hand, the outputs of 2nd Velar Palatalization and Iotation are actually alveolar rather than postalveolar affricates. On the other hand, the prepalatals produced by Coronal Palatalization are ultimately also non-anterior coronals, but they are not affricates. Thus, more needs to be said about Affrication. We postpone this discussion till the sections on 2nd Velar Palatalization, Iotation, and Coronal Palatalization. We show there that the difficulty in defining correctly the class of stops that undergo Affrication is only apparent. The desired class emerges from solutions that are independently motivated, such as the statement of the rules and their interaction.

4.2. FIRST VELAR PALATALIZATION

Under this heading we consider three independent rules: the velar palatalization itself, the assimilation of fricatives, and the dissimilation of stops. We discuss them in this order.

4.2.1. The statement of First Velar Palatalization

This rule cuts across the whole morphological system of Slovak. It is found in nouns, adjectives, and verbs. It appears in both derivation and inflection. Below we list some examples:

(4) k → č   človek 'man'—človieč+ik (dimin.), človeč+í 'human',
            človeč+en+stv+o 'humanity', človieč+a 'children', človeč+e
            'man' (voc.)
            bok 'side'—boč+i+t' 'keep away'
            vnuk 'grandson'—vnúč+ik (dimin.), vnúč+a (dimin.)
            zvuk 'sound'—zvuč+a+t' 'to sound'
            piek+l+a 'she baked'—peč+iem 'I bake'
            mäkk+ý 'soft'—mäkč+i+t' 'soften', mäkč+en 'soft diacritic'
    g → ʒ   strig+a 'witch' (-a is the nom. sg. ending)—stridž+í (Adj.),
            strídž+a 'child of a witch'
            cveng 'sound'—cvendž+a+t' 'to sound'
    x → š   strach 'fright'—straš+i+t' 'frighten', straš+i+dl+o 'monster'
            blch+a 'flea' (-a is the nom. sg. ending)—blš+í (Adj.), blš+a
            'small flea'
            ropuch+a 'toad'—ropuš+í (Adj.)
    ɣ → ž   sneh 'snow'—snež+i+t' 'to snow'
            beh 'run' (N)—bež+a+t' 'to run'
            drah+ý 'expensive'—draž+ie+t' 'become expensive'
            strieh+l+a 'she guarded'—strež+iem 'I guard'
            pstruh 'trout'—pstrúž+ik (dimin.)
            Boh 'God'—Bož+e (voc.)
            batoh 'bag'—batôž+ik 'bundle', batož+in+a 'luggage'

Palatalization takes place before front vowels and *j* (for this environment,
see 4.6.2). Most suffixes are self-explanatory from the phonological point
of view. We wish to comment only on three suffixes. The diminutive *-a*
and the verbalizing *-a* look as if they have back vowels and hence seem
to contradict the generalization that palatalization is triggered by front
vowels: *vnúč+a* 'grandchild' (dimin.), *zvuč+a+t'* 'to sound'. This is only
apparent. At a deeper stage of derivation the suffixes have a front //ä//.
Thus, the suffix in *vnúč+a* is the same as in *chláp+ä* 'man' (dimin.). The
surface [a] is derived by *ä*-Backing (2/13). This rule turns //ä// into [a]
after non-labial consonants. Our data show that *ä*-Backing must follow
rather than precede 1st Velar Palatalization.

The third potentially controversial suffix is *-í*, as in *človeč+í* 'human'. It
looks like an inflectional *-í* but in fact is not. We analyse this suffix in 6.4,
where we show that the adjectivization of *človek* 'man' is due to the
suffix *-i*, and *-í* is merely an inflectional ending. Thus, the underlying
representation of *človeč+í* is //človek+i+í//.

One further comment is in order. Notice that the surface [ɦ], a voiced
laryngeal fricative, is interpreted in (4) as an underlying //ɣ//, a voiced
velar fricative. We discuss this interpretation in 9.3, where we describe
Voice Assimilation. Here let us merely note that 1st Velar Palatalization
lends strong support to such an interpretation. By regarding surface [ɦ] as

derivable from underlying //ɣ// we are able to bring out the parallel in the changes exhibited in (4): velars are turned into postalveolars.

We may complement the data in (4) by observing that 1st Velar Palatalization applies regularly before yer suffixes, which we discussed in 3.3. Our examples involve the adjectivizing //En// and //Isk//, the nominal //Eb//, //IstEv//, and //Ec//, as well as the diminutive and the feminine //Ek//. Recall that capital letters stand for yers, the fleeting vowels that surface when followed by a yer and delete otherwise.

(5) Boh 'God'—bož+sk+ý (Adj.)—bož+stv+o 'supernatural being'
druh 'friend'—druž+b+a 'friendship'—druž+stv+o 'social life'
súbeh 'competition'—súbež+n+ý 'parallel' (Adj.)—súbež+ec
'adherent'
jazyk 'tongue'—jazýč+ek (dimin.)—jazyč+n+ý (Adj.)
mliek+o 'milk'—mlieč+k+o (dimin.)—mlieč+n+y (Adj.)
černoch 'black' (N)—černoš+k+a (fem.)—černoš+sk+ý (Adj.)
útech+a 'happiness'—úteš+n+ý (Adj.)

The examples in (4) and (5) are all instances of 1st Velar Palatalization applying in a derived environment. This is a generalization rather than a coincidence. The only exception to this generalization is the fem. loc. sg. ending -e. Velars remain unchanged before this ending: v Amerik+e 'in America', o noh+e 'about the leg'. The exceptionality of -e lies in the fact that the ending is palatalizing with respect to Coronal Palatalization: o žen+e [n'] 'about a woman'. One way of solving this problem is to mark -e as an exception to 1st Velar Palatalization. Another way is to attempt a phonological solution. We return to this problem in 6.6, where we discuss non-palatalizing suffixes.[2]

First Velar Palatalization systematically fails to apply morpheme-internally, regardless of whether the vowel is a yer or not:

(6) //k// kin+o 'cinema', kiahne 'smallpox', okiadz+a+t' 'smoke' (DI),
kedy 'when', cirkev 'Orthodox church', laket' 'elbow',
sukien+k+a 'dress' (dimin.), ker 'bush' (the last four examples
have yers: compare the gen. sg. cirkv+i, lakt'+a, kr+a, and the
base form sukň+a)

//g// gitar+a 'guitar', gestikul+ova+t' 'gesticulate', general 'general',
tiger 'tiger' (a yer: compare the gen. sg. tigr+a), dogiem (the
gen. pl. of dogm+a 'dogma': a yer)

---

[2] In that section we also discuss some other surface violations of 1st Velar Palatalization, for example the fact that in adjectives k remains unchanged before the -ý[í] of the masc. nom. sg. and the -ého of the gen. sg., as in sladk+ý 'sweet'—sladk+ého. These endings are different from the loc. sg. -e just mentioned, since they are systematically non-palatalizing with respect to all rules.

//x// chichot 'laughter', chirurg 'surgeon', chemik 'chemist', práchen+n+ý (an adjective from práchn+o 'tinder': *e*–zero alternation, hence a yer)

//ɣ// histόri+a 'history', hierarchi+a 'hierarchy', her+ec 'actor' (a yer: compare hr+a 'play'), bahen+n+ý 'swampy' (a yer: compare bahn+o 'swamp'), ihiel (gen. pl. of ihl+a 'needle': a yer)

We conclude that 1st Velar Palatalization is cyclic and hence does not apply in non-derived environments. As we shall see later on numerous occasions, the cyclicity of 1st Velar Palatalization is predictable from the ordering relations into which this rule enters. It applies before other rules that are cyclic and thus it must be cyclic itself. The data in (6) merely confirm this prediction.

The consequence of cyclicity is that words such as *čist+ý* 'clean' that could be derived from //ki-// in Proto-Slavic, when the rule was not cyclic, are now lexicalized with an underlying affricate. Morpheme-internal affricates in borrowings such as *gin* [ʒin] 'gin' are also interpreted as underlying. The analysis is thus not abstract, in the sense that surface representations correspond to underlying representations in a direct fashion.

Let us now turn to the problem of how to state 1st Velar Palatalization formally. The fact that stops turn into affricates (*k, g* → *č, ʒ*) need not be included in the statement of the rule. This fact is predictable from Affrication (3). It suffices to assume that 1st Velar Palatalization turns dorsals (that is, velars) into non-anterior coronals. Thus, //x, ɣ// become /š, ž/ and the stops //k, g// appear as /t̩, d̩/, where the dot means non-anterior.

(7) First Velar Palatalization

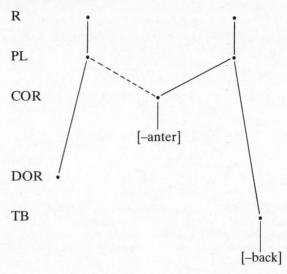

The node CORONAL and the feature [–anter] that have been assigned to the front vowel or glide by rule (2) spread to the velar (see (7)). An open question is whether the node DORSAL should be delinked simultaneously with the spreading or whether this is effected by some later rule. In other words, is 1st Velar Palatalization merely a spreading or a spreading-cum-delinking rule? We investigate this problem in 4.3.

4.2.2. Fricative Assimilation and Stop Dissimilation

Considerations such as simplicity and generality have led us to break up the changes of //k, g// → [č, ǯ] into two steps: //k, g// → /ṭ, ḍ/ by 1st Velar Palatalization and /ṭ, ḍ/ → [č, ǯ] by Affrication. We shall now show that this reasoning is additionally supported by the need to account for the dissimilation that affects the outputs of 1st Velar Palatalization when they appear in clusters with dental fricatives.

The clusters //sk// and //zg// turn into [št'] and [žd'] before front vowels:

(8) lesk 'glamour'—lešt+i+t' (V), lešt+in+a ~ lešt+ie 'glamour'
   (collective)
   rusk+ý 'Russian'—rušt+in+a 'Russian language'
   dosk+a 'board'—došt+ičk+a (dimin.)
   pisk 'scream'—pišt'+a+t' (V), UR //pisk+ä+t'//
   pan+sk+ý 'lord' (Adj.)—s+pan+št+ie+t' 'become lord-like', UR
   //-sk+ej+t'//[3]
   rázg+a 'dry branch'—ražd+in+a ~ ražd+ie 'dry branches' (collective)
   mliazg+a 'pulp'—mliažd+i+t' 'squeeze'
   druzg 'crack' (N)—družd'+a+t' (V), UR //druzg+ä+t'//

How should we analyse these alternations? In particular, would it be advisable to turn //sk, zg// into [št', žd'] directly by a special rule? Undoubtedly, this would be a false step. On the one hand, the alternation of k and t' is independent of the alternation of s and š. This is shown by examples such as hrušk+a 'pear'—hrušt+ičk+a (dimin.), where //š// already exists in the underlying representation. On the other hand, there are words in which sk turns into č, for instance latin+sk+ý 'Latin'— latin+č+in+a 'Latin language', which contrasts with rušt+in+a 'Russian language' in (8). Words such as latin+č+in+a must lose their š prior to the rule which dissimilates č (or rather /ṭ/) from š by turning it into t. The dissimilation is thus conditioned directly by the presence of š. Once it has been lost (interconsonantally), the dissimilation does not take place.

---

[3] The verbalizing suffix is -ej: compare s+pan+št+ej+ú 'they become lord-like'. The //j// is deleted before consonants and the e undergoes lengthening: recall our analysis in 3.1.1 and 3.1.2.

Let us look in detail at the derivational steps in the change of //sk, zg// into [št′, žd′]. The first step is the application of 1st Velar Palatalization. We thus obtain /st̨, zd̨/, where the stops are postalveolar. Now we need an assimilation rule that turns alveolar //s, z// into postalveolar /š, ž/ before postalveolar /t̨, d̨/: see (9).

(9) Fricative Assimilation

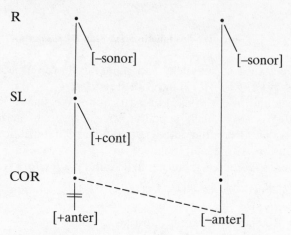

The next step is to dissimilate the /t̨, d̨/. As indicated by the contrast *rušt+in+a* 'Russian language'—*latin+č+in+a* 'Latin language', the dissimilation is conditioned by the presence of /š/: see (10).

(10) Stop Dissimilation

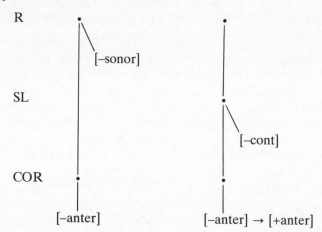

Stop Dissimilation derives /t, d/. These are now subject to Coronal Palatalization, which turns them into [t′, d′]. The derivation of *lešt+i+t′*, a verb from *lesk* 'glamour', illustrates the particular steps just described. We bypass the infinitive cycle:

(11) lesk+i WFR: Verbalization
     lest̩+i 1st Velar Palatalization (7)
     lešt̩+i Fricative Assimilation (9)
     lešt+i Stop Dissimilation (10)
     lešt'+i Coronal Palatalization (2/29)

Notice that the rules must apply in precisely this order. These rules are cyclic since, as we show in 4.5, Coronal Palatalization is cyclic. We thus have an example demonstrating that the cyclicity of 1st Velar Palatalization can be predicted from the ordering relations among rules.

The independence of Fricative Assimilation from Stop Dissimilation is further supported by the fact that there are words, admittedly only two or three, which are exceptions to the latter but not to the former rule. Thus, the adjectives from *tresk+a* 'type of fish' and *glezg* 'type of bird' are *trešč+í* and *gleždž+í* (both in Dvonč *et al.* 1966: 227). The intermediate /t̩, d̩/ resist Stop Dissimilation and hence they undergo Affrication (3). This brings us to the most interesting result of our analysis. The fact that underlying //k, g// may dissimilate to /t, d/ is a strong argument in favour of postulating Affrication as a separate rule from the palatalization rules. It also supports the statement of 1st Velar Palatalization in the form as given in (7). If Affrication had not existed and consequently 1st Velar Palatalization would have had to turn //k, g// directly into [č, ž], the dissimilation process expressed in (10) would have been unnecessarily complex. The dissimilation rule would have had to 'de-affricate' its inputs. Given our account, this is not necessary. Affrication is simply ordered after Stop Dissimilation. Data such as those discussed in this section provide interesting evidence for the reality of intermediate stages in phonological derivation.

4.3. SECOND VELAR PALATALIZATION

Masculine nouns exhibit an alternation in the nom. pl. between velar and alveolar consonants, with an additional affrication of stops:

(12) x → s Čech 'Czech'—Čes+i, mních 'monk'—mnís+i, valach
            'shepherd'—valas+i, hajdúch 'footman'—hajdús+i
     k → c Slovák 'Slovak'—Slovác+i, logik 'logician'—logic+i, žiak
            'pupil'—žiac+i, prorok 'prophet'—proroc+i

The corresponding rule, known in Slavic as 2nd Velar Palatalization, is clearly conditioned morphologically, since normally velars change into postalveolars before front vowels (1st Velar Palatalization). The question is whether the rule environment is purely morphological or whether it is mixed, that is, partly phonological and partly morphological, applying before the front-vowel ending of the nom. pl. There is no doubt that only the second alternative is correct. This is best shown by words that can take both -*i* and -*ovia* as free variants in the nom. pl., for example *klasik* 'classicist'—*klasic+i* ~ *klasik+ovia*. The former but not the latter variant exhibits palatalization. This generalization is confirmed further by velar stems that end in -*h* and -*g*. They always take -*ovia* in the nom. pl. and the velar is never palatalized: *vrah+ovia* 'enemies', *biológ+ovia* 'biologists'.

In Chapter 3 (sections 3.2.1.4 and 3.2.3.1) we pointed out that the nom. pl. of masculine nouns has both the palatalizing allomorph -*i* and the non-palatalizing allomorph -*y* [i]. The former is added to [+personal] nouns and the latter appears elsewhere. One may wonder whether a simpler interpretation is not available. We might assume that there is only one high-vowel allomorph of the nom. pl. and that it is the non-palatalizing -*y*. The palatalizing property of -*y* can then be written into the statement of 2nd Velar Palatalization by making the rule sensitive to the fact that the input noun must be [+personal]. That is, the morphological environment would include reference to both nom. pl. and [+personal]. This would account correctly for instances of 2nd Velar Palatalization with animals when they are personified, for example *vlk* 'wolf'—*vlc+i* (alongside *vlk+y*). This explanation would not have adverse effects for 2nd Velar Palatalization since in Slovak the rule applies exclusively in the nom. pl. (In certain other Slavic languages, such as Polish or Czech, 2nd Velar Palatalization also applies in the dat. /loc. sg. to non-personal nouns: compare Polish *ręk+a* 'hand'—*ręc+e*, Czech *ruk+a*—*ruc+e* vs. Slovak *ruk+a* —*ruk+e*.) A decisive argument against this interpretation comes from the observation that not only 2nd Velar Palatalization but also Coronal Palatalization applies under personification, for example *orl+i* [l'] 'eagles', *had+i* [d'] 'reptiles'. If the nom. pl. ending were a non-palatalizing -*y* and palatalization were triggered by the additional [+personal] feature, then this feature would have to be written into Coronal Palatalization. This would be a false step, however. Coronal Palatalization is a general rule and it cannot be conditioned by non-phonological properties (see 4.5).

The statement of 2nd Velar Palatalization introduces certain problems. There are two alternatives: either (i) velars change directly into alveolars, or (ii) 2nd Velar Palatalization acts on the output of 1st Velar Palatalization and hence it fronts postalveolars to alveolars.

The first alternative does not seem to be attractive. The problem is that 2nd Velar Palatalization would have to effect four different changes simultaneously: spread the node CORONAL, change [–anter] into [+anter], delink the node DORSAL, and change stops into affricates. The co-occurrence of these mutually unrelated changes is implausible. Recall that the delinking of DORSAL is independently necessary for the outputs of

1st Velar Palatalization and that Affrication is a rule in its own right. It is not possible to assume that 2nd Velar Palatalization would merely front the stop and Affrication would then apply. The //k// fronted to /t/ would not undergo Affrication because this rule applies only to non-anterior stops. (Needless to say, anterior /t, d/ are phonemes in Slovak.)

Let us investigate the second alternative. The assumption here is that 2nd Velar Palatalization acts on the outputs of 1st Velar Palatalization. Prior to 2nd Velar Palatalization, the //k// has thus been changed into non-anterior /ṭ/, which can now undergo Affrication. Only at this stage, that is, after the /ṭ/ has been affricated to /č/, does 2nd Velar Palatalization apply and front the /č/ to [c]. In the case of underlying //x//, 1st Velar Palatalization derives /š/, which is then changed into [s] by 2nd Velar Palatalization.

(13) Second Velar Palatalization

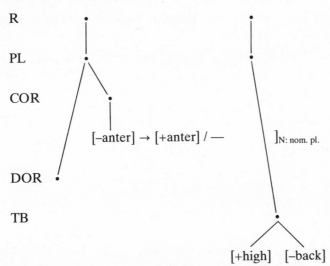

R

PL

COR

[–anter] → [+anter] / —   ]N: nom. pl.

DOR

TB

[+high] [–back]

The derivation of surface [c, s] from //k, x// requires one more step: the node DORSAL must be delinked. Recall that in section 4.2 we asked whether this delinking should be effected simultaneously with the spreading of CORONAL by 1st Velar Palatalization or whether it should go by a later rule. Undoubtedly, only the latter assumption is correct. The evidence comes from the fact that underlying //č, š// remain unaffected by 2nd Velar Palatalization:

(14) volič 'elector'—volič+i
      zbrojnoš 'armed man'—zbrojnoš+i
      papež 'pope'—papež+i

The reference to DORSAL in the statement of 2nd Velar Palatalization excludes the data in (14). The outputs of 2nd Velar Palatalization as well as 1st Velar Palatalization undergo a late rule of Dorsal Delinking. Finally, we need to establish the status of 2nd Velar Palatalization. The rule is conditioned morphologically. Therefore it is lexical and cyclic.

We should point out that, in spite of being fully productive, 2nd Velar Palatalization is not a rule of spreading. The reason is that it effects a phonologically arbitrary change. This is not surprising, given the fact that the rule is in part conditioned morphologically, which is a consequence of the loss of diphthongs in Proto-Slavic.

4.4. AFFRICATE PALATALIZATION

Slovak, like Polish, has a rule of Affricate Palatalization that turns //c, ʒ// into [č, ǯ] before front vowels and glides. (There are very few examples for ʒ → ǯ.) The rule operates throughout the whole morphological system: nouns, adjectives, and verbs.

(15) koniec 'end'—konč+i+t' 'finish', konč+it+ý 'having a sharp end'
        (Adj.)
      zajac 'hare'—zajač+ik (dimin.), zajač+in+a (fem.)
      chlap+ec 'boy'—chlap+č+e (voc. sg.), chlap+č+ek (dimin.),
        chlap+č+a (dimin.), chlap+č+isk+o (augmentative)
      otec 'father'—otč+e (voc. sg.), otč+in+a 'home country'
      dravec 'beast of prey'—dravč+ek (dimin.), dravč+í (Adj.)
      ovc+a 'sheep'—ovč+í (Adj.), ovč+iar 'shepherd', ovč+iak 'shepherd'
        (dog), ovč+in+ec 'flock of sheep'
      sác+a+t' 'push'—sáč+e 'he pushes'
      hádz+a+t' 'throw'—hádž+e 'he throws'
      hranic+a 'border'—hranič+n+ý (Adj.), hranič+i+t' (verb), hranič+iar
        'inhabitant of the border region'
      ulic+a 'street'—ulič+k+a (dimin.), ulič+n+ý (Adj.)
      noc 'night'—noč+n+ý (Adj.)
      dispozíc+i+a 'disposal'—dispozič+n+ý (Adj.)
      deriuác+i+a 'derivation'—deriuač+n+ý (Adj.)

Attention should be drawn to the last five examples. They indicate that Affricate Palatalization, like all other phonological palatalization rules, applies before yers: here the diminutive //Ek// and the adjectivizing //En// (see 3.3 and Chapter 5). The last two examples in (15) are blatant borrowings, and yet Affricate Palatalization takes effect.

The statement of the rule is uncontroversial. Alveolar //c, ʒ// are turned into postalveolar [č, ǯ] by delinking [+anter] and spreading [−anter], which has been previously assigned to the front vowels by Coronal Specification (2): see (16).

(16) Affricate Palatalization

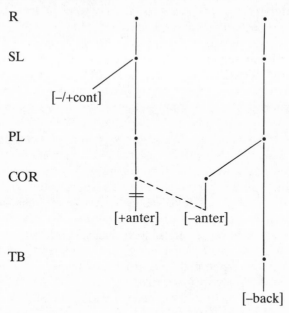

Affricate Palatalization enters into a counterfeeding relation with Fronting (see 6.5) as well as with 2nd Velar Palatalization and Dentalization (see 4.6). It must be ordered before all these rules. Thus, the fronting of //-ám// in *ulic+iam* 'street' (dat. pl.) does not feed Affricate Palatalization. Neither do the other two rules that derive [c, ʒ] for example *žiac+i*, the nom. pl. of *žiak* 'pupil'. We have noted that 2nd Velar Palatalization is lexical and cyclic, and consequently Affricate Palatalization must be lexical and cyclic as well. Therefore it is not surprising that the rule has some exceptions, for instance *pomoc+n+ý* 'helpful', UR //pomoc+En-//, and that morpheme-internal [c, ʒ] are found before both back and front vowels, as in *cap* 'goat', *cest+a* 'way', and *cic+a+ť* 'suck'.

4.5. CORONAL PALATALIZATION

In Slovak, palatalization is more restrictive than in some other Slavic languages, for example Polish. Labials do not palatalize at all. In the class of dento-alveolars //s, z// palatalize to [s', z'] only in the dialects of Eastern Slovak, that is in the region bordering Poland. Central Slovak, which is regarded as the norm, permits the palatalization of //t, d, n, l//. Other dialects restrict this class even further by excluding the //l//. Thus, *posl+i* 'envoys', *nies+l+i* 'they carried', and *bál+e* 'ball' (loc. sg.) have a hard [l] rather than a soft prepalatal [l']. D'urovič (1975) and de Bray (1980) observe that there is a persistent tendency not to palatalize *l* before *i, e, ie*, and *ia* in the speech of all educated speakers. However, the pronunciation norm for Central Slovak is to subject *l* to palatalization (Král' 1988). There is a general agreement on this issue on the part of all authors, for example Letz (1950), Pauliny (1968), Dvončová *et al.* (1969), Sabol (1989). And yet, the question remains why it is //l// and not //t, d, n// that tends to escape palatalization. A look at the places of articulation of Slovak consonants provides the answer.

In terms of phonetics [l] is like [š, ž, č, ǯ], that is, it is postalveolar, while [t, d, n] are dental (Král' 1988). Coronal Palatalization takes [+anter] sounds as an input, hence //l// does not fit in. In order to subject //l// to palatalization, we must stipulate that it is [+anter] at the underlying level. Moreover, we must postulate a late spell-out rule that changes [+anter] *l* to [−anter], wherever it has not been palatalized. The dialects that do not permit the palatalization of *l* are simpler than standard Slovak in the sense that they have an underlying [−anter] *l*. Consequently, the underlying representation corresponds directly to the phonetic representation and there is no need for any spell-out rule.

In this book we analyse the standard variety of Slovak as described most recently by Král' (1988). To subject *l* to palatalization, we assume that it is [+anter] at the underlying level. It then forms a class with //t, d, n//. The input to Coronal Palatalization consists of non-continuant anterior coronals. The rule applies before front vowels and *j*: see (17).

(17) Coronal Palatalization

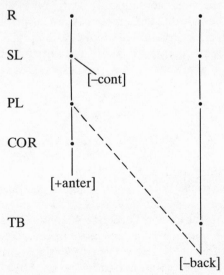

Coronal Palatalization raises some formal problems.[4] I assume with Czaykowska-Higgins (1988) that palatals are complex segments (cf. Sagey 1986) in that they are linked to both COR and TB with the value [–back].[5] (The TB node is inserted automatically by convention when [–back] has been spread.) As pointed out to me by Ellen Kaisse, an alternative view would be to spread [–back] to COR rather than to PL and, more generally, to assume that [–back] hangs off COR rather than off TB. Either of these views is compatible with the facts of Slovak. Observe further that Coronal Palatalization spreads [– back] and thus derives anterior /t', d', n', l'/. However, at the phonetic level [t', d', n', l'] are [+high, –anter], that is they are prepalatal. Consequently, we need a late spell-out rule which brings the outputs of Coronal Palatalization into agreement with the phonetic facts:

(18) Prepalatal Spell-out $\begin{bmatrix} -\text{contin} \\ -\text{back} \end{bmatrix} \rightarrow \begin{bmatrix} -\text{anter} \\ +\text{high} \end{bmatrix}$

One may wonder why the change from underlying //t, d, n, l// to surface [t', d', n', l'] is effected by two rules rather than by one. This derivation is motivated from three independent sources. First, in theoretical terms one would want to assume that a palatalization rule that actually produces soft consonants is a rule of spreading. If Coronal Palatalization were to derive the prepalatals in one step, then it could not be conceived as spreading. The crucial observation here is that Coronal Palatalization applies not only before /i, j/ but also before /e, ä/, which are [–high] (see the examples in (19) below). Second, by factoring out the features [–anter, +high] from Coronal Palatalization and assigning them to /t', d', n', l'/ by Prepalatal Spell-out, we can extract redundancies at the underlying level. The underlying //t', d', n', l'// in t'ah 'feature', chut' 'taste', etc. can be analysed as [+anter, –back], that is as palatalized dentals rather than as prepalatals. Prepalatal Spell-out, which is a late non-cyclic rule, applies not only to the outputs of Coronal Palatalization but also to underlying palatalized consonants.

The third and the most important reason for keeping Prepalatal Spell-out as a separate rule from Coronal Palatalization comes from the observation that the outputs of Coronal Palatalization do not affricate. Nevertheless, the ordering relations (see 4.6) are such that Coronal Palatalization applies before Affrication. The latter affects [–anter] stops, both palatalized and non-palatalized. If Coronal Palatalization itself produced [–anter] outputs, then these outputs would incorrectly fall within the scope of Affrication. In sum, Prepalatal Spell-out must be a different rule from Coronal Palatalization.

[4] I would like to thank Ellen Kaisse for her discussion of this issue with me.
[5] There is a technical difference. Czaykowska-Higgins (1988) uses DOR rather than TB as the location of vowel features.

Below we give examples illustrating the application of Coronal Palatalization. They are drawn from all areas of the morphological system of Slovak: nouns, verbs, adjectives; derivation and inflection:

(19) t → t'   advokát 'lawyer'—advokát+i (nom. pl.), advokát+ik (dimin.)
              brat 'brother'—brat+ia //brat+å]// (nom. pl.), brat+ec
              //brat+Ec// 'friend'
              miest+o 'place'—miest+e (loc. sg.), u+miest+i+t' 'to place',
              miest+en+k+a 'seat reservation'
              Egypt 'Egypt'—Egypt'+an //egipt+än// 'Egyptian'
              plet+ú 'they weave'—plet' //plet+I// (imper.; note: the
              imperative morpheme is a yer—see Chapter 7)

     d → d'   hrad 'castle'—hrad+e (loc. sg.), hrad+isk+o 'the place where
              a castle stood'
              had 'reptile'—hád'+a /had+ä/ 'young reptile', had+í (Adj.),
              had+ík (dimin.), had+isk+o (augmentative), had+ic+a
              (fem.), had+i+t' sa 'weave', had+í sa 'it weaves', had+it+ý
              ~ had+iv+ý 'similar to a reptile'

     n → n'   baran 'ram'—baran+e (loc. sg.), baran+ec //baran+Ec//
              'young ram', baran+ic+a 'fur cap', baran+in+a 'mutton',
              baran+í (Adj.), baran+iar 'shepherd'
              žen+a 'wife'—žen+e (dat. sg.), žen+ič+k+a (dimin.), žen+ích
              'bridegroom', žen+i+t' sa 'marry'
              bahn+o 'swamp'—bahn+e (loc. sg.), bahn+i+t' 'make
              muddy', bahn+isk+o (augmentative), bahn+it+ý ~
              bahn+ist+ý (Adj.)

     l → l'   sokol 'falcon'—sokol+e (loc. sg.), sokol+ík (dimin.),
              sokol+ic+a (fem.), sokol+í (Adj.), sokol+iar 'hunter for
              falcons'
              stál+y 'constant'—stál+ejš+í 'more constant', stál+e
              'constantly', u+stál+i+t' 'decide', u+stál+im 'I decide',
              stál+ec //stal+Ec// 'permanent member'
              strel+a 'shot' (N)—strel+i+t' 'shoot', strel'+b+a
              //strel+Eb+a// 'shooting', strel+ec //strel+Ec// 'shooter',
              strel+iv+o 'ammunition'

The examples in (19) testify that Coronal Palatalization applies in a derived environment. This is a generalization. Formerly the rule operated morpheme-internally but it no longer does. The result is that the occurrence of prepalatals before front vowels inside morphemes is no longer predictable. Prepalatals are found in native words such as *tich+ý* 'silent', *teles+o* [t'el'es+o] 'body', *nit'* [n'it'] 'thread', *desat'* [d'esat'] 'ten', etc. However, hard [t, d, n, l] can also occur in front-vowel environments morpheme-internally, in both historically Slavic and historically non-Slavic words (cf. Kráľ 1988: 140 ff., D'urovič 1975: 17):

(20) teraz 'now', ten 'that', temer 'almost', všeteč+n+ý 'inquisitive', terč
'aim', titul 'title', rutin+a 'routine'

Likewise with //d, n, l//:
dekan 'dean', diván 'sofa', odinakial 'elsewhere'
nerv 'nerve', nikotín 'nicotine', nit+ova+t 'sew together'
legend+a 'legend', lig+a 'league', liter+a 'letter'

That Coronal Palatalization does not apply in non-derived environments cannot be attributed to any special status of the words in (20) such as the fact that many of them are borrowings. This is not possible on both theoretical and descriptive grounds. The term 'borrowing' is a notion from diachronic linguistics and in this book we are concerned with a synchronic account of modern Slovak. One might, however, talk about a special lexical class if the words in (20) could be identified as belonging to one for independent reasons. Evidently, this is not the case. The non-occurrence of palatalization is the only property that the words in (20) have in common. But let us assume for the moment that, regardless of the arbitrariness, we would want to pursue the interpretation that the words in (20) are marked diacritically as [+foreign]. We would then expect that [+foreign] is lost once the items become 'nativized', that is, integrated into the native system. Such a 'nativization' could proceed on several independent planes, for example morphology, segmental phonology (that is, the structure of underlying representations), and phonological rules. However, all the tests indicate that the words in (20) are fully integrated into the system of Slovak.

Morphological nativization, that is, the addition of native affixes, does not affect the behaviour of the non-palatalizing words *vis-à-vis* Coronal Palatalization. Thus, *t* is not palatalized not only in *titul* 'title' but also throughout the inflectional paradigm, for example in the loc. sg. *titul+e*. Neither does it change under derivational affixation: *titul+n+ý* (Adj.), *titul+ova+t'* (V), *pod+titul* 'subtitle', etc.

In terms of segmental make-up words such as those in (20) are not different from the rest of the Slovak vocabulary. They are composed entirely of the sounds that are underlying segments. Could this be a coincidence in the sense that the source language had the same underlying inventory as Slovak? Hardly. The best proof is that Latinate or English borrowings have developed yers and we know that these yers did not exist in the source languages. Thus, we have *tiger* [tiger] 'tiger'—*tigr+a* (gen. sg.), *sveter* [sveter] 'sweater'—*svetr+a* (gen. sg.). The underlying representations are therefore //tigEr// and //svetEr//.

Non-palatalizing words such as those in (20) can undergo and trigger native phonological rules. Thus, *politik* 'politician'—*politič+k+a* [politič+k+a] (fem.) illustrate the operation of 1st Velar Palatalization before the feminine yer suffix //Ek//; compare the gen. pl. *politič+iek*.

On the other hand, *disciplín+a* 'discipline' triggers the Rhythmic Law and yet neither *d* nor *l* are palatalized: *disciplín+am* (dat. pl., underlying //-ám//; compare *žen+ám*, the dat. pl. of *žen+a* 'wife').

In sum, all attempts to find independent motivation for the lexical diacritic [+foreign] in words such as those in (20) fail. Could we perhaps simply mark these words as exceptions to Coronal Palatalization? This would fare well with cases such as *politič+k+a* 'woman politician' that we mentioned above. The root morpheme could be marked [–Coronal Palatalization] since Coronal Palatalization is independent of 1st Velar Palatalization. Consequently, there would not be any adverse effects. That this line of reasoning is untenable also is best shown by examples such as the following:

(21) *a.* Nom. pl.: dekan+i [dekan'+i] 'deans', delegát+i [delegát'+i] 'delegates'
  b. Loc. sg.: disciplín+e [disciplín'+e] 'discipline', oktet+e [oktet'+e] 'octet', test+e [test'+e] 'test'
  c. Dimin.: hotel+ík [hotel'+ík] 'hotel', dekrét+ik [dekrét'+ik] 'decree', telefón+ik [telefón'+ik] 'telephone'

The same words systematically resist Coronal Palatalization morpheme-internally and undergo it at morpheme boundaries. Examples such as *test+e* are particularly telling, since the otherwise identical sequences of *t* and *e* turn out to have two different phonetic manifestations: [te] vs. [t'+e].

We conclude that Coronal Palatalization is a classic example of a cyclic rule in the sense that it applies exclusively in derived environments. It is also a good example of a rule that used to be non-cyclic but became cyclic in the course of historical development. This thesis is best illustrated by comparing the nativization of borrowings that came into the language at different stages of its history. Thus, *latina*, a borrowing from the early Middle Ages, has a prepalatal [t'] in *latin+sk+ý* (Adj.) and in *latin+č+in+a* 'Latin language'. In contrast to this, *detektiv* 'detective' and *telegram*, which are undoubtedly recent borrowings, have non-palatal [d, t, l]. Even more interestingly, *latin+izmus* 'Latinism', a late reborrowing of the same stem, has a non-palatal [t]. These facts follow automatically if we assume that Coronal Palatalization simply changed its status from a non-cyclic to a cyclic rule. Evidence along the same lines could be built up for 1st Velar Palatalization, but to save space we shall not do this here.

As regards interaction with other phonological rules, we pointed out in 4.2.2 that Coronal Palatalization must apply after 1st Velar Palatalization, Fricative Assimilation, and Stop Dissimilation (see derivation (11) above). Since Coronal Palatalization is cyclic, it follows from the rule ordering that these rules are also cyclic. The cyclicity of 1st Velar Palatalization that we justified on descriptive grounds can now be seen as predictable.

The same conclusion emerges from the analysis of palatalization in the verbal system. In addition it becomes clear that Vowel Deletion must also be a cyclic rule because it applies before Coronal Palatalization. The relevant examples are the 3rd pl. forms of the present tense in the class of C-verbs. Slovak is different from Polish here in that it permits 1st Velar Palatalization to apply to these forms. However, as in Polish, Coronal Palatalization is blocked. In (22) we look at the derivation of *peč+ú* 'they bake' and *plet+ú* 'they weave'. The underlying representation of *peč+ú* has a velar, as shown by the alternation in *piek+l+a* 'she baked'.[6] For comparison we also derive the 1st sg. *peč+iem* 'I bake' and *plet+iem* 'I weave'.

(22)

pek+ú	plet+ú	pek+m	plet+m	
pek+éú	plet+éú	pek+ém	plet+ém	Extension (3/24)
peč+éú	—	peč+ém	—	1st Velar Palatalization (7)
peč+ú	plet+ú	—	—	Vowel Deletion (3/8)
—	—	—	plet'+ém	Coronal Palatalization (17)
—	—	peč+iem	plet'+iem	Diphthongization (2/25)

It is crucial that Vowel Deletion should apply before Coronal Palatalization, since otherwise the *t* of *plet+ú* would be incorrectly palatalized. On the other hand, 1st Velar Palatalization must precede Vowel Deletion and hence Coronal Palatalization. The rule ordering which we established earlier on the basis of a completely different set of data is thereby confirmed. We return to some further details of deriving prepalatal consonants in Chapter 8. It is also there that we discuss Depalatalization.

Finally, we may note that Coronal Palatalization never applies across prefix boundaries. Thus, words such as *pod+is+t'* 'come up', *pod+jazd* 'driveway', and *pod+izb+a* 'antechamber' have [d] rather than [d']. As we explain in the next chapter, there is a systematic reason why palatalization is blocked across prefixes. We discuss this problem as a blocking effect of the yers in 5.2.

4.6. IOTATION

4.6.1. *j*-Insertion

Slovak, like other Slavic languages, exhibits a type of palatalization which is known as Iotation or *j*-Palatalization. The relevant pattern of consonant alternations is illustrated in (23) below. The examples are drawn from the class of *a*-stem verbs (recall 3.1.1). We look at five conjugational forms:

---

[6] For the alternation between *e* and *ie* in the root, see Closed Syllable Lengthening in 6.1.1.3.

the infinitive, the 1st sg. present, the 3rd pl. present, the gerund, and the imperative. These forms are made up of the verb stem (root + the verbalizing suffix -*a*) followed by the conjugational suffix: //t′// for the infinitive, //m// for the 1st sg., //ú// for the 3rd pl., //úc// for the gerund, and the yer //I// for the imperative (see 3.1.2, 3.1.8, 3.1.7, and 3.1.3). There is no need to look at any further conjugational forms since the pattern of alternations in the 1st sg. is exactly the same as in all the other persons of the present paradigm. The present participle has the same form as the gerund. The past, the perfect, and the passive participles have consonantal suffixes and they do not trigger any alternations. Our examples are the verbs *česat'* 'comb', *pratat'* 'hide', *plakat'* 'weep', *brechat'* 'bark', *sácat'* 'push' and *klamat'* 'lie'. In the infinitive the underlying representation corresponds to the spelling form.

(23) infinitive: čes+a+t', prat+a+t', plak+a+t', brech+a+t' //brex+a+t'//, sác+a+t', klam+a+t'

1st sg.: češ+em //čes+a+m//, prac+em //prat+a+m//, plač+em //plak+a+m//, breš+em //brex+a+m//, sáč+em //sác+a+m//, klam+em //klam+a+m//

3rd pl.: češ+ú //čes+a+ú//, prac+ú //prat+a+ú//, plač+ú //plak+a+ú//, breš+ú //brex+a+ú//, sáč+u //sác+a+ú//, klam+ú //klam+a+ú//

gerund: češ+úc //čes+a+úc//, prac+úc //prat+a+úc//, plač+úc //plak+a+úc//, breš+úc //brex+a+úc//, sáč+uc //sác+a+úc//, klam+úc //klam+a+úc//

imperative: češ //čes+a+I//, prac //prat+a+I//, plač //plak+a+I//, breš //brex+a+I//, sáč //sác+a+I//, klam //klam+a+I//

As might be expected, the pattern of alternations with verbs whose roots end in voiced obstruents corresponding to those in (23) is parallel. We look at the infinitive and the 1st sg. only:

(24) rez+a+t' 'cut'—rež+em //rez+a+m//
vlád+a+t' 'rule'—vládz+em //vlád+a+m//
luh+a+t' 'cheat'—luž+em //luɣ+a+m//
sádz+a+t' 'put'—sádʒ+em //sáʒ+a+m//

Let us list the consonant alternations in (23) and (24). Recall that the consonant spelled *h* is underlying //ɣ//, a voiced velar fricative (see 4.2):

(25) *a.* //s, z// → [š, ž]
    //t, d// → [c, ʒ]
b. //k, x, ɣ// → [č, š, ž] (there are no examples for *g* → *ǯ*)
c. //c, ʒ// → [č, ǯ]
d. //m// does not alternate

The alternations in (25*a*) are new. So far we have seen that //t, d// are turned into [t′, d′] by Coronal Palatalization. However, in (25*a*) they become alveolar affricates [c, ʒ]. Note also that Coronal Palatalization does not affect //s, z//, and yet these alternate with [š, ž] in (25a). We are therefore dealing with a new palatalization pattern, which, as we argue below, is derived by means of Iotation.

The remaining alternations in (25) do not unveil any new facts: (25b–c) are clearly explicable in terms of 1st Velar Palatalization (7) and Affricate Palatalization (16). The fact that //m// in (25d) does not alternate is not a surprise. Slovak does not have a rule of labial palatalization. The other labials, as well as //r//, which is not included in any palatalization rule, do not alternate either.[7]

(26) šib+a+t' 'beat'—šib+em //šib+a+m// 'I beat'
klep+a+t' 'tap'—klep+em //klep+a+m// 'I tap'
rev+a+t' 'scream'—rev+em //rev+a+m// 'I scream'
žobr+a+t' 'beg'—žobr+em //žobr+a+m// 'I beg'

The intriguing question is how it is possible to have the palatalization in (25) if the alternating consonant is always followed by a back vowel in (23) and (24). The first step towards clarifying this mystery is the observation that Extension, rule (24) in Chapter 3, applies throughout the present-tense conjugation and in the gerund. Recall that Extension inserts //í// if the stem ends in a front vowel and //é// in the remaining types of stems. Recall also that Extension is motivated not by the alternations in (25) but rather by the fact that the vowels //í// and //é//, surface [ie], actually appear phonetically and trigger palatalization rules. This is particularly clear with C-stems such as //pek// 'bake': peč+iem 'I bake', peč+ú 'they bake', peč+úc 'baking', etc.

After the application of Extension the verbs in (23), for example plak+a+t' 'weep' and sác+a+t' 'push', have the following representations:

(27) 1st sg.: /plak+a+ém/, /sác+a+ém/
3rd pl.: /plak+a+ém/, /sác+a+ém/
gerund: /plak+a+éúc/, /sác+a+éúc/

The representations in (27) are now parallel to the imperatives in (23). In all these cases we have a sequence of a back vowel followed by a front vowel. The solution seems obvious. Slovak has a rule of Vowel Deletion and if this rule applies before the palatalization rules, then the root consonant of the verb will be adjacent to a front vowel. Consequently, palatalization can ensue:

(28) plak+a+ém → plak+ém (Vowel Deletion) → plač+ém (1st Velar Palatalization)

---

[7] We discuss //l, n// in 4.6.3 below.

Unfortunately, this explanation is incorrect. First, the alternations in (25a) could not be explained. If the *t* of *prat+a+t'* 'hide'—*prac+em* 'I hide' in (23) becomes adjacent to the extension vowel /é/, then Coronal Palatalization is applicable and we derive [t'] instead of the correct [c]:

(29) prat+a+ém → prat+ém (Vowel Deletion) → *prat'+ém (Coronal Palatalization)

Second, we argued in 4.5 that 1st Velar Palatalization must apply before and not after Vowel Deletion: see derivation (22). Third, in the 3rd pl. and in the gerund in (27) Vowel Deletion would truncate not only *a* but also *é*, and consequently palatalization would be incorrectly blocked. We take *sáč+u* 'they push' and Affricate Palatalization as an example:

(30) sác+a+éú → *sác+u

A crucial and as yet unexplained argument comes from the observation that all the examples discussed in this chapter, regardless of whether they do or do not trigger consonant alternations, that is, also the examples in (26), show an effect of Glide Shortening (2/27). This rule shortens non-high vowels after a glide and it is motivated independently by alternations in nouns (see 8.2). It must be Glide Shortening that derives a short *e* in *plač+em* /plak+a+ém/ 'I weep' and all the other examples in (23–7). Given the following two facts: (i) that we need a glide in order to explain vowel shortening, and (ii) that we need to account for the occurrence of palatalization, it becomes clear that the glide must be /j/. The /j/ is inserted by a rule which applies before a certain configuration of vowels. This configuration includes *a*-stems but not other types of verb stems. Consequently, for example, C-stems are not subject to *j*-Insertion. We thus obtain the contrast -*em* vs. -*iem* in *plač+em* 'I weep' and *peč+iem* 'I bake'. This is shown informally in (31).

(31) plak+a+m	pek+m	
plak+a+ém	pek+ém	Extension (3/24)
plakj+a+ém	—	*j*-Insertion (see below)
plačj+a+ém	peč+ém	1st Velar Palatalization (7)
plačj+ém	—	Vowel Deletion (3/8)
plačj+em	—	Glide Shortening (2/27)

The rules of Diphthongization and *j*-Simplification (see 8.2) complete the derivation.

Apart from explaining length relations, this analysis has a number of other advantages. First Velar Palatalization need not be ordered after Vowel Deletion, hence the paradox mentioned earlier is resolved. The application of Affricate Palatalization presents no difficulty either: the rule is triggered by /j/. The alternations in (25a), /s, z, t, d/ → [š, ž, c, ȝ], can now be seen as occurring in a different environment from that of front vowels in Coronal Palatalization. They can therefore be kept apart from the alternations of [t, d] and [t', d']. The rule that we have called Iotation is now stated informally in (32):

(32) Iotation $\begin{Bmatrix} s, z \\ t, d \end{Bmatrix} \rightarrow \begin{Bmatrix} š, ž \\ c, ʒ \end{Bmatrix} / \underline{\quad} j$

We shall postpone the formal statement of Iotation till later. Let us now take a closer look at *j*-Insertion. We shall use Iotation as a diagnostic test for this rule.

Apart from the conjugational forms of *a*-stems, Iotation and hence *j*-Insertion are also found in derived imperfectives of *i*-stem verbs. The imperfective suffixes are //aj// and //ova// (see 3.1.12).[8] Examples are tabulated in (33).

(33)   *Perfective*   *Imperfective*

t → c   strat+i+t' 'lose'   strác+a+t' //strat+i+aj+t'//
         s+plat+i+t' 'pay back'   s+plác+a+t' //-plat+i+aj+t'//
         s+krát+i+t' 'shorten'   s+krac+ova+t' //-krat+i+ova+t'//
         za+chvát+i+t' 'catch'   za+chvac+ova+t' //-xvat+i+ova+t'//
d → ʒ   pre+ced+i+t' 'sift through'   pre+ciedz+a+t' //-ced+i+aj+t'//
         o+kad+i+t' 'incense'   o+kiadz+a+t' //-käd+i+aj+t'//
         o+slobod+i+t' 'free'   o+slobodz+ova+t' //-d+i+ova+t'//
         od+súd+i+t' 'condemn'   od+sudz+ova+t' //-sud+i+ova+t'//
Likewise s, z → š, ž
         za+has+i+t' 'extinguish'   za+háš+a+t' //-ɣas+i+aj+t'//
         od+raz+i+t' 'repel'   od+ráž+a+t' //-raz+i+aj+t'//

Let us put together the vowel configurations that trigger *j*-Insertion:

(34)   a+é: present-tense conjugation of *a*-stems and the gerund/present participle
        a+I: imperative of *a*-stems
        i+aj: derived imperfectives with *-aj*
        i+ova: derived imperfectives with *-ova*

We are now ready to state *j*-Insertion. Only one further condition needs to be imposed. The *j* is inserted in verbs and not in nouns. Words such as *parti+a* 'party' and *porci+a* 'portion' must be excluded. Had *j* been inserted there, the *t* of *parti+a* and the *c* of *porci+a* would have undergone Iotation and Affricate Palatalization, respectively. The restriction to verbs can be pinpointed even further. As shown by (34), the first vowel of the vowel sequence is a verbalizing suffix. This is a significant observation since it explains why *j* is not inserted not only in *porci+a* but also in the

---

[8] Recall that *-aj* causes lengthening while *-ova* triggers shortening; see 3.1.12.

verb *porci+ova+t'* 'to portion': the *i* is not a verbalizing suffix.[9] The rule of *j*-Insertion is now stated as follows (the final version is given in (40) below):

(35) *j*-Insertion $\emptyset \rightarrow$ j / — [−cons, α back]$_{\text{VERB}}$ [−cons, −α back]

Rule (35) covers the vowel configurations in (34): the vowels must disagree in the value for [back].[10] All the other configurations of vowels do not trigger *j*-Insertion. We give some examples in (36).

(36) *a.* pís+a+t' 'write'—od+pis+ova+t' //-pís+a+ova+t'// 'write back'
        (DI); compare *od+pís+a+t'* (perfective), *od+píš+em* 'I write back'
        (DI), where the representation after Extension has applied is
        /pís+a+ém/ and hence *j*-Insertion and Iotation apply as required
      b. vid+ie+t' 'see':
        present tense: vid+í+š 'you see' //vid+e+š// → /vid+e+íš/ by
            Extension
        vid+ia 'they see' //vid+e+ắ// → /vid+e+íắ/ by Extension
        imperative: vid' 'see' //vid+e+I//
        past participle: vid+en+ý //vid+e+en-//
        gerund/present participle: vid+iac //vid+e+ắc// → /vid+e+íắc/ by
            Extension

Neither in the imperfective *odpisovat'* nor in any of the forms of *vidiet'* is *j*-Insertion applicable, which is correct. There is little point in multiplying examples. For the interested Slavist suffice it to say that the scope of *j*-Insertion and hence Iotation in Slovak is smaller than, for example, in Polish (see Rubach 1984).

A question arises how *j*-Insertion should be represented in prosodic terms. We argue in Chapter 7 that Slovak has a *j*-Constraint which blocks the application of Regressive Gliding (i → j / — V) if as a result of gliding /Cj-/ onset would arise. This is shown schematically in (37).

(37) *j*-Constraint   *Onset

Given such a constraint, *j*-Insertion seems to be a problem. Notice that the insertion of /j/ by (35) results in /Cj-/ onsets when syllable structure is

---

[9] Also, *j*-Insertion is then inapplicable to the intermediate forms /pek+éú/ *peč+ú* 'they bake' and /plet+éú/ *plet+ú* 'they weave' since *é* is not a verbalizing suffix: see derivation (22). This is correct: the [č] in the first example is derived by 1st Velar Palatalization and the application of Iotation in *plet+ú* is avoided.

[10] Some exceptions to *j*-Insertion must be noted, for example *o+hlás+i+t'* 'announce'—*o+hlas+ova+t'* (DI) //-s+i+ova+t'//, *po+cít+i+t'* 'feel'—*po+cit'+ova+t'* (DI) //-t+i+ova+t'//.

reassigned. Taking *češ+em* 'I comb' as an example we obtain the derivation given in (38) (see 23)).

(38) Cycle 2   čes+a
                 (no rule applies)
                 _____

      Cycle 3   čes+a+m
                 čes+a+ém   Extension (3/24)
                 česj+a+ém   *j*-Insertion (35)

                 σ σ
                 /| /|
                 česj+a+ém   Syllable Structure (partial)

Abandoning *j*-Insertion as a rule is not an option. We need the /j/ to trigger not only Iotation but also Glide Shortening (see the derivation in (31) above). Fortunately, three-dimensional representations make a solution of our dilemma possible.

Observe that *j*-Constraint is defined on skeletal slots. If we assumed that the /j/ from (35) had no skeletal slot of its own, then no violation of (37) would arise. Using a related analysis of Polish by Bethin (1992) as an inspiration,[11] we propose to associate the inserted /j/ with the skeletal slot of the preceding consonant. That is, the consonant and the /j/ form a contour segment. The representation of the relevant stage of derivation in (38) is then as given in (39),

(39)   σ   σ
        /\   /\
       X X X   X
       | | |\ |
       č e sj + a + é m

and the statement of *j*-Insertion must be corrected: see (40).

(40) *j*-Insertion   X   X
      (final) | /\
                       C → C j / — [–cons, α back]$_{VERB}$ [–cons, –α back]

In later derivations we shall omit reference to the X slot in order to save space.

4.6.2. Iotation: the rule

Now we return to the statement of Iotation given provisionally in (32): //s, z// are turned into postalveolar [š, ž] while //t, d// become affricates.

---

[11] Bethin's analysis of Polish is different since, first, /j/ comes from gliding and not from insertion and, second, the conflation of /j/ with the preceding consonant under one X slot is effected by Iotation.

The derivation of [š, ž] is straightforward. Iotation must simply change [+anter] into [–anter]. This suggests a solution to the affrication of //t, d//. Suppose the stops also become [–anter]: then they are subject to Affrication (3). We thus derive intermediate /č, ǯ/ from //t, d//. A further rule that we call Dentalization (see below) fronts the affricates, deriving the surface [c, з]. Iotation is then represented by (41).

(41) Iotation

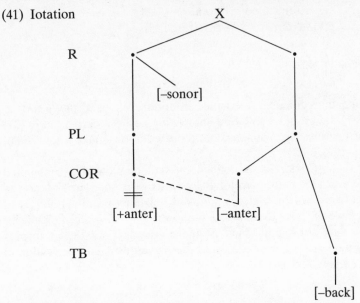

The statement of Iotation refers to the spreading of [–anter]. In section 4.1 we postulated the rule of Coronal Specification that assigns the node CORONAL and the feature [–anter] to front vowels, that is, to melody segments which are characterized as [–cons, –back]. Our intention was to extract a redundancy that would otherwise have existed at the underlying level. In other words, we were led by purely theory-oriented considerations. Now we have evidence that this step was correct. Coronal Specification must be a rule and not merely a statement of some facts concerning the underlying representation. If the latter were true, the rule of *j*-Insertion would have to be additionally complicated by specifying that the *j* (that is, /i/ at the melodic tier) had the node CORONAL and was [–anter]. Such a complication is avoided if Coronal Specification as a rule applies after *j*-Insertion.

Iotation (41) derives the final output in the case of the fricatives: //s, z// → [š, ž]. However, //t, d// are turned into postalveolar /ţ, ḑ/. They are further subject to Affrication (3), which produces /č, ǯ/. Now we need a rule of Dentalization that will change /č, ǯ/ into the [c, з] which are found on the surface. At this stage a problem seems to arise, but, as we show below, this is only apparent. The difficulty is that Dentalization must affect only those /č, ž/ that derive from underlying //t, d//. Dentalization must not apply to the /č, ž/ that derive from //k, g// via 1st Velar Palatalization or from //c, ʒ// via Affricate Palatalization. The problem is illustrated by examples in (42). In the case of *a*-stems we give the representation after Extension has applied.

(42) t → ţ → č → c: strat+i+t' 'lose'—strac+a+t' /strat+i+aj+t'/ (DI); see
      (33)
      prac+em /prat+a+ém/ 'I hide'; see (23)
   k → č bok 'side'—od+boč+i+t' //-bok+i+t'// 'push aside'—
      od+boč+ova+t' //-bok+i+ova+t'// (DI)
      plač+em /plak+a+ém/ 'I weep'; see (23)
   c → č koniec 'end'—za+konč+i+t' //-konEc+i+t'// 'to end'—
      za+konč+ova+t' //-konEc+i+ova+t'// (DI)
      sáč+em /sác+a+ém/ 'I push'; see (23)

The problem seems to be serious: how do we identify the /č, ž/ from //t, d// after Affrication has applied? Notice that no manipulation in the ordering of the rules can help solve this dilemma. The reason is that in the case of derived imperfectives in (42), 1st Velar Palatalization and Affricate Palatalization apply already in the second cycle and, consequently, prior to *j*-Insertion and Iotation. The latter two first become applicable in the third cycle, where the required vowel configuration arises. Thus, by the time the //t// of *strác+a+t'* in (42) has a chance to undergo Iotation and change into /ţ/, the /ţ/ in *od+boč+ova+t'* as well as the /č/ in *za+konč+ova+t'* have already been derived. If Affrication applies now, the various derived /č/ segments become indistinguishable. In the case of the /č/ from //k// we might yet attempt to preserve the required distinction by assuming that the node DORSAL has not been delinked, hence the /č/ from //k// and the /č/ from //t// are distinct. This analysis fails in the case of the /č/ from //c// as there the node DORSAL is not represented at any level of derivation.

The answer to our dilemma lies in the details of cyclic derivation. Notice that not only 1st Velar Palatalization and Affricate Palatalization but also Coronal Palatalization apply in the second cycle in derived imperfectives. A partial derivation of the examples in (42) makes this clear. Recall that Affrication is cyclic since it applies before cyclic 2nd Velar Palatalization (see (43)). Incidentally, this derivation demonstrates that ordering Iotation at some early stage is pointless since we cannot avoid the derivation of the affricates by 1st Velar Palatalization (and Affrication) and by Affricate Palatalization anyway. These affricates arise in an earlier cycle. On the other hand, precisely the derivation in (43) provides the key to our dilemma. Since in cycle 2 the application of Coronal Palatalization, like that of 1st Velar Palatalization and Affricate Palatalization, cannot be avoided either, we begin cycle 3 with a [−back]

(43)

	strat+i+aj+t′	-bok+i+ova+t′	-konEc+i+ova+t′	
Cycle 2	strat+i	bok+i	konEc+i	WFR: Verbaliz.
	—	—	—	j-Inser. (40)
	—	boṭ+i	—	1st Velar Pal. (7)
	—	—	konEč+i	Affric. Pal. (16)
	—	—	—	Vowel Del. (3/8)
	strat′+i	—	—	Coronal Pal. (17)
	—	—	—	Iotation (41)
	—	boč+i	—	Affrication (3)
Cycle 3	strat′+i+aj	boč+i+ova	konEč+i+ova	WFR: DI
	strat′j+i+aj	bočj+i+ova	konEčj+i+ova	j-Insertion
	—	—	—	1st Velar Pal.
	—	—	—	Affricate Pal.
	strat′j+aj	bočj+ova	konEčj+ova	Vowel Deletion
	(vacuous)	—	—	Coronal Pal.
	straṭ′j+aj	—	—	Iotation
	strač′j+aj	—	—	Affrication
	stracj+aj	—	—	Dentalization (see below)

t. Consequently, [–back] is also present at the stage when Affrication applies. The effect of Affrication in the case of /t′/, that is, palatalized postalveolar *t* from //t//, is now different from the parallel effect in the output of 1st Velar Palatalization. It is also different from the /č/ from //c//. The affricate that arises from /t′/ is [–back] and hence distinct from all the other affricates. The rule of Dentalization acts on [–back] affricates. It fronts the affricates and erases [–back] in order to bring the intermediate segment /č′/ into agreement with phonetic facts, that is, in order to derive [c]: see (44). There is no direct proof that the rule is cyclic. However, it applies exclusively to phonologically derived segments, hence it fits naturally into the class of cyclic rules. In connection with Dentalization let us now return to the observation that we made at the beginning of this chapter. We pointed out that different palatalization rules spread different nodes or features of the front vowels constituting the rule environments. Our motivation then was rule simplicity: why should we assume that //k// or //c// changing into [č] is [–back] at an earlier derivational stage if phonetically it is not palatalized? Spreading [–back] in these cases would thus be a spurious complication. The discussion of Dentalization provides strong support for this particular understanding of various palatalization rules. Had [–back] been allowed to spread by 1st Velar Palatalization or by Affricate Palatalization, the statement of Dentalization would have been impossible, because the relevant derivational information—the fact that the /č/ from //t// had previously

(44) Dentalization

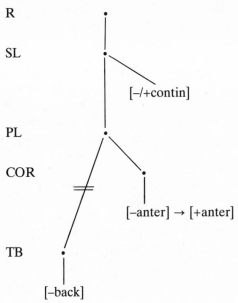

undergone Coronal Palatalization and hence was /č/—would have been obliterated.

To sum up the discussion of Iotation and the other palatalization rules we shall now look at a few sample derivations. All our examples are the 1st sg. present forms. First, let us establish the underlying representations:

(45) *a.* kreš+em //kres+a+m// 'I engrave', an *a*-stem; compare the
infinitive *kres+a+t'*
krút+im //krút+i+m// 'I roll', an *i*-stem; compare the infinitive
krút+i+t'
s+krúc+a+m //-krút+i+aj+m// 'I roll together' (we ignore the
prefix), a derived imperfective; compare the infinitive
s+krúc+a+t', an imperfective from *krút+i+t'*; in sum,
s+krúc+a+m has the following structure: Prefix + Root +
Verbalizing Suffix + DI Suffix + Present Tense Ending
b. trepoc+em //trepot+a+m// 'I hum', an *a*-stem; compare the
infinitive *trepot+a+t'*, a verb from the noun *trepot* 'hum'
let+ím //let+e+m// 'I fly', an *e*-stem; compare the infinitive
let+ie+t' //let+e+t'// (the *ie* is an effect of *e*-Lengthening, see
3.1.2, and Dipthongization); *let+ie+t'* is a verbalization from
the noun *let* 'flight'
pišt+ím //pisk+ä+m// 'I scream', an *a*-stem; compare the infinitive
pišt'+a+t' //pisk+ä+t'//, a verbalization of the noun *pisk* 'scream'

In addition to the rules discussed in this chapter, the following other rules are applicable: Extension (3/24), which applies in the present tense and inserts /í/ after front vowels and /é/ elsewhere (see 3.1.9); Vowel Deletion (3/8), whose function is to simplify sequences of vowels (see 3.1.3); *aj*-Coalescence (3/32), which turns *aj+é* into *á* (see 3.1.8); the Rhythmic Law (2/26), which shortens vowels after a long vowel (see Chapter 6); Glide Shortening (2/27), which shortens a non-high vowel after a glide; and *j*-Simplification, which deletes /j/. The last two rules are definitely post-cyclic. We discuss them in 8.2. Now let us look at the derivations of the words in (45*a*): see (46). Recall that *j*-Insertion requires that the sequence of vowels should disagree in the value for [back]. Consequently, it applies to *kreš+em* and *s+krúc+a+m* in (46) but not to *krút+im*.

In (46) we see a good illustration of the mechanics and the principles of cyclic derivation. All the rules apply in derived environments in accordance with the provisions of the Strict Cyclicity Constraint (SCC). The environments are derived either morphologically or phonologically. In the former case they arise through the application of word-formation rules. For instance, Verbalization turns the root *krút* into a verb and hence cyclic Coronal Palatalization can apply. In the latter case they are created in the course of derivation by cyclic rules that apply earlier. For example, Affrication applies to the output of Iotation and Dentalization to the output of Affrication. In both instances the structural description and the structural change of the rules are contained wholly within one morpheme, but the crucial point is that the representation is derived and hence the SCC permits the rules to apply. An exactly opposite function of the SCC is seen in the derivation on the right in (46). In cycle 4 the SCC blocks Iotation since /j/ has been derived in an earlier cycle and all the changes effected in cycle 4 are non-feeding. If we had tried to apply Affricate Palatalization, then the same effect would have been obtained for the sequence /cj/ in cycle 4. Affricate Palatalization, which must be ordered before Dentalization, would have been blocked, as the structure /cj/ arose in cycle 3. On the other hand, *j*-Insertion may effect a change within the scope of cycle 2 when it applies in cycle 3. Such an application of *j*-Insertion is permitted by the SCC since the rule is sensitive to a sequence of vowels and the relevant sequence first arises in cycle 3. In other words, the addition of the derivational suffix *-aj* as well as the application of Extension in cycle 3 are feeding changes with respect to *j*-Insertion. The later rules in this cycle, for example Iotation, act on the structure derived by *j*-Insertion, and hence the requirement of derived environment imposed by the SCC is fulfilled.

Now we derive the examples listed in (45*b*): see (47). These derivations are a useful review of the rule ordering discussed in this chapter. To this we add two further rules. As pointed out in connection with derivation (46), Affricate Palatalization must crucially apply before Dentalization.

(46)

Cycle 2	kres+a	krút+i	krút+i	WFR: Verbalization
	—	—	—	Extension
	—	—	—	*j*-Insertion
	—	—	—	Vowel Deletion
	—	—	—	*aj*-Coalescence
	—	krút′+i	krút′+i	Coronal Pal.
	—	—	—	Iotation
	—	—	—	Affrication
	—	—	—	Rhythmic Law
	—	—	—	Dentalization

Cycle 3	kres+a+m	krút′+i+m	krút′+i+aj	WFRs: 1st sg. and DI
	kres+a+ém	krút′+i+ím	—	Extension
	kresj+a+ém	—	krút′j+i+aj	*j*-Insertion
	kresj+ém	krút′+ím	krút′j+aj	Vowel Deletion
	—	—	—	*aj*-Coalescence
	—	—	—	Coronal Pal.
	krešj+ém	—	krút′j+aj	Iotation
	—	—	krúč′j+aj	Affrication
	—	krút′+im	—	Rhythmic Law
	—	—	krúcj+aj	Dentalization

Cycle 4	—	—	krúcj+aj+m	WFR: 1st sg.
			krúcj+aj+ém	Extention
			—	*j*-Insertion
			—	Vowel Deletion
			krúcj+á+m	*aj*-Coalescence
			—	Coronal Pal.
			(BLOCKED by SCC)	Iotation
			—	Affrication
			krúcj+a+m	Rhythmic Law
			—	Dentalization

				Postcyclic
	krešj+em	—	—	Glide Shortening
	kreš+em		krúc+a+m	*j*-Simplif. (8.2)

We argued in 4.4 that it must also apply before 2nd Velar Palatalization and Fronting, a very early rule that we discuss in 6.5. On the other hand, 2nd Velar Palatalization must apply after Affrication (see 4.3). We thus arrive at the following set of ordered rules:

(47)

Cycle 2	trepot+a	let+e	pisk+ä	WFR: Verbalization
	—	—	—	Extension (3/24)
	—	—	—	*j*-Insertion (40)
	—	—	pisṭ+ä	1st Velar Pal. (7)
	—	—	—	Vowel Del. (3/8)
	—	—	pišṭ+ä	Fric. Assim. (9)
	—	—	pišt+ä	Stop Dissim. (10)
	—	let'+e	pišt'+ä	Coronal Pal. (17)
	—	—	—	Iotation (41)
	—	—	—	Affrication (3)
	—	—	—	Dentalization (44)

Cycle 3	trepot+a+m	let'+e+m	pišt'+ä+m	WFR: 1st sg. pres.
	trepot+a+ém	let'+e+ím	pišt'+ä+ím	Extension
	trepotj+a+ém	—	—	*j*-Insertion
	—	—	—	1st Velar Pal.
	trepotj+ém	let'+ím	pišt'+ím	Vowel Deletion
	—	—	—	Fricative Assim.
	—	—	—	Stop Dissimilation
	trepot'j+ém	—	—	Coronal Pal.
	trepoṭ'j+ém	—	—	Iotation
	trepoč'j+ém	—	—	Affrication
	trepocj+ém	—	—	Dentalization

				Postcyclic
	trepocj+em			Glide Shortening (2/27)
	trepoc+em			*j*-Simplification (8.2)

(48) *j*-Insertion
  1st Velar Palatalization
  Vowel Deletion
  Affricate Palatalization
  Fricative Assimilation
  Stop Dissimilation
  Coronal Palatalization
  Iotation
  Affrication
  2nd Velar Palatalization
  Dentalization

Of these rules only the status of Dentalization might be debatable (the rule could be postcyclic). Coronal Palatalization in particular is a classic example of a cyclic rule since it exhibits a syndrome of properties that characterize this type of rule. Although the motivation for the cyclicity of 2nd Velar Palatalization is not as spectacular as for Coronal Palatalization, the cyclic status of this rule is clear. Recall that it is assumed in this book with Booij and Rubach (1987) that rules form blocks, that is, in the unmarked case the rule is either only cyclic or only postcyclic or only postlexical (see Chapter 1). Given this concept and the independently necessary ordering in (48), we predict that all the rules preceding the last rule in this block must be cyclic. This is a significant generalization and an important theoretical result. The descriptive evidence provided in this chapter confirms our predictions at full length.

4.6.3. Residual problems

In this section we discuss briefly some alternations which, we claim, must be accounted for by allomorphy rather than by phonological rules. Consider the words in (49):

(49) *a.* pust+i+t' 'let go'—pušt'+a+t' (DI)
   vy+čist+i+t' 'clean'—vy+čišt'+a+t' (DI)
 b. trest+a+t' 'punish'—tresc+em 'I punish'
   chl'ast+a+t' 'drink'—chl'asc+em 'I drink'
   chvast+a+t' 'boast'—chvasc+em 'I boast'

The words in (49*a*), the only two such verb stems, seem to suggest that Iotation should precede Fricative Assimilation and Stop Dissimilation, since then the alternation *s* ~ *š* can be explained:

(50) st → sṭ (Iotation) → šṭ (Fricative Assimilation) →
  šṭ (Stop Dissimilation) → št' (Coronal Palatalization)

This, however, is contradicted by the data in (49*b*), where the derivation proceeds exactly as reported in 4.6.2: *t* changes into *c* by Iotation and *s* remains unaffected. We conclude that the stems in (49*a*) are instances of allomorphy, that is, /št'/ in these stems is no longer derivable via the present-day phonological rules of Slovak. This conclusion is additionally supported by the fact that the cluster [št'] is also found in environments in which it could not be derived along the lines suggested in (50), for example *vy+trešt+i+t'* 'stare': a perfective *i*-stem, hence *j*-Insertion and Iotation are inapplicable.

The data in (51) are largely parallel to those in (49):

(51) *a.* posl+a+t' 'send'—pošl+em 'I send', pošl+ú 'they send'
     mysl+ie+t' 'think'—roz+mýšl'+a+t' 'ponder' (DI)
  b. zauzl+i+t' 'complicate'—zauzl'+ova+t' (DI)
     od+kresl+i+t' 'strike off'—od+kresl'+ova+t' (DI)
     mazn+a+t' 'spoil'—mazn+em 'I spoil', mazn+ú 'they spoil'

The two verbs in (51*a*), the only such examples, seem to indicate that not
only /s, z/ and /t, d/ but also sonorant non-continuants undergo Iotation,
since *s* alternates with *š*; hence the derivation should be along the lines
of (50). This account would be incorrect. First, the verbs in (51*a*) are irregular in some ways. Thus, *posl+a+t'* 'send' comes from *posol* 'envoy'—
posl+a (gen. sg.); that is, it has a yer between the *s* and the *l*. In order
to derive /š/ in *pošl+em* 'I send' Fricative Assimilation would have to
be complicated by making reference to the skeleton, as only then would
the yer not be able to break up the adjacency of the fricative and the lateral. The second stem, //misl+e// 'think', shows a predictable alternation between *s* and *š* in the derived imperfective. However, in the related noun
myšl+ien+k+a 'thought' the [š] could not be derived, since the environment of *j*-Insertion and further Iotation is not met. Thus, the verb stems in
(51*a*) are irregular in ways that could not be corrected by Iotation.

A second argument against deriving [š] from //s// in (51*a*) comes from
the data in (51*b*). If sonorants were permitted to undergo Iotation, then
we should also find [š, ž] in (51*b*), but we do not. We conclude that *poslat'*
and *mysliet'* show allomorphy and the [š] in the related forms can no
longer be derived from //s// by the rules of Slovak. No doubt, Iotation
historically applied also to *l*. This is presumably the explanation why
words such as *okrašl'+ova+t'*, a derived imperfective from *okrášl+i+t'*
'adorn', and *kašl+a+t'* 'cough' have acquired their *š*. Today, there are no
related forms in which *š* would alternate with *s* and the contexts in which *š*
appears do not fall within the scope of Iotation.

Finally, we note a certain subregularity in the 3rd pl. of the present
tense with the verb stems that end in //l, n//:

(52) pipl+a+t' sa 'tinker'—pip[l']+em sa 'I tinker', pip[l']+eš sa 'you
     tinker', etc. *versus* pip[l]+ú sa 'they tinker'
     sten+a+t' 'sigh'—ste[n']+em 'I sigh', ste[n']+eš 'you sigh', etc. *versus*
     ste[n]+ú 'they tinker'

The words in (52) are *a*-stems and hence they undergo *j*-Insertion in various conjugational forms. The presence of /j/ can be diagnosed from the
fact that the extension vowel //é// surfaces as short, hence Glide Shortening must have applied. The consonants are palatalized as predicted by
Coronal Palatalization, which applies not only before /i/ and /e/ but also
before /j/. In Slovak, as in Polish, the palatalization effects in the class
of sonorants (but not obstruents) are the same, regardless of whether the

palatalizing segment is a vowel or a glide. In this sense the data in (52) are perfectly regular. The irregularity consists in the fact that the sonorant is not palatalized in the 3rd pl. of the present tense. Consequently, Slovak must have a rule that deletes /j/ after a sonorant and before the 3rd pl. ending prior to Coronal Palatalization. That at earlier stages of the historical development such a rule did not exist can be deduced from the fact that *pošl+ú*, the 3rd pl. of *posl+a+t'* 'send', has retained the *š*. As mentioned earlier, Iotation also used to apply to sonorants. The only remnant of this state of affairs is the alternation *s ~ š* precisely in the conjugation of *poslat'* (see (51) above). The by-products of the historical changes affecting Iotation are the handful of irregular formations discussed in this section.[12]

---

[12] Two C-stems, *min+út'* 'pass' and *zhrn+út'* 'put together', exhibit palatalization in the derived imperfective forms: *miň+a+t'* and *zhŕň+a+t'*. Either they are instances of allomorphy or, as suggested by Isačenko (1966), Slovak has the suffix //äj// alongside the regular //aj// in derived imperfectives.

MELODY–SKELETON INTERACTION: THE YERS

5.1. BACKGROUND

The claim that the skeleton is a separate tier of representation from the melody is justified by the fact that the relationship between the skeleton and the melody need not be one-to-one (see 1.3). Thus, three-dimensional theory permits, among others, analyses that postulate floating melodies, that is, melody segments without associated X slots. In fact, it is to be expected that languages should make use of floating matrices. If it had been discovered that no language used this type of representation, the motivation for keeping the skeleton as a separate tier would have been weakened.

The concept of floating matrices finds strong support in the analysis of Slovak. We show in this chapter that Slovak yers must be interpreted precisely as melody segments without associated X slots. The term 'yer' is used in Slavic to describe fleeting vowels; that is, vowels that alternate with zero. Historically, yers are a pair of high lax (short) vowels usually represented as /ĭ, ŭ/, where the diacritic above the vowel means [–tense]. They underwent the law known as Havlík's Law, whereby even-numbered yers (counting from the right) lowered to merge with other vowels and odd-numbered yers deleted. It was Lightner's (1965) discovery that yers form part of the underlying structure of contemporary Slavic. Analysing Russian, Lightner postulated the rule known as Lower, whose function was to vocalize a yer before a yer in the next syllable. Unvocalized yers deleted context-freely.

Surface effects of Lower are different in different Slavic languages. Below we give examples from Russian, which represents East Slavic, from Polish, which belongs to West Slavic, and from Serbo-Croat, which is a member of the South Slavic subgroup. The examples are in the nom. sg. and the gen. sg.:

(1) *a.* Russian: ĭ, ŭ → e, o

      den' 'day'—dn'+a; son 'dream'—sn+a

  b. Polish: ĭ, ŭ → e

      pies [p'jes] 'dog'—ps+a; bez 'lilac'—bz+u

  c. Serbo-Croat: ĭ, ŭ → a

      pas 'dog'—ps+a; zamak 'castle'—zamk+a

In Russian, as in Slovak, the historical distinction between front and back yers is paralleled in the modern language, though because of later changes the present distribution of [e] and [o] does not always correspond with the former. In Polish the two yers merge into phonetic [e] but their front/back quality is carried over into surface representations as the presence versus the absence of palatalization on the preceding consonant. In Serbo-Croat the merger into [a] is complete, at least in the context of labials, since no surface palatalization is found.[1]

That yers have not ceased to play a role in modern Slovak can be seen from the fact that they are found also in borrowings, some of which are of relatively recent date. That is, yers have developed in words in which they never existed historically. Note the *e*–zero alternation in (2):

(2) *Nom. sg.*   *Gen. sg.*
    sveter 'sweater'   svetr+a
    motocykel 'motorcycle' motocykl+a
    semester 'semester'   semestr+a
    september 'September' septembr+a

Thus, the alternating vowels described here as 'yers' are very much alive as a pattern in contemporary Slovak and no phonological theory can afford to ignore this fact. At this point two lines of reasoning are possible:

  (i) *Vowel insertion.* The vowels that alternate with zero are epenthetic.
  (ii) *Vowel deletion.* The fleeting vowels are present underlyingly and Slovak has a rule of deletion which deletes them in some contexts.

To put it differently, the question is whether yers can (hypothesis (i)) or cannot (hypothesis (ii)) be predicted from surface phonological structure. We argue below that only hypothesis (ii) is correct.

5.2. VOWEL INSERTION: A REJECTED HYPOTHESIS

Evidence from several typologically different sources can be adduced against the insertion hypothesis:

Triggering effects

Not only vocalized but also unvocalized yers trigger the application of phonological rules. Thus, the //l// of *strel+a* 'shot' undergoes Coronal

---

[1] As pointed out to me by Andrew Spencer, in some other contexts we still need a front yer //ĭ// in order to explain velar palatalization in words such as *straš+an* 'terrible' (masc., nom. sg., short form)—*straš+n+a* (fem., nom. sg.), both derived from *strach* 'fear'. An alternative would be to assume that the Serbo-Croatian yer is a front *ä* vowel (the one found in Slovak). Yer Vocalization would then be simpler as it would be a rule of backing and not backing plus lowering. More exactly, Yer Vocalization would presumably be the same as in Slovak, that is, rule (13) below, and Backing would be a late spell-out rule.

Palatalization not only in *strel+ieb* 'shooting' (gen. pl.), where the yer in *-ieb* has vocalized,[2] but also in those cases where the yer does not surface, such as the nom. sg. *strel'+b+a*.

As a further example we take the adjectivizing suffix *-n/en*. The *e*–zero alternation is seen in the adjectives *dlž+en* 'indebted' (masc. short form) —*dlž+n+á* (fem. nom. sg.), both of which are derived from the noun *dlh* 'debt'. Notice that the effects of 1st Velar Palatalization (here: *h → ž*) are present in both forms, regardless of whether the yer has or has not vocalized. The same observation is true when we look at the operation of other rules. Vowel Lengthening (and Diphthongization), which is triggered by a yer, applies to *hôr+n+y*, an adjective from *hor+a* 'forest'. Affricate Palatalization changes //c// into [č] in *noč+n+ý*, an adjective from *noc* 'night'. Yer Hiatus, a rule that inserts /j/ between two vocalic segments, applies before *-n* in *múzej+n+ý*, an adjective from *múze+um* 'museum' (see 5.7 below). Notice that with the assumption that yers are underlying in Slovak the application of all of these rules is understandable.

Blocking effects

If the yers are underlying, as proposed in (ii), then they can block the application of phonological rules also in those instances where yer vocalization does not take place. It becomes clear why Postvocalic *j*-Deletion, which deletes /j/ before consonants (see rule (4) in Chapter 3), does not apply to words such as *zbroj+n+ý*, an adjective from *zbroj* 'armour'. Neither can Nasal Deletion, a rule that deletes nasals before consonants (see 5.6), apply to *pís+om+n+ý*, an adjective from *pís+m+o* 'letter'. Recall that the adjectivizing *-n* is precisely one of the yer suffixes.

Yet another mysterious fact can be explained on the assumption that yers are underlying. Coronal Palatalization, which has the effect, amongst others, of turning *d* into *d'* before *i*, does not apply to prefixal structures such as *pod+ist'* 'come up'. An explanation can be sought in the fact that the prefix *pod-* contains a back yer after *d*. The yer is postulated on the strength of the alternation *pod-* vs. *podo-*, for example *pod+ist'* 'come up', *podo+tknúť* 'mention'. If the yer *o* is present in the underlying representation of the prefix, then understandably Coronal Palatalization cannot affect the *d* in *pod+ist'* since the stop is not followed directly by the front vowel *i*.

---

[2] The vocalized yer is diphthongized further by Vowel Diphthongization, hence we have *-ieb* rather than *-eb*; see Chapter 6.

Alternations

The front/back distinction of the yers exists in modern Slovak: we have *e* and *o*, respectively. This poses a problem, since both of these vowels are found in the same phonological environment, for example after labials and after coronal fricatives:

(3) *Nom. sg.*   *Gen. sg.*
   a. pes 'dog'   ps+a
      bobor 'beaver' bobr+a
   b. sen 'dream'   sn+a
      blázon 'fool' blázn+a

The occurrence of the fleeting *e* and *o* is unpredictable because Slovak, unlike Polish, has lost the palatalization of labials and coronal fricatives. Neither is it possible to deduce whether the yer is *e* or *o* from the following consonant. In (4a) below, the front yer appears before both a 'hard' *n* and the 'soft' *ň*. Moreover, there are also instances in which a hard consonant follows *e* while a soft consonant follows *o*, as in (4b):

(4) *a.* sen 'dream'—sn+a (gen. sg.)
      peň 'trunk'—pň+a (gen. sg.)
   b. priemysel 'industry'—priemysl+u (gen. sg.)
      uhoľ 'coal'—uhľ+a (gen. sg.)

The change of status of Coronal Palatalization from originally non-cyclic to cyclic also has its share in contributing to the unpredictability of the fleeting *e* and *o*. With the cyclicity of Coronal Palatalization hard stops occur before both the front and the back yer:

(5) liter [t] 'litre'—litr+a (gen. sg.)
    lotor 'rascal'—lotr+a (gen. sg.)

The environment of velars leads to the same type of problem: both yers appear in the same context:

(6) *a.* ker 'bush'—kr+a (gen. sg.)
      cukor 'sugar'—cukr+u (gen. sg.)
   b. šláger 'hit'—šlágr+a (gen. sg.)
      švagor 'brother-in-law'—švagr+a (gen. sg.)

The pair in (7) is even more spectacular:

(7) prí+jem 'receipt'—prí+jm+u (gen. sg.)
    ná+jom 'hiring'—ná+jm+u (gen. sg.)

Historically, the roots *jem/jm* and *jom/jm* come from the same source, but synchronically they must be treated as unrelated since they have developed two different yers.

In sum, the facts adduced in (3)–(7) make the theory of vowel insertion untenable as an account of the yers.

Putative insertion environments

The final argument against the insertion hypothesis comes from consideration of the environment in which the yer would have to be inserted. At first glance it seems that the insertion hypothesis could explain the facts of syllable structure. Notice that in most of our examples the yer surfaces phonetically in contexts that would otherwise lead to the rise of extra-syllabic consonants. Thus, assuming for the moment that *blázon* 'fool' and *cukor* 'sugar' derive from underlying //blázn// and //cukr//, respectively, one could hypothesize that the *o* is inserted in order to improve the syllable structure. That is, *o*-insertion is triggered by *n* and *r*, which cannot be syllabified since they stand after an obstruent and hence violate the Sonority Sequencing Generalization (see 1.3). In the gen. sg. *blázn+a* and *cukr+u* the *o* is not inserted since the sonorants can syllabify as onsets of the following syllable.

Unfortunately, this syllable-based approach cannot be maintained in view of the fact that fleeting vowels occur also in environments that do not warrant the occurrence of extrasyllabic consonants. In (8*a*) all consonants can be syllabified, even if the underlying representations contain no yers. The words in (8*b*) show that the relevant clusters are permitted syllable-finally.

(8)   *Nom. sg.*   *Gen. sg.*   *Putative UR*
  a. faloš 'dishonesty'   falš+e   //falš//
     ocot 'vinegar'   oct+u   //oct//
     Turek 'Turk'   Turk+a   //turk//
     Portugalec 'Portuguese' Portugalc+a //portugalc//
     Japonec 'Japanese'   Japonc+a   //japonc//
  b. falš 'foul', pôct 'distinction' (gen. pl.), park 'park', filc 'felt', kredenc 'cutlery'

Finally there are words in which the occurrence of the fleeting vowel is conditioned grammatically and not phonologically. Thus, in *zámk+a*, the gen. sg. of *zámok* 'lock', no vowel surfaces between the *m* and the *k*. This, one would say, is due to the fact that the cluster *mk* can be parsed easily by the syllabification rules: $(zám)_\sigma (ka)_\sigma$. However, in the derived imperfective form of the related verb, *y* breaks up the *mk* cluster: *zamyk+a+t'* 'to lock'.[3]

Summing up the discussion in this section, we conclude that the vowel

---

[3] For an analysis of vowel alternations in derived imperfectives, see 5.5 below.

insertion hypothesis cannot be maintained. Vowel–zero alternations must be accounted for by a deletion rule. The yers are present in the underlying representation. In some contexts they surface phonetically and in some other contexts they delete. The details of this analysis are presented in the following section.

5.3. UNDERLYING YERS

Given that the yers are underlying, the simplest analysis of the vowel–zero alternations is to postulate a rule of deletion. This, however, turns out to be impossible since the rule cannot be formulated. That the deletion of the vowel is unpredictable is shown by the pairs of words in (9), where in the same context the *e* and *o* delete in some instances but not in others.

(9) *Nom. sg.*   *Gen. sg.*
   a. semester 'semester' semestr+a
       jeseter 'sturgeon' jeseter+a
   b. šev 'seam' šv+u
       lev 'lion' lev+a
   c. kotol 'cauldron' kotl+a
       atol 'atoll' atol+u
   d. bahor 'felly' bahr+a
       bachor 'belly' bachor+a

Thus, the fleeting *e* and *o* must somehow be made distinct from the non-fleeting *e* and *o*. At this point we might follow the traditional approach to the Slavic yers which originated with Lightner's (1965) analysis of Russian and assume that the yers in Slovak, as in Russian, are high lax vowels. The feature [–tense] makes them distinct from the 'regular', non-fleeting //i, u//. The underlying yers, which we now transcribe as // ĭ, ŭ //, change into [e, o] by Lightner's rule known as Lower (cf. Lightner 1965, 1972):

(10) Lower $\begin{Bmatrix} ĭ \\ ŭ \end{Bmatrix} \rightarrow \begin{Bmatrix} e \\ o \end{Bmatrix} / - C_0 \begin{Bmatrix} ĭ \\ ŭ \end{Bmatrix}$

Thus, yers vocalize as [e, o] if they are followed by a yer in the next syllable. An associated assumption here is that the so-called zero endings are themselves yers. As pointed out in Chapter 3 (see 3.2.1.9) and amply motivated in Chapter 6 (see 6.1.1.3), this analysis is strongly corroborated by the analysis of vowel lengthening. The zero endings are represented by the back yer //ŭ// since the word-final consonant is never palatalized. Let us look at *vápen+ec* 'limestone' as an example. It contains a chain of three yers. The root has a yer since the *e* alternates with zero in *vápn+o* 'lime'. The *-ec* suffix also has a yer because it appears as *c* in the gen. sg. *vápen+c+a*. The third yer is that of the inflectional ending, here the masc. nom. sg. The derivation is now as in (11). We apply Lower (10) cyclically.

(11) UR *v*ápĭn+ĭc+ŭ
  Cycle 2 *v*ápĭn+ĭc
      *v*ápen+ĭc   Lower
  ─────────────────────────
  Cycle 3 *v*ápen+ĭc+ŭ
      *v*ápen+ec+ŭ Lower

Yers which are not followed by a yer and hence are unable to vocalize delete context-freely:

(12) Yer Deletion ĭ, ŭ → ∅

This analysis in the spirit of Lightner (1965, 1972) can account correctly for all the facts of vowel–zero alternations. However, it leads to certain system-internal difficulties. First, it calls for introducing the otherwise redundant feature [tense] as a distinction at the underlying level. (Recall that the yers //ĭ, ŭ// are distinct from the regular //i, u// solely by being [–tense].) Second, it disturbs the symmetry of the long/short correspondence in the underlying inventory of Slovak. As pointed out in Chapter 2, all short vowels have their long counterparts (long vowels or diphthongs). In the case of yers, however, there is no evidence that there is a pair of corresponding long vowels. How can we explain this peculiarity? The matter is straightforward in the framework of three-dimensional representations.

Recall that length is represented at the skeletal rather than at the melodic tier (see 1.3). A long vowel is a melody segment that is linked to two X slots while a short vowel is linked to one X slot. Suppose yers are floating matrices at the underlying level; that is, they are melody segments without an associated X slot (Kenstowicz and Rubach 1987, Rubach 1986). It is now predicted that yers as underlying segments can never be long. This prediction follows precisely from the fact that length is expressed not at the melodic tier but at the skeleton and that yers have no representation at the skeletal tier. We also avoid introducing [tense] as a distinctive feature. The distinction between the yers //ĭ, ŭ// and the 'regular' vowels //i, u// is now expressed in structural terms: the absence versus the presence of an X slot. At the melodic tier the yers and the regular vowels are identical.

Surface reflexes of yers which actually appear in phonetic representations must receive an X slot in the course of phonological derivation. This follows from the widely accepted assumption that in order to be pronounced a segment must be licensed prosodically (Itô 1986). That is, it must be part of the prosodic structure; for instance, part of the syllable. Prosodic structure is erected over X slots because the task of syllabification rules is to organize Xs into syllables (recall 1.3). The vocalization of yers in surface representations must therefore be a rule of X-slot assignment. In (13) we quote the statement of this rule after Kenstowicz and Rubach (1987). The circled V stands for a floating vowel, that is, a melody segment without an associated X slot:

(13) Yer Vocalization X
$$\textcircled{V} \rightarrow V \: / — C \: \textcircled{V}$$

In its statement, (13) expresses the generalization given earlier in (10): a yer vocalizes before a yer.

An immediate advantage of the new representation of the yers is that Yer Deletion has become superfluous as a rule. The yers that have not undergone (13) remain without an X slot. They cannot be licensed prosodically and hence are never realized phonetically. At the end of phonology they are deleted by convention: Steriade's (1982) Stray Erasure.

Interpreting yers as floating matrices at the underlying level has yet another advantageous consequence. There is no need to assume that the surface reflexes of the vocalized yers derive from high vowels. At the melodic tier the underlying representation and the phonetic representation are identical. The yers are distinct from the other vowels since they do not have X slots. Thus, the nom. sg. *centimeter* 'centimetre' and the gen. sg. *centimetr+a* are represented underlyingly as follows. Recall that the nom. sg. ending is a yer. Note the contrast between the regular *e* and the yer *e*:

(14)

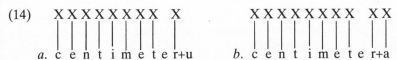

Yer Vocalization applies to (14*a*) but not to (14*b*). Unvocalized yers—the *u* in (14*a*) and the *e* in (14*b*)—are stray-erased at the end of the derivation.

The derivation of *vápen+ec* 'limestone' given earlier in (11) is now replaced by (15).

The interpretation of yers as floating matrices makes two predictions, both of which turn out to be correct. First, in principle it is no longer necessary to limit yers to the class of fleeting mid vowels *e* and *o*. Second, unvocalized yers should be invisible to rules which operate at the skeletal tier only. This follows from the fact that unvocalized yers have no representation there. Let us look at these two predictions in some detail.

With the assumption that the yer is defined in structural and not in phonetic terms—that is, as a floating matrix and not as a lax vowel—it is to be expected that not only the traditional mid vowels but also other vowels may take on the property of being a yer. To put this differently, in principle all vowels may show alternations with zero and may be subject to Yer Vocalization (13). This prediction is borne out. We find

(15)

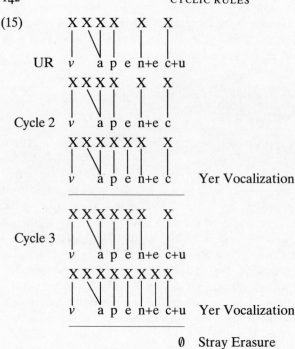

UR   v   a p e n+e c+u

Cycle 2   v   a p e n+e c

v   a p e n+e c   Yer Vocalization

Cycle 3   v   a p e n+e c+u

v   a p e n+e c+u   Yer Vocalization

∅   Stray Erasure

alternations of *a* and zero on a large scale. Some examples are given in
(16). They are all neuter and feminine nouns.[4] Note that in the gen. pl. the
vocalized yers are lengthened.

(16)   *Nom. sg.*   *Gen. pl.*
   a. jedl+o 'food'   jedál
       vreck+o 'bag'   vrecák
       brvn+o 'beam'   brván
   b. tehl+a 'brick'   tehál
       dosk+a 'board'   dosák
       kart+a 'card'   karát[5]

The development of an *a* yer is unexpected in the traditional account.
Slovak has two low vowels in its original phonological system: //ä// and
//a//. Adding a third low vowel, the yer *a*, that would have to be made
phonetically distinct at the underlying level from the original //ä// and //a//

---

[4] The yer *a* appears less often in masculine nouns: *chrbát* 'back' (vocalization and
lengthening before the nom. sg. yer)—*chrbt+a* (gen. sg.).
[5] Most of these words also have an alternative form with the yer *e*. For instance, the gen.
pl. of *kart+a* may also be *kariet* (vocalization, lengthening, and diphthongization).

is difficult to imagine, particularly since *ä* may also be either a regular vowel or a yer:

(17) päst' 'fist'—päst+e (gen. sg.) *versus*
      odo+pä+t' 'undo'—odo+pn+út' 'undo' (perfective): *ä*–zero
      alternation

In our account the matter is simple: the defining property of yers is structural and not phonetic, hence any vowel may in principle be a yer.

Summing up, we have found so far that *e*, *o*, *a*, and *ä* all have their corresponding yers. One wonders whether the remaining vowels in Slovak, *i* and *u*, can also exhibit the yer property of alternating with zero. Indeed, they can. In (18) we give examples of the regular *i*, *u* and the yers *i*, *u* (with *i* there is some dialectal variation):

(18) *a.* hák 'hook'—háč+ik (dimin.)—háč+ik+a (gen. sg.) *versus*
       chudák 'poor man'—chudáč+ik (dimin.)—chudáč+k+a (gen. sg.)
       bok 'side'—bôč+ik (dimin.)—bôč+k+a (gen. sg.)
     b. luk 'bow'—luk+u (gen. sg.) *versus*
       k ~ ku:[6] k riek+e 'to the river'—ku káv+e 'to the coffee'

We conclude that all Slovak vowels can appear in the capacity of yers. This is exactly what one would expect, given the interpretation that the distinction between yers and regular vowels is made at the skeleton and not at the melody.

The new interpretation of the yers makes yet another important prediction: rules that manipulate X slots must treat yers as invisible. The Rhythmic Law is precisely this type of a rule. Recall that the Rhythmic Law shortens long vowels after a long vowel or a diphthong. To put it in syllabic terms: complex syllable nuclei are shortened after complex nuclei. We shall postpone the details of this analysis till Chapter 6. For the moment we simply assume that the Rhythmic Law is indeed stated in syllabic terms (N stands for 'nucleus'):

(19) Rhythmic Law

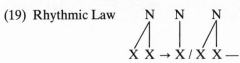

In (20) we give examples which illustrate that unvocalized yers are treated as invisible by the Rhythmic Law; that is, the rule applies 'across' them. We hasten to add that for a number of reasons (see Chapters 7 and 9) it cannot be assumed that unvocalized yers are deleted prior to the application of the Rhythmic Law. We look at the dat. pl. suffix *-ám*, which is underlyingly long, as shown by *lan+ám* 'cable' (dat. pl.). Recall that yers

---

[6] This alternation is discussed further in 9.1.

are vocalized before the gen. pl. yer. Floating matrices are transcribed as capital letters.

(20) *Nom. sg.*   *Gen. pl.*   *Dat. pl.*   *UR*

	Gen. pl.	*Dat. pl.*	*UR*
sídl+o 'trap'	sídel	sídl+am	//sídEl+ám//
pásm+o 'strand'	pásem	pásm+am	//pásEm+ám//
plátn+o 'cloth'	pláten	plátn+am	//plátEn+ám//
hálk+a 'porch roof'	hálok	hálk+am	//ɣálOk+ám//
srvátk+a 'whey'	srvátok	srvátk+am	//srvátOk+ám//

Syllable structure is created over Xs and not directly over melody segments. Thus, N-placement (1/30), which assigns the nucleus, ignores yers. The derivation of *sídl+am* 'trap' (dat. pl.) is now as given in (21).

(21)
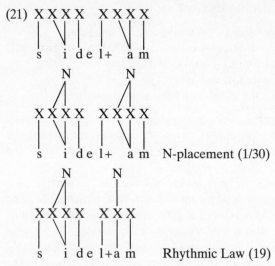

The Rhythmic Law applies across unvocalized yers and yields the desired result. This is possible because yers have been defined as floating matrices. Our interpretation of the yers has thus gained new evidence in its favour.

5.4. EXCURSUS: THE MORA AND THE YERS

We show in the next chapter that Slovak has a rule of lengthening which is triggered by yers (recall rule (24) in Chapter 2). Schematically:

(22) Vowel Lengthening

$$\begin{matrix} N & & N \\ | & & /\,| \\ X & \rightarrow & X\ X \end{matrix}\ /\ -\!\!-\ C\ yer$$

Lengthening takes place in the gen. pl. of feminine and neuter nouns and, as we pointed out earlier, the gen. pl. ending is a yer. The lengthened mid vowels diphthongize to *ie* and *ô* [uo]. Compare the nom. sg. with the gen. pl. in (23):

(23) fabrik+a 'factory'—fabrík
      chat+a 'cottage'—chát
      čel+o 'forehead'—čiel
      kol+o 'circle'—kôl

These examples look like instances of compensatory lengthening,[7] since there is a convergence of two facts. The yer, which after all is a vocalic segment, does not vocalize, and the preceding vowel is lengthened. If a yer carried an X slot and hence had a timing unit of its own (a mora), then the lengthening of the vowel could be an instance of compensation: the X slot of the yer is linked to the vowel which thus becomes long. On the other hand, the yer which is a donor of the X slot cannot vocalize as it has become a floating segment. The logic of this reasoning is attractive. If correct, it provides a strong argument against our interpretation of yers as floating segments at the underlying level. Thus, to uphold our theory we must demonstrate that in spite of its appeal the interpretation of rule (22) as an instance of compensatory lengthening is incorrect.

The argument is rather complex. Let us begin by explaining that vocalized and lengthened yers undergo the Rhythmic Law. Compare:

(24) vedr+o 'bucket'—vedier (gen. pl.) *versus*
      krídl+o 'wing'—krídel (gen. pl.)

The derivation of the gen. pl. forms is given in (25). We assume for the sake of the argument that yers carry X slots in the underlying representation. We ignore the problem of how to make yers distinct from the regular (non-fleeting) vowels. The yers appear in italics. We take up the derivation at the point when the node N has already been assigned. In (25a) the lengthened yer remains long since it is not preceded by a long vowel. In (25b) it shortens in accordance with the Rhythmic Law. Mid vowels diphthongize, but only when they are long. We thus obtain the contrast: *ie* in *vedier* versus *e* in *krídel*. The theory of compensatory lengthening looks plausible.

An argument against compensatory lengthening comes from the observation that the yer which causes lengthening may itself surface as long. This happens if there is a chain of three yers. We look at the diminutives of the examples from (24):

---

[7] We shall not be concerned with stating rule (22) formally as a rule of compensatory lengthening. As we show below, compensatory lengthening as a mechanism is not appropriate for Slovak.

(25) *a.*

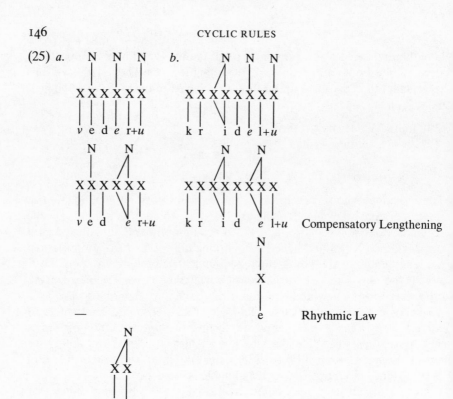

Compensatory Lengthening

Rhythmic Law

Diphthongization

(26) vedier+c+e 'bucket'—vedier+ec (gen. pl.) *versus*
    krídel+c+e 'wing'—krídel+iec (gen. pl.)

The diminutive suffix is //ec// and *e* is a yer, as shown by the alternation with zero and the fact that it causes the lengthening of the root yer. The suffixal yer vocalizes since it is followed by the yer of the gen. pl. A partial derivation is given in (27). We assume that the rules apply cyclically (see Chapter 6). In cycle 3 Compensatory Lengthening has the effect of moving an X slot from the final to the preceding yer. At this point the derivation collapses. We are not able to derive the long (and subsequently diphthongized) yer in the diminutive suffix of *krídel+iec*. Instead we obtain the incorrect form **krídel+ec*. This is due to the fact that the yer of *-ec* passed on its mora (X slot) to the root yer in cycle 2. Thus, in cycle 3 it may survive only because it receives an X slot from the gen. pl. yer *u*. This, however, is insufficient. In order to diphthongize to *ie* it must have two X slots (moras) and not one. The theory of compensatory lengthening as an explanation of the Slovak facts is simply incorrect. We conclude that Vowel Lengthening does not provide a counterargument to our

(27)   *a.*   *b.*

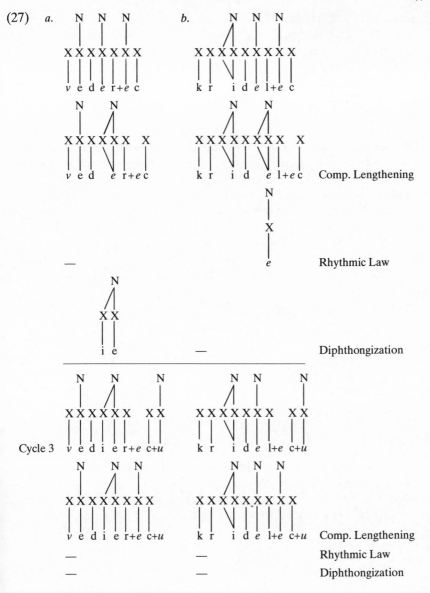

Comp. Lengthening

Rhythmic Law

Diphthongization

Cycle 3

Comp. Lengthening
Rhythmic Law
Diphthongization

interpretation of yers as floating matrices. The analysis laid out in the preceding section is upheld.

Finally let us see whether our interpretation of the yers could be translated into the moraic theory recently proposed by Hayes (1989), who develops Hyman's (1985) theory. The essence of Hayes's approach is the claim that a fully structured skeleton as a tier of representation is not necessary in phonological theory. Instead of X slots that are assigned to consonants and vowels alike, we have moras (marked μ) that are universally assigned to vowels only (marginally, also to long consonants). Consonants in onsets are built into syllable structure directly from the melody, without an intermediate representation at the skeletal tier. Consonants in codas may carry a mora but only in weight-sensitive languages in which they need to produce a heavy cluster effect. In Slovak they do not contribute to syllable weight and hence they are linked to the mora of the vowel (cf. Rubach, forthcoming). Thus, the Slovak roots *kus* 'bit' and *kút* 'angle' have the representation of (28*a*) at the underlying level, and that of (28*b*) after syllable structure has been assigned.

(28) *a.*

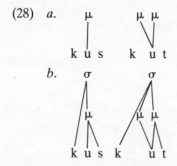

b.

Our interpretation of yers as floating matrices can be translated into the moraic framework without difficulty. A yer is then a vocalic melody without an associated mora. The root *vedr* of *vedr+o* 'bucket', which has an *e* yer between *d* and *r* (see (24) above), is represented as follows:

(29)   μ
         |
         |
    v e d e r

Yer Vocalization is then a rule of mora assignment. The moraic theory thus makes the same prediction as the X-skeletal theory with regard to the facts discussed in the preceding section.

The difference between the two theories comes to light when we consider the problem of adjacency. The X-skeletal framework permits us to establish adjacency of consonants across yers by referring to the X slots. Thus, C_1 and C_2 are adjacent in a hypothetical C–yer–C string:

(30) $\begin{array}{ccc} X & & X \\ | & & | \\ C_1 & V & C_2 \end{array}$

A rule that treats C_1 and C_2 as adjacent must simply refer to Xs since it is there that floating matrices are not visible. In a moraic framework this possibility is not open to us because consonants do not have any representation at the skeleton. For C_1 and C_2 to be adjacent, the yer must first be deleted. The evidence in Chapters 8 and 9 suggests that there are phonological rules which treat C_1 and C_2 as adjacent at the stage of derivation at which the unvocalized yers are still present. It comes from the observation that postcyclic lexical rules, which of necessity apply before postlexical rules, must treat yers as invisible (Anterior Depalatalization in Chapter 8). It cannot be assumed that the yers have been deleted, since they play a role in the operation of postlexical rules (Vowel Vocalization in Chapter 9). In the remainder of this book we shall adhere to the X-skeletal theory rather than to the moraic framework of Hayes (1989).

5.5. DERIVED IMPERFECTIVE RAISING

In this and in the following two sections we discuss further evidence for yers in Slovak. For typographic convenience we shall transcribe yers as capital letters, with the understanding that capitalization denotes a floating matrix. We begin with derived imperfectives (DI).

In Slovak, as in other Slavic languages, yers vocalize before the DI suffix -aj. Compare the perfective and the DI forms in (31):

(31) *a.* za+tk+nú+t' 'imprison'—za+týk+aj+ú 'they imprison' (DI)
      b. vy+sch+nú+t' 'to dry'—vy+sych+aj+ú 'they dry' (DI)

The vocalized yer Y is subsequently lengthened by *aj*-Lengthening, rule (53) in Chapter 3. That yer vocalization in derived imperfectives and *aj*-Lengthening are two distinct processes is shown by the fact that a morpheme may undergo one but not the other rule. This is the case in (31*b*), where *sYch* is an exception to *aj*-Lengthening.

In addition to the vocalization of yers we find vowel alternations in derived imperfectives: see (32). The vowels [e] and [o] of the nouns alternate with [i] in the verbs. Recall that in Slovak, by contrast with Russian and Polish, the earlier distinction between [i] and [i] in the verbs corresponding to the [e] and [o] in the nouns has been lost. It survives in the spelling only, *y* and *i* both being pronounced [i]. If the underlying yer had the melody representation //i//—that is, if we took the segment appearing in the verb as underlying—then we would not be able to predict where the putative *i* yer should lower to [e] and where to [o] in the nouns

(32)   *Nom. sg.*   *Gen. sg.*   *DI: 3rd pl.*

     a. ná+zov 'name'   ná+zv+u   na+zýv+aj+ú

        zá+mok 'lock'   zá+mk+a   za+myk+aj+ú[8]

     b. prí+jem 'receipt'   prí+jm+u   pri+jím+aj+ú

        ná+jom 'hiring'   ná+jm+u   na+jím+aj+ú

---

in (32). This is made particularly clear by the fact that, as shown by (32*b*), [e] and [o] may appear in exactly the same environment. We conclude that the underlying melodic segment in the alternations in (32) is that of the noun; hence it is either the yer *E* or the yer *O*. These yers are not only vocalized but also neutralized to [i] before the DI suffix *-aj*.

(33) DI Raising

$$\underset{\textstyle |}{X}$$

$$ⓥ → \begin{bmatrix} +\text{high} \\ -\text{back} \end{bmatrix} / \text{— C aj]}_{\text{DI}}$$

With DI Raising (33) and Yer Vocalization (13) we are now able to account for the alternations in (32). We take the first word as an example and simplify the derivation by omitting the prefix cycle. As usual, floating matrices are transcribed as capital letters in order to save space. Recall that the nom. sg. ending is the yer *U*. The regular *u* is the ending of the gen. sg.: see (34).

(34)

(ná+)z*Ov*+U	(ná+)z*Ov*+u	(na)z*Ov*+aj (+ú)	
zo*v*+U	—	—	Yer Vocalization (13)
—	—	zi*v*+aj	DI Raising (33)
—	—	zí*v*+aj	*aj*-Length. (3/53)
ná+zo*v*	ná+z*v*+u	na+zí*v*+aj+ú	Stray Erasure

Liquids are a special context in Slavic. They trigger a lowering rule which turns /i/ into /e/:

(35) Liquid Lowering

$$\underset{[-\text{back}] → [-\text{high}] / \text{—}}{V} \begin{bmatrix} +\text{cons} \\ +\text{sonor} \\ -\text{nas} \end{bmatrix}$$

In derived imperfectives the lowered *e* is subsequently lengthened by *aj*-Lengthening. As a long mid vowel it is further subject to Diphthong-

---

[8] This verb, whose perfective form is *za+mk+nú+t'* 'to lock', belongs to a small class of verbs which gave an alternative form with *-yn* in the derived imperfective: *za+mk+ýn+aj+ú* 'they lock'. Such alternative forms arise when the perfective suffix *-n* fails to delete in the derived imperfective. It is then expanded by augmenting *y* which subsequently undergoes *aj*-Lengthening.

ization (2/25). We look at the 3rd pl. of the perfective and imperfective aspects:

(36) u+mr+ú 'they die'—u+mier+aj+ú
     na+tr+ú 'they rub'—na+tier+aj+ú
     vy+pr+ú 'they push out'—vy+pier+aj+ú
     pošl+u 'they send'—posiel+aj+ú

The last word is a particularly telling example. The underlying yer is *O* since the verb is derived from the noun *posol* 'envoy'; compare the gen. sg. *posl+a*: *o*–zero alternation. The derivation to *posiel+aj+ú* 'they send' (DI) is therefore as shown in (37).

(37) Cycle 2   posOl+aj
               posil+aj   DI Raising (33)
               posel+aj   Liquid Lowering (35)
               posél+aj   *aj*-Lengthening (3/53)
               posiel+aj   Diphthongization (2/25)

     _____

     Cycle 3   posiel+aj+ú
               (no rule applies)

We have assumed that all the rules in (37) are cyclic. This assumption is undoubtedly correct, although the decisive argument has not yet been given. It comes in Chapter 6, where we demonstrate that Diphthong-ization is a classic example of a cyclic rule. DI Raising, Liquid Lowering, and *aj*-Lengthening must be ordered before it (a feeding order); hence they are cyclic.

Liquid Lowering is an interesting example of a cyclic rule.[9] It applies in derived environments in the sense 'derived by an earlier rule': note that the vowel /i/ is an output of DI Raising. Although the cyclicity of Liquid Lowering has been established on purely theoretical grounds (rule ordering), it is fully confirmed by descriptive data. Examples such as *sirot+a* 'orphan', *sirup* 'syrup', *cirkev* 'Orthodox church', and *syr* 'cheese' show that the rule does not apply in non-derived environments. On the other hand, words such as *teraz* 'now' document the fact that at a certain point in the history of Slovak Liquid Lowering was not a cyclic rule, and that indeed it did apply in non-derived environments. Historical change was therefore a change in the status of the rule: from non-cyclic to cyclic.

---

[9] Andrew Spencer has drawn my attention to the fact that Liquid Lowering does not apply before the past tense *l*, as in *pros+i+l* 'he asked'. Neither does it apply to the prefix-plus-stem structure: *pri+radiť* 'coordinate'. While the former failure to apply must be treated as an exception, the latter need not be. In Slovak, as in other Slavic languages, all lexical rules fail to apply across prefix junctures; see Booij and Rubach (1984) for a suggestion of how such problems can be solved.

5.6. COMPENSATORY VOCALIZATION

Both consonantal and vocalic alternations are found in the class of C-stem verbs that end in a nasal: see (38).

(38) *Infinitive*   *1st sg. pres.*   *Past part.*   *Passive part.*
    za+ča+t' 'begin'   za+čn+em   za+ča+l   za+ča+t+ý
    na+pä+t' 'strain'   na+pn+em   na+pä+l   na+pä+t+ý
    vy+ža+t' 'mow'   vy+žn+em   vy+ža+l   vy+ža+t+ý
    t'a+t' 'cut'   tn+em   t'a+l   t'a+t+ý

Observe that the nasal of the root does not appear before consonants. This is confirmed further by other inflected forms such as *za+ča+vš+í* 'having begun' vs. *za+čn+úc* 'beginning'. The nasal is either *n*, as in (38), or *m*, as in *po+jm+em* 'I take'—*po+ja+t'* 'take'. We account for the alternating nasals by postulating a rule of deletion:

(39) Nasal Deletion $[+\text{nasal}] \rightarrow \emptyset\ /\ — \text{C}$

Rule (39) is seen to apply at morpheme junctures. Morpheme-internal clusters of nasals and consonants are commonplace:

(40) mliek+o 'milk', mráz 'frost', inform+ova+t' 'inform', temn+ý 'dark', tendenci+a 'tendency', nonsens 'nonsense', revanš 'revenge', pomst+i+t' 'avenge', koncert 'concert'

The explanation for the words in (40) is that Nasal Deletion is cyclic and hence cannot apply in non-derived environments. However, this explanation seems to be contradicted by the examples in (41):

(41) jam+k+a 'hole' (dimin.), kon+sk+ý 'horse' (Adj.), šialen+stv+o 'madness', zem+n+ý 'earthly', obran+c+a 'defender', hon+b+a 'chasing'

In fact, these words are only apparent exceptions. They all contain suffixes that begin with a yer (see 3.3). The yer surfaces wherever the environment of Yer Vocalization is met, for instance in the gen. pl. *jam+iek* 'hole' (dimin.) In sum, the words in (41) support rather than contradict our analysis.[10]

Now we return to the vowel alternations in (38). The vowels *a* and *ä* alternate with zero. Consequently, they are yers. This conclusion is supported further by the fact that A and Ä trigger Yer Vocalization in

---

[10] Note that words such as *han+liv+ý* 'defamatory' and *klam+liv+ý* 'illusory' are not exceptions to Nasal Deletion. In the case of the suffix *liv*, underlying //Eliv//, the presence of the yer can be determined only indirectly by looking at the palatalization effects. We see the effects of 1st Velar Palatalization in words such as *straš+liv+ý* 'frightful' and *úteš+liv+ý* 'compassionate', the adjectives derived from *strach* 'fright' and *útech+a* 'compassion'. The yer of *-Eliv* can never surface since it is always followed by a 'regular' vowel.

prefixes. For example, the prefixes *s(o)-* and *od(o)-* have yers. This is shown by the fact that the vowel deletes when no yer follows: *s+tlie+t'* 'burn down', *od+del+ie+t'* 'separate'. When appended to the roots in (38) the prefix yer vocalizes: *so+ža+t'* 'reap', *odo+pä+t'* 'undo' (see 5.8 below).

Although it is clear that *A* and *Ä* in (38) are yers, it is by no means obvious how they vocalize. Yer Vocalization is not at play here, which is best documented by the passive participle, where the inflectional ending is a 'regular' vowel: *za+ča+t+ý* 'begun'. Let us establish the underlying representations of the forms in (38). We take *za+ča+t'* 'begin' as an example. The first observation is that the yer in *-ča-* is *Ä* rather than *A*. This is shown by the related noun *za+čia+t+ok* 'beginning'. The yer of *-ča-* vocalizes here as [ia]. Both the vocalization and the diphthongization are understandable when we realize that the nominalizing suffix *-ok* contains a yer: compare the gen. sg. *za+čia+t+k+u*. The yer of *-ča-* must be a front rather than a back vowel: //čÄ//. It undergoes Yer Vocalization and Vowel Lengthening before the yer of the suffix *-Ok*. The lengthened /ä/ is further diphthongized by rule (2/25). In the infinitive *za+ča+t'* the *Ä* is vocalized but not lengthened. Consequently, it undergoes *ä*-Backing (2/13): *ä* → *a* after non-labials.

Returning to the underlying representation of the inflected forms of *za+ča+t'*, let us recall that the nasal consonant is present underlyingly. Its distribution in surface representations is governed by Nasal Deletion (39). Consequently, the underlying representations are as follows:

(42) UR: *a.* za+čÄn+t'   *b.* za+čÄn+em   *c.* za+čÄn+l   *d.* za+čÄn+t+í
       Surface: *a.* za+ča+t'   *b.* za+čn+em   *c.* za+ča+l   *d.* za+ča+t+í

We must now face the basic question: why does *Ä* vocalize? Returning to the data in (38), observe that there is a direct relationship between the deletion of the nasal consonant and the vocalization of *Ä*: the former induces the latter. Things begin falling into place when we realize that yers are floating matrices and that Nasal Deletion (39) deletes the melody segment, leaving the skeletal slot intact. That is, after Nasal Deletion we have a floating X slot in the immediate neighbourhood of a floating melody segment, the one representing the yer. Such a configuration is (presumably) universally impossible, and hence the yer docks onto the free skeletal slot by convention.[11] This is illustrated in (43), where we contrast the examples given earlier in (42*a*) and (42*b*), the former with and the latter without the vocalization of *Ä*; relevant here is cycle 3. We have now identified a new mechanism for the vocalization of the yers, a mechanism that we might dub compensatory vocalization. The compensatory effect consists in passing the slot of the nasal onto the floating yer.

[11] If it turned out that the docking could not be assumed to follow from the universal convention, then the linking of the floating X slot and the floating yer would have to be effected by a rule of Slovak.

(43)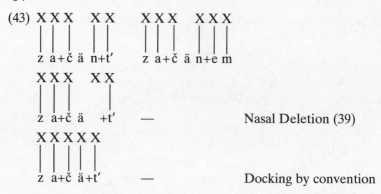

Our analysis of the yer *Ä* in the class of C-stem verbs can be extended rather easily to the suffix -*ä* which forms neuter nouns with the meaning 'young (of a creature)'. Such an extension is motivated by the fact that -*ä* behaves like a yer in that it causes Vowel Lengthening (for details see Chapter 6). We thus have the following parallel:

(44) *a.* nom. sg.: ryb+a 'fish', žab+a //žäb+a// 'frog'; -*a* is the fem. nom. sg. ending

    b. gen. pl.: rýb, žiab (diphthongization after lengthening); Vowel Lengthening applies before the gen. pl. yer

    c. 'young creature' -*ä* derivational suffix: rýb+ä 'young fish', žiab+ä 'young frog'; the inflectional ending is zero

If the root consonant is not a labial, *ä*-Backing turns *ä* into *a*. The presence of /ä/ at a deeper stage of derivation is then manifested by palatalization. The forms on the right in (45) have the -*ä* derivational suffix:

(45) pan 'man'—páň+a
    žen+a 'woman'—žieň+a
    had 'reptile'—hád'+a
    vnuk 'grandson'—vnúč+a
    vták 'bird'—vtáč+a

If we assume that the derivational -*ä* is a yer in the underlying representation, then we can explain the lengthening of the root vowel, but the question is how the surface vowel is derived from the yer. The easiest solution is to assume that compensatory vocalization is at play here, but then we need to have the structure '*Ä* followed by a nasal and a consonant' at the underlying level, so that Nasal Deletion can take effect. The consonant is easy to discover: in all inflected forms except the nom. sg.

-ä/a surfaces as -ät/at.[12] For example, rýb+ä 'young fish' has the following declension in the plural:

(46) nom./acc.   rýb+ät+á
     gen.   rýb+ät
     dat.   rýb+ät+ám
     loc.   rýb+ät+ách
     instr.   rýb+ät+ami

We thus find -ät on the surface. The consonant is there but the nasal is not. This, however, is not a surprise. Slovak has a rule of Nasal Deletion (39) and the Strict Cyclicity Constraint permits it to apply to affixes. Consequently, the nasal is always deleted. The underlying representation of the suffix under consideration can therefore be safely assumed to be //Änt//, where Ä is a yer which vocalizes to ä as a consequence of applying Nasal Deletion.

We still need to explain why the t of //Änt// does not surface in the nom. sg. rýb+ä. This clearly requires an allomorphy rule since there is no restriction against t appearing at the end of a word. In the morpheme //Änt// t is deleted only in the nom. sg., where the ending is zero.[13] The rule is therefore as follows:

(47) Änt-Allomorphy   t → ∅ / —]

Finally, the question is why the t is not dropped in the gen. pl.: rýb+ät. The explanation here is that, as mentioned several times before, the gen. pl. ending is a yer. It is this yer that blocks the deletion of t. The derivation of the nom. sg. rýb+ä, the nom. pl. rýb+ät+á, and the gen. pl. rýb+ät is now given in (48). Length and lengthening are represented as an additional X slot linked to the vowel. Note that the ordering of Vowel Lengthening before Nasal Deletion (which is cyclic) assigns Vowel Lengthening to the class of cyclic rules.

5.7. YER HIATUS

Yers can claim yet another argument in their favour: the operation of the rule that we call Yer Hiatus. Consider the alternation of j and zero in the following examples:

---

[12] In the oblique cases of the singular the obstruent is t′ rather than t, an effect which can be achieved by postulating an allomorphy rule.

[13] This is the case in the class of neuter nouns, but not in masculine or feminine nouns, which have a yer as the nom. sg. ending.

(48)

	X X X X X	X X X X X X X	X X X X X	
UR	r i b+ä n t	r i b+ä n t+ a	r i b+ä n t+u	

	X X X X X	X X X X X	X X X X X	
Cycle 2	r i b+ä n t	r i b+ä n t	r i b+ä n t	

	X X X X X X	X X X X X X	X X X X X X	
	r i b+ä n t	r i b+ä n t	r i b+ä n t	V. Length. (2/24)

	X X X X X X	X X X X X X	X X X X X X	
	r i b+ä t	r i b+ä t	r i b+ä t	Nasal Del. (39) and docking
	—	—	—	Rhythmic Law (2/26)

		X X X X X X X X	X X X X X X	
Cycle 3		r i b+ä t+ a	r i b+ä t+u	WFRs: inflection
			X X X X X X X	
		—	r i b+ ä t+u	V. Lengthening
		—	—	Nasal Deletion
			X X X X X X	
		—	r i b+ä t+u	Rhythmic Law

	X X X X X			
Postcyclic	r i b+ä	—	—	Änt-Allomorphy (47)
			X X X X X X	
	—	—	r i b+ä t	Stray Erasure

(49) štúdi+um 'study'—študij+n+ý (Adj.)
múze+um 'museum'—múzej+n+ý (Adj.)
Jude+a 'Judea'—judej+sk+ý (Adj.)
rádi+o 'radio'—rádij+k+o (dimin.)
Ázi+a 'Asia'—ázij+sk+ý (Adj.), Ázij+k+a 'Asian' (N, fem.)

The [j] cannot be present in the underlying representation. This is documented by the fact that Glide Shortening (2/27), a rule that shortens vowels after /j/, does not apply in the inflected forms of the examples in (49), for instance *štúdi+um*:

(50) nom. pl.   štúdi+á
     dat. pl.   štúdi+ám
     loc. pl.   štúdi+ách

The /j/ in the examples on the right in (49) must therefore arise in the course of derivation. These examples have a common denominator in the sense that they all contain suffixes which begin with a yer (see 3.3). Could we therefore assume that the yer is turned into /j/? This might be prompted particularly by the adjectivizing suffix *-sk* //Isk//. The underlying representation of, for example, *judej+sk+ý* 'Judean' is //jude+Isk-//. Upon closer examination this hypothesis becomes untenable. It would predict that the derivation of [j] and the vocalization of the yer are mutually exclusive—that is, when one occurs, the other cannot, since they both come from the same source. This is incorrect:

(51) rádi+o 'radio'—rádij+k+o (dimin.)—rádij+ok (gen. pl.)
     Ázi+a 'Asia'—Ázij+k+a 'Asian' (N, fem.)—Ázij+ok (gen. pl.)

The examples on the right in (51) indicate that the occurrence of [j] and the vocalization of the yer may coincide. The [j] must therefore come from insertion and not from an underlying yer. The environment of the rule is that of a vowel followed by a yer (the circle round the vowel denotes a floating segment, that is, a yer):

(52) Yer Hiatus $\emptyset \rightarrow j / V — \text{Ⓥ}$

Perhaps our statement is too strong, and /j/ is simply inserted between two vowels, regardless of whether one of them is a yer or not?[14] But that this is not true is shown by contrasts such as the following:

(53) Ázi+a 'Asia'—Ázi+e (gen. sg.)—Ázij+ec 'Asian' (N, masc.), where
     -ec has a yer; compare the gen. sg. Ázij+c+a

The crucial forms here are the gen. sg. *Ázi+e* and the personal noun *Ázij+ec*. Only the latter has /j/, yet in surface terms the context is identical: *i* followed by *e*. Yer Hiatus must therefore apply at the stage at which the yer of *-Ec* in *Ázij+ec* has not yet been vocalized. Reference to a yer in (52) is thus crucial.

---

[14] In some dialects of Slovak there is indeed a hiatus rule that inserts [j] between two vowels one of which is *i*. This, however, is a purely surface phenomenon and it has nothing to do with our rule of Yer Hiatus. First, Yer Hiatus is true of all dialects, whereas Surface *j*-Insertion applies only in some dialects. (Surface *j*-Insertion is disapproved of by Král' 1988.) Second, the /j/ from Yer Hiatus must be inserted prior to Glide Shortening since it shortens the vocalized and lengthened yer in the gen. pl. *Ázij+ok* (N, fem.). As shown by the data in (50), Surface *j*-Insertion does not have this effect. It must therefore apply after Glide Shortening. Third, Surface *j*-Insertion would not be able to account for the [j] in words such as *múzej+n+ý* 'museum' (Adj.), since the underlying representation here has no *i*. As pointed out in section 3.3 and earlier in this chapter, the adjectivizing *-n* is //En// and hence *múzej+n+ý* has the representation //múze+En-//.

In (54) we give a few sample derivations. Our examples are the words *Ázi+e* (gen. sg.), *Ázij+k+a* (N, fem., nom. sg.; the *-Ok* suffix, see 51), *Ázij+ec* (N, masc., nom. sg.), and *Ázij+c+a* (gen. sg.). Recall that the nom. sg. of masculine nouns is a yer.

(54)

	UR	ázi+e	ázi+Ok+a	ázi+Ec+U	ázi+Ec+a	
	Cycle 2	ázi+e	ázi+Ok	ázi+Ec	ázi+Ec	
		—	ázij+Ok	ázij+Ec	ázij+Ec	Yer Hiatus (52)
		—	—	—	—	Yer Voc. (13)
	Cycle 3		ázij+Ok+a	ázij+Ec+U	ázij+Ec+a	
			—	—	—	Yer Hiatus
			—	ázij+ec+U	—	Yer Vocaliz.
		—	ázij+k+a	ázij+ec	ázij+c+a	Stray Erasure

In the next section and in Chapter 6 (section 6.8) we demonstrate that Yer Vocalization is a cyclic rule. Yer Hiatus interacts with Yer Vocalization and hence it must also be cyclic.

5.8. SUMMARY: THE PREFIXES

We summarize our discussion by showing that evidence for postulating yers in stems is also drawn from the alternations of vowels in prefixes. Consider the following examples:

(55) od/odo: od+plat+i+t' 'pay back'—odo+hr+at' 'play back'
roz/rozo: roz+plak+a+t' 'weep'—rozo+dn+i+t' 'to dawn'
pod/podo: pod+pál+i+t' 'burn'—podo+tk+nú+t' 'mention'
z/zo: z+mraz+i+t' 'freeze'—zo+sch+nú+t' 'dry up'
v/vo: v+pad+nú+t' 'fall into'—vo+pcha+t' 'to stick'

The vowel–zero alternations indicate that the prefixes end in a yer. The prefix yer vocalizes before the yer of the root. That the root has a yer can in most cases be shown independently. Thus, in the first two examples in (55) the roots are nouns and they themselves show vowel–zero alternations: *hr+a* 'play' (fem., nom. sg.)—*hier* (gen. pl.), *deň* 'day' (masc., nom. sg.) —*dň+a* (gen. sg.), etc.

Given that the prefixes end in yers, we can now use them as corroborating evidence for postulating yers in the roots. For example, in section 5.6 above we established that the root *pä*, as in *na+pä+t'* 'strain', had a yer (see 38). The evidence came from the *ä*–zero alternation in *na+pä+t'* 'strain'—*na+pn+em* 'I strain'. This conclusion is now corroborated by the behaviour of the prefix *od-*:

(56) odo+pä+t' 'undo'—odo+pn+em 'I undo'—odo+pín+aj+ú 'they undo'
(DI)—odo+pín+a+t' 'undo' (DI, *j* deleted before a consonant by
rule (4) from Chapter 3)

The alternations in (56) sum up our discussion of the yers since they illustrate the operation of all the major rules discussed in this chapter. In (57)
we look at a partial derivation of the first three forms in (56). We consider
cycles 2 and 3, as only these cycles are relevant. As was the case previously, long vowels are represented as two skeletal slots.

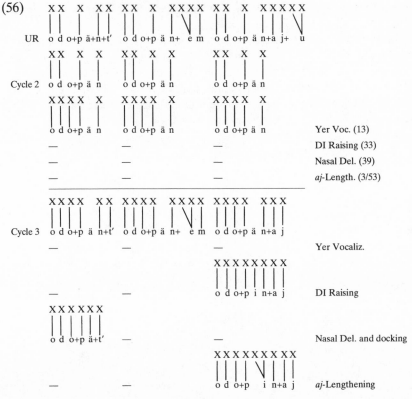

From the point of view of the Slavist it is interesting to note that in
Slovak, by contrast with Polish and Russian, prefixes do not present any
problem for cyclic derivation.[15] The order of phonological rules is in perfect agreement with the order of phonological operations; in particular,

[15] This is not to say that the phonological behaviour of prefixes is always straightforward.
In fact, many prefix-plus-stem structures behave irregularly. For instance, it has been pointed
out to me by Andrew Spencer that *odo+pínat'* 'undo' has an alternative (now dated) form
od+pínat' in which, exceptionally, the prefix yer does not surface. However, irregularities
of this type are a problem for any theory and they are in no way enhanced by Lexical
Phonology. Incidentally, the surfacing of the yer in certain prefixes is also due to a rule that
is independent of Yer Vocalization. We discuss this rule in 9.1.

prefixation comes before inflectional suffixation. In Polish the situation is more complex. The forms corresponding to those in (57) are *od+pią+ć* 'undo', *ode+pn+ę* 'I undo', *od+pin+aj+ą* 'they undo' (DI). The yer of the prefix vocalizes only when the yer of the root has not vocalized: *ode+pn+ę*. This creates a problem, since from the point of view of morphology prefixation precedes suffixation, while from the point of view of phonology prefixes can be processed only after the cycle 'root plus suffixation'. It is in this cycle that the rules corresponding to the Slovak Nasal Deletion and DI Raising apply, thereby blocking Yer Vocalization from applying to the prefixes on the next cycle (see Rubach 1984 for an analysis).

The derivation in (57) closes our discussion of the yers. It has demonstrated that the yers form a complex but a regular system in the grammar of Slovak. On the theoretical side the yers illustrate the advantages of operating with three-dimensional representations. In particular, they corroborate the concept of a floating melody segment. We shall return to the problem of the yers in the next chapter.

6

SKELETON–SYLLABLE INTERACTION

In this chapter we look at the interaction between the skeletal and the syllabic tiers. On the descriptive side we deal with various lengthening and shortening rules. We conclude that these rules must be stated in terms of the relations between the X slots and the nucleus (N) and that they are independent of the melodic tier. This provides strong motivation for three-dimensional representations. We also demonstrate the superiority of Lexical Phonology over the traditional *SPE* paradigm. Evidence comes from the classic syndrome of behaviour: derived-environment application, reference to lexical information, and cyclic derivation. The latter property is illustrated most clearly by the Rhythmic Law and its interaction with Yer Vocalization. The analysis shows how ordering paradoxes can be resolved and how lexical properties of rules can be derived from ordering, a result that can be obtained in the version of Lexical Phonology which assumes the subtheory of blocks of rules.

In section 1 we present the data and draw basic generalizations. Section 2 deals with the problem of representation. Section 3 is a discussion of Diphthongization as well as the status of diphthongs in Slovak phonology. Sections 4 and 5 summarize the results that can be obtained by using the paradigm of Lexical Phonology.

6.1. DATA AND BASIC GENERALIZATIONS

In this section we review all rule-governed productive patterns of alternation which involve either lengthening or shortening of syllable nuclei.[1] Some of these rules have been mentioned before, others are new. For clarity of discussion we have so far used only vowels as examples for lengthening/shortening. However, in this regard diphthongs and syllabic liquids behave exactly like vowels.

As explained in Chapter 2, the lengthened /e, o, ä/ diphthongize. We repeat the rule below:

(1) Diphthongization é, ó, ä́ → ie, uo, ia

---

[1] For example, there is shortening before the agentive suffix -ač: trúb+i+t' 'play the trumpet'—trub+ač, pod+pál+i+t' 'set fire to'—pod+pal+ač. However, Pauliny (1968: 112) observes that the rule applies only to older words. Newer formations systematically resist the rule, for instance fúk+a+t' 'blow'—fúk+ač, viaz+a+t' 'bind'—viaz+ač. Such lexically governed rules that are in the process of dying out and are limited to a handful of words will not be discussed here.

On the other hand, the diphthongs /ie, uo, ia/ lose their onglide and become [e, o, a] when they are shortened.

Slovak has a fully developed system of long and short liquids. In an exact parallel to vowels and diphthongs, length relations in liquids are either rule-governed or underlying. The latter case is illustrated in (2):

(2) *a.* short: dlh 'debt', pln+ý 'full', tlst+ý 'fat', tlm+i+t' 'to silence';
      krv 'blood', krk 'neck', vrch 'summit', srn+a 'deer'

   b. long: kĺb 'joint', plz+nu+t' 'get dyed', hĺb+av+a 'depth',
      vy+bĺk+nu+t' 'catch fire'; pŕhl+i+t' 'burn', hŕb+a 'pile',
      z+hŕk+nu+t' 'fall down'

In what follows we shall exemplify length relations in the three parallel classes of nuclei: vowels, diphthongs, and liquids. However, phonological rules will be stated informally by reference to vowels only, since, as we show in section 6.2, such statements generalize easily to diphthongs and liquids. We begin with the class of lengthening rules.

6.1.1. **Lengthening**

Three types of environment can be distinguished in lengthening rules: purely morphological, mixed morphological and phonological, and phonological. We discuss them in this order.

6.1.1.1. *Morphological environments*

Recall that in Chapter 3 we posited two rules of vowel lengthening before the infinitive suffix -*t'*: *e*-Lengthening (3) and *u*-Lengthening (36). We argued that in spite of the common environment the two rules must be regarded as distinct. This conclusion follows from different orderings: *e*-Lengthening applies after Postvocalic *j*-Deletion (3/4) and the Rhythmic Law (2/26), while *u*-Lengthening is ordered before both of these rules. Additionally, *e*-Lengthening provides inputs to Diphthongization (here: *é* → *ie*). To save space we shall not repeat these rules here. For discussion the reader is referred to sections 3.1.2 and 3.1.9.

A third rule of lengthening in Chapter 3 is *aj*-Lengthening (53), which applies to derived imperfectives. We complement the discussion in section 3.1.12 by adducing examples that illustrate the rise of diphthongs and long liquids. The forms on the right are derived imperfectives: the infinitive and the 3rd pl. of the present tense.

(3) *a.* od+beh+nú+t' 'run away'—od+bieh+a+t' //-bey+aj-//, od+bieh+aj+ú
   za+men+i+t' 'exchange'—za+mieň+a+t' //-men+i+aj-//,
      za+mieň+aj+ú
   o+kad+i+t' 'scent'—o+kiadz+a+t' //o+käd+i+aj-//, o+kiadz+aj+ú
   čľap+nú+t' 'make a noise'—čliap+a+t' //čľ'äp+aj-//, čliap+aj+ú
   pre+glg+nú+t' 'swallow'—pre+glg+a+t' //-glg+aj-//, pre+glg+aj+ú

b. na+pl̥n+i+t' 'fill up'—na+pĺń+a+t' //-pln+i+aj-//, na+pĺń+aj+ú
pre+vr̥h+nú+t' 'turn over'—pre+vŕh+a+t' //-vr̥ɣ+aj-//, pre+vŕh+aj+ú
vy+str̥č+i+t' 'stick out'—vy+stŕč+a+t' //-strk+i+aj-//, vy+stŕč+aj+ú

The 3rd pl. forms in (3) show that the DI suffix is *-aj*. In the infinitive the
j is deleted by Postvocalic *j*-Deletion (3/4). The verbs in (3) are either
C-verbs (see *n*-verbs in 3.1.9) or *i*-verbs. The addition of *-aj* in the latter
class of stems creates a vowel configuration that triggers *j*-Insertion and
Iotation, rules (40) and (41) in Chapter 4. Finally, *ä*-Backing (2/13)
conceals the fact that in words such as *o+kad+i+t'* 'incense' (perfective)
the surface [a] derives from the underlying //ä//. Recall that *ä*-Backing
turns //ä// into [a] after [–labial] segments. A sample derivation of
o+kiadz+a+t' 'incense' (DI) and *na+pĺń+a+t'* 'fill up' sums our discussion:
see (4). Both are *i*-stems (compare (3) above). We omit the prefix cycle.

(4) UR (o+)käd+i+aj+t' (na+)pln+i+aj+t'

Cycle 2	käd+i	pln+i	WFR: Verbalization
	—	—	*j*-Insertion (4/35)
	—	—	Vowel Deletion (3/8)
	—	—	*aj*-Lengthening (3/53)
	käd'+i	pln'+i	Coronal Palataliz. (4/17)
	—	—	Iotation (4/41)
	—	—	Affrication (4/3)
	—	—	Dentalization (4/44)
	—	—	Postvocalic *j*-Del. (3/4)
	—	—	Diphthongization (1)
Cycle 3	käd'+i+aj	pln'+i+aj	WFR: DI
	käd'j+i+aj	pln'j+i+aj	*j*-Insertion
	käd'j+aj	pln'j+aj	Vowel Deletion
	kä́d'j+aj	pĺn'j+aj	*aj*-Lengthening
	—	—	Coronal Palatalization
	kä́ḍ'j+aj	—	Iotation
	kä́ʒ'j+aj	—	Affrication
	kä́ʒj+aj	—	Dentalization
	—	—	Postvocalic *j*-Deletion
	kiaʒj+aj	—	Diphthongization
Cycle 4	kiaʒj+aj+t'	pĺn'j+aj+t'	WFR: infinitive
	kiaʒj+a+t'	pĺn'j+a+t'	only Postvocalic
			j-Deletion can apply

The derivation is completed by applying a postcyclic rule of *j*-
Simplification, which we discuss in 8.2.

Looking at *o+kiadz+a+t'* in (4) we notice that the surface [ia] is derived
by Diphthongization from the front /ä́/ rather than from the back /á/.

This, however, is no more than an assumption. We may interpret the verb root as an underlying //ä// since all the surface forms can be derived by independently motivated rules. Recall that the evidence for ä-Backing in Chapter 2 was based primarily on distributional facts: [ä] is found phonetically only after labials. We repeat the rule in (5):

(5) ä-Backing   ä → a / [–lab] —

Given this rule we may safely assume that *o+kiadz+a+t'* has an underlying //ä//. The surface [a] in the diphthong [ia] as well as in the perfective form *o+kad+i+t'* which does not undergo lengthening can be derived by rule (5). Deriving the diphthong [ia] from /ä́/ certainly makes more sense than deriving it from /á/, since it is more natural for a front onglide [i] to develop before a front vowel than before a back vowel. In fact, we have evidence that the onglide [u] arises before a back vowel, because the lengthened *ó* turns into [uo]. The statement of Diphthongization given in (1) can now be improved as follows:

(6) Diphthongization   é, ä́, ó → ie, iä, uo

Notice, however, that our evidence for the diphthongization of /ä́/ to [iä] is indirect. It comes from general phonological considerations. Direct evidence is provided by Numeral Lengthening. Among the inputs to this rule there are also words with an underlying //ä// that is found directly on the surface in the non-lengthened forms:

(7) pät' 'five'—piat+i 'fifth'
    devät' 'nine'—deviat+i 'ninth'
    desat' 'ten'—desiat+i 'tenth'
    šest' 'six'—šiest+i 'sixth'
    osem 'eight'—ôsm+i 'eighth'

Both *pät'* and *desat'* contain an underlying //ä//, but in the latter word this fact is masked by ä-Backing. The lengthening rule is as follows:

(8) Numeral Lengthening V → V́ / —]ORDINAL NUMERAL

That rule (8) must be ordered before the Rhythmic Law can be deduced both from exceptional formations such as *tret+í* 'third' (compare *tri* 'three') and, more generally, from the fact that ordinal numerals take an adjectival declension. The *i* in *piat+i* 'fifth' is thus underlyingly long, as in *cudz+í* 'foreign' (see 3.2.2).

Yet another lengthening rule operates before the diminutive suffix *-ik*:

(9) vlak 'train'—vláč+ik, znak 'sign'—znáč+ik, pluh 'plough'—plúž+ik,
    puk 'bud'—púč+ik;
    človek 'man'—človieč+ik, sneh 'snow'—sniež+ik, krok 'step'—
    krôč+ik, most 'bridge'—môst+ik;
    hrb 'hill'—hŕb+ik, krk 'neck'—kŕč+ik, vlk 'wolf'—vĺč+ik

A closer examination of the data reveals that the lengthening suffix is itself long. This can be deduced, on the one hand, from words such as *ps+ík*[2] 'dog', where *-ík* has no chance to shorten since, by contrast with (9), no long nucleus precedes. On the other hand, the long *-ík* is found in words which are exceptions to lengthening, such as *chlap+ík* 'man', *les+ík* 'forest', and *meč+ík* 'match'. The diminutive suffix is thus underlyingly long. The lengthening rule is now given in (10):

(10) *ík*-Lengthening V → V́ / — ík

The derivation of *vláč+ik* 'train' is therefore as given in (11) (see (9) above).

(11) vlak+ík
    vlaṭ+ík   1st Velar Palatalization (4/7)
    vlač+ík   Affrication (4/3)
    vláč+ík   *ík*-Lengthening (10)
    vláč+ik   Rhythmic Law (2/26)

The ordering of *ík*-Lengthening before the Rhythmic Law is essential.

6.1.1.2. *Partially phonological environments*

In this section we discuss two rules whose environments are both phonological and morphological. The phonological part of the environment is the same in both cases, and it is the requirement that the syllable must be open. The rules are nevertheless different. This follows not only from the fact that the morphological environments are distinct but also, rather interestingly, from their different ordering: one rule applies before Diphthongization and the other after it. We begin with Prefix Lengthening.

A prefix vowel is lengthened when it appears in an open syllable of a noun: see (12).

(12) za+bav+i+t' 'have fun'—zá+bav+a 'fun'
    vy+plat+i+t' 'to pay'—vý+plat+a 'pay' (N)
    za medz+ou 'over the border'—zá+medz+i+e 'out' (in sport)
    za mor+om 'overseas' (Adv.)—zá+mor+i+e 'overseas countries'
    Likewise:
    vy+buch+nú+t' 'explode'—vý+buch 'explosion'
    u+trat+i+t' 'lose'—ú+trat+a 'loss'
    pre+chod+i+t' 'cross'—prie+chod 'crossing'
    pri+del+i+t' 'assign'—prí+del 'assignment'
    po+rod+i+t' 'bear'—pô+rod 'birth'
    na roh+u 'at the corner'—ná+rož+i+e 'corner space'

---

[2] The underlying representation of the root is //pEs//; that is, it contains a yer: compare *pes* (nom. sg.)—*ps+a* (gen. sg.). However, unvocalized yers do not erect a syllable and hence they cannot lengthen; see section 6.2 below.

The restriction to open syllables is necessary since the prefixes *od-*, *pod-*, *nad-*, *roz-*, *bez-*, and *ob-* never lengthen. We thus have contrasts such as the following:

(13) od+let+ie+t' 'fly away'—od+let 'departure' *versus*
     na+let+ie+t' 'fly over'—ná+let 'air raid'

The lengthening rule is in (14):

(14) Prefix Lengthening $V \rightarrow \acute{V} / — [$
     Condition: nouns

Prefix Lengthening has a considerable number of exceptions, for instance *za hranic+ou* 'abroad'—*za+hranic+a* 'foreign countries'. In fact, as pointed out to me by Andrew Spencer, it should probably be regarded as a minor rule.

The words in (12) show that the prefix vowel must be lengthened prior to Diphthongization since the lengthened *e, o* surface as [ie, uo]. In fact Prefix Lengthening is ordered even earlier. It precedes the Rhythmic Law, as is made clear by the following examples:

(15) za+brán+i+t' 'avoid'—zá+bran+a 'avoidance'
     u+tráp+i+t' 'to plague'—ú+trap+a 'plague'
     vy+rúb+a+t' 'cut out'—vý+rub (N)

A different type of rule operates in (16).

(16) *Noun*   *Adjective*
   a. degenerác+i+a 'degeneration'   degenerač+n+ý
      dispozíc+i+a 'disposal'   dispozič+n+ý
      revolúc+i+a 'revolution'   revoluč+n+ý
   b. konferenc+i+a 'conference'   konferenč+n+ý
      konstrukc+i+a 'construction'   konstrukč+n+ý
      atrakc+i+a 'attraction'   atrakč+n+ý
   c. bibliofil 'bibliophile'   bibliofíl+i+a (derived noun)
      megaloman 'megalomaniac'   megalomán+i+a (derived noun)

A comparison of (16*a*) and (16*b*) makes it clear that the lengthening is triggered by the melodic configuration: a consonant followed by *i* and by a vowel. The data in (16*c*) show that lengthening takes place under suffixation. This is strengthened by the observation that the rule does not operate morpheme-internally: for example, the *e* of *pediater* 'paediatrician' does not lengthen (*ia* is a sequence of vowels and not a diphthong). Consequently, the lengthening rule is cyclic:

(17) *CiV*-Lengthening $V \rightarrow \acute{V} / — C i V$

The interest of (17) lies in the fact that lengthening does not lead to diphthongization:

(18) hyster+ik 'hysterical person'—hystér+i+a 'hysteria'
kavaler+ist+a 'cavalryman'—kavalér+i+a 'cavalry'
histor+ik 'historian'—histór+i+a 'history'
kolon+ist+a 'colonist'—kolón+i+a 'colony'

The rule must therefore be ordered after Diphthongization. It should also be noted that *CiV*-Lengthening has a number of exceptions, for instance *komis+i+a* 'committee', *izotop+i+a* 'isotopy'.

The reader may have noticed that *CiV*-Lengthening affects words which from the etymological point of view are borrowings. This, however, is of little interest. On the one hand, in most borrowings length is an unpredictable property. On the other hand, etymologically foreign words are well integrated into the system of Slovak. We substantiate this point in 6.2 below.

6.1.1.3. *Phonological environments*

In this section we consider a number of diagnostic suffixes which trigger lengthening. A common factor of these suffixes is the presence of a yer. Consequently, we propose that the lengthening before these suffixes should be expressed in phonological rather than in morphological terms. We then analyse a case for which a phonological explanation is no longer available.

Lengthening is triggered by both inflectional and derivational suffixes. We begin in (19) with the gen. pl. of feminine and neuter nouns. The second word of each pair is in the gen. pl.

(19) *a. Feminine nouns*

hal+a 'hall'—hál
par+a 'steam'—pár
slin+a 'saliva'—slín
ryb+a 'fish'—rýb
ruk+a 'hand'—rúk
pokut+a 'repentance'—pokút
žen+a 'woman'—žien
včel+a 'bee'—včiel
noh+a 'leg'—nôh
šop+a 'shed'—šôp
žab+a 'frog'—žiab
pät+a 'heel'—piat
slz+a 'tear'—sĺz
črt+a 'feature'—čŕt

b. Neuter nouns

lan+o 'rope'—lán
blat+o 'mud'—blát
piv+o 'beer'—pív
koryt+o 'trough'—korýt
bruch+o 'belly'—brúch
put+o 'chain'—pút
čel+o 'forehead'—čiel
teles+o 'body'—telies
kol+o 'circle'—kôl
lon+o 'lap'—lôn
čar+o 'magic'—čiar
mäs+o 'meat'—mias
jablk+o 'apple'—jabĺk
zrn+o 'grain'—zŕn

Some exceptions should be noted, for instance *katastrof+a* 'catastrophe' —*katastrof* (gen. pl.), *boler+o* 'bolero'—*boler* (gen. pl.).

Lengthening before the nom. sg. yer of masculine nouns is limited to a small class of words; that is, the majority of the masc. sg. forms do not undergo the rule.[3] Below we look at the regular cases. The second word in each pair is the gen. sg. form:

(20) mráz 'frost'—mraz+u, kôň 'horse'—koň+a, vôl 'ox'—vol+a, kôš 'basket'—koš+a, stôl 'table'—stol+a, nôž 'knife'—nož+a, chlieb 'bread'—chleb+a

Vowels are lengthened also before the nom. sg. yer of masculine adjectives (the so-called 'short form'). We thus have contrasts such as the following (note that the feminine nom. sg. ending is -a):

(21) rad+a 'pleased' (fem.)—rád (masc.)
     sam+a 'alone' (fem.)—sám (masc.)

Lengthening in derivational morphology is illustrated most clearly by the diminutive suffixes which begin with a yer (see 3.3). In (22) we give the base form followed by the diminutive in two different cases so that the yer (vowel–zero alternation) becomes clear.

(22) a. *Masculine: base form*

	Dimin. nom. sg.	*Gen. sg.*
hlas 'voice'	hlás+ok	hlás+k+a
sud 'cup'	súd+ok	súd+k+a
snop 'sheaf'	snôp+ok	snôp+k+a
kvet 'flower'	kviet+ok	kviet+k+a
chlp 'hair'	chĺp+ok	chĺp+k+a
srp 'sickle'	sŕp+ok	sŕp+k+a

b. *Feminine: base form*

	Dimin. nom. sg.	*Gen. pl.*
hlav+a 'head'	hláv+k+a	hláv+ok
košeľ'+a 'shirt'	košieľ'+k+a	košieľ'+ok
sirot+a 'orphan'	sirôt+k+a	sirôt+ok
pamät' 'memory'	pamiat+k+a	pamiat+ok
žrd' 'stick'	žŕd+k+a	žŕd+ok

c. *Neuter: base form*

	Dimin. nom. sg.	*Gen. pl.*
želez+o 'iron'	želiez+k+o	želiez+ok
plec+e 'back'	pliec+k+o	pliec+ok
hoväd+o 'beast'	hoviad+k+o	hoviad+ok

The requirement that the diminutive suffix must begin with a yer is made clear by contrasts such as *hor+a* 'forest'—*hôr+k+a* (dimin.) vs. *hor+ičk+a* (dimin.). The diminutive suffix *-Ec* behaves in a parallel fashion: see (23).

---

[3] One way of describing this fact is to assume that a yer and a zero ending are both representations of the nom. sg. The former but not the latter would then trigger lengthening.

(23) ramen+o 'shoulder'   ramien+c+e (nom. sg.)—ramien+ec (gen. pl.)
                          ramien+k+o (nom. sg.)—ramien+ok (gen. pl.)
     drev+o 'wood'   driev+c+e (nom. sg.)—driev+ec (gen. pl.)
                          driev+k+o (nom. sg.)—driev+ok (gen. pl.)
     čel+o 'forehead'   čiel+c+e (nom. sg.)—čiel+ec (gen. pl.)
                          čiel+k+o (nom. sg.)—čiel+ok (gen. pl.)

However, even though vowel lengthening before the diminutive yers is quite regular, exceptions can also be found, for instance *čln+ok* 'boat', *mäs+k+o* 'meat'.[4]

Lengthening before the adjectival suffixes //Isk// and //En// as well as before the collective nominalizing //IstEv// (see 3.3) is limited to a small class of words. Some examples are given in (24):

(24) občan 'citizen'—občian+sk+y—občian+stv+o
     mešt'an 'city-dweller'—meštian+sk+y—meštian+stv+o
     hor+a 'forest'—hôr+n+y

The suffix //-Änt//, spelled *-a/ä* and denoting young creatures, is a productive environment for lengthening (recall the discussion of this suffix in 5.6):

(25) had 'reptile'—hád'+a, hus 'goose'—hús+a, ryb+a 'fish'—rýb+ä, zver 'animal'—zvier+a, vlk 'wolf'—vĺč+a
     Exceptions: kur+a 'hen'—kur+a, and a few others

The appearance of yers in the suffixes discussed in this section (data in 19–25) makes it possible to subsume the lengthening contexts under a single environment. Schematically:

(26) Vowel Lengthening $V \rightarrow \acute{V} / — C$ yer

One or two yer suffixes are exceptions to (26). Thus, the imperative does not cause lengthening. In another context, that of the infinitive, rule (26) is no longer applicable since, we claim, the yer environment has been lost.

Consider the verbs presented in (27). The passive participle is given in the masc. nom. sg., while the past participle appears in the fem. nom. sg. (*-a* gender marker).[5] There are two options: either we posit a morphologically conditioned lengthening rule which operates in the infinitive and in the past participle, or we attempt to state the environment in phonological terms by referring to a closed syllable. Let us pursue this latter

---

[4] The diminutive suffix *-Ek* does not generally induce lengthening, for example *ryb+a* 'fish'—*ryb+k+a* (dimin.)—*ryb+iek* (gen. pl.), *much+a* 'fly'—*muš+k+a* (dimin.)—*muš+iek* (gen. pl.).

[5] The reason for giving the feminine rather than the masculine form is that in the latter a postcyclic rule of *o*-Insertion applies and obliterates the picture, for example *pás+ol* 'he grazed'. We discuss *o*-Insertion in Chapter 7.

(27) *Passive participle*   *Infinitive*   *Past participle*
     pas+en+ý   pás+t' 'graze'   pás+l+a
     nes+en+ý   nies+t' 'carry'   nies+l+a
     (pre+)mož+en+ý   môc+t' 'can'   môh+l+a
     prad+en+ý   prias+t' 'weave'   prias+l+a
     tlč+en+ý   tĺc+t' 'beat'   tĺk+l+a

option—although not much is at stake here, since, as we explain below,
the rule must be in part morphologically conditioned anyway.

(28) Closed Syllable Lengthening $V \rightarrow \acute{V} / \text{— C)}_{\sigma]}$ CLASS 1 VERBS

Some comments are in order. First, the rule is limited to Class 1 verbs (see
3.1.1), since it does not apply to, for example, *pi+t'* //*pij+t'*// 'drink' and
pad+n+em 'I fall'. Second, Closed Syllable Lengthening applies before
Diphthongization and, as we explain in 6.2 below, it is cyclic. How can we
then avoid the lengthening of the vowel in the root cycle, for example
the *a* of //pas// 'graze'? If this lengthening were permitted, not only the
infinitive and the past participle but all the conjugational forms should
show lengthening. The solution is easy if we assume with Borowsky (1986)
that a final consonant is universally extrametrical (see also 7.6 and 7.7).
Slovak is then not an exception to this generalization. The derivation of
the first example in (27) is as given in (29). We look at cycles 1 and 2 and
assume that Syllabification reapplies after every rule (see 1.3.).

(29)

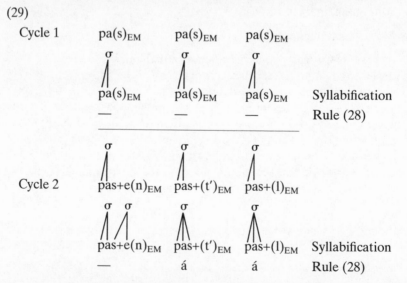

A further question is whether it would be well-advised to assume that
the infinitive suffix is //tI //, in other words that it contains a yer as it might

have done in Proto-Slavic. We could then ascribe the lengthening in the infinitive in (27) to the general rule of Vowel Lengthening (26). The answer is clearly negative. On the one hand, the lengthening does not take place in the infinitives of *i*-verbs, *a*-verbs, *ä*-verbs, and *ova*-verbs (see 3.1.1). On the other hand, if lengthening does take place in the infinitive, then it is governed by rules whose ordering is incompatible with an attempt to express them as a single generalization; compare *e*-Lengthening and *u*-Lengthening in 6.1.1.1 above. The infinitive is thus a good example illustrating the thesis that phonological environments may weaken in the course of historical development and their role may be taken over by partly or fully morphological rules.

6.1.2. Shortening

Shortening rules confirm the generalization that has emerged from the study of lengthening rules: long vowels, diphthongs, and syllabic liquids behave in exactly the same way. Another parallel concerns the environments: they can be either morphological or phonological.

6.1.2.1. *Morphological environments*

In order to save space we shall refrain from stating the particular shortening rules. Two of them have actually been stated previously: CC-Shortening (43) in 3.1.9 and *ova*-Shortening (61) in 3.1.12. While there is nothing to add to the former, the latter should be complemented by pointing out that not only long vowels but also diphthongs and liquids shorten before the DI suffix *-ova*:

(30) roz+štiep+i+t' 'split'—roz+štep+ova+t'
  pre+sviet+i+t' 'enlighten'—pre+svec+ova+t'
  po+tiah+nu+t' 'pull'—po+t'ah+ova+t'
  u+viaz+a+t' 'bind'—u+väz+ova+t'
  vy+bík+nu+t' 'fade'—vy+blk+ova+t'
  z+hŕk+nu+t' sa 'gather'—z+hrk+ova+t' sa

Attention should be drawn to *u+viaz+a+t'* 'bind'. It supports the interpretation of Diphthongization in 6.1.1.1 that the vowel corresponding to the diphthong [ia] is [ä] rather than [a].

Shortening is found also before the nominalizing *-ák* and, less regularly, before the agentive *-ár*[6] and the nominal *-ec/c*, underlying //Ec//: see (31).

---

[6] See Dvonč (1966), who lists exceptions such as *fréz+ár* 'milling cutter' and *bábk+ár* 'doll-maker'. These words are doubly exceptional since neither *ár*-Shortening nor the Rhythmic Law applies. Dvonč notes, however, that these forms tend to be regularized in favour of the Rhythmic Law, that is, the innovating pronunciations are *fréz+ar* and *bábk+ar*.

(31) *a.* túl+a+t' sa 'wander'—tul+ák 'wanderer'
         múdr+y 'wise'—mudr+ák 'sage'
         biel+y 'white'—bel+ák 'white hare'
         vŕt+a+t' 'drill'—vrt+ák 'driller'
     b. vín+o 'wine'—vin+ár 'wine-grower'
         múr 'wall'—mur+ár 'bricklayer'
         džbán 'pot'—džban+ár 'potter'
         hviezd+a 'star'—hvezd+ár 'astronomer'
         liek 'medicine'—lek+ár 'physician'
         drôt 'wire'—drot+ár 'tinsmith'
     c. kúp+i+t' 'buy'—kup+ec 'merchant'—kup+c+a (gen. sg.)
         Also the *-Ec* that takes the feminine declension:
            súd+i+t' 'judge'—sud+c+a 'judge' (N)
            za+stúp+i+t' 'replace'—za+stup+c+a 'deputy'
         BUT: vlád+nu+t' 'rule'—vlád+c+a 'ruler' and a few other
         exceptions

The agentive *-Ec* in (31c) is interesting in the sense that we normally have
lengthening rather than shortening before yer suffixes. The correct outputs can be derived by ordering *Ec*-Shortening after Vowel Lengthening.[7]
   Finally, shortening occurs before the comparative-degree suffix *-š*:

(32) blíz+k+y 'near'—bliž+š+í, úz+k+y 'narrow'—už+š+í, krát+k+y
     'short'—krat+š+í, ried+k+y 'rare'—red+š+í, biel+y 'white'—bel+š+í [8]

In the next section we look at the Rhythmic Law, which undoubtedly is a
purely phonological rule.

6.1.2.2. *Phonological environments: Rhythmic Law*

This is probably the best-known rule of Slovak. It has been discussed in
detail by descriptive grammarians, for instance by Peciar (1946), Dvonč
(1955, 1963), Pauliny (1968), and many others. The Rhythmic Law has
also found its way into the generative literature: Isačenko (1966), Browne
(1970), Kenstowicz (1972), Anderson (1974), Kenstowicz and Kisseberth
(1977, 1979), and Kenstowicz and Rubach (1987). The generalization
is that long vowels, liquids, and diphthongs shorten after long vowels,
liquids, and diphthongs. We state the rule informally in (33):

(33) Rhythmic Law $\acute{V} \rightarrow V \: / \: \acute{V}$ —

---

[7] One other suffix, the nominalizing *-Eb*, has the same effect. However, there are only
a few relevant examples: *mlát+i+t'* 'thresh'—*mlat+b+a* 'threshing', *šial+i+t'* 'lie'—*šal'+b+a*
'lie' (N), and some two or three other words.
[8] If not for the last example these data could be interpreted in a different way. Assuming
that the *-k* suffix, which is regularly deleted in the comparative degree, has a yer, as it does in
Polish, the words in (32) might be analysed as instances of Vowel Lengthening.

The Rhythmic Law is a sweeping generalization about Slovak phonology. It accounts for alternations in both inflectional and derivational morphology of all major lexical categories: adjectives, nouns, and verbs.

The declension pattern of adjectives was introduced in 3.2.2 (Tables 3*a* and 3*b*). In (34) we extend the data by adding examples with diphthongs and liquids. In order to save space we present only the masculine and feminine nom. sg. and the masculine dat. sg. of adjectives.

(34) *Masculine*   *Feminine*   *Masc. dat. sg.*

     mal+ý 'small'   mal+á   mal+ému

                   versus

     čír+y 'clear'   čír+a   čír+emu

     čiern+y 'dark'   čiern+a   čiern+emu

     priam+y 'direct'   priam+a   priam+emu

     mĺkv+y 'silent'   mĺkv+a   mĺkv+emu

In the case of nouns the relevant examples are found in the feminine and in the neuter. The declension patterns were discussed in Chapter 3 (sections 3.2.3.2 and 3.2.3.3). In (35) we show the dat. pl. and the loc. pl. of feminine nouns.

(35) *Nom. sg.*   *Dat. pl.*   *Loc. pl.*

     par+a 'steam'   par+ám   par+ách

                versus

     lúk+a 'meadow'   lúk+am   lúk+ach

     riek+a 'river'   riek+am   riek+ach

     kôr+a 'surface'   kôr+am   kôr+ach

     vŕb+a 'willow'   vŕb+am   vŕb+ach

In the class of neuter nouns the relevant cases are the nom. pl., dat. pl., and loc. pl.: see (36).

(36) *Nom. sg.*   *Nom. pl.*   *Dat. pl.*   *Loc. pl.*

     zlat+o 'gold'   zlat+á   zlat+ám   zlat+ách

                    versus

     vín+o 'wine'   vín+a   vín+am   vín+ach

     miest+o 'place'   miest+a   miest+am   miest+ach

In the verbal system the extension vowels *é* and *í*, the 3rd pl. ending -*ú*, as well as the *á* from *aj*-Coalescence shorten in accordance with the Rhythmic Law (see 3.1.8). In (37) we give the forms with the extension vowel *é* and the 3rd pl. ending -*ú*. The effect of the Rhythmic Law on the extension vowel *í* and the *á* from *aj*-Coalescence is illustrated in (38):

(37) *1st sg.*   *3rd pl.*
      plet+iem 'I weave'   plet+ú
      versus
      driem+em 'I sleep'   driem+u
      môž+em 'I can'   môž+u
      viaž+em 'I bind'   viaž+u

---

(38) *a.* pros+ím 'I ask' *vs.* chvál+im 'I praise', ciel+im 'I aim'
      b. vol+á+m 'I call' *vs.* rát+a+m 'I count', siah+a+m 'I reach'

In derivational morphology the Rhythmic Law is seen to operate with the nominalizing suffix -*ník* in (39a) and the diminutive -*ík* in (39b). As pointed out in 6.1.1.1 above, -*ík* triggers lengthening and then shortens by the Rhythmic Law. To keep these two facts apart, in (39b) we use examples which have long nuclei at the underlying level; that is, length in these is independent of -*ík*. The word *chleb+ík* 'bread' given for comparison is an exception to *ík*-Lengthening.

(39) *a.* Agentive -*ník*:
         hut+a 'steel works'—hut+ník

         versus

         čalún 'wallpaper'—čalún+nik
         montáž 'assembling'—montáž+nik
         papier 'paper'—papier+nik
         požiar 'fire'—požiar+nik

      b. Diminutive -*ík*:
         chleb 'bread'—chleb+ík

         versus

         múr 'wall'—múr+ik
         džbán 'pot'—džbán+ik
         chliev 'pigsty'—chliev+ik
         galôn 'bow'—galôn+ik
         tŕň 'thorn'—tŕn+ik

The Rhythmic Law confirms the earlier-stated generalization that long vowels, diphthongs, and long liquids behave in a parallel fashion. Like other shortening rules, the Rhythmic Law is not free of exceptions. Some of them are genuine, others are only apparent. Amongst the genuine exceptions we have, for example, the gen. pl. ending -*í*, the 3rd pl. present desinence -*ia*, the present gerund -*iac*, and the agentive -*ár* (de Bray 1980):

(40) básn+í 'nonsense' (gen. pl.), kúp+ia 'they buy', súd+iac 'judging', mliek+ár 'milkman'

Dvonč (1963) adds that in the gen. pl. of feminine and neuter nouns some words show variation where one of the forms is a violation of the Rhythmic Law, for instance *sídl+o* 'trap'—*sídel* ~ *sídiel*. However, side by side with these legitimate exceptions descriptive grammars adduce a number of what we may characterize as pseudo-exceptions. Thus, to return to de Bray (1980), the following are listed next to the cases in (40):

(41) *a.* fem. instr. sg. *-ou*: krásn+ou brán+ou 'beautiful gate';
　　 b. a complete declension of adjectives on the *páv+í* pattern: see the declension of *had+í* in Table 3*b* in 3.2.2;
　　 c. certain neuter nouns such as *liatie* 'pouring' and *prútie* 'twigs' which belong to the *čítanie* declension pattern: see Table 9 in 3.2.3.3;
　　 d. the verbalizing suffix *-ie* in words such as *zmúdriet'* 'become wise'.[9]

We shall show that these are not true exceptions.

6.2. REPRESENTATION: *SPE* VERSUS LEXICAL PHONOLOGY

In this section we discuss the interpretation of lengthening and shortening rules in the framework of the *SPE* theory and in the framework of Lexical Phonology. We conclude that only the latter is compatible with the data. We then present a compelling argument for three-dimensional representations in phonology.[10] As we shall shortly see, the distinction between diphthongs and vowel sequences is crucial for our arguments. To facilitate the reading of this section, we shall adopt the convention of putting a dot between vowel sequences whenever ambiguity could arise. Thus, *dialekt* 'dialect', which is trisyllabic, will be represented as *di.alekt*, while *diabol* 'devil', which is disyllabic, will be left as it is in the orthography.

6.2.1. The *SPE* analysis

The *SPE* analysis expresses a parallel between long vowels and liquids on the one hand and diphthongs on the other by assuming that there are

---

[9] To add one more case, words such as *tisíc+násobný* 'thousandfold' and *tisíc+krát* 'thousand times' quoted as exceptions by de Bray (1980) can be straightforwardly accounted for by assuming that the Rhythmic Law does not apply across constituents of a compound.
[10] This section in part summarizes and in part extends and revises the arguments presented in Kenstowicz and Rubach (1987).

no underlying diphthongs in Slovak (Kenstowicz 1972, Kenstowicz and Kisseberth 1979). Rather, all diphthongs are derived from long vowels by Diphthongization (6). Further, diphthongization is ordered after the Rhythmic Law so that the rhythmic shortening can bleed Diphthongization. This is in fact the only possible ordering. Otherwise the consequences would be disastrous. Every shortening/lengthening rule would have to refer to disjoint environments: a long vowel or a diphthong. In the case of the Rhythmic Law itself this disjunction would have to be stated twice: in the input and in the environment. In short, there would be enormous redundancies in the statement of a number of rules. Furthermore, the rise/ loss of a diphthong would have to be treated as two formally distinct operations: one affecting length and the other a diphthongal onglide. This step is obviously incorrect since the parallel between long vowels and diphthongs, patently the same type of alternation, would be lost to sight. In sum, the *SPE* theory assumes that all diphthongs arise from Diphthongization, which applies after all shortening rules.

The *SPE* framework offers two possible representations of length: either by means of the feature [long], an option adopted by Kenstowicz (1972), or by gemination, an option exploited by Isačenko (1968). Neither representation is particularly fortunate.

As pointed out by Kenstowicz and Rubach (1987), using the feature [long] would require that Diphthongization should encompass two simultaneous operations: an onglide is inserted and at the same time the vowel is shortened. This difficulty can be avoided if long vowels are interpreted as geminates. Then, *é* is /ee/ and Diphthongization is a simple feature change in the first member of the geminate: /ee/ → [ie]. However, lengthening and shortening become hopelessly difficult to state. Lengthening is then an insertion of an identical segment. Thus, *slín*, the gen. pl. of *slin+a* 'saliva', is transformed from /slin/ into [sliin]. But *vín*, the gen. pl. of *vín+o* 'wine' (underlying long vowel), would also undergo the same rule, which is incorrect: /viin/ → [viiin]. The generalization is that only underlying short vowels can lengthen. This is easily expressed by the feature [long] as lengthening is vacuous for words that are [+long] at the input to the rule. With the geminate theory we must look at the surrounding context in order to know if the lengthening should take place. This is not a simple procedure either, since Slovak permits sequences of *i* and *í*, as in the gen. pl. *akci+í* 'action'. Given the geminate theory the representation is /i+ii/. Furthermore, shortening could not be understood as a rule that applies after a geminate. There are clear counterexamples, for instance *pann+ám* 'Miss' (dat. pl.), *tortill+ám* 'tortilla' (dat. pl.): the geminate *n* and *l* do not trigger the Rhythmic Law. Neither are geminate sequences inputs to the Rhythmic Law, for example *Mári+in* 'Mary's', *indivídu+um* 'individual' (pejorative).

In sum, the *SPE* analysis runs into difficulty with the representation of length. However, the idea that all diphthongs derive from underlying long vowels is insightful. With the ordering of Diphthongization after lengthening/shortening rules, we arrive at a single and elegant analysis. Could we then assume that, once the problem of the representation of length is solved by introducing the X-skeleton, the *SPE* analysis becomes flawless? Hardly. As we show in the next section, the correct framework is that of Lexical Phonology.

6.2.2. Lexical Phonology

In this section we demonstrate that Diphthongization is a cyclic rule in the sense that it applies exclusively in derived environments. This raises the question of how to represent diphthongs, since morpheme-internal diphthongs must be underlying. We pursue this question in the next section.

The problem with the *SPE* analysis is that it is limited to the etymologically native vocabulary. Such a limitation was often assumed as perfectly natural in the 1960s and 1970s. However, even then some morphemes would have to be analysed as exceptions. For example, in the native *dcér+a* 'daughter' as well as in the adjectival masc. gen. sg. *-ého*, masc. dat. sg. *-ému*, neuter nom. sg. *-é*, and non-virile nom. pl. *-é* the long vowel does not diphthongize. If we expand the data base to include etymological loanwords, the number of exceptions to Diphthongization rises to literally hundreds of lexical items. Long mid vowels are perfectly stable and they do not show any symptoms of a tendency towards diphthongization:

(42) trén 'military carriages', bazén 'pool', afér+a 'affair', krém 'cream', Grék 'Greek', majonéz+a 'mayonnaise', tón 'tone', perón 'platform', gól 'goal', póz+a 'pose', mór+a 'mora', mód+a 'fashion', chór 'space near the organ in church'

An *SPE* type of explanation—that these words have not been integrated into the grammatical system of Slovak and hence do not undergo Diphthongization—must be rejected. There are no clues, short of etymological studies, to indicate that these words can be identified as borrowings. Thus, assigning them to a special lexical class would be equivalent to treating them as exceptions. This follows from two types of observation. First, these words are composed entirely of segments that appear in the native part of the Slovak lexicon. In many cases they also conform to the canonical shape of native roots. Second, by any imaginable test, morphological or phonological, they are fully integrated into the grammatical system of Slovak.

Morphological integration manifests itself in the fact that, on the one hand, these words have the same inflection as the native words (43a) and, on the other hand, they may undergo all kinds of native derivational affixation (43b).

(43) *Etymologically foreign*   *Etymologically native*

a. tón 'tone'—tón+y (pl.)   dom 'house'—dom+y
b. krém 'cream'   obed 'dinner'
   krém+ov+ý (Adj.)   obed+ov+ý (Adj.)
   krém+ova+t' (V)   obed+ova+t' 'dine'
   balón 'balloon'   stôl 'table'
   balón+ov+ý (Adj.)   stol+ov+ý (Adj.)
   balón+ik (dimin.)   stol+ík (dimin.)
   Švéd 'Swede'   Čech 'Czech'
   švéd+sk+y (Adj.)   čes+k+ý
   švéd+č+in+a 'Swedish'   češ+t+in+a 'Czech'
   režisér 'director'   pis+ár 'writer'
   režisér+k+a (fem.)   pis+ár+k+a (fem.)
   režisér+sk+y (Adj.)   pis+ár+sk+y (Adj.)
   režisér+stv+o 'directing'   pis+ár+stv+o 'writing'
   vagón 'carriage'   hlad 'hunger'
   vagón+ov+ý (Adj.)   hlad+ov+ý (Adj.)
   vagón+ova+t' (V)   hlad+ova+t' (V)

Evidence for phonological integration of loanwords is no less compelling. It is seen both at the level of segmental representation and in the sphere of phonological rules. With regard to the former the word *tégel'* 'crucible' is a particularly telling example. The second *é* has developed into a yer, yet the first *é* remains undiphthongized; compare the gen. sg. *tégl'+a: e*–zero alternation, hence the underlying representation is //tégEl'//. Even more intriguing is the observation that etymological borrowings both trigger and undergo all shortening rules, exactly like native words. Our examples in (44a) are the loanwords *protéz+a* 'crutch', *póz+a* 'pose', *sapér+sk+y* 'miner' (Adj.), *európ+sk+y* 'European', *kupón* 'coupon', *balón* 'balloon', *lén+o* 'fief', and *likér* 'liqueur'. They are accompanied by native words with short vowels, which makes it clear that the affixes have long vowels in the underlying representation. The glosses for the native words are as follows: *skaz+a* 'flaw', *dvor+sk+ý* 'courtly', *chleb* 'bread', and *robot+ník* 'worker'.

(44) *a.* Rhythmic Law
      (i) noun inflection
          dat. pl.: protéz+am, póz+am *vs.* skaz+ám
          loc. pl.: protéz+ach, póz+ach *vs.* skaz+ách
      (ii) adjective inflection
          nom. sg.: sapér+sk+y, európ+sk+y *vs.* dvor+sk+ý
          gen. sg.: sapér+sk+eho, európ+sk+eho *vs.* dvor+sk+ého
          dat. sg.: sapér+sk+emu, európ+sk+emu *vs.* dvor+sk+ému

(iii) diminutive -*ík*
    kupón—kupón+ik, balón—balón+ik *vs.* chleb — chleb+ík
(iv) agentive -*ník*
    lén+o —lén+nik, likér—likér+nik *vs.* robot+ník
b. *ár*-Shortening (*ár* carries an agentive meaning)
    scén+a 'scene'—scen+ár, planét+a 'planet'—planet+ár, mili.ón
    'million'—mili.on+ár, betón 'concrete'—beton+ár
    Similarly: slovník 'dictionary' (a native word)—slovnik+ár

To summarize briefly, considerations such as segmental inventory and all kinds of morphological and phonological tests lead clearly to the conclusion that etymological borrowings have been thoroughly integrated into the system of Slovak. But then, given the *SPE* analysis, the borrowings that have long mid vowels should diphthongize. Yet, as the data in (42–4) show, they do not. A solution to this dilemma suggests itself. Diphthongization is a cyclic rule and hence it is limited to derived environments. The long vowels in (42–4) are morpheme-internal; that is, length is not derived via a phonological rule. The failure to diphthongize is now understandable. Given this result we predict that vowels in etymological borrowings should lengthen and, if they are mid, also diphthongize whenever they meet the environment of one of our lengthening rules. This prediction is borne out. In (45*a–b*) the form on the left is in the nom. sg. and the one on the right in the gen. pl. Recall that the dot represents vowel sequences (as opposed to diphthongs).

(45) *a.* kompozit+um 'compound'—kompozít
      ru.in+a 'ruin'—ru.ín
      nu.ans+a 'nuance'—nu.áns
      pyžam+a 'pyjamas'—pyžám
      mili.ard+a 'milliard'—mili.árd
   b. cigaret+a 'cigarette'—cigariet
      oper+a 'opera'—opier
      adres+a 'address'—adries
      bomb+a 'bomb'—bômb
      not+a 'note'—nôt
   c. bok 'side'—bôč+ik (dimin.)
      krok 'step'—krôč+ik (dimin.)
   d. vagón 'carriage'—vagón+ik (dimin.)
      telefón 'telephone'—telefón+ik (dimin.)

Quite intentionally we have selected as our examples in (45*a–b*) those words which seem to be recent borrowings or have a clear foreign structure, such as sequences of vowels (a generally non-Slavic phenomenon). And yet, all words behave exactly as predicted. In (45*b*) Diphthongization takes effect after Vowel Lengthening since the long vowel is derived, hence the Strict Cyclicity Constraint opens the vowel to Diphthongization, a classic instance of a cyclic application. The examples in (45c–d) confirm this conclusion. In (45c) the long vowel is derived by *ík*-Lengthening and hence it diphthongizes. However, in (45d) the *ó* is long already in the underlying representation. The length is thus not a derived property and consequently Diphthongization is blocked by the Strict Cyclicity Constraint.

Given our conclusion that Diphthongization is cyclic and consequently does not apply in non-derived environments, all instances of diphthongs in roots must be present in the underlying representation. Thus, the *SPE* analysis of *liek* 'medicine', *žiar* 'heat', and *bôb* 'bean' as underlying //lék//, //žár//, and //bób// is no longer open to us. We must assume //liek//, //žiar//, and //buob// at the underlying level.[11] The advantage is that these representations are much less abstract than those in the *SPE* analysis. However, the disadvantages are quite disastrous. We face the duplication problem outlined in the preceding section and lose one of the most significant results of our descriptive analysis: that long vowels and diphthongs behave in a parallel fashion. Fortunately, these negative repercussions of recognizing underlying diphthongs can be eliminated by assuming that length is expressed at the skeletal tier. We turn to this problem in the next section.

6.2.3. Skeletal representations

It will be recalled that with three-dimensional representations length distinctions are expressed at the skeletal tier (see 1.3). Short vowels are associated with one skeletal slot while long vowels and diphthongs are linked to two skeletal slots. In other words, complex syllable nuclei are represented as two moras since skeletal X slots are timing units. We achieve the desired effect: at the skeletal tier long vowels and diphthongs have an identical representation. A further advantage is that long liquids have the same structural representation as long vowels and diphthongs. This is a good result since the parallel between long vowels/diphthongs and the syllabic liquids described in 6.1 can now be expressed. In sum, *Grék* 'Greek', *liek* 'medicine', and *kĺb* 'joint' are represented as follows:

(46) skeleton:

This system of representation makes a prediction that the so-called floating matrices—that is, melody segments that are not associated with any X

---

[11] Actually, these representations can be considerably simplified. We sharpen the analysis in 6.3 below.

slot—cannot play a role in shortening rules since they are invisible at the skeletal tier, and shortening rules count Xs and not segmental melodies. As documented in Chapter 5, Slovak yers are precisely such floating matrices. Recall that yers vocalize—that is, receive an X slot—if followed by another yer. Otherwise they delete. The deletion of unvocalized yers is effected by Stray Erasure, which, as we demonstrate in Chapter 9, does not take place until the postlexical component. Unvocalized yers are thus present during the lexical derivation. We show in 6.8 below that the Rhythmic Law is a cyclic lexical rule. Consequently, it applies in the presence of unvocalized yers. The prediction of the skeletal representation exemplified in (46) is that vocalized yers are visible to the Rhythmic Law and unvocalized yers are not. This prediction is fully borne out.

In (47) we take complex adjectives as examples and show that vocalized yers block the Rhythmic Law. Recall that the adjectivizing -*n* is //En// at the underlying level (see 3.3):

(47) čísl+o 'number'—čísel+n+ý
    krídl+o 'wing'—krídel+n+ý
    vápn+o 'calcium'—vápen+n+ý
    pís+m+o 'letter'—pís+om+n+ý

On the other hand, unvocalized yers have no X slots and hence are invisible to the Rhythmic Law, which takes effect 'over the yer'. Again we look at the //En// adjectives:

(48) stád+o 'flock'—stád+n+y
    klík 'embryo'—klíč+n+y
    múk+a 'flour'—múč+n+y
    jód 'iodine'—jód+n+y
    epizód+a 'episode'—epizód+n+y
    mliek+o 'milk'—mlieč+n+y
    pôst 'fast'—pôst+n+y
    klb 'joint'—klb+n+y

Needless to say, the same regularity is found with all instances of yers and not only with the adjectival suffix //En//. In (49) we present a partial derivation of *čísel+n+ý* 'number' (Adj.) and *čísl+am*, the dat. pl. of *čísl+o* 'number'. Recall that the dat. pl. ending has an underlying long vowel: compare *blat+ám* 'mud'.

To summarize briefly, by introducing the skeletal tier into representation we arrive at a common parameter for the classes of segments that behave in a parallel way: long vowels, diphthongs, and long liquids. We correctly predict that unvocalized yers are invisible to shortening and hence are skipped over by the Rhythmic Law. Does the appeal to the X-skeleton provide sufficient machinery to resolve the problems that arise when the traditional linear representations are posited? At first glance

(49)

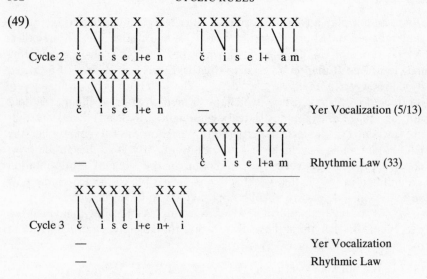

it seems that the machinery is indeed sufficient. We could now define the three classes of segments as instances of two slots linked to the melody, which is characterized by the feature set [+sonor, −nas]. (Note that [−cons] would not be enough, as liquids would be excluded.) But this is clearly incorrect. Of the many possible reasons for rejecting this proposal, let us mention only two. First, (50a–b) shows that it is not true that simply any doubling of slots with the melody [+sonor, −nas] can play a role in the Rhythmic Law. Second, (50c) demonstrates that the Rhythmic Law is sensitive to the syllable tier.

(50) *a.* kre.ol+sk+ý 'creole' (Adj.), po.et+ám 'poet' (dat. pl.), lan+ám
         'rope' (dat. pl.)
    b. múze+um 'museum', gymnázi+um 'secondary school'
    c. vý+sln+n+ý 'sunny place' (Adj.), ú+mr+t+n+ý 'dead'

Clearly a sequence of two X slots with the melody [+sonor, −nas] can neither trigger nor undergo the Rhythmic Law: compare (50a) and (50b), respectively. On the other hand, the blocking of the Rhythmic Law in (50c) must certainly be attributed to the fact that the liquid intervening between the two long vowels is syllabic. The liquid is short and consequently the final -ý follows a short and not a long nucleus: the Rhythmic Law does take effect.

We have now identified the correct parameter for the Rhythmic Law. It is a nucleus that is associated with two X slots. The Rhythmic Law looks exclusively at the relation that obtains at the interface of the skeletal and the syllabic tiers. Representations at the melodic tier are irrelevant. We quote the rule after Kenstowicz and Rubach (1987):

(51) Rhythmic Law (final)

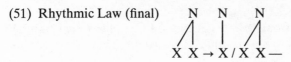

In (51) we have presented the nuclei as right-headed with a satellite slot to the left. This does justice to the fact that Slovak diphthongs are rising; that is, the component to the left is less sonorous. We shall explain later in this chapter that the segmental make-up of this component is largely predictable. Given the right-headed nuclei, shortening rules can now be construed as a deletion of the satellite slot. On the other hand, lengthening rules are the contrary operation—they add a satellite slot.

The representation of our three examples in (46) is now as given in (52). Recall that N″ is the syllable node and N′ is the coda (see 1.3).

(52)

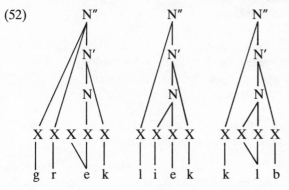

From the point of view of the Rhythmic Law the only essential relationship is between the N and the X slots. Consequently, the rule applies to the projection of syllable nuclei. This captures the observation that segments which do not belong to the nucleus (consonants in onsets and codas) are skipped by the Rhythmic Law. In (53) we look at the dat. pl. forms *téz+am* 'thesis', *riek+am* 'river', and *vŕb+am* 'willow'. The dat. pl. suffix is *-ám*. A projection of nuclei gives the representations to which the Rhythmic Law applies.

(53)

The requirement that the target and the trigger be adjacent is fulfilled in (53) by scanning the Ns.

With our conclusion that the Rhythmic Law is sensitive only to the geometric relationship between the N and the X slots, we expect that this geometry might in general play a role in the system of Slovak. Indeed it does, since it distinguishes (i) long vowels from combinations of identical vowels, (ii) diphthongs from vowel sequences, (iii) *j* plus vowel from *iV* diphthongs, and (iv) *j* plus vowel from *i* plus vowel.[12] These contrasts are exemplified in (54).

(54) *a.* long *ú, í, ó* versus *uu, ii, oo* (two syllables):
　　　　Chartúm (name)—indivídu+um 'individual' (pejorative)
　　　　kmín 'caraway'—Mári+in 'Mary's'
　　　　ozón 'ozone'—entozo+on 'parasite'
　　b. diphthong (one syllable) versus vowel sequence (two syllables):
　　　　riek+a 'river'—paci.ent 'patient'
　　　　hygiena 'hygiene'—hy.en+a 'hyena'
　　　　ziap+a+t' 'weep'—entuzi.azmus 'enthusiasm'
　　　　diabol 'devil'—di.alekt 'dialect'
　　c. *j* plus vowel versus diphthong:
　　　　jeden 'one'—kiež 'when'
　　　　jasn+ý 'bright'—čiar+a 'line'
　　　　pri+jat' 'accept'—priat' 'wish' (Král''s 1988 example)
　　d. diphthong versus vowel sequence versus *j* plus vowel:
　　　　biel+y [ie] 'white'—bi.enále [i-e] 'biennial'—objektív+n+y [je]
　　　　　'objective'
　　　　občian+sk+y [ia] 'citizen' (Adj.)—indi.an+sk+ý [i-a] 'Indian'—
　　　　vojan+sk+ý [ja] 'referring to midsummer'

We conclude that Slovak fully exploits the geometric relations between the skeleton and the syllable tier that are permitted within the framework of three-dimensional representations. The three-way contrasts in (54*d*) are particularly interesting. It will be recalled that the difference between diphthongs and vowels on the one hand and glides on the other is construed as a geometric relation: diphthongs and vowels occupy a nuclear and glides a non-nuclear position. As shown in (54*d*), the segmental representation at the melodic tier may be identical in the three classes of cases: see (55).

The contrasts in (55) lead to the following expectation. While diphthongs are limited to the melodic representations [ie, ia],[13] the sequences

---

[12] Attention should be drawn to the fact that in some dialects of Slovak the distinction between the diphthongs *ie* and *ia* and the glide–vowel sequences *je* and *ja* is not made (see 2.3.2). Further, there are certain distributional gaps. With the exception of labials, *j* does not occur after consonants in the morpheme-internal position. The contrast between long vowels and sequences of identical vowels is restricted in that these occur only in intramorphemic and intermorphemic positions, respectively. Thus, some contrasts in (54) are explicable in terms of the Syllable Structure Algorithm (see 1.3).

[13] For the third diphthong, [uo], the contrasts exhibited in (54–5) do not obtain, at least in the standard dialect. Unlike Kenstowicz and Rubach (1987), I assume that the surface [*v*] derives from underlying //*v*//, a labiodental approximant. Thus, *svork+a* 'pack' and *kôrk+a* 'bread crust' are different underlyingly at the segmental tier: [*vo*] vs. [uo]. Kenstowicz and Rubach (1987) believe that all instances of surface [*v*] derive from the glide /u̯/, that is, from the melody representation [u]. We discuss the status of [*v*] in Chapter 7.

(55)

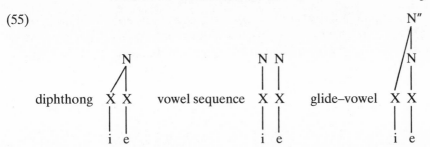

of *i* plus vowel or *j* plus vowel should appear quite freely with different vowels. The former should have the same combinatorial possibilities as any other vowel sequences. The latter should be unrestricted since, in general, syllable onsets and rhymes collocate freely. These expectations are confirmed by the data:

(56) *a.* audi.enci+a 'audience', di.alóg 'dialogue', Júli.us (name)
  Compare: po.et+a 'poet', kre.ol 'creole', pne.umatik+a 'tyre', fe.udal+n+ý 'feudal', silu.et+a 'silhouette'
 b. jed 'poison', ja 'I', jogurt 'yoghurt', juh 'south'

Furthermore, if our interpretation is correct that various length-sensitive rules of Slovak are defined on syllabic nuclei, then we predict that neither vowel sequences nor sequences of *j* plus vowel can trigger the Rhythmic Law, since the rule looks at the nucleus only and the nucleus is short. This is borne out:

(57) mili.ard+a 'milliard'—mili.ard+ám (dat. pl.)
  Si.am 'Siam'—si.am+sk+ý (Adj.)
  hy.en+a 'hyena'—hy.en+sk+ý (Adj.)
  jedl+o 'meal'—jedl+ám (dat. pl.)
  trojak 'kind of plough'—trojak+ý (Adj.)

Finally, heterosyllabic vowel-plus-vowel sequences and *j*-plus-vowel sequences should, we predict, be able to occur in combination with long vowels. This prediction also is borne out. In (58*a*) the long vowel is underlying, while in (58*b*) it is derived by Vowel Lengthening before the gen. pl. yer.

(58) *a.* bari.ér+a 'barrier', tri.ád+a 'triad', di.ód+a 'diode';
  júl 'July', Ján 'John', rajón 'region'
 b. pi.an+o 'piano'—pi.án (gen. pl.)
  jazd+a 'travel'—jázd (gen. pl.)
   versus
  rias+a 'cassock'—rias (gen. pl.)
  dám+a 'lady'—dám (gen. pl.)

Lengthening is possible in *pi.an+o* and *jazd+a* since the nucleus is short. On the other hand, *rias+a* contains a diphthong and *dám+a* a long vowel; that is, the nucleus dominates two X positions. These roots are represented in (59).

(59)
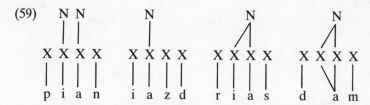

The failure of Vowel Lengthening to apply to *rias* and *dám* is now explained as a general constraint on the size of a prosodic unit. We stipulate that it may contain at most two skeletal slots. This stipulation is confirmed by the fact that there are no triphthongs in Slovak. Furthermore, as mentioned earlier, we assume that complex nuclei are right-headed; that is, the less sonorous onglide has a satellite position to the left in the nucleus. This predicts that if a less sonorous element appears to the right of the more sonorous element, then such a combination cannot be a diphthong. It is hence either a sequence of heterosyllabic vowels or a pseudo-diphthong; that is, a sequence of a vowel and a glide that occupies a coda position in the syllable. This prediction is correct. The combinatorial possibilities in these cases are essentially unrestricted:

(60) *a.* V plus V: na.ivn+ý 'naïve', kale.idoskop 'kaleidoscope', celulo.id 'celluloid', koka.ín 'cocaine', kafe.ín 'caffeine'
   b. V plus glide: tajg+a 'taiga', taj+n+ý 'secret', čuj+n+ý 'sensitive', olej 'oil', stroj+ník 'mechanic'

It is also understandable that words such as those in (60) cannot trigger the Rhythmic Law since they do not have complex nuclei. On the contrary, these words should be able to undergo Vowel Lengthening. Both predictions are borne out:

(61) *a.* tajg+a 'taiga'—tajg+ám (dat. pl.) *versus* rias+a 'cassock'—rias+am (dat. pl.)
      stroj+ník 'mechanic' *versus* požiar+nik 'fireman'
   b. tajg+a 'taiga'—tájg (gen. pl.)
      ru.in+a 'ruin'–ru.ín (gen. pl.)

In (61*b*) Vowel Lengthening identifies the nucleus as short and hence can apply. The rule is triggered by the yer of the gen. pl. We now restate Vowel Lengthening, given earlier in (26). The final version in (62) is quoted after Kenstowicz and Rubach (1987):

(62) Vowel Lengthening

N   N

X → X X / — C Ⓥ

The circled V stands for a vocalic segment which is unassociated with the skeletal tier. Recall that this is how yers are represented.

To summarize: in order to avoid duplication in shortening and lengthening rules we have proposed that the common parameter for long vowels, diphthongs, and long liquids is their geometric structure at the interface of the skeletal and the syllabic tiers.[14] The shared property is the type of nucleus: an N dominating two skeletal positions. The nucleus is right-headed; that is, the satellite position is to the left. Length-sensitive operations manipulate the satellite X slot. They delete it in the case of shortening and add it in the case of lengthening. The segmental make-up of the nucleus at the melodic tier is irrelevant. It may be a single vocalic segment (long vowel), a combination of vocalic segments (diphthong), or a liquid. The claim that rules affecting quantity operate at the interface of the nucleus and the skeletal slots has gained new strength in the light of the fact that Slovak distinguishes both phonetically and phonologically between diphthongs, vowel sequences, and combinations of glides and vowels (in whichever order). In the next section we look more closely at the representation of diphthongs and long vowels at the melodic tier. We also investigate the problem of how the rule of Diphthongization should be stated.

6.3. DIPHTHONGIZATION

Consider our statement of Diphthongization (6), which we now repeat as rule (63):

(63) Diphthongization   é, ä́, ó → ie, iä, uo

Given the fact that, after lengthening, the vowel (for instance é) has the structure in (64),

(64)

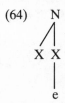

---

[14] To save space we refrain from restating all shortening rules along the lines of the Rhythmic Law (51) and all lengthening rules along the lines of Vowel Lengthening (62).

Diphthongization consists in inserting an onglide vowel under the empty skeletal slot. Notice that the value for the feature [back] of the onglide is predictable in a straightforward way from the value of this feature of the vowel in the head position. The onglide is front before the front vowels /e, ä/ and back before the back vowel /o/. In other words, the value for [back] spreads to the onglide from the vowel in the head position. What is unpredictable is the fact that the onglide vowel is high. This feature must therefore be inserted under the empty satellite slot. The structure in (64) is now altered as in (65).

(65)

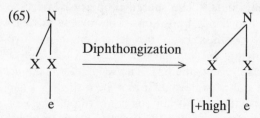

The value for [back] is spread from the vowel in the head position by a rule that we call Diphthong Spell-out. The relevant node is that of Tongue Body: see (66).

(66) Diphthong Spell-out

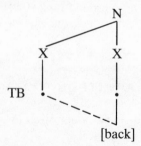

Returning now to Diphthongization proper (that is, the insertion of [+high]), notice that the rule need not be restricted to long /é, ä̆, ó/. No harm is done if it applies to long /i, u/ since, after Diphthong Spell-out has also applied, we obtain a geminate structure that is collapsed into a long vowel by the Obligatory Contour Principle (OCP). The OCP (Leben 1973, McCarthy 1986) prohibits two adjacent segments at the melodic tier, and hence the change in (67) follows automatically.

(67)

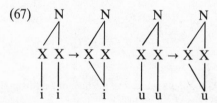

While the OCP does not generally hold for intermorphemic adjacent segments, it is believed to be true for morpheme-internal segments, and certainly it is true for nucleus-internal segments such as those in (67). Given this result, we may safely assume that Diphthongization applies not only to long /é, ä̃, ó/ but also to /í, ú/. The segment that must be excluded from Diphthongization is a long /á/, since otherwise we would derive the diphthong *[ua] in, for example, *pár* *[puar], the gen. pl. of *par+a* 'steam'. The exclusion of /á/ is achieved by requiring that the vowels undergoing Diphthongization must agree in the value for [back] and [round]: see (68).

(68) Diphthongization

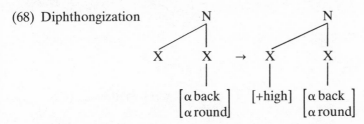

Recall now that Diphthongization is cyclic (see 6.2.2 above). It applies exclusively in derived environments: to the output of all lengthening rules with the exception of *CiV*-Lengthening (a cyclic rule), which is ordered after it. With the version of the Strict Cyclicity Constraint that treats affixes as a derived environment, Diphthongization may also apply to affixes. However, root-internal diphthongs must be underlying. The representations of *liek* 'medicine' vs. *Grék* 'Greek' are now as shown in (69).

(69)

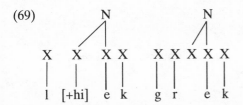

Two comments are in order. First, nothing stands in the way of regarding Diphthong Spell-out (66) as a postcyclic rule. Thus, the specification of the onglide in the underlying representation of root-internal diphthongs is minimal: only [+high].[15] Second, the linking of the melody /e/ to the first slot of the vowel in words such as *Grék* 'Greek' can be regarded as a postcyclic default rule. Such a linking is necessary independently for a derived long *á*, since lengthening rules add a slot but do not link the melody segment to the added slot.

---

[15] In instances in which underlying root-internal diphthongs are subject to shortening rules, the X slot over the [+high] onglide is deleted. The floating [+high] is subsequently stray-erased.

We summarize our discussion by showing in (70) the derivation of *liet* and *lán*, the gen. pl. forms of *let+o* 'summer' and *lan+o* 'rope' (irrelevant information is omitted). Recall that the gen. pl. ending is a yer.

(70)

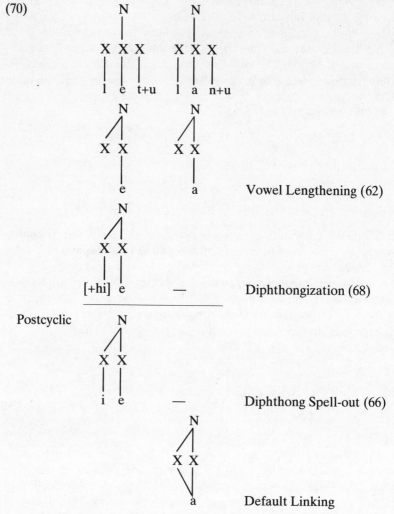

In the next two sections we investigate other sources of surface diphthongs: Contraction and Fronting. We put forward a claim that [iu] is not an underlying diphthong.

6.4. CONTRACTION AND THE *IU* DIPHTHONG

Diphthongs arise not only through the diphthongization of the lengthened vowels but also through a contraction of *i* and a vowel. Relevant here is the *čítan+i+e* 'reading' pattern of neuter nouns and the *had+í* declension of adjectives that we discuss later. Complete paradigms were given in 3.2.3.3 and 3.2.2. Below we repeat the nominal declension, but only in the singular. Our examples for contraction are the words *čes+a+n+i+e* 'combing' and *per+i+e* 'feathers'. We contrast them with the morphologically simple noun *plec+e* 'shoulder'.

(71) nom./acc.   *a.* plec+e   *b.* čes+a+n+i+e   *c.* per+i+e
    gen.   plec+a   čes+a+n+i+a   per+i+a
    dat.   plec+u   čes+a+n+i+u   per+i+u
    loc.   plec+i   čes+a+n+í   per+í
    instr.   plec+om   čes+a+n+ím   per+ím

We should stress that *ie*, *ia*, and *iu* in the morphologically complex words in (71) are diphthongs, which contrast sharply with heterosyllabic vowel sequences such as *ia* in *di.alekt* 'dialect'. There is no doubt that the three diphthongs come from the contraction of the vowel *i* and the vowel of the inflectional ending. As observed by Browne (1971), the *i* is a separate morpheme. In (71*b*) it denotes resultative nouns that are built on the passive participle. In (71*c*) it forms collectives. Compare the examples in (72) (-*ý* is an adjectival inflectional ending).

(72) *a.* čes+a+n+ý 'combed'—čes+a+n+i+e 'combing'
        mil+ova+n+ý 'loved'—mil+ova+n+i+e 'loving'
        pros+en+ý 'asked'—pros+en+i+e 'asking'
        pre+let+en+ý 'flown'—pre+let+en+i+e 'flying'
        pad+nu+t+ý 'fallen'—pad+nu+t+i+e 'falling'
        pi+t+ý 'drunk'—pi+t+i+e 'drinking'
    b. per+o 'feather'—per+i+e 'feathers'
        chrast 'bush'—chrast+i+e 'bushes'
        smrek 'spruce'—smreč+i+e 'spruces'

The morpheme *i* falls together, as it were, with the vocalic inflectional ending to form a diphthong: see (73).

(73) Contraction $N_1 N_2$ $N_1 N_2$

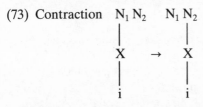

Some comments are in order. First, if the ending happens to be *i*, (73) produces a long vowel, for instance in the loc. sg. of (71*b*–*c*): /i+i/ → [í]. Second, Contraction is the source of the surface diphthong [iu] in the dat. sg. in (71*b*–*c*). Third, the rule applies also when the vowel *i* is followed by a long vowel of the ending. Compare the dat. pl. and the loc. pl. forms of

blat+o 'mud' with those of *čes+a+n+i+e* 'combing' and *per+i+e* 'feathers'
in (74):

(74) dat. pl.   blat+ám   čes+a+n+i+am   per+i+am
     loc. pl.   blat+ách   čes+a+n+i+ach   per+i+ach

Upon contraction the long vowel of the ending shortens automatically.
This is not surprising. As pointed out in 6.2.3, Slovak restricts the size of a
prosodic unit to a maximum of two slots; that is, there are no triphthongs.

Finally, Contraction must be a cyclic rule because it systematically does
not apply to morpheme-internal sequences of *i* and a vowel, hence *di.alekt*
'dialect' is trisyllabic. Still, a few exceptions remain. For example, *kuli*
'coolie' does not undergo Contraction in the nom. pl. *kuli+ovia* or in the
instr. pl. *kuli+ami*. On the other hand, Latinate words such as *akci+a*
'action', *depresi+a* 'depression', *demonštráci+a* 'demonstration', *obligáci+a*
'obligation', etc., which are supposed to have disyllabic endings in the
standard dialect (cf. Kráľ 1988), do in fact undergo Contraction in the
speech of many educated speakers. This has come to light in a syllabification test that I administered to twenty people. In close to 80 per cent of
answers the syllabification of *akci+a* was *ak.cia* rather than *ak.ci.a*.

Contraction is also found in the class of denominal adjectives. Compare
the feminine singular declension of *pekn+ý* 'beautiful' with that of *had+í*
'reptilian'. A complete paradigm was given in 3.2.2.

(75) nom.   pekn+á   had+i+a
     gen./dat./loc.   pekn+ej   had+ej
     acc.   pekn+ú   had+i+u
     instr.   pekn+ou   haď'+ou

Adjectives of the *had+í* type are denominal derivatives: see (76).

(76) *a.* had 'reptile'—had+í, leopard 'panther'—leopard+í, vran+a
        'crow'—vran+í, medveď 'bear'—medveď+í, včel+a 'bee'—včel+í,
        zajac 'hare'—zajač+í, Boh 'God'—bož+í, vlk 'wolf'—vlč+í, blch+a
        'flea'—blš+í
     b. pes 'dog'—ps+í, orol 'eagle'—orl+í, mravec 'ant'—mravč+í

The underlying representation of these adjectives is 'root + adjectivizing
suffix + inflectional ending', for example *had+í* 'reptilian' //had+i+í//. The
adjectivizing *i* cannot be seen on the surface because it has fallen together
with the inflectional ending owing to Contraction. What we see on the surface is a reflex of the *i* manifested as palatalization (Coronal Palatalization,
Affricate Palatalization, and 1st Velar Palatalization in (76)). Clearly, the
palatalization is not due to the inflectional ending since, as pointed out in
3.2.2, adjectival endings are non-palatalizing. Thus, *pekn+ý* 'beautiful', an
inherent adjective, ends in [n], while *vran+í* 'crow', a derived adjective,
ends in [n']. It should be added that the adjectivizing suffix is the vowel *i*

and not the yer *I*. This is made clear by the examples in (76*b*), where the root yer does not surface by Yer Vocalization. That is, *ps+í*, an adjective from the noun *pes* 'dog' (compare the gen. sg. *ps+a*), is //pEs+i+í// rather than //pEs+I+í//. (Recall that yers are vocalized if they are followed by a yer in the next syllable.)

The data in (75) unveil yet another regularity. The adjectivizing *i* is deleted before a suffix that begins with a short vowel. The presence of *i* at an earlier stage of derivation is manifested indirectly by palatalization, for example *had'+ou* 'reptile' (Adj., fem. instr. sg.). The deletion of *i* must take place before Contraction and it cannot be generalized to nouns. There, the *i* undergoes Contraction also before short vowel endings: compare the data in (71) above.

We summarize our discussion by showing in (77) a partial derivation of *per+i+e* 'feathers', *had+i+a* 'reptilian' (fem. nom. sg.), and *had+i+u* (acc. sg.). We take up the derivation in cycle 3, that is, after Coronal Palatalization has palatalized the //d// to [d'].

(77)

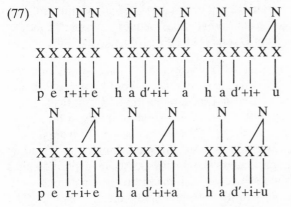

Contraction (73)

Finally, it should be noted that, in addition to the declension of neuter nouns in (71), the declension of denominal adjectives in (75) is another source of the surface diphthong [iu]. The third and last source is the declension of soft-stem adjectives. This is discussed in the following section. We suggest that in these adjectives [iu] is an effect of Fronting, a rule that applies to all long vowels. We begin with a general presentation of the problem.

6.5. FRONTING

In section 6.3 we put forward a claim that diphthongs arise from /é, ã̌, ó/ but not from /á/. It is therefore surprising to discover that there are regular correspondences between /á/ and /ia/. In (78) we look at some selected cases in the declension of feminine and neuter nouns. Complete paradigms were given in 3.2.3.2 and 3.2.3.3. Our examples are the words *vod+a* 'water' and *ulic+a* 'street' in the feminine class, and *blat+o* 'mud' and *plec+e* 'shoulder' in the neuter class.

(78) *a.* nom. sg.   vod+a   ulic+a
     instr. sg.   vod+ou   ulic+ou
     dat. pl.   vod+ám   ulic+iam
     loc. pl.   vod+ách   ulic+iach
     instr. pl.   vod+ami   ulic+ami

   b. nom. sg.   blat+o   plec+e
     nom. pl.   blat+á   plec+ia
     dat. pl.   blat+ám   plec+iam
     loc. pl.   blat+ách   plec+iach
     instr. pl.   blat+ami   plec+ami

Likewise, we find the *ulica* pattern in: medz+a 'border', baň+a 'mine', kad'+a 'container', Kat'+a (name), alej+a 'avenue', rol'+a 'field', depeš+a 'telegram', ryž+a 'rice', papuč+a 'slipper', gundž+a 'knot' (examples from Dvonč *et al.* 1966: 105)

We begin by observing that in the vowel–diphthong alternation the vowel is always long. If this vowel had been /á/ it would have diphthongized to [ia] via the familiar rule of Diphthongization. We notice further that the diphthong appears in the class of soft-stem nouns. Now, accepting the suggestion made by Kenstowicz (1972), we can derive /á/ from //á// by Fronting. However, the question is how the environment of Fronting should be expressed. In particular, should we insist on a phonological solution and state it as the occurrence of [–back] on the final consonant, or should we rather operate with the morphological diacritic SOFT? The facts speak for the latter solution.

On the one hand, it seems that Fronting indeed takes place after [–back] segments, since /t', d', n', l', j/ are phonetically [–back] and they cause Fronting. But, on the other hand, the rule applies also after /c, ʒ, š, ž, č, ǯ/, which were palatalized in Old and Middle Slovak but are no longer soft (cf. Pauliny 1963). Consequently, if we assumed that they were [–back] in the underlying representation, then we would also have to assume that there is a late rule which deletes [–back] before the phonetic representation is reached. Further, if [–back] were really the correct environment for Fronting, then the rule should also apply to stems that end in *i* and *e*. However, it does not. The sequences of *i* and *á* are heterosyllabic: see (79). Yet another argument against expressing the environment of Fronting by means of [–back] derives from the observation that there are no cases on record in which Fronting would have to apply in the environment of derived segments such as those that come

(79)

		Nom. sg.	*Dat. pl.*
a.	feminine	parti+a 'party'	parti+ám
		ide+a 'idea'	ide+ám
b.	neuter	štúdi+um 'study'	štúdi+ám
		múze+um 'museum'	múze+ám

from Coronal Palatalization. The segment that triggers Fronting is always stem-final and it is an underlying palatal or an underlying formerly palatalized consonant. Finally—and this is a decisive argument—Fronting applies to a small but entirely arbitrary class of words that end in all kinds of consonants. Dvonč *et al.* (1966) list the following, amongst others:

(80)

Nom. sg.	*Dat. pl.*		*Nom. sg.*	*Dat. pl.*
mor+e 'sea'	mor+iam		par+a 'steam'	par+ám
krv 'blood'	krv+iam	*versus*	krav+a 'cow'	krav+ám
hus 'goose'	hus+iam		kos+a 'scythe'	kos+ám

In (80), Fronting is clearly governed lexically.

We conclude that Fronting is triggered by the morphological diacritic SOFT, which is motivated independently by a number of inflectional sub-regularities that we discussed in Chapter 3. The diacritic SOFT characterizes the final consonant of the stem. We may construe it as being either present in the lexicon or assigned by a redundancy rule. In fact, both of these options seem to occur. In (80) SOFT is undoubtedly lexical. On the other hand, in the class of stems ending in /t′, d′, n′, l′, j/ as well as /c, ʒ, š, ž, č, ǯ/ SOFT may be assigned by a redundancy rule. Fronting can now be stated as rule (81). (We omit the intermediate nodes.)

(81) Fronting

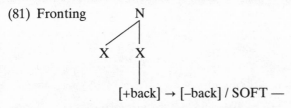

$$[+\text{back}] \rightarrow [-\text{back}] \ / \ \text{SOFT} \ —$$

Given this general statement, Fronting applies to all long back vowels, hence not only to /á/ but also to /ó/ and /ú/. The former does not occur in the relevant contexts but the latter does. In (82) we look at the feminine singular declension of adjectives. Complete paradigms were given in 3.2.2. Our examples are the words *mlad+ý* 'young' and *cudz+í* 'foreign':

(82)

nom.	mlad+á	cudz+ia
gen./dat./loc.	mlad+ej	cudz+ej
acc.	mlad+ú	cudz+iu
instr.	mlad+ou	cudz+ou

The fem. acc. sg. form is the third and last source of the surface diphthong [iu] (the other sources were discussed in the previous section). Notice that [iu] comes from underlying long //ú//. After Fronting we obtain /ǘ/, a front rounded vowel. The diphthong can now be interpreted as an instance of spreading within the nucleus. The features [+high, –back] are spread onto the empty skeletal slot from /ǘ/. This is shown informally in (83).

(83) ü-Spreading

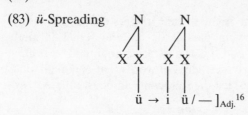

The intermediate /ü/ must be spelled out phonetically as [u]. This can be achieved by a late redundancy rule which expresses a surface generalization of Slovak that the features [round] and [back] correlate phonetically in the class of non-low vowels; that is, segments are either [+round, +back] or [–round, –back]:

(84) Round/Back Redundancy $\begin{bmatrix} -\text{cons} \\ -\text{low} \end{bmatrix} \rightarrow \begin{bmatrix} \alpha\,\text{round} \\ \alpha\,\text{back} \end{bmatrix}$

In sum, all instances of the surface diphthong [iu] are derivable by rules.

While ü-Spreading and Round/Back Redundancy may be postcyclic, Fronting must definitely be cyclic. The reason is that it applies before Diphthongization, which is cyclic: recall that the /ǻ/ from //á// diphthongizes to [ia]. Naturally, Diphthongization is inapplicable if the /ǻ/ is shortened by the Rhythmic Law. Compare the data in (78) and (82) with those in (85).

(85) a. Fem. nom. sg.   Dat. pl.
          sviec+a 'candle'   sviec+am
          tôň+a 'shadow'   tôň+am
          dielň+a 'workshop'   dielň+am

      b. fem. nom. sg.: rýdz+a 'pure', dúž+a 'big', sviež+a 'fresh'

To summarize our discussion so far we present three sample derivations in (86). The examples are mlad+á 'young', cudz+ia 'foreign', and rýdz+a 'pure' in the fem. nom. sg.

With our statement of Fronting we can eliminate the verbalizing morpheme //äj// which was postulated by Isačenko (1966) for verbs such as večer+a+ť 'eat supper'. The reason behind Isačenko's suggestion is that

---

[16] The rule does not apply to verbs, for example bij+ú 'they beat'.

(86)

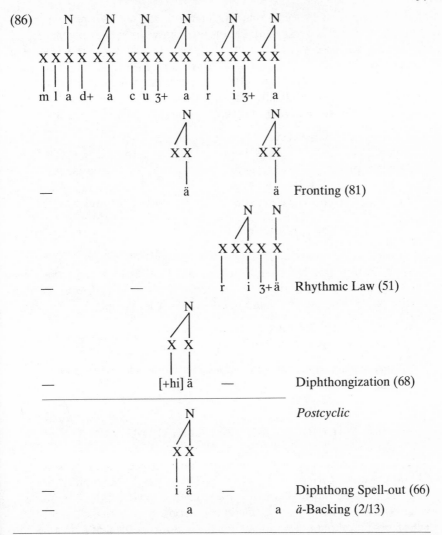

—	ä	ä Fronting (81)
—	—	r i ʒ+ä Rhythmic Law (51)
—	[+hi] ä	— Diphthongization (68)

Postcyclic

—	i ä	— Diphthong Spell-out (66)
—	a	a ä-Backing (2/13)

večer+a+t' contrasts with the 'ordinary' *aj*-stem verbs in that it surfaces with the diphthong [ia] in the present-tense conjugation. Compare:

(87) večer+a+t' 'eat supper'—večer+iam 'I eat supper'—večer+aj+ú 'they eat supper' *versus*
vol+a+t' 'call'—vol+ám 'I call'—vol+aj+ú 'they call'

In Isačenko's statement the long vowel in the 1st sg. comes from Coalescence: *aj+é → á* and *äj+é → ä́* (later diphthongized to [iä]), where *é* is the extension vowel (see 3.1.8). However, it should be noted that *večer+a+t'* 'eat supper' is a verbalization of the noun *večer+a* 'supper', which belongs to the lexical class of stems that trigger Fronting (see (80) above). Thus, the dat. pl. form is *večer+iam*. Given this observation it is not necessary to assume that *večer+a+ť* has an underlying //äj//. Rather, the verbalizing morpheme is //aj//, as in *vol+a+ť* 'call', and Fronting, which is now ordered after *aj*-Coalescence (3/32), derives /á/, which is subsequently diphthongized. This is illustrated in (88), where to save space we omit reference to the skeletal and the syllabic tiers and consider cycle 3.

(88) vol+aj+m 'I call'   večer+aj+m 'I eat supper'
      vol+aj+ém   večer+aj+ém   Extension (3/24)
      vol+á+m   večer+á+m   *aj*-Coalescence (3/32)
      —   večer+ắ+m   Fronting (81)
      —   večer+ia+m   Other rules:
                                                 Diphthongization
                                                 (68) and Diphthong
                                                 Spell-out (66)

Thus, Fronting is fed by *aj*-Coalescence. However, at the same time Fronting is in a counterfeeding relationship *vis-à-vis* Affricate Palatalization (4/16). The //c, ʒ// remain unaffected in, for example, the dat. pl.:

(89) feminine: ulic+iam 'street', skic+iam 'short story'
      neuter: srdc+iam 'heart', medz+iam 'border'

We return briefly to Fronting in connection with Glide Shortening in 8.2.

6.6. EXCURSUS: NON-PALATALIZING VOWELS

Slovak has a small class of suffixes which have surface front vowels [e] and [i] and yet do not trigger palatalization. This seems to be an arbitrary fact since, as pointed out by D'urovič (1975: 15), we have 'minimal pairs' such as *siln+ejš+í* [n'] 'stronger' vs. *siln+ej* [n] 'strong' (fem. gen. sg.). An adherent of 'concrete' phonology might conclude at this point that palatalization rules should not be construed as applying in the phonological context of front vowels and glides, but rather should simply be made sensitive to a list of suffixes. Then, the palatalizing comparative-degree suffix *-ejš* in our example would be included in the list of environments of Coronal Palatalization, while the non-palatalizing fem. gen. sg. *-ej* would not. This is not a particularly attractive analysis. First, it makes the whole system of palatalization entirely arbitrary and thus conflicts with the facts. In terms of phonetic (but not necessarily underlying) representations this system is only partly arbitrary, since by and large front-vowel suffixes do indeed trigger palatalization rules. Second, an analysis of this type would not be

able to explain why the same suffixes must be listed in different phonological rules.[17] For example, the verbalizing -*i*:

(90) Coronal Palatalization: rad+a 'advice'—rad+i+t' 'advise'
     1st Velar Palatalization: muk+a 'torture'—muč+i+t' 'to torture'
     Affricate Palatalization: koniec 'end'—konč+i+t' 'to end'

Let us look at the facts in greater detail. We take the masc. dat. sg. -*ému*
suffix of the adjectival declension as an example. It systematically resists
all the palatalization rules:

(91) *a.* Coronal Palatalization: pekn+ému [n] 'beautiful'
     b. 1st Velar Palatalization: sladk+ému 'sweet'
     c. Affricate Palatalization: súc+emu 'wise'

Is there a single generalization that underlies the behaviour of -*ému*? With
Halle's (1987) distinction of cyclic versus postcyclic affixes, one possibility
would be to assume that the suffix -*ému* is postcyclic. This, however, is a
false path. Notice that in (91*c*) -*ému* is shortened by the Rhythmic Law
and, as we point out in 6.7 below, the Rhythmic Law is cyclic. Consequently, -*ému* must be available in the cyclic component. In short, it seems
that -*ému* must be listed as an exception to the three rules in (91).
However, this means giving up an attempt to account for the facts in (91)
in terms of a single generalization. Notice that the rules in (91) are independent of each other. This follows from, amongst others, their different
ordering in the grammar of Slovak (see Chapter 4).

Listing -*ému* as an exception to the three palatalization rules does not
solve the problem. There are two other entirely independent facts that
need to be accounted for. First, -*ému* resists Diphthongization in (91*a–b*).
This cannot be attributed to the fact that it is an affix. The Strict Cyclicity
Constraint correctly does not exclude affixes from the operation of cyclic
rules. For example //ǽ//, the 3rd pl. suffix in the present tense, diphthongizes in *vid+ia* 'they see'. Second, -*ému* appears as diphthongal -*iemu* with
soft-stem adjectives, for example *cudz+iemu* 'foreign'.

In sum, there are five independent facts that need to be accounted for
in the case of -*ému*: Coronal Palatalization, 1st Velar Palatalization, Affricate Palatalization, and the absence of the surface diphthong in some
environments versus its presence in some other environments. A solution
suggests itself. Let us assume that -*ému* has a mid back unrounded vowel
in the underlying representation—that is, it is //-ɤmu//. There is internal
support in the system of Slovak for introducing this vowel. Recall that all

---

[17] As pointed out in 3.2.1.8, there is only one suffix which is non-palatalizing with respect
to one rule but palatalizing with respect to another rule. It is the fem. loc. sg. ending in the
nominal declension; compare *vod+e* 'water' vs. *Amerik+e*—Coronal Palatalization applies
but 1st Velar Palatalization does not.

vowels can be either short or long. The back mid unrounded vowel fits
well into this system. It is long in -*ému* as well as in the masc. acc. sg. -*ého*,
the fem. nom. pl. -*é*, and the fem. acc. pl. -*é* in the adjectival declension
(see 3.2.2). On the other hand, it is short in the fem. gen. sg. -*ej* that we
quoted at the beginning of this section, as well as in a number of nominal
suffixes (see 3.2.3.1). A natural question at this point is how we propose to
derive the surface [e] and [é] from the underlying //ɤ// and //ɤ́//.[18] The
difficulty is only apparent. In the previous section we suggested that
Slovak has Round/Back Redundancy (84). This rule was motivated, on
the one hand, by surface generalizations and, on the other hand, by the
need to account for the diphthong [iu] in *cudz+iu* 'foreign' (fem. acc. sg.).
Nothing more needs to be said. Round/Back Redundancy, a postcyclic
rule, derives surface [e] and [é] without difficulty.

With //ɤ́// as an underlying segment we account for the behaviour of our
diagnostic example -*ému* (as well as other non-palatalizing mid-vowel
suffixes) in a straightforward manner. Palatalization rules, which are
cyclic, are inapplicable because //ɤ́// is a back vowel. Neither can Diphthongization (68) apply since its environment is simply not met (see the
statement of the rule in 6.3). The occurrence of the diphthong [ie] in
cudz+iemu //cuʒ+ɤ́mu// 'foreign' follows from the ordering of Fronting
before Diphthongization, a fact that is independently motivated from the
interaction of Fronting and the Rhythmic Law. (The latter is ordered
before Diphthongization.) Fronting turns //cuʒ+ɤ́mu// into /cuʒ+ému/,
which is then subject to Diphthongization: *é* → *ie*.

In the case of non-palatalizing [i] suffixes the situation is not really
comparable to that of the non-palatalizing [e] suffixes. The similarity lies
in the fact that some of the [i] suffixes resist all palatalization rules. We
take the masc. nom. sg. [í] suffix as an example:

(92) *a.* Coronal Palatalization: pekn+ý [pekn+í] 'beautiful'
      b. 1st Velar Palatalization: sladk+ý [slatk+í] 'sweet'
      c. Affricate Palatalization: súc+y [súc+i] 'wise'

However, there is no comparable evidence from the facts of Diphthongization. Furthermore, in the case of some non-palatalizing [i] suffixes
Halle's (1987) solution is readily available. This solution is not open to the
[í] in (92) since it shortens rhythmically in (92*c*) and the Rhythmic Law is
cyclic. However, nothing stands in the way of regarding, for instance,
-*izmus* as in *patriot+izmus* [t] 'patriotism' as a postcyclic suffix. A solution
along the lines proposed for the non-palatalizing [e], that is, interpreting

---

[18] These two vowels must therefore be added to the inventory in (16) in Chapter 2. The
feature [round] contrasts ɤ/ɤ́ with o/ó. Note that [round] is necessary in any case, since it is
distinctive in the statement of Diphthongization (68).

the non-palatalizing [i] as an underlying high back unrounded vowel //ɨ//, while tempting for an adherent of 'abstract' phonology, is not particularly well supported. Rather, a handful of non-palatalizing [i] suffixes are genuine exceptions to palatalization rules.

6.7. RULE INTERACTION

The aim of this section is to investigate various interactions and build up an ordered block of rules. We use Booij and Rubach's (1987) concept of rule blocks to predict the status of particular rules (cyclic or postcyclic). It is shown that cyclicity follows from rule ordering. Theoretical predictions go hand in hand with the descriptive evidence accumulated in this and in the preceding chapters.

We begin by looking at the interaction of Contraction (73) and Rhythmic Law (51). Consider the data presented in (93).

(93) *a. Noun*   *Adj.: masc. nom. sg.*   *Fem. nom. sg.*

kohút 'rooster'	kohút+í	kohút+i+a
muflón 'moufflon'	muflón+í	muflón+i+a
žeriav 'crane'	žeriav+í	žeriav+i+a

    b. prút 'twig'—prút+i+e 'twigs'
        práv+o 'law'—bez+práv+i+e 'lawlessness'
        tŕň 'thorn'—tŕn+i+e 'thorns'

Long vowels and diphthongs in the derived words come from Contraction. The examples in (93*a*) are parallel to those in (76*a*) with the underlying representation of the type //-C+i+í// in the masculine and //-C+i+á// in the feminine form. Recall that //í// is an adjectivizing morpheme. The words in (93*b*) are parallel to those in (72*b*), where //i// is the morpheme for collective nouns.

The interest of the data in (93) lies in the fact that the Rhythmic Law is systematically inapplicable in these examples. Traditional grammars such as de Bray (1980) quote such cases as exceptions. There is, however, a much simpler explanation: the Rhythmic Law is ordered before Contraction. It can never apply in (93) since prior to Contraction we have vowel sequences and not long vowels or diphthongs.

Rule ordering can also explain another class of traditional exceptions to the Rhythmic Law:

(94) múdr+y 'wise'—z+múdr+ie+t' 'become wise'
     príkr+y 'hard'—príkr+ie+t' 'become hard'
     váž+n+y 'important'—z+váž+n+ie+t' 'become important'

The examples in (94) were discussed briefly in Chapter 3 (see derivation (6) in 3.1.2). The diphthong [ie] is derived by *e*-Lengthening (3/3).
Since the 'exceptions' in (94) are systematic, simple listing is not a solution. We can explain them easily by ordering *e*-Lengthening after the
Rhythmic Law. At the stage when the Rhythmic Law applies the verbalizing morpheme is a short vowel /e/. It is subsequently lengthened and
diphthongized.

To summarize, we have established the following ordering relationships:
Rhythmic Law, Contraction, *e*-Lengthening, and Diphthongization. The
remaining rules that we discuss below are ordered before the Rhythmic
Law.

Dvonč *et al.* (1966: 102, 116) note that in the gen. pl. of the type *par+a*
'steam'—*pár* Vowel Lengthening (62) does not apply if the preceding
syllable is long or diphthongal:

(95) *Nom. sg.*   *Gen. pl.*
      nížin+a 'lowland'   nížin
      písmen+o 'letter'   písmen
      dial'+av+a 'big distance'   dial'+av
      rieč+isk+o 'river bed'   rieč+isk

These 'exceptions' to the Rhythmic Law are systematic and they require
explanation. The solution is simple: Vowel Lengthening is ordered before
the Rhythmic Law. Thus, the gen. pl. *nížin* 'lowland' is first lengthened
and then shortened. The words in (95) turn out to be regular rather than
exceptional.

A similar explanation can be offered for yet another class of exceptions
to Vowel Lengthening quoted by Dvonč *et al.* (1966: 102, 116):

(96) *Nom. sg.*   *Gen. pl.*
      ú+tech+a 'joy'   ú+tech
      zá+hrad+a 'garden'   zá+hrad
      prie+zv+isk+o 'nickname'   prie+zv+isk

These words are parallel to those in (95) except for the fact that the length
in the base forms on the left in (96) comes from Prefix Lengthening (14);
compare, for example, *u+teš+i+t'* 'bring joy to'. Prefix Lengthening applies
in the cycle which precedes the inflectional cycle, as the latter comes last
in the derivation. When the stem vowel becomes long by Vowel Lengthening, the Rhythmic Law takes effect and the length is lost.

Finally, Yer Vocalization must be ordered before Vowel Lengthening
since vocalized yers lengthen and, if they are mid, diphthongize. In (97),
Vowel Lengthening is triggered by the inflectional yers of the fem./neuter
gen. pl. and the masc. nom. sg.

(97) a. *Fem./neuter: nom. sg.*   *Gen. pl.*
      ihl+a 'needle'   ihiel
      bedr+o 'hip'   bedier
      kvapk+a 'drop'   kvapôk
      sestr+a 'sister'   sestár

    b. *Masculine: nom. sg.*   *Gen. sg.*
      čepiec 'cap'   čepc+a
      hrniec 'pot'   hrnc+a
      veniec 'wreath'   venc+a
      chrbát 'back'   chrbt+a

To summarize, we have established the following set of ordered rules:

(98) Yer Vocalization
     Vowel Lengthening
     Prefix Lengthening
     Rhythmic Law
     Contraction
     e-Lengthening
     Dipthongization

Recall now that Dipthongization as a derived environment rule shows a classic syndrome of cyclic properties. It is also the last ordered rule in (98). (However, it is not the last cyclic rule: recall that Diphthongization is followed by *CiV*-Lengthening (17).) Given the theory of blocks of rules (Booij and Rubach 1987, see 1.2), a prediction is made that all the rules in (98) are lexical and cyclic. This is a non-trivial prediction and it shows that Lexical Phonology imposes a significant limitation on the power of the grammar. We pointed out in Chapter 1 that cyclic rules exhibit certain diagnostic properties. Like all lexical rules they are sensitive to lexical information; that is, they may have exceptions and/or apply in the environment of specified morphemes. They are also limited to derived environments and apply in a cyclic fashion. These properties are independent of each other, and hence they need not be overtly characteristic for every rule. That is, it may be the case that no relevant evidence is found for each of these properties in every single rule. However, a prediction is made that no counterevidence will be found either.

Descriptive evidence confirms our theoretical predictions. With the exception of *e*-Lengthening and Diphthongization all the rules in (98) have lexical exceptions (see Chapter 5 and sections 6.1 and 6.4 in this chapter). The rules of *e*-Lengthening and Prefix Lengthening are sensitive to lexical information of a different type. The former applies before a specified morpheme (the infinitive suffix -*t'*), the latter is limited to prefixes. For Contraction, Diphthongization, and the Rhythmic Law there is evidence that they apply exclusively in derived environments. Thus, morpheme-internal vowel sequences in (54*b*–*c*), (56*a*), and (57) earlier in this chapter do not contract. Words such as *dialekt* 'dialect' remain tri-syllabic. Neither may morpheme-internal //é, ó// diphthongize: for example, *Grék* 'Greek', *tón* 'tone'—see the examples in (42–4) in 6.2.2. On the other hand, if morpheme-internal /é, ó/ arise as an effect of Vowel Lengthening they do, predictably, diphthongize, for instance *cigaret+a* 'cigarette'— *cigariet* (gen. pl.) (see the examples in (45*b*) in 6.2.2). The Rhythmic Law is similar in this respect. Although we do not know of any sequences of two long vowels morpheme-internally, we do find the Rhythmic Law to be applicable morpheme-internally when length is due to Vowel Lengthening. The relevant examples are the gen. pl. forms such as *nížin* 'lowland' in (95) above. Cyclicity as a property is independent of the other diagnostics just discussed: lexical information and derived-environment application. We investigate this claim in the following section.

6.8. THE CYCLE: YER VOCALIZATION AND THE RHYTHMIC LAW

Recall that Yer Vocalization and the Rhythmic Law contrast in their environments in the sense that the former is, as it were, 'regressive' while the latter is 'progressive'. That is, Yer Vocalization is sensitive to what follows whereas the Rhythmic Law is sensitive to what precedes. Yer Vocalization applies *before* a yer while the Rhythmic Law applies *after* a long nucleus. If the rules are cyclic, then we predict that Yer Vocalization should vocalize all vocalic melodies in a chain of yers in the direction as predicted by the order in which word-formation rules have applied. Thus, in the case of root plus suffixes all yers should vocalize from left to right.

With regard to the Rhythmic Law cyclic application makes the opposite prediction. In a chain of long nuclei such as $[[[\acute{V}]_1 \ \acute{V}]_2 \ \acute{V}]_3$. We should obtain an alternating pattern; that is, we should derive $[[[\acute{V}]_1 \ V]_2 \ \acute{V}]_3$. The middle long vowel shortens since it is preceded by a long vowel on the second cycle. The last long vowel cannot shorten because by the time we come to the third cycle the relevant environment has already been lost and the preceding vowel is short. This result can only be obtained if the Rhythmic Law applies cyclically. A non-cyclic application would have produced the sequence $\acute{V}VV$, that is, a long vowel followed by two short vowels. In sum, the mode of rule application has empirical consequences, and cyclicity is a property that is independent of the other diagnostics such as lexical information and derived-environment limitation. Descriptive evidence testifies to the correctness of this claim. We first look at Yer Vocalization.

The gen. pl. *okien+eč+iek* 'window' (double diminutive) is a rather spectacular example. It contains a chain of four yers. Compare:

(99) *a.* okn+o 'window'—okien (gen. pl.), UR //okEn+U//, where -*U* is
the gen. pl. yer
  b. okien+c+e (dimin.)—okien+ec (gen. pl.), UR //okEn+Ec+U//
  c. okien+eč+k+o (double dimin.)—okien+eč+iek (gen. pl.), UR
//okEn+Ec+Ek+U//

That (99*c*) has a chain of four yers can be seen from the alternations
in (99*a*–*b*). The root has a yer that surfaces in the gen. pl. in (99*a*)
as well as before the diminutive yer in (99*b*–*c*). The diminutive suffixes are
-*Ec* and -*Ek* (for discussion see 3.3). Their yers surface in accordance with
Yer Vocalization. In addition they trigger palatalization rules (Coronal
Palatalization and Affricate Palatalization) and Vowel Lengthening. The
gen. pl. inflectional yer -*U* cannot vocalize since it is not followed by a yer.
  Slovak has many words with a chain of yers. Below we give a few more
examples.

(100) *a.* spol+u 'together'—spol+ok 'community'—spol+k+a (gen. sg.)
—spol+oč+n+á 'common' (fem. nom. sg.)—spol+oč+en+sk+á
'social' (fem. nom. sg.), UR //spol+Ok+En+Isk+á//, where -*Ok* is
a nominalizing suffix while -*En* and -*Isk* are adjectival
morphemes (see 3.3)
  b. skl+o 'glass'—skiel (gen. pl.)—skiel+c+e (dimin)—skiel+ec
(gen. pl.), UR //skEl+Ec+U//
  c. vedr+o 'bucket'—vedier (gen. pl.)—vedier+c+e (dimin.)
—vedier+ec (gen. pl.), UR //*v*edEr+Ec+U//
  d. hrst' 'handful'—hŕst+k+a (dimin.)—hŕst+ok (gen. pl.)
—hŕst+oč+k+a (double dimin.)—hŕst+oč+iek (gen. pl.), UR
//xrst'+Ok+Ek+U//

This pattern is the same as in (99): all but the final yer vocalize. Historically the situation was different. In the tenth–twelfth centuries the Slavic
languages were subject to the law known as Havlík's Law (Havlík 1889),
according to which Yer Vocalization applied from right to left, vocalizing
every equal-numbered yer and thereby producing an alternating pattern.
Pauliny (1963) points out that a former double diminutive of the word
dom 'house' was *dom+č+ek* (nom. sg.): compare the gen. sg. *dom+eč+k+a*.
The representation //dom+Ek+Ek+U//, where the last morpheme is the
inflectional yer of the nom. sg., is an example of this early pattern.
According to Pauliny the nom. sg. form *dom+č+ek* changed later to
dom+eč+ek (nom. sg.): compare again the gen. sg. *dom+eč+k+a*. This
later change, which Pauliny unfortunately does not date, is precisely the
point at which Yer Vocalization becomes cyclic and hence the direction
of application changes from right-to-left to left-to-right, as predicted by
the cycle. This illustrates one type of historical change: a non-cyclic
rule becomes cyclic (cf. Rubach 1981, Kiparsky 1982, Rubach 1984).

Unfortunately, today the yer of the second diminutive has turned, apparently under Czech influence, into a 'full' vowel and hence the yer of the first diminutive cannot vocalize. In the standard dialect it is no longer a yer and the pattern is *dom+č+ek* (nom. sg.)—*dom+č+ek+a* (gen. sg.: the *e* of *-ek* does not alternate with zero). However, Polish has preserved the form from the time when Yer Vocalization became cyclic: compare the Polish *dom+ecz+ek* (nom. sg.)—*dom+ecz+k+a* (gen. sg.; note: *cz* stands for *č*). Evidence for the cyclicity of the Rhythmic Law is similar. Compare the examples in (101).

(101) *a.* rol'+a 'field'   osad+a 'settlement'
        rol'+ník 'farmer'   osad+ník 'settler'
        rol'+níc+k+y (Adj.)   osad+níc+k+y (Adj.)

        úrad 'office'   dover+a 'trust'
        úrad+ník 'official'   dover+ník 'trustee'
        úrad+níc+k+y (Adj.)   dover+níc+k+y (Adj.)

   b. pút' 'pilgrimage'   práv+o 'law'
        pút+nik 'pilgrim'   práv+nik 'lawyer'
        pút+nic+k+ý (Adj.)   práv+nic+k+ý (Adj.)

        papier 'paper'   likér 'liqueur'
        papier+nik 'stationer'   likér+nik 'producer of liqueur'
        papier+nic+k+ý (Adj.)   likér+nic+k+ý (Adj.)

The words in (101*a*) demonstrate that the suffix *-ník*[19] triggers the Rhythmic Law: the inflectional *-ý* surfaces as short. However, in (101*b*) the *-ý* remains long. This effect can be obtained easily if the Rhythmic Law applies cyclically.

The cycle gives a rationale for two otherwise very peculiar properties of the Rhythmic Law: stepwise rather than simultaneous application and left-to-right directionality. Both of them follow from the fact that word-formation rules interact with cyclic phonological rules. Thus, it is only on the last cycle that we have a complete word. On earlier cycles we see merely chunks of the word. The rules must therefore apply in a stepwise fashion. The directionality need not be stipulated either. It is dictated by the order of affixation operations.

Returning to the facts in (101*b*), notice that on the second cycle when *-ník* is added the Rhythmic Law shortens the vowel of the suffix and derives *-nik*. Consequently, on cycle 3 the preceding vowel is short and the Rhythmic Law cannot take effect: the *-ý* surfaces as long.

---

[19] The suffix is actually //En+ík//, where //En// is the adjectivizing morpheme. Compare *súkn+o* 'cloth'—*súken+n+ík* //súkEn+En+ík//: the //En// triggers Yer Vocalization of the root yer. The fact that *-n+ík* has a yer is of no significance for the Rhythmic Law because unvocalized yers do not project a nuclear slot and are hence invisible to the Rhythmic Law.

The cyclicity of the Rhythmic Law can also be seen in its interaction with Vowel Lengthening: see (102).

(102)   *Nom. sg.*   *Gen. pl.*
   a. čel+o 'forehead'   čiel
       čiel+c+e (dimin.)   čiel+ec
   b. jazer+o 'lake'   jazier
       jazier+c+e (dimin.)   jazier+ec
   c. polen+o 'log'   polien
       polien+c+e (dimin.)   polien+ec

The derivation of *čiel+ec* 'forehead' (dimin. gen. pl.) proceeds as shown in (103). We simplify the derivation by leaving out reference to the skeletal tier and by ignoring the details of diphthongization. Recall that *U* is the gen. pl. ending.

(103) Cycle 2   čel+Ec   WFR: diminutivization
                 —   Yer Vocalization (5/13)
                čél+Ec   Vowel Lengthening (62)
                 —   Rhythmic Law (51)
                čiel+Ec   Diphthongization (68)

      Cycle 3   čiel+Ec+U   WFR: gen. pl.
                čiel+ec+U   Yer Vocalization
                čiel+éc+U   Vowel Lengthening
                čiel+ec+U   Rhythmic Law
                 —   Diphthongization

                čiel+ec   Stray Erasure

The diminutive suffix *-Ec* causes lengthening of the root vowel on cycle 2. On cycle 3 *-Ec* vocalizes and lengthens because of the gen. pl. yer *-U*. That the lengthening of the vocalized *-ec* is real can be seen by looking at *pláten+iec* 'cloth' (dimin. gen. pl.) in (106) below. The lengthening of *-ec* in (103) is undone by the Rhythmic Law. The mechanism of the cycle is essential for the derivation of *čiel+ec* in (103). The reason is that Vowel Lengthening is triggered by a yer and in this example the yer of *-Ec* acts both as an environment and as an input. The *E* of *-Ec* functions as an environment for the lengthening of the root yer. At the same time this yer itself is an input to Vowel Lengthening after Yer Vocalization. In a non-cyclic derivation Yer Vocalization should both follow and precede Vowel Lengthening. Let us clarify this point.

In the derivation of forms such as the gen. pl. *stebiel* 'stalk' (gen. pl., see (106*a*) below), Yer Vocalization must precede Vowel Lengthening: see (104).

(104) stebEl+U
       stebel+U   Yer Vocalization (5/13)
       stebél+U   Vowel Lengthening (62)
       stebiel+U   Diphthongization
       _____
       stebiel   Stray Erasure

Notice that the ordering of Yer Vocalization before Vowel Lengthening is
feeding. The latter cannot apply until the former has provided an X slot
over the yer, because lengthening is an operation at the skeleton. When
we now look at the derivation of *čiel+ec* 'forehead' (dimin. gen. pl.) and
ignore the cycle, it seems that Vowel Lengthening must precede Yer
Vocalization. This is necessary since otherwise the root vowel cannot
lengthen. (Recall that Vowel Lengthening applies before a yer.) The
derivation in (105a) arrives at the correct output, but the one in (105b)
does not.

(105) *a.* čel+Ec+U   *b.* čel+Ec+U
             čél+Ec+U   V. Lengthening   čel+ec+U   Yer Vocalization
             čél+ec+U   Yer Vocalization   čel+éc+U   V. Lengthening
             čiel+ec+U   Diphthongization   čel+iec+U   Diphthongization
             _____   _____
             čiel+ec   Stray Erasure   *čel+iec   Stray Erasure

If we now compare (104) and (105a) we see an ordering paradox. In (104)
Yer Vocalization must precede while in (105a) it must follow Vowel
Lengthening. This ordering paradox is solved by the cycle, as shown by
(103). We may add that a different instance of an ordering paradox is
discussed in 7.6.

    The best proof for the cyclicity of the Rhythmic Law can be drawn from
the complex pattern of interacting rules illustrated in (106).

(106) *a.*   'stalk'   'beam'   'awl'
              nom. sg.   stebl+o   brvn+o   šidl+o
              gen. pl.   stebiel   brvien   šidiel
              dimin. nom. sg. stebiel+c+e   brvien+c+e   šidiel+c+e
              dimin. gen. pl. stebiel+ec   brvien+ec   šidiel+ec
       b.   'cloth'   'tissue'   'wing'
              nom. sg.   plátn+o   vlákn+o   krídl+o
              gen. pl.   pláten   vláken   krídel
              dimin. nom. sg. pláten+c+e   vláken+c+e   krídel+c+e
              dimin. gen. pl. pláten+iec   vláken+iec   krídel+iec

The contrast between the dimin. gen. pl. forms in (106*a*) and (106*b*) can be derived if the rules apply cyclically. In (106*a*) the roots are short, hence the root yer vocalizes and lengthens before the diminutive -*Ec*. This suffix is in turn vocalized and lengthened before the gen. pl -*U*. However, it is subsequently shortened by the Rhythmic Law. In (106*b*) the derivation is similar but the root vowel is long. Therefore the vocalized yer in the second syllable of the root is shortened rhythmically still on cycle 2. In consequence of this fact the vocalized and lengthened yer of the diminutive -*Ec* cannot shorten on cycle 3. In (107) we derive the dimin. gen. pl. forms of the words for 'stalk' and 'cloth' in (106). As in the previous derivation, irrelevant information is omitted and the representations are simplified by ignoring reference to the skeleton. We begin with cycle 2.

(107) Cycle 2

(107)	Cycle 2	stebEl+Ec	plátEn+Ec	WFR: diminutivization
		stebel+Ec	pláten+Ec	Yer Vocalization (5/13)
		stebél+Ec	plátén+Ec	Vowel Lengthening (62)
		—	pláten+Ec	Rhythmic Law (51)
		stebiel+Ec	—	Diphthongization (68)
	Cycle 3	stebiel+Ec+U	pláten+Ec+U	WFR: gen. pl.
		stebiel+ec+U	pláten+ec+U	Yer Vocalization
		stebiel+éc+U	pláten+éc+U	Vowel Lengthening
		stebiel+ec+U	—	Rhythmic Law
		—	pláten+iec+U	Diphthongization
		stebiel+ec	pláten+iec	Stray Erasure

To summarize, we have demonstrated that cyclicity as a property is independent of the other diagnostics for identifying cyclic lexical rules: derived-environment application and lexical information. In (108) we list the properties of the cyclic rules that we have discussed in this and in the preceding section. The Rhythmic Law has a unique position among the rules since it checks positively for all the three properties. We should point out, however, that in the case of the Rhythmic Law 'derived environment' is used in the sense described in the discussion of (95) and (96) in the preceding section. That is, the Rhythmic Law applies morpheme-internally to the structures derived by Vowel Lengthening. The other type of proof for derived-environment application—the presence of a chain of long nuclei morpheme-internally—does not, to the best of my knowledge, exist. As pointed out to me by Andrew Spencer, this may be due to the fact that there are rather few polysyllabic roots in the native Slavic lexicon.

(108)

	Cyclicity	Derived-environment application	Lexical information
Yer Vocalization	yes	—	yes
Vowel Lengthening	—	—	yes
Prefix Lengthening	—	—	yes
Rhythmic Law	yes	yes	yes
Contraction	—	yes	yes
e-Lengthening	—	—	yes
Diphthongization	—	yes	—

Let us repeat: the fact that Diphthongization applies in derived environments and hence is cyclic assigns all the earlier-ordered rules to the class of cyclic lexical rules. This rather spectacular prediction is confirmed fully by descriptive evidence. The advantages of using the framework of Lexical Phonology are now clear.

7

SYLLABLE STRUCTURE

In this chapter we look at Slovak syllable structure. A general outline is presented in 7.1. We then proceed to investigate the properties of the Syllable Structure Algorithm. Specifically, we address the questions of whether it applies cyclically and whether it is continuous (sections 7.2 and 7.3). In 7.4 we look at the domain of syllabification and conclude that prefixes as well as constituents of compounds constitute separate domains. Glides are discussed in 7.5. We then pursue the problem of how extrasyllabic consonants are treated in various components of phonology. We conclude that some liquids are made syllabic in the cyclic component (section 7.6), while other liquids trigger a postcyclic rule of vowel insertion (section 7.7). The status of *v*—whether *v* is a glide or not—is discussed in 7.8. On a more general level, this problem occasions a debate of adjunction and resolving extrasyllabicity by changing the feature composition of a segment.

7.1. THE SYLLABLE STRUCTURE ALGORITHM

The Syllable Structure Algorithm (SSA) was introduced in 1.3, but now we shall extend it by including language-specific rules. The Sonority Sequencing Generalization (SSG) will be supplemented by the Obstruent Sequencing Principle. We shall then proceed to demonstrate how these principles operate in Slovak by analysing native-speaker judgements on permissible syllabification and by indicating that the application of certain rules is connected in crucial ways to the occurrence of extrasyllabic consonants. We shall then address the problem of variation.

The SSA includes two universal rules (N-Placement and the CV Rule) and language-specific rules for deriving onsets and codas. The reason some rules are language-specific is that not all languages have complex onsets (that is, other than predicted by the CV Rule) or codas. However, every language must have the CV Rule, even if it does not have CV syllables. The point is that, according to Levin (1985), the CV Rule erects the syllable node N″ and hence it must apply even if no consonant precedes the vowel, as in the English word *ant* (see 1.3).

In (1) we state the SSA formally. The language-specific rules—the Onset Rule, the Coda Rule, and the Complex Coda Rule—are based on

Polish (Rubach and Booij 1990*a*). While the formal statement of these rules is the same regardless of the language, their ordering with respect to one another is a parameter in the sense that languages differ in this ordering, as we demonstrate later in this section.

(1) SSA (Polish)

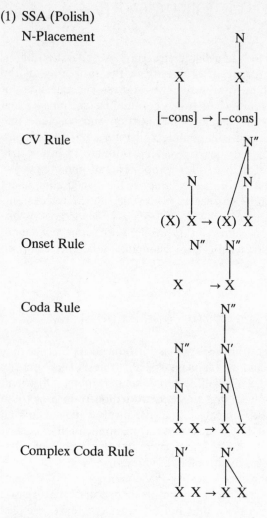

N-Placement

CV Rule

Onset Rule

Coda Rule

Complex Coda Rule

N-Placement applies to every [–cons] segment. In consequence of this fact, it overgenerates for languages which have glides [j] and [u̯]. As mentioned in 1.3, these glides are represented as //i// and //u//, respectively, at the melodic tier. They differ from the vowels *i* and *u* precisely by the fact that they do not carry an N; that is, they are either in the onset or in the coda. However, given the statement in (1), all instances of [–cons] segments are assigned an N. Deriving the glides [j] and [u̯] requires gliding rules that we discuss in 7.5.

If Levin (1985) is right and the CV Rule is universally endowed with the power to resyllabify strings, then in its capacity as a resyllabification mechanism, the CV Rule in Slovak is restricted to the cyclic component because, on the one hand, all word-formation is cyclic in Slovak and, on the other hand, Slovak, like Polish but unlike French, does not permit syllabification across word boundaries.

The Onset Rule is in fact a complex onset rule, as simple onsets are derived by the CV Rule. The Coda Rule corresponds to the CV Rule in that it adjoins the segment which is immediately adjacent to the nucleus. If a language has codas that are larger than one member, then it requires the Complex Coda Rule. Such codas could not be derived by the Coda Rule for formal reasons: the environment of the Coda Rule is not met because the relevant segment is not directly postnuclear. Although a separation of the Coda Rule and the Complex Coda Rule looks like a complication that is motivated by what seems to be a shortcoming of the formal apparatus, we shall see that it is supported on descriptive grounds by evidence from Slovak.

The application of the SSA is governed by both the universal and the language-specific principles. The universal principle is the Sonority Sequencing Generalization given as (29) in 1.3 and now repeated for convenience in (2):

(2) SSG:
> The sonority of segments must decrease towards the edges of the syllable in accordance with the following scale:
>
> nucleus—liquids—nasals—fricatives—stops.

Notice that we use the term 'nucleus' rather than the traditional term 'vowel' in the statement of the SSG. This is significant, as we demonstrate later in this chapter.

The SSG is overridden by the Obstruent Sequencing Principle, which has the status of a language-specific principle, though we should note that it is applicable not only in Slovak but also in Polish (Rubach and Booij 1990a).

(3) The Obstruent Sequencing Principle:
> With obstruents there is no requirement of sonority distance.

The effect of (3) is that fricatives and stops may occur in clusters in either order and that obstruents of the same class may cluster together. That it is necessary to relax the SSG at this point is shown by the examples in (4):

(4) *a.* starý 'old', spev 'song', skala 'rock', zdar 'success', zbytok 'surplus', zgerba 'bastard', štyri 'four', špára 'slit', škoda 'damage', žblnk 'ripple', žgrloš 'miser', vták 'bird', chciet' 'want', psota 'distress', pšochár 'wretch', kšeft 'business', džgat' 'pierce', džbán 'jar', čkat' 'hiccup', ktorý 'which', tkat' 'weave', bdiet' 'drudge away', dbat' 'care', vzor 'pattern', vše 'always', pstruh 'trout', bzdiet' 'stink'

   b. biceps 'muscle', keks 'type of cake', produkt 'product', text 'text', skúbst' 'twitch'

The largest onset has four and the largest coda three consonants. They are derived by reiteration of the Onset Rule and Complex Coda Rule, respectively.

While the Obstruent Sequencing Principle is generally correct in opening the way to all possible combinations of segments within the class of obstruents, it must be restricted in two significant ways. First, sequences of identical intervocalic consonants are always heterosyllabic. This is not a stipulation for Slovak but rather a universal principle (Kuryłowicz 1947). It predicts that words such as *brutto* 'gross' must be syllabified *brut-to* and not **bru-tto*. Second, in the case of Slovak not only identical but also near-identical consonants are not permitted to form onsets and codas. Thus, no word may begin with **sš*, **zž*, **vf*, or **gk*.

While it is clear from our examples that the Obstruent Sequencing Principle operates in Slovak, it must yet be demonstrated that the SSG, a superordinate principle, applies as well. We demonstrate this by drawing evidence from two sources: native-speaker judgements on permissible syllabification and the operation of allomorphy/phonological rules.

Judgements on permissible syllabification are based, on the one hand, on the descriptions available in the standard literature, such as Letz (1950), Zauner (1966), Stanislav (1977), and Pauliny (1979), and, on the other hand, on the results of a questionnaire that was administered to a group of twenty native speakers of Slovak.[1] The questionnaire was a written test in which speakers were asked to divide words into syllables, indicating if more than one option was available. With three speakers the same test was repeated three times at intervals of several weeks. The intention was to see whether variation exists in the speech of the same informant. The results of the investigation are summed up in (5). The number of informants who chose each variant is given in parentheses, but it should be noted that the same type of variation was found in the tests done by the same informant with different words, or (in the case of the three informants who repeated that test) with the same words.

[1] I would like to thank my Slovak consultants for their assistance. In particular, I would like to single out L'ubomir D'urovič and Peter Durčo, who provided interesting discussion in addition to filling out the questionnaires on several separate occasions.

(5)   Variation   VC-CV as the only
      ─────────────────────────────────────   possibility

      VC-CV   V-CCV

---

a. myd-lo (12)   my-dlo (8) 'soap'   fal-da 'fold'
      sed-lo (11)   se-dlo (9) 'saddle'   ol-tár 'altar'
      dub-le-ta (9)   du-ble-ta (11) 'double'   kol-ba 'butt'
      cyk-lus (14)   cy-klus (6) 'cycle'   bal-kón 'balcony'
      ih-la (15)   i-hla (5) 'needle'   kul'-hat' 'limp'
      mys-liet' (18)   my-sliet' (2) 'think'   bol'-še-vik 'bolshevik'
      jad-ro (9)   ja-dro (11) 'core'   kar-ta 'card'
      mod-rý (13)   mo-drý (7) 'blue'   čar-dáš 'csardas'
      kob-ra (14)   ko-bra (6) 'cobra'   far-ba 'paint'
      strieb-ro (12)   strie-bro (8) 'silver'   tur-bí-na 'turbine'
      ob-raz (11)   o-braz (9) 'picture'   fir-ma 'firm'
b. boč-ný (19)   bo-čný (1) 'side' (Adj.)   pán-ča 'master'
      blúz-nit' (16)   blú-znit' (4) 'wander'   men-za 'canteen'
      kom-pro-mis-ný (18)   kom-pro-mi-sný (2)   in-ter-nat 'boarding
                               'compromise' (Adj.)   house'

Notice that the words showing variation and those whose syllabification is constant often form 'minimal pairs' in the sense that the consonants involved are the same but their sequential ordering is different, for instance *dl* in *mydlo* 'soap' vs. *ld* in *falda* 'fold'. Evidently, variation is permitted only when the SSG is not violated.

A different type of evidence documenting the operation of the SSG is drawn from the application of allomorphy and phonological rules. This evidence is overwhelming and it will accumulate as we proceed. For the moment let us merely indicate what we have in mind. In (6) we briefly introduce the imperative allomorphy that we shall discuss in detail in 7.2 and 7.3.

(6)   *a.* nes 'carry', plet' 'weave', žeň 'marry', kop 'dig', lom 'break'
      b. mysl+i 'think', namydl+i 'soap', padn+i 'fall', mr+i 'die', spomn+i
            'remember'

The imperative manifests itself on the surface as a zero ending in (6a) and as the vowel *i* in (6b). This pattern of distribution becomes understandable if we consider syllable structure at the stage when the *i* ending has not yet been added. While the words in (6a) can be fully syllabified, those in (6b) cannot, since a violation of the SSG would occur. An application of the SSA to the roots *nes* 'carry' and *mysl* 'think' reveals this difference clearly: the *l* is extrasyllabic. We can now pursue the following line of reasoning. A vowel needs to be inserted in order to 'rescue' the *l* by building a syllable into which the *l* can be syllabified. Consequently, the *l* is licensed prosodically (Itô 1986), that is, it is part of prosodic structure. In this way it can escape Stray Erasure, which deletes all unlicensed material at the end of phonological derivation. Now the term 'rescue' makes sense. We state the *i*-Insertion rule in (7) as the first approximation. It will be revised as rule (22) in 7.2. The asterisk means that the consonant is extrasyllabic:

(7) Imperative Allomorphy $\emptyset \rightarrow i / *C —$

The derivation of *nes* and *mysl+i* is now shown in (8). (It is simplified; for details, see 7.2.)

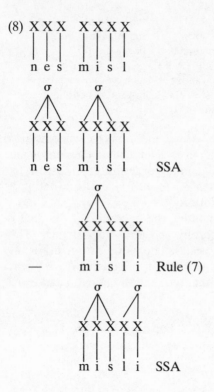

This straightforward account of the difference between (6*a*) and (6*b*) is possible only if we assume that Slovak obeys the SSG, because otherwise the consonants triggering rule (7) could not be identified as extrasyllabic.

Now we return to the discussion of the SSA rules listed in (1). In particular, we ask the question how the language-specific rules are ordered with respect to each other. The results of the questionnaire are in agreement with the standard descriptive grammars such as Stanislav (1977) that the following division of consonant clusters is the normal (unmarked) pattern:

(9) *a.* VCCV → VC-CV

  *puš-k*ar-ský 'rifle shop' (Adj.), *puš-ný* 'shooting' (Adj.)

  Note: *šk-* and *šn-* would be well-formed onsets; compare: škola
  'school', šnorovat' 'to lace'

 b. VCCCV → VC-CCV[2]

  *ab-st*i-nent [ap-sti-] 'teetotaller', ko*m-pr*o-mis 'compromise',
  ko*n-tr*akt 'contract'

  Note: *-ps*, *-mp*, and *-nt* would be well-formed codas; compare: klips
  'ear-ring', púmp 'pump' (gen. pl.), asistent 'assistant'

The syllabification in (9*a*) is derived by the SSA if the Coda Rule
precedes the Onset Rule. Furthermore, the pattern in (9*b*) requires that
the Onset Rule should precede the Complex Coda Rule. In sum, the SSA
is as follows:

(10) SSA (Slovak)   N-Placement
                     CV Rule
                     Coda Rule
                     Onset Rule
                     Complex Coda Rule

A sample derivation of *kompromis* 'compromise' and *klips* 'ear-ring' is
now shown in (11). To save space we omit reference to the X-tier.

(11) *a.*

 b.

If the Complex Coda Rule preceded the Onset Rule, then the *p* of
kompromis would be in the first rather than in the second syllable:
*komp-ro-mis.

---

[2] However, one should note the pervasive tendency to avoid onsets consisting of two stops.
Thus, *egyptka* 'Egyptian' (fem.) is normally syllabified as *egypt-ka*.

Our analysis is confirmed by preference ratios in instances which permit variation: see (5). Recall that the VC-CV pattern was prevalent. The same conclusion emerges from yet another instance of variation: clusters of *s* (or *z*) and stops:

(12) a-sis-tent (16)   a-si-stent (4) 'assistant'
      bis-kup (15)   bi-skup (5) 'bishop'
      des-po-ta (13)   de-spo-ta (7) 'despot'

Interestingly, the words in (12) are identical in Slovak and in Polish, but the prevalent pattern in the case of Polish is V-CCV (cf. Rubach and Booij 1990*a*). Thus, *bi-skup* is the first choice and *bis-kup* the second. This fact can be expressed by ordering the Onset Rule before the Coda Rule in Polish, which is the opposite of the ordering established for Slovak. We thus confirm our earlier observation that the mutual relationship between the Onset Rule and the Coda Rule is a language-specific matter and hence constitutes a parameter along which languages may differ.

Now we address the problem of variation. In the course of the analysis we have uncovered three contexts in which it occurs: (5*a*), (5*b*), and (12). There is a clear hierarchy of preference, which we list in (13):

(13) *a*. obstruent plus liquid
      b. *s* plus stop
      c. obstruent plus nasal

The hierarchy in (13) corresponds in part to what Murray and Vennemann (1983) call contact laws, which assign preference to clusters composed of strongest and weakest segments, where strong/weak denotes the greatest/smallest distance from the nucleus in the SSG. Also, clusters of *s* and stops are a well-known pattern in the world's languages in the sense that these segments typically cluster together even if a language does not have the Obstruent Sequencing Principle.

There are two further formal questions that need to be addressed in connection with the statement of the SSA: (i) does the SSA operate directly on the melodic tier or rather on the skeletal tier?; and (ii) is it essential that the SSG should specify a nucleus rather than simply a vowel (the traditional view) as being in the central position of the syllable?

There is no doubt that syllable structure is constructed on the skeleton and not directly on the melodic representations. If the latter were true, then there would be no way of distinguishing between short and long vowels, since both are represented identically at the melody. Yet this distinction is crucial in order to define, for example, a heavy cluster, which determines the placement of stress in English. Recall that a heavy cluster is either a sequence of a short vowel followed by a consonant, or a long vowel (see 3.1). If syllable structure is constructed on the skeleton, these two instantiations of a heavy cluster can be conveniently defined as the presence of branching. In sum, the task of the SSA is to group skeletal Xs into syllables. Melodic representations play an indirect role in the sense that the SSA checks them only in order to determine whether a violation of the SSG does not take place. If it does, then the segment remains unsyllabified; that is, it remains extrasyllabic.

Given this view of syllabification, a prediction is made that unvocalized yers, which are floating (X-less) melodic segments, cannot influence the construction of syllables. This is borne out. Recall that unvocalized yers are deleted by Stray Erasure only at the end of phonological derivation. Consequently, they are present at the stage when syllables are erected. Thus, for instance, *striebr+o* 'silver' has a yer between *b* and *r*. The yer vocalizes in the adjective *striebor+n+ý*. In contrast, *obraz* 'picture' has no yer between *b* and *r*. This difference is irrelevant for syllabification and both *striebr+o* and *obraz* and syllabified in the same way: *strieb-ro ~ strie-bro*, *ob-raz ~ o-braz* (see (5)).

Now we turn to the question of whether the SSG should be defined with respect to the vowel or, more generally, with respect to the nucleus. A potential difference between these two views comes to light when we consider syllabic consonants. Assume for the moment that Slovak has *v*-Gliding, a rule that we state informally in (14) and motivate in detail in 7.8. Recall that *v* is a labiodental approximant, hence it is a sonorant:

(14) *v*-Gliding   Coda
$$\text{Coda}$$
$$v \rightarrow \underset{\sim}{u} / \;\overline{\quad\quad}$$

Consider now the phonetic realization of *v* in (15):

(15) *a.* only [u̯]: krv 'blood', prv 'first', brv (gen. pl. of brv+a 'eyebrow'),
        mrv (imper. of mrv+i+t' 'crumble')
    b. only [u̯]: lev 'lion', stav 'rank', cirkev 'Orthodox church'
    c. variation [u̯] ~ [v]: serv 'serve', nerv 'nerve', červ 'maggot', rezerv
        (gen. pl. of rezerv+a 'reserve'), sálv (gen. pl. of salv+a 'salute'),
        vúlv (gen. pl. of vulv+a 'clitoris'))

A comparison of (15a) with (15b) indicates that *v*-Gliding applies in both classes of words in exactly the same way. This means that *v* is in a coda and (14) is applicable. In (15a) the nucleus of the syllable is *r*. That is, *r* and *v* constitute a well-formed syllable. Notice, however, that *r* and *v* are in the same class of segments from the point of view of the SSG since approximants are classed together with liquids with regard to sonority. If the SSG were defined in purely melodic terms on relations holding between adjacent segments, then the sequence *rv* would constitute a violation and hence it could not be syllabified. Evidently, this is not the case. We conclude that the SSG refers to the relations holding between members of onsets and codas. That is, *rv* is a permissible sequence if *r* is syllabic, since it is then a nucleus and hence no violation of the SSG takes place.[3]

A question can now be raised whether we could not pursue a different line of reasoning. We could manipulate the sonority hierarchy and assume that, at least in the case of Slovak, approximants and liquids form separate sonority classes such that *v* is stronger (further removed from the nucleus) than liquids. Then, sequences such as *-rv* would be well-formed from the point of view of the SSG, regardless of whether *r* were syllabic or not. The data in (15*c*) indicate that this is a false step. There is no doubt that in words such as *serv* 'serve' both *r* and *v* are in a non-nuclear position and hence the SSG applies. The only way to explain why *v* is realized as [*v*], a prevalent pronunciation, is to assume that *v* is not in a coda. This result is obtained automatically if *r*, *l*, and *v* are in the same sonority class of approximants, as then the SSG takes effect and blocks the syllabification of *v* into the coda. The realization of *v* as [u̯] in (15*c*), a less-favoured variant, is derived by a rule of adjunction that overrides the SSG and puts *v* forcefully into the coda.

Thus, the SSG is defined with respect to members of onsets and codas. The central position in the hierarchy in (2) is occupied by the nucleus, which is either a vowel or a syllabic consonant. Universal sonority classes such as that for approximants, including liquids, should not be overridden by a language-specific suspension of this classification. Only then can the relevant difference between (15*a*) and (15*c*) be adequately made.

Finally, let us clarify the role of morpheme boundaries in syllabification. Traditional descriptive grammarians such as Letz (1950) and Stanislav (1977) recommend that morpheme boundaries should be respected when dividing words into syllables. However, the results of our questionnaire show that this is not borne out. Rather, whenever morpheme boundaries coincide with the syllabic division, then this is for independent reasons such as the fact that VCCV is syllabified as VC-CV or the fact that the final consonant is extrametrical on an earlier cycle. Compare the morpheme division with the syllabic division in (16). The syllabifications in parentheses are the marked patterns.

(16) vod+a 'water': vo-da (the only admissible variant)
     teles+n+ý 'corporal': te-les-ný (te-le-sný)
     šťast+liv+ý 'happy': šťas-tli-vý (šťast-li-vý)

The unmarked patterns are readily generated by our rules. This follows from the assumption made in Chapter 6 and motivated further in 7.6 below that constituent-final consonants are extrametrical in Slovak. Thus, for instance, *vod+a* is *vo(d)*$_{EM}$ on the first cycle. On cycle 2, when *a* is added, the CV Rule puts *d* into the onset.

---

[3] A similar conclusion has also emerged from a study of German: see Rubach (1990).

The question may be asked how we are to account for the variation in (16) as well as in (12) and (5) given earlier. The less-favoured variants can be derived if we assume that the Onset Rule may optionally resyllabify strings and that this resyllabification follows the hierarchy of preference in (13). The Complex Coda Rule may also sometimes resyllabify strings, but such resyllabifications are less typical.

7.2. CYCLIC SYLLABIFICATION

Now we address the question of whether the SSA is cyclic or non-cyclic and conclude that it is cyclic. That this conclusion is correct is shown by the operation of allomorphy and phonological rules. Below we look first at Imperative Allomorphy, then consider Liquid Syllabification.

The cyclicity of the SSA is motivated by the structure of the imperative. In (6) we indicated briefly that the occurrence of i as the imperative ending is governed by rule (7), which is triggered by an extrasyllabic consonant. The data in (17) corroborate this conclusion:[4]

(17) *a.* dr+ú 'they tear'—dr+i
      mr+ú 'they die'—mr+i
      žn+ú 'they cut'—žn+i
      pad+n+ú 'they fall'—pad+n+i
      za+čn+ú 'they begin'—za+čn+i

    b. mydl+i+t' 'to soap'—mydl+i
      vy+svetl+i+t' 'explain'—vy+svetl+i
      mysl+ie+t' 'think'—mysl+i
      zo+smieš+n+i+t' 'ridicule'—zo+smieš+n+i
      u+zem+n+i+t' 'connect to earth'—u+zem+n+i

    c. kresl+i+t' 'describe'—kresl+i
      u+rýchl+i+t' 'speed up'—u+rýchl+i
      ob+jasn+i+t' 'clarify'—ob+jasn+i
      u+skromn+i+t' 'become modest'—u+skromn+i

The words in (17*a–b*) are all yer roots. This is shown by vowel–zero alternations in (18). The vocalization of the root yer is effected by DI Raising (5/33) and Liquid Lowering (5/35) in (18*a*), and by Yer Vocalization (5/13) in (18*b*):

(18) *a.* dr+ú 'they tear'—vy+dier+aj+ú 'they tear out' (DI)
      žn+ú 'they cut'—vy+žín+aj+ú 'they cut out' (DI)

    b. mydl+o 'soap'—mydiel (gen. pl.)—mydl+i+t' 'to soap'
      svetl+o 'light'—svetiel (gen. pl.)—vy+svetl+i+t' 'explain'

---

[4] Here and below we compare the imperatives with those forms of their base verbs which show the structure of the stem most clearly. Sometimes it is the 3rd pl. of the present tense, at other times it is the infinitive or the past tense.

One may therefore wonder whether the root yer may have something to do with the surfacing of the *i* in the imperative. This is contradicted by (17*c*), where the roots clearly do not contain yers. Compare, for example, *ob+jasn+i+t'* 'clarify' and *jasn+ý* 'clear' as well as *u+rýchl+i+t'* 'speed up' and *rýchl+y* 'fast'. In sum, the appearance of *i* in the imperative is conditioned by syllable structure rather than by the occurrence of a yer in the root. This becomes particularly clear when we realize that the *i* is not inserted if the verb can be fully parsed by the SSA:

(19) nes+ú 'they carry'—nes
　　　čuj+ú 'they feel'—čuj
　　　vol+aj+ú 'they call'—vol+aj
　　　rozum+ej+ú 'they understand'—rozum+ej

Now we know that the occurrence of *i* in the imperative is linked to the presence of an extrasyllabic consonant. A comparison of *kresl+i* 'describe' and *nes* 'carry' after the SSA but prior to Imperative Allomorphy (7) brings out the relevant difference: see (20).

(20)

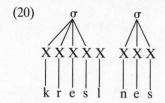

While it is clear that Imperative Allomorphy (7) has extrasyllabic consonants as its environment, it remains to be established how the input to the rule looks. The verbs in (21) indicate that the imperative triggers palatalization rules: Coronal Palatalization (4/17) in (21*a*) and 1st Velar Palatalization (4/7) in (21*b*):

(21) *a.* klad+ú 'they put'—klad'
　　　　　min+ú 'they pass'—miň
　　　　　kol+ú 'they gore'—kol'
　　　b. tiek+l+a 'she flowed'—teč
　　　　　strieh+l+a 'she guarded'—strež

The palatalization in (21) must be due to the presence of a front vowel at an earlier stage of the derivation. Clearly the front vowel must be an imperative suffix because the examples in (21) are imperative verbs. They all belong to the class of C-verbs, hence they do not contain a verbalizing suffix that might have caused palatalization on an earlier cycle. The palatalizing vowel in (21) seems to be peculiar at first glance because it does not surface phonetically. This fits the description of a yer. As documented in Chapter 5, yers do not surface if they are not followed by a yer. In sum, the imperative ending must be a front yer.[5] The statement of Imperative Allomorphy in (7) must now be revised. The rule inserts an X over a yer rather than inserting a vowel.[6] That is, the imperative yer is vocalized if it is preceded by an extrasyllabic consonant:[7]

(22) Imperative Vocalization

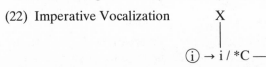

$$ⓘ → i / *C —$$

Our analysis claiming that the imperative suffix is a yer is supported additionally from three independent sources. In (23) we give the imperative forms of the 1st pl. and the 2nd pl.

(23)
	1st pl.	*2nd pl.*	*Gloss*
a.	čuj+me	čuj+te	'feel'
	rozum+ej+me	rozum+ej+te	'understand'
b.	miň+me	miň+te	'pass'

In (23a) the rule of Postvocalic j-Deletion (3/4) and in (23b) Nasal Deletion (5/39) are blocked, even though in surface terms their environments are met: the j and the ň are followed by a consonant. This blocking is understandable precisely if we assume that the imperative suffix is a yer. The representations of *čuj+me* 'let's feel' and *miň+me* 'let's pass' are thus as follows: //čuj+I+me//, //miň+I+me//, where -me is the 1st pl. ending and *I* is the imperative suffix. The yer of the imperative intervenes between the j/n and the consonant and hence the environments of Postvocalic j-Deletion and Nasal Deletion are in fact not met.

A third independent reason why we would like to posit a yer as the imperative suffix is the derivation of complex verbs which come from nouns or adjectives and hence contain verbalizing suffixes:

(24) kos+a 'scythe'—kos+i+t' 'mow'—kos (imper.)
let 'flight'—let+ie+t' 'fly'—let' (imper.)

The imperative is derived from verb stems which contain the verbalizing suffixes -i and -ie //él//. We face the problem of how to explain why

---

[5] The yer is necessary also for the derivation of the imperative in a-stem verbs such as *čes+a+t'* 'comb'—*češ* which show a reflex of Iotation. The imperative form is //čes+a+I//. The sequence of vowels triggers j-Insertion (4/40) and Iotation (4/41).

[6] This analysis has been inspired by Bethin's (1990) discussion of a similar but not identical problem in Polish.

[7] According to the standard sources, such as Stanislav (1977), *i* may appear phonetically as the ending of the imperative also in verbs which end in a consonant cluster that can be syllabified from the point of view of the SSG. However, the appearance of *i* is always then optional, hence a contrast with verbs such as those in (18) is always maintained. For example, *urč+i+t'* 'determine': *urč ~ urč+i*, *rozmliažd+i+t'* 'crush': *rozmliažd ~ rozmliažd+i*. This variation can be accounted for if we assume that the Complex Coda Rule is optional for the speakers who use the *i* forms.

the verbalizing suffixes do not appear phonetically in the imperative. Evidently, they are deleted by Vowel Deletion (3/8), which applies before a vowel. However, the vowel which triggers the rule is not seen on the surface. Again, this fact emerges straightforwardly from our analysis if we assume that the imperative suffix is a yer. The imperatives in (24) are represented as //kos+i+I// and //let+é+I//, respectively.

Now we return to the problem of whether the SSA is cyclic or not. The derivation of yer-stem verbs in (17) provides the required evidence. There is no doubt that Imperative Vocalization (22) must be ordered before Yer Vocalization (5/13), as in (25a); otherwise the latter would take effect and an incorrect form would be derived, as in (25b). Our example is the verb *dr+i* //dEr+I// 'tear', which we contrast with *nes* //nes+I// in (25c).

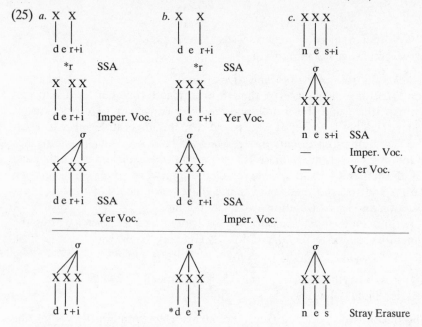

Recall that Yer Vocalization is a cyclic rule. Given the ordering in (25a), Imperative Vocalization must also be cyclic. But Imperative Vocalization is sensitive to syllable structure and hence requires that the SSA should apply before it. We conclude that the SSA is cyclic.

7.3. CONTINUOUS SYLLABIFICATION

The conclusion from the preceding section that the SSA is cyclic raises the question whether the SSA applies only once at the beginning of a cycle or rather reapplies automatically at all intermediate stages. If the latter is true, then a further question is whether the SSA reapplies also in the postcyclic and the postlexical components.

That the SSA must apply more than once is evident from the derivation in (25): the yer in (25a) must be syllabified after it has been vocalized by rule (22). Could we therefore assume that the SSA applies twice: at the beginning and at the end of the cycle? Derivation of complex verbs makes it clear that this hypothesis is untenable. The relevant examples were given in (24). In (26) we contrast the derivation of the first example in (24) with that of the first example in (17b): *kos* 'mow' and *mydl+i* 'soap' (a yer stem, see (18b)); compare the infinitives *kos+i+t'* and *mydl+i+t'*.

(26) Cycle 1   *a.* kos   *b.* midEl

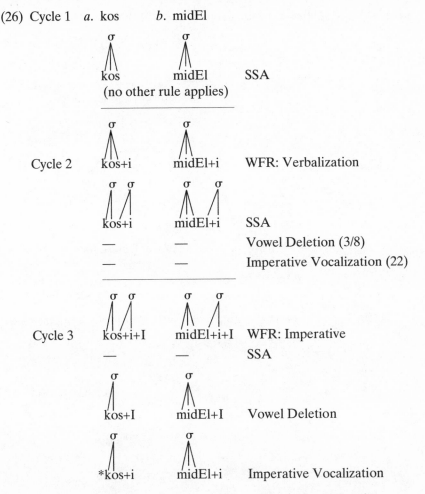

Cycle 2   kos+i   midEl+i   WFR: Verbalization

                              SSA

—   —   Vowel Deletion (3/8)

—   —   Imperative Vocalization (22)

Cycle 3   kos+i+I   midEl+i+I   WFR: Imperative

—   —   SSA

kos+I   midEl+I   Vowel Deletion

*kos+i   midEl+i   Imperative Vocalization

The derivation in (26a) is incorrect as we obtain **kos+i* for the correct *kos*. The situation can be remedied easily if we permit the SSA to reapply after Vowel Deletion. The stranded *s* in (26a) resyllabifies into the coda while the stranded *l* in (26*b*) does not, because the SSA is blocked by the SSG. After Imperative Vocalization the SSA must reapply again in order to syllabify the vocalized yer and derive the surface syllabification (myd)$_\sigma$ (l+i)$_\sigma$.

Reapplication of the SSA is required also by *v*-Gliding, rule (14), which turns /v/ into [u̯] in a coda:

(27) *a.* bav+i+t' sa [v] 'play'—bav sa [u̯] (imper.)
　　b. páv+a [v] 'peacock' (gen. sg.)—páv [u̯] (nom. sg.)

The derivation of the words in (27*a*) is shown in (28).

(28) Cycle 1　　*a.* bav　　　*b.* bav

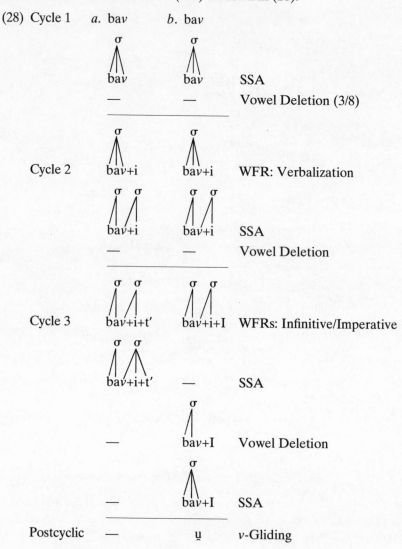

	SSA
— —	Vowel Deletion (3/8)
Cycle 2　bav+i　bav+i	WFR: Verbalization
bav+i　bav+i	SSA
— —	Vowel Deletion
Cycle 3　bav+i+t'　bav+i+I	WFRs: Infinitive/Imperative
bav+i+t'　—	SSA
—　bav+I	Vowel Deletion
—　bav+I	SSA
Postcyclic　—　u̯	*v*-Gliding

Notice that the *v* in (28*a*) is first in a coda but ultimately in an onset. The derivational stages of the *v* in (28*b*) are even more complex: coda, onset, coda. Reapplication of the SSA is crucial in order to derive the correct outputs. As we shall see, the SSA also reapplies postcyclically (7.7) and postlexically (7.8). In sum, the SSA is continuous. It begins applying in the cyclic component and keeps reapplying after every rule until the end of the derivation. Thus, Slovak confirms the conclusion reached by Itô (1986) and for Polish by Rubach and Booij (1990*a*) that syllabification is continuous.

7.4. DOMAIN OF SYLLABIFICATION

In the preceding sections we established the SSA and determined how it should apply. The last formal question is in what domain the SSA applies. Slovak as well as Polish (cf. Rubach and Booij 1990*b*) are cumbersome in this regard because prefixes, most of which come historically from prepositions, constitute separate domains of syllabification. This conclusion emerges from the results of the questionnaire (see the description in 7.1). The observation is that the CV Rule is systematically violated at prefix–stem junctures. In (29) we mark the relevant morphological and syllable boundaries.

(29) | *Morphology* | *Gloss* | *Syllabification* |
|---|---|---|
| bez+oký | 'eyeless' | bez-o- (20), be-zo- (0) |
| nad+individuálny | 'supraindividual' | nad-i- (20), na-di- (0) |
| pred+ostatný | 'penultimate' | pred-o- (19), pre-do- (1) |
| roz+iskrený | 'sparked' | roz-is- (19), ro-zis- (1) |
| od+učiť | 'unlearn' | od-u- (18), o-du- (2) |

Although the generalization is clear, we should comment on the marginal syllabification in (29) which seems to obey the CV Rule in one or two instances in a sample of words which were used in the questionnaire. The situation in Slovak parallels that in Polish, in the sense that the CV Rule may apply across what a linguist might analyse as a prefix juncture if the morphemic division into the prefix and the stem is not clear. For instance, *rozum+ie+ť* 'understand' comes historically from *roz* 'apart' and *umieť* 'know' but is now fully lexicalized and there is no perception of the prefix boundary. In sum, the degree to which the CV Rule is violated is directly related to the transparency of morphological structure.

Returning to the basic generalization, we face the problem of how to account for the fact that prefixes form a separate domain from the point of view of syllabification. Given that the situation in Slovak and Polish is practically identical, it seems that the easiest solution is to adopt the proposal of Rubach and Booij (1990*b*), who postulate the following constraint:

(30) Prosodification Constraint:
Derivation of prosodic structure is blocked by the constituency bracket [

The prediction of (30) is that the CV Rule is blocked not only in prefix–stem structures such as [[*bez*[*ok*]]*ý*] 'eyeless' but also in compounds, which is correct. Stanislav (1977) states that in, for example, [[*šesť*] [*uholník*]] 'hexagon' the final *ť* belongs to the first syllable. At the end of the cyclic component the Bracket Erasure Convention erases internal brackets and, consequently, (30) has no effect in postcyclic phonology. This, however, is not a problem, since in Slovak, as in Polish, all word-formation is cyclic and it is only in the cyclic component that the CV Rule may work as a resyllabification mechanism.

7.5. GLIDING

As we remarked in 1.3, N-Placement overgenerates in that it assigns a nucleus to every [–cons] segment. Consequently, if a language has glides, then they must be derived by a mechanism that we have not discussed yet. In this section we look at the derivation of [j] in Slovak. An account of [u̯] is given in 7.8.

If we disregard a small class of exceptions (which we address below), the distribution of [j] and [i] is complementary. Specifically, the following environments permit [i] but not [j]:

(31) *a.* # — C: ihl+a 'needle', istot+a 'essence', iskr+a 'spark'
    b. C — C: sirota 'orphan', pisk 'scream', plat+i+t' 'pay'
    c. C — #: kuli 'coolie', pan+i 'lady', dekan+i 'deans'
    d. C — V: dialekt 'dialect', pian+o 'piano', miniatur+a 'miniature',
        miliard+a 'milliard', triumf 'triumph', kiosk 'stand', biológ
        'biologist', kuli+ovia 'coolies', diét+a 'children', hyen+a
        'hyena'[8]

The question arises where [j] *can* appear. Ignoring for the moment (31*d*), the generalization is that [j] occurs when adjacent to a vowel:

(32) *a.* V —: kraj 'country', čaj 'tea', tajga 'taiga'
    b. — V: jak 'how', jasn+ý 'bright', juh 'south'
    c. V — V: boj+ov+ník 'fighter', čuj+ú 'they feel', doj+i+t' 'to milk'

---

[8] All the words in (31*d*) are instances of vowel sequences; that is, *i* is not part of a diphthong. Contrast *dialekt* 'dialect' (three syllables) vs. *diabol* 'devil' (two syllables).

N-Placement treats all the [–cons] segments alike. The glide [j] is then derived by removing the nucleus node. This is effected by gliding rules. (Recall that the sole difference between *i* and *j* is their place in syllable structure: *i* is a nucleus while *j* is either an onset or a coda.)

(33) *a.* Progressive Gliding

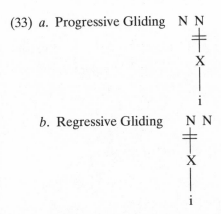

    b. Regressive Gliding

The rules in (33) should probably be stated as one rule with a mirror-image effect. Then, the regressive expansion must apply first, because (33*b*) is ordered before (33*a*), as we point out below. Furthermore, one may wonder why gliding is not stated as a resyllabification rule that effects two changes simultaneously: delinking of N and placing the delinked segment in the onset. This complication is not necessary if we include gliding in the SSA and order it before the Onset Rule and the Coda Rule. The SSA is now given in its final version:

(34) SSA (final)   N-Placement
                    CV Rule
                    Regressive Gliding
                    Progressive Gliding
                    Coda Rule
                    Onset Rule
                    Complex Coda Rule

The ordering of Regressive Gliding before Progressive Gliding is motivated by the fact that in words such as *jiríčka* 'linnet' the sequence //ii// of two *i* vowels (after N-Placement) is changed into [ji] rather than [ij]. The CV Rule precedes Regressive Gliding because it must be able to check whether *j*-Constraint, which restricts the operation of Regressive Gliding, is applicable. We discuss this problem below.

    We sum up our discussion by presenting in (35) the first cycle of the derivation for *jajč+a+t'* 'whine'.

(35)

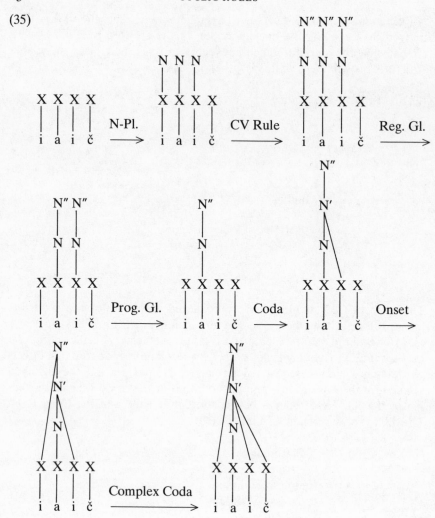

Gliding rules interpret not only underlying but also derived representations. For example, Yer Hiatus (5/52) inserts an *i* segment which is interpreted as [j] by Regressive Gliding; compare *Kore+a* 'Korea'—*korej+sk+ý* 'Korean' (see 5.7).

There is a small class of exceptional words in which *i* remains syllabic in spite of the fact that it stands next to a vowel:

(36) *a.* druid 'druid', naivn+ý 'naïve', stoik 'Stoic', Kain 'Cain' (vs. [j] as expected in *Kaifaš*)

  b. variation [i] ~ [j]: koktail 'cocktail', email 'enamel' (vs. only [j] in the corresponding adjective *email+ov+ý*)

  c. ego+ist+a 'egoist', ego+izmus 'egoism', proza+ik 'writer', ide+i 'idea' (loc. sg.)

  d. ioniz+ova+t' 'ionize', ión+sk+y 'Ionian'

The only genuine exceptions are the words in (36*a*). Those in (36*b*) are listed by Král' (1988) as examples of variation. The suffixes in (36*c*) are all non-palatalizing: compare, for example, *ulic+i* 'street' (gen. sg.—no Affricate Palatalization). We suggested in 6.6 that they should be regarded as postcyclic in the sense of Halle (1987). If we now assume that Progressive Gliding is turned off postcyclically, an assumption that is supported by the behaviour of prefixes,[9] then the occurrence of [i] rather than [j] in (36*c*) is explained. Finally, the examples in (36*d*) taken from Král' (1988) contradict Regressive Gliding, but they are pronounced with [j] rather than with [i] by many speakers, and hence they are not exceptions (L'ubomir D'urovič and Martin Votruba, personal communication). No such conclusion can be drawn about the words listed earlier in (31*d*). The generalization is that *i* never glides to *j* if it is preceded by a consonant, hence *dialekt* [dia-] 'dialect' contrasts with *jak* [jak] 'how'.[10] This generalization is expressed formally by postulating *j*-Constraint.

(37) *j*-Constraint   *N″

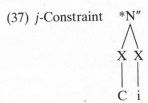

---

[9] Relevant here are the prefixes *za-* and *po-* as in *za+interesovat'* 'get interested' and *po+ihrat'* 'play'. In the cyclic component Progressive Gliding is blocked by Prosodification Constraint (30). In the postcyclic component (that is, after the internal brackets have been erased) Progressive Gliding would apply if it were still operative.

[10] A handful of exceptions should be listed: *subjekt* 'subject', *objektívn+y* 'objective', *adjektivum* 'adjective', *injekci+a* 'injection', and perhaps one or two other morphemes. The *j* is unstable in examples of this type. Thus, *fjeld* 'field' shows the variation [je] ~ [ie]. In *evanjelium* 'gospel' and *anjel* 'angel' the [je] pronunciation has been ousted and [ie] appears as the only variant (cf. Král' 1988). Still, the question remains how the exceptional words such as *subjekt* can be treated. One way is to assume that the first syllable is extrametrical. The *b* is then invisible to Regressive Gliding, which can therefore apply: *(sub)jekt* is parallel to *jak* 'how'. We may note in this connection that prefix–stem structures with *j* such as *ob+jasnit'* 'explain' and *od+jechat'* 'go away' are not exceptional in any way. The occurrence of *j* after a consonant is a consequence of the cyclic SSA: on the cycle when *j* is derived the prefix has not yet been added.

Thus, the application of Regressive Gliding is blocked in *dialekt* by (37). In *jak*, which is represented as //iak//, there is no onset and hence Regressive Gliding takes effect. This means that the CV Rule must apply before Regressive Gliding in order to be able to form an onset in *dialekt* and hence make the word available for blocking by *j*-Constraint.

In sum, gliding rules complement the SSA, and the version given in (34) can be regarded as final.[11] In the following three sections we look at the consequences of applying the SSA. Specifically, we identify three different types of situation in which the SSA unveils the existence of extrasyllabic consonants. These consonants are rescued back to the syllable in different ways: syllabification of the consonant (7.6), insertion of a vowel (7.7), and change in the feature content (7.8).

7.6. SYLLABIC LIQUIDS

We have noted before on a number of occasions that liquids stand out among Slovak consonants. One distinguishing property is that they can be underlyingly short and long, which makes them similar to vowels. Another characteristic feature is their ability to function as syllable nuclei (see Rubach and Booij, 1992):

(38) *a.* prst 'finger', hrb 'hunch', Srb 'Serbian', prv 'first', krv 'blood',
         tvrd+i+t' 'claim', smrt' 'death', smrd+ie+t' 'stink', chlp 'hair', tlst+ý
         'fat', tlm+i+t' 'muffle', pln+ý 'full', vlk 'wolf'
     b. Sartre [sartr], Sèvre [sevr], double [dabl] or [debl]

These words contrast with those in (39), in which the liquids are not syllabic:

(39) *a.* mrak 'darkness', plec+e 'shoulder', koncern 'company', šturm
         'attack', film 'film'
     b. rmut 'sadness', rdest 'water-pepper', rdie+t' 'become rusty', lka+t'
         'sob', l'stiv+ý 'crafty'

Ignoring (39*b*) for the moment, we arrive at a straightforward generalization: extrasyllabic liquids become syllabic.[12] This includes all the words in (38) and excludes those in (39*a*):

---

[11] An alternative to gliding would be to postulate two different N-Placement rules: one for *i* and the other for the remaining vowels (including *u*). This does not seem to be a particularly attractive solution since, first, it loses sight of the fact that N-Placement is a universal rule and, second, it leads to complications in that the statement of the general N-Placement Rule requires baroque disjunctions.

[12] The rule is indeed limited to liquids if we ignore the onomatopoeic *hm* 'hm'.

(40) Liquid Syllabification

$$*L \rightarrow L$$

That the occurrence of syllabic consonants is rule-governed is shown by the examples in (41). They exhibit an alternation between syllabic and non-syllabic liquids (on the left and on the right, respectively):

(41) jadr+n+ý 'tough'—jadr+o 'nucleus'
mudr+c 'sage'—mudr+ák 'sage' (pejor.)
jabl+k+o 'apple'—jabl+oň 'apple-tree'

To accommodate these alternations we must assume either (i) that liquids are underlyingly syllabic and that Slovak has a rule of desyllabification, or (ii) that Slovak has rule (40). Clearly the latter option is superior as it is both simpler and more extensive than (i). However, the data in (41) highlight a certain problem. It seems that we can determine the syllabicity of liquids only at the word level, because only then it is clear whether affixation rules have added a vocalic suffix or a consonantal one. Liquids are syllabic in the latter but not in the former case. In short, Liquid Syllabification must be a postcyclic rule. Unfortunately, this conclusion is incompatible with several important facts in the phonology of Slovak. In particular, it runs counter to our understanding of lengthening and shortening rules. As we pointed out earlier (see Chapter 6), syllabic liquids behave like vowels in that they can lengthen by Vowel Lengthening (6/62) as in (42a–b), and they can trigger the Rhythmic Law (6/51) as in (42c).

(42) a. hal+a 'hall'—hál (gen. pl.)
    srn+a 'deer'—sŕn (gen. pl.)
    slz+a 'tear'—slz (gen. pl.)
  b. hlas 'voice'—hlás+ok (dimin.)—hlás+k+a (gen. sg.)
    srp 'sickle'—sŕp+ok (dimin.)—sŕp+k+a (gen. sg.)
    chlp 'hair'—chĺp+ok (dimin.)—chĺp+k+a (gen. sg.)
  c. lúk+a 'meadow'—lúk+am (dat. pl.), UR //ám//; compare hal+a
    'hall'—hal+ám (dat. pl.)
    riek+a 'river'—riek+am (dat. pl.)
    vŕb+a 'willow'—vŕb+am (dat. pl.)

Words such as hal+a 'hall' and hlas 'voice' indicate that liquids do not lengthen if they are non-syllabic. That is, Liquid Syllabification must precede Vowel Lengthening. But Vowel Lengthening is cyclic (see Chapter 6). Consequently, Liquid Syllabification must also be cyclic. The operation of the Rhythmic Law in (42c) leads to the same conclusion. Recall that the rule must crucially act at the interface of the skeleton and the syllabic tier in order not to distinguish between long vowels and liquids. The underlying long *r* in *vŕb+a* 'willow' must therefore be syllabic when the Rhythmic Law applies, and we know that the Rhythmic Law is a cyclic rule.

Interestingly, our claim that, counter to the facts in (41), Liquid Syllabification must be cyclic is corroborated by purely descriptive evidence drawn from the derivation of syllabic liquids themselves. The relevant example here is the word *u+mr+l+c+a* 'dead person' (gen. sg.). In surface terms there is an ambiguity as to whether the *r* or the *l* should be syllabic, because both meet the environment of rule (40). However, the fact is that it is only *r* which can be syllabic (Pauliny 1979; L'ubomir D'urovič, personal communication). This result can be obtained easily if Liquid Syllabification is cyclic: on the cycle when *l* is considered, the *r* has already been made syllabic. The *l* is then syllabified into the coda and the correct output is derived. Note, incidentally, that we thereby confirm our earlier observation (see (15)) that sonority relations are defined between members of syllable margins (onsets and codas) but not between the nucleus and syllable margins, hence syllabic *r* can take *l* as a coda even though both are in the same sonority class.

To summarize, there is compelling evidence that Liquid Syllabification is cyclic (see also (47) below). This is in conflict with the observation made in connection with (41) that the syllabicity of liquids can be determined only postcyclically. How can we resolve this conflict?

Our dilemma is solved by the universal convention of Final Consonant Extrametricality (Borowsky 1986), which we found to be applicable to Slovak also in our earlier analysis (see 6.1.1.3). The effect of this convention is that root-final consonants first become available to syllable-oriented rules on cycle 2, because only then does the Peripherality Condition erase extrametricality. The derivation of *jadr+n+ý* 'tough' and *jadr+o* 'nucleus', the first pair of words in (41), proceeds as shown in (43). We simplify the derivation by omitting irrelevant parts of representation and ignoring unvocalized yers, because they do not play any role in syllabification.

(43) Cycle 1   jad(r)_{EM}   jad(r)_{EM}

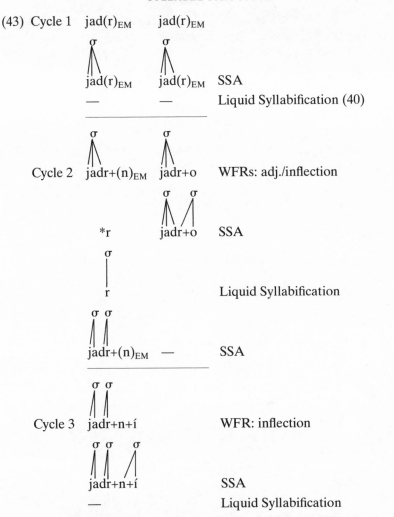

Cycle 2   jadr+(n)_{EM}   jadr+o   WFRs: adj./inflection

Cycle 3   jadr+n+í   WFR: inflection

Final Consonant Extrametricality also has beneficial effects for explaining the relation between Yer Vocalization and Liquid Syllabification. Consider the examples in (44):

(44) sveter 'sweater'—svetr+a ((gen. sg.)
     kotol 'cauldron'—kotl+a (gen. sg.)
     kufor 'trunk'—kufr+a (gen. sg.)

The root yers in the words on the left are vocalized before the nom. sg. yer //U//. Without final extrametricality the liquid would become syllabic on cycle 1, and hence we would need to posit a rule of desyllabification which would desyllabify consonants on cycle 2 after the root yer has been vocalized. With final extrametricality these complications are avoided by ordering Liquid Syllabification after Yer Vocalization. In (45) we derive the yer stem *sveter* 'sweater' and compare it with the derivation of the straightforward examples *srn+a* 'deer' and *Sartre*. The yer //U// is the ending of the masc. nom. sg. and the *-a* of the fem. nom. sg.

(45)

Cycle 1	$svetE(r)_{EM}$	$sr(n)_{EM}$	$sart(r)_{EM}$	

σ $\qquad\qquad$ σ

$svetE(r)_{EM}$ $\quad$ *r $\qquad$ $sart(r)_{EM}$ $\qquad$ SSA

— $\qquad$ — $\qquad$ — $\qquad$ Yer Vocalization (5/13)

σ

— $\qquad$ r $\qquad$ — $\qquad$ Liquid Syllabification (40)

σ

— $\qquad$ $sr(n)_{EM}$ $\qquad$ — $\qquad$ SSA

σ $\qquad$ σ $\qquad$ σ

Cycle 2 $\quad$ $svetEr+U$ $\quad$ $srn+a$ $\quad$ $sartr+U$ $\qquad$ WFRs: inflection

$\sigma\ \sigma$

*r $\qquad$ $srn+a$ $\qquad$ *r $\qquad$ SSA

σ

$sveter+U$ $\qquad$ — $\qquad$ — $\qquad$ Yer Vocalization

$\sigma\ \sigma$

$sveter+U$ $\qquad$ — $\qquad$ — $\qquad$ SSA

σ

— $\qquad$ — $\qquad$ r $\qquad$ Liquid Syllabification

$\sigma\ \sigma$

— $\qquad$ — $\qquad$ $sartr+U$ $\qquad$ SSA

This derivation highlights two points of theoretical interest. First, we confirm our earlier assertion that the SSA is continuous: it must reapply to *sveter* in the middle of cycle 2 in order to syllabify the vocalized yer and thereby pre-empt the application of Liquid Syllabification. Second, the addition of a yer counts as a violation of the Peripherality Condition and extrametricality must be erased. Only then can the *r* of *Sartre* be made syllabic on cycle 2. This finding is corroborated by our analysis in 7.2, where the addition of the imperative yer must open the structure for inspection by the SSA in order to determine whether the final consonant is syllabifiable.

The application of Liquid Syllabification in the imperative leads to an unexpected strengthening of our analysis. Recall that the imperative yer is vocalized when preceded by an extrasyllabic consonant. Liquid Syllabification plays a role here in that it pre-empts Imperative Vocalization by creating a syllable with a liquid as its nucleus:

(46) tĺc+t' 'pestle'—tlč
 tlm+i+t' 'muffle'—tlm
 skrč+i+t' 'crumple'—skrč

Liquid Syllabification and the SSA derive a well-formed syllable from the intermediate representation /tlč+I/: *č* is syllabified into the coda and we obtain *tlč* rather than **tlč+i*. Crucial in this derivation is the ordering of Liquid Syllabification before Imperative Vocalization. But now we have an ordering paradox. It is clear from (45) that Liquid Syllabification applies after Yer Vocalization. Thus, according to (45) and (46) the ordering of the rules is: Yer Vocalization, Liquid Syllabification, Imperative Vocalization. This runs counter to the ordering given earlier in (25), where Imperative Vocalization must apply before Yer Vocalization. According to (25) and (46) the order of the rules is: Liquid Syllabification, Imperative Vocalization, Yer Vocalization. However, this ordering paradox only arises if the rules apply non-cyclically. Given the cycle, the order of the rules is: Imperative Vocalization, Yer Vocalization, Liquid Syllabification, and all the forms can be derived without difficulty. Consider the imperative *tlč* 'pestle', the derivation of which is given in (47). The final consonant is //k// and not //č//, as shown by the alternation in *tĺk+l+a* 'she pestled'.

Now we address the problem raised by the data in (39*b*): how are we to avoid the application of Liquid Syllabification to word-initial consonants in words such as *rmut* 'sadness'? Of course, one can always rewrite Liquid Syllabification in a way that would exclude word-initial consonants:

(47) Cycle 1   tl(k)$_{EM}$

              *l   SSA

              —   Imperative Vocalization (22)

              —   Yer Vocalization (5/13)

              σ
              |
              l   Liquid Syllabification (40)

              σ

              tl(k)$_{EM}$ SSA

              σ

Cycle 2   tlk+I   WFR: imperative

              σ

              tlk+I   SSA

              —   Imperative Vocalization

              —   Yer Vocalization

              —   Liquid Syllabification

              σ

              tlč +I   1st Velar Palatalization (4/7)

              σ

              tlč   Stray Erasure

---

(48)   σ
          |
   *L → L / C —

Rmut is not now an input to Liquid Syllabification, because *r* is not pre-ceded by a consonant. But while the formulation in (48) avoids the problem under discussion, it is unacceptable on general theoretical grounds. As predicted by the SSA, no consonant can be extrasyllabic after a vowel. Consequently, 'writing in' the environment of a consonant in (48) is simply an embarrassment. It is reminiscent of Halle's (1959) argument against the phoneme in the sense that the same generalization is stated twice.

Our problem is to find a way of saying that word-initial extrasyllabic liquids do not count for the purposes of Liquid Syllabification. At first glance it seems that positing word-initial extrametricality might be a solution. However, this step is unacceptable. First, unlike word-final extrametricality, which is universal, word-initial extrametricality would have to be a stipulation that is specific to Slovak, hence we have a complication of the grammar. Second, word-initial extrametricality does not solve the problem but merely delays it to later stages of the derivation. Given Itô's (1986) assumption that segments must be licensed prosodically in order to be realized phonetically, we have to posit a rule of adjunction which applies after the extrametricality has been erased at the end of the cyclic component. Third—and this argument is decisive—word-initial extrametricality would in effect contradict the generalization subsumed under *j*-Constraint (37). Recall that the proper application of gliding rules requires that it must be possible to determine whether there is a word-initial onset or not. Gliding takes effect only in the latter case, hence in *jak* 'how' but not in *dialekt* 'dialect'. If the word-initial consonant is extrametrical, then the distinction between *jak* and *dialekt* is lost as the *d* is invisible to the SSA. In sum, word-initial extrametricality is not an option.

Given this conclusion, we might just as well assume that adjunction, which would be necessary at later stages of the derivation anyway, applies in the cyclic component. We state the rule in (49):

(49) Initial Adjunction: adjoin initial *C to the syllable node

Our decision to adjoin *C to the syllable node is arbitrary in the sense that *C could just as well be adjoined to the phonological word node, as is the case in Polish (cf. Rubach and Booij 1990*b*). We return to this problem in 7.8.[13]

We have now analysed all the data adduced in (38) and (39). This analysis has led to the following conclusions. Liquid Syllabification is cyclic. Its application is mediated by Final Consonant Extrametricality and Initial Adjunction. The SSA applies continuously and is not ordered among phonological rules. However, Liquid Syllabification as well as Initial Adjunction are ordered: the latter precedes the former. Moreover, Liquid Syllabification applies after Imperative Vocalization and Yer Vocalization. This is an important observation. Steriade (1982) assumes

[13] In the case of the morpheme *lož* 'lie', Initial Adjunction cannot fulfil its task of excluding *l* from Liquid Syllabification. The problem is that *lož* has a yer: compare *lž+i* (gen. sg.). Consequently, no syllable is erected on the root cycle and hence Initial Adjunction is inapplicable. The morpheme *lož* must be simply an exception to Liquid Syllabification.

that syllable-structure rules may be ordered among phonological rules. This is correct with respect to Liquid Syllabification and Initial Adjunction. However, it is incorrect with respect to the SSA, which must be continuous. Thus, syllable-structure rules are of two types: phonological rules such as Liquid Syllabification and Initial Adjunction, and the rules of the SSA. That is, syllable-oriented rules have more structure than has hitherto been assumed. Finally, it may be observed that Liquid Syllabification is a 'rescue strategy' in the sense that it licenses prosodically segments that would otherwise have remained extrasyllabic. Liquid Syllabification applies to word-medial and word-final but not to word-initial extrasyllabic segments, an effect of Initial Adjunction. This asymmetry between the word-medial and word-final position on the one hand, and the word-initial position on the other, is not at all untypical. It is exhibited also by several unrelated rules in Polish and Czech (cf. Rubach and Booij 1990*b*).

7.7. POSTCYCLIC INSERTION

In this section we look at the environment in which the Peripherality Condition has no effect. Final extrametricality is then erased by convention at the end of the cyclic component, which leads to a rise of extrasyllabicity postcyclically. However, now the extrasyllabicity is resolved in a different way: the liquid is not syllabified, rather a vowel is inserted (see Rubach and Booij, 1992). Consider the forms of the past participle set out in (50).

(50) Infinitive   Past participle   Gloss

	Masculine	Feminine	Neuter	
hús+t'	húd+ol	húd+l+a	húd+l+o	'hum'
liez+t'	liez+ol	liez+l+a	liez+l+o	'crawl'
viez+t'	viez+ol	viez+l+a	viez+l+o	'transport'
nies+t'	nies+ol	nies+l+a	nies+l+o	'carry'
piec+t'	piek+ol	piek+l+a	piek+l+o	'bake'

The problem is how to account for the occurrence of *o* in the masculine gender and its absence in the feminine and the neuter genders. An offhand suggestion is to assume that *o* is a yer, because the pattern of vowel–zero alternation typically falls under Yer Vocalization. An immediate consequence of such an analysis is the necessity to assume that the past participle *l* is followed by a yer in the masculine gender. The yer is postulated in order to trigger the vocalization of the putative *o* yer. Thus, *húd+ol* 'he hummed' would have to be represented as /fiúd+Ol+U/. Unfortunately, there is strong evidence that this representation is incorrect: neither the alternating *o* nor the masculine gender marker can be a yer. The correct representation is simply /ñúd+l/ and the gender marker for the masculine is zero.

That the alternating *o* cannot be a yer is shown by the fact that the nasal consonant is deleted before *l*:

(51) stih+nú+t' //stiɣ+n+t'//[14] 'manage'—stih+ol—stih+l+a—stih+l+o
 pad+nú+t' 'fall'—pad+ol—pad+l+a—pad+l+o
 chud+nú+t' 'lose weight'—chud+ol—chud+l+a—chud+l+o

If a yer intervened between the nasal and the *l*—that is, if the representation were //stiɣ+n+Ol// for *stih+ol* 'he managed'—then the nasal could not delete because it would not be adjacent to the lateral. Incidentally, we may observe that *l* is extrametrical in *stih+ol* /stifi+n+(l)$_{EM}$/ and yet it triggers the deletion of *n*. There is nothing disturbing about this fact. Extrametricality is invisible at the skeletal and, consequently, also at the syllabic tier; the melodic tier is not affected.

A similar type of evidence indicates that the masculine gender marker cannot be a yer either.[15] The roots in (52) contain yers:

(52) zámok 'lock'—zámk+a (gen. sg.)—zamk+nú+t' 'to lock'
 zamk+ol 'he locked'—zamk+l+a 'she locked'—zamk+l+o 'it locked'
 Also: vy+sch+nú+t' 'to dry'—vy+sch+ol 'he dried'
 dotk+nú+t' 'to touch'—dotk+ol 'he touched'

If the masculine gender had a yer, the representation of *zamk+ol* 'he locked' would be //zamOk+n+l+U//. The root yer would then be subject to Yer Vocalization and we would derive the incorrect *[zamok+l]. The correct representation is therefore //zamOk+n+l// and Yer Vocalization is inapplicable, as desired.

To summarize, an attempt to interpret the *o*–zero alternation in (50) as derivable from an underlying yer is untenable. Consequently, the *o* must be an effect of an insertion rule which operates in the environment of an extrasyllabic liquid:

(53) *o*-Insertion   X
               |
          $\emptyset \rightarrow o$ / — *L

---

[14] The *ú* comes from *u*-Insertion (3/37).

[15] As mentioned in Chapter 3, only one stem seems to suggest that the masculine gender has a yer ending. We have stem-internal vowel–zero alternations in *šie+l* 'he went'—*š+l+a* 'she went'—*š+l+o* 'it went'. However, this alternation is best analysed as suppletion, since the stem is heavily irregular anyway; compare the infinitive *is+t'* 'go' and the 3rd sg. present tense *id+e* 'he goes'.

(54)

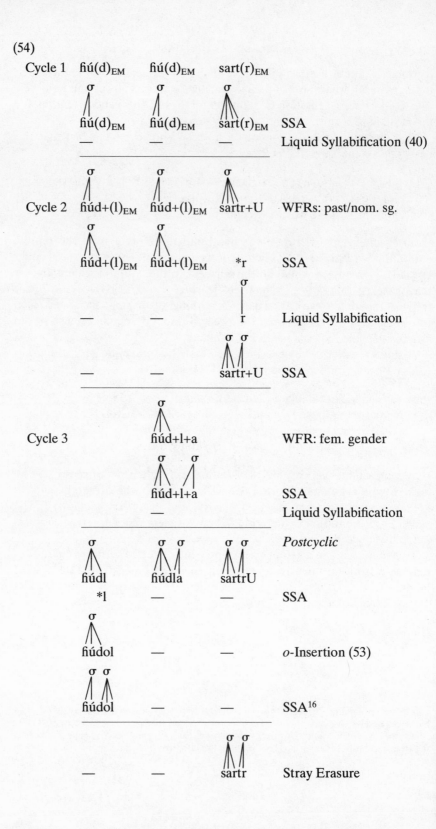

Cycle 1	fiú(d)$_{EM}$	fiú(d)$_{EM}$	sart(r)$_{EM}$	
	σ	σ	σ	
	fiú(d)$_{EM}$	fiú(d)$_{EM}$	sart(r)$_{EM}$	SSA
	—	—	—	Liquid Syllabification (40)
Cycle 2	σ fiúd+(l)$_{EM}$	σ fiúd+(l)$_{EM}$	σ sartr+U	WFRs: past/nom. sg.
	σ fiúd+(l)$_{EM}$	σ fiúd+(l)$_{EM}$	*r	SSA
	—	—	σ r	Liquid Syllabification
	—	—	σ σ sartr+U	SSA
Cycle 3		σ fiúd+l+a		WFR: fem. gender
		σ σ fiúd+l+a		SSA
		—		Liquid Syllabification
Postcyclic	σ fiúdl	σ σ fiúdla	σ σ sartrU	
	*l	—	—	SSA
	σ fiúdol	—	—	*o*-Insertion (53)
	σ σ fiúdol	—	—	SSA[16]
	—	—	σ σ sartr	Stray Erasure

Rule (53) turns /fiúd+l/ into [fiúd+ol] *húd+ol* 'he hummed' and /zamOk+l/ (after the deletion of *n*) into [zamk+ol] *zamk+ol* 'he locked'.

A comparison of *o*-Insertion (53) and Liquid Syllabification (40) leads to a striking observation: both rules apply in the same environment, yet their effects are distinct. How can this be reconciled? A solution is readily provided by the framework of Lexical Phonology.

Observe that *o*-Insertion is a postcyclic and not a cyclic rule. This is shown by the fact that *o*-Insertion is triggered only by the extrasyllabic liquid which is found at the word level, hence in *húd+ol* /fiúd+l/ 'he hummed' but not in *húd+l+a* 'she hummed' and *húd+l+o* 'it hummed', in which the *l* has been syllabified into the onset of the last syllable. On the other hand, Liquid Syllabification is cyclic. Thus, *o*-Insertion and Liquid Syllabification apply in different components and consequently they are not in conflict in spite of the identical environment.

One further problem requires explanation. Words such as *Sartre* /sartr/ and *double* /dabl/ 'double game' undergo Liquid Syllabification, while *húd+ol* /fiúd+l/ does not. How can we avoid the syllabification of *l* in /fiúd+l/? The answer lies in Final Consonant Extrametricality and inflectional yers. The *l* of /fiúd+l/ remains extrametrical throughout the cyclic derivation because, as argued above, the masculine gender has a zero ending rather than a yer and hence the Peripherality Condition is inapplicable. The *l* loses extrametricality by convention at the end of the component (here, the cyclic component). On the other hand, *Sartre* is a noun, and hence, like all other masculine nouns, it takes the nom. sg. yer ending. The extrametricality of the final *r* is erased by the Peripherality Condition and the *r* is open to Liquid Syllabification. We sum up our discussion by deriving *húd+ol* 'he hummed' and *húd+l+a* 'she hummed', which we contrast with *Sartre*: see (54). We may observe in passing that the assignment of Initial Adjunction to the cyclic component has beneficial effects for our analysis in this section. It makes it clear why *o*-Insertion does not apply to words such as *rmut* 'sadness': the *r* is adjoined and hence the environment of *o*-Insertion is not met.

The task of *o*-Insertion and of the SSA is to license prosodically the *l* in (54). Consequently, the *l* can escape Stray Erasure. This is not the case in East Slovak. According to Pauliny (1963) the past participle *l* is deleted in this dialect:

(55) | *Central Slovak* | *East Slovak* | *Gloss* |
|---|---|---|
| piek+ol | pik | 'he baked' |
| nies+ol | nis | 'he carried' |
| vied+ol | vid | 'he led' |

---

[16] The *d* of *húdol* is delinked from the coda by a universal convention which stipulates that syllable margins are redetermined whenever a vowel is inserted between consonants. The CV Rule puts the floating *d* into the onset of the final syllable.

The deletion of *l* need not be a rule. It suffices to assume that East Slovak has no *o*-Insertion and hence *l* stays unprosodified, which makes it subject to Stray Erasure.

To summarize, *o*-Insertion, like Liquid Syllabification, has the function of rescuing extrasyllabic consonants from being deleted. Both rules apply in the same environment. This, however, does not cause any difficulty if one assumes the framework of Lexical Phonology: *o*-Insertion is post-cyclic while Liquid Syllabification is cyclic.

7.8. THE PROBLEM OF *v*

In this section we look at *v* and conclude that it is represented as a labiodental approximant at the underlying level. An intricate pattern of alternations is accounted for by postulating a rule which changes //*v*// into a glide in syllable coda and into an obstruent context-freely. The latter change is undone by a special rule applying before non-nasal sonorants. We begin by presenting the basic facts.

In terms of phonetic representation *v* is realized in four different ways:

(56) *a.* [*v*]: labiodental approximant (a sonorant, cf. Král' 1988, Isačenko 1968, Dvončová *et al.* 1969, Sabol 1989[17]): vad+a 'drawback', vlas 'hair', svet 'world'
   b. [u̯]: labiovelar glide: šev 'seam', stav 'state', archív 'archive'
   c. [v]: labiodental voiced fricative:[18] vzor 'pattern', v+beh+nú+t' 'run into', v+znik 'origin'
   d. [f]: labiodental voiceless fricative: v+pad+nú+t' 'fall into', vták 'bird', vtip 'wit'

This is a rather spectacular range of differentiation: from a glide to a voiceless obstruent. However, there is no reason for concern. As is well known, Proto-Slavic had only the glide [u̯]. In the course of historical development [u̯] changed into the fricative [v], but the extent to which this happened is different in different Slavic languages. In Polish the change is complete in the sense that the fricative [v] has been restructured as the underlying representation.[19] Russian, for example, has not gone so far: the

---

[17] In the past there was some controversy regarding the status of *v*: see Sabol (1964). The matter is complicated, since in East Slovak (the region bordering on Poland) *v* is an obstruent in all positions, which is an exact parallel to Polish. As regards the facts of Central Slovak, which is the dialect under consideration, I follow the remarkably detailed transcriptions in Král"s (1988) pronouncing dictionary.

[18] Note the transcription: [v] is an obstruent while [*v*] is a sonorant (a labiodental approximant).

[19] This is shown by the fact, amongst others, that Polish, unlike all the other Slavic languages, has a rule of progressive devoicing; compare Polish *bitw+a* [-tf-] 'battle' and Russian *bitv+a* [-tv-] 'battle'.

glide is still present at the underlying level, although it is always realized phonetically as a fricative. Slovak is least different from Proto-Slavic: the glide appears phonetically, albeit in a restricted context. This is demonstrated by the data in (57):

(57) [v]   [u̯]
    zdrav+ý 'healthy'   zdrav+š+í 'healthier'
    stav+a+t' 'build'   stav+b+a 'building'
    zabav+i+t' 'play'   zabav (imper.)
    sport+ov+ec 'athlete'   sport+ov+c+a (gen. sg.)
    hlav+a 'head'   hláv (gen. pl.), hláv+k+a (dimin.)

The generalization is clear: [v] occurs in onsets and [u̯] in codas. Given this complementary distribution we can assume that either [v] is derived from the underlying glide //u̯// or the other way round: [u̯] from approximant //v//. The former assumption requires rule (58a) while the latter calls for rule (58b).

(58) *a.* u̯-Strengthening   Onset

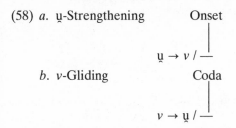

                   u̯ → v / —

  b. *v*-Gliding   Coda

                   v → u̯ / —

Rule (58a) is closer to the historical facts, but it requires some further assumptions. In particular, it is necessary for u̯-Strengthening to be preceded by a gliding rule because, given the present-day syllable theory, the glide [u̯] differs from the vowel [u] in exactly the same way as [j] differs from [i]. That is, [u̯] and [u] are represented in the same way at the melodic tier but in different ways at the syllabic tier: [u̯] is either an onset or a coda while [u] is a nucleus. Therefore we expect that the relation between [u̯] and [u] should parallel that between [j] and [i]. This, unfortunately, is not the case. First, [u̯] occurs in contexts in which [j] is never permitted and, second, [u̯] contrasts with [u] in a way that precludes the possibility of deriving the former from the latter. The relevant contexts and contrasts are summarized in (59):

(59) *a.* # — C: vlak 'train' *vs.* ulic+a 'street'
    b. C — C: nerv+stv+o 'nervous system' *vs.* rusk+ý 'Russian'
    c. C — #: sálv 'salute' (gen. pl.) *vs.* bal+u 'ball' (gen. sg.)

That [u̯] cannot be derived from [u] was observed originally by Isačenko (1968), who pointed out that Slovak has 'minimal pairs' such as *v+bit'* 'hammer in'[20] vs. *u+bit'* 'kill'. This conclusion is strengthened further by arguments which are independent of surface phonotactics. First, an assumption that [j] and [u̯] come from the respective high vowels makes it impossible to derive words such as *juh* 'south'. The melodic representation would be //iuy// and an ambiguity would arise as to whether the gliding of *i* or the gliding of *u* should take precedence. To guarantee that the derivation was correct we would need to introduce *ad hoc* conditions and stipulations. Second, if [u̯] is //u// at the underlying level, then Liquid Syllabification is blocked incorrectly in words such as *krv* [kru̯] 'blood' and *prv* [pru̯] 'first'. Final Consonant Extrametricality is inapplicable to the representations //kru// and //pru// because //u// is not a consonant. Worse, the //u// undergoes N-Placement and we derive the incorrect [kru] and [pru]. Third—and this is decisive—the rule of *u*-Gliding is practically impossible to state, since evidently Slovak tolerates sequences of *u* and a vowel: compare *duel* 'duel', *individuál+n+y* 'individual', *evaku+ova+t'* 'evacuate', *mauzóle+um* 'mausoleum', all of which contain the vowel *u*.

We conclude that *u̯*-Strengthening is untenable. Consequently, the approximant //v// is underlying and [u̯] is derived by *v*-Gliding:[21]

(60) *v*-Gliding

$$v \rightarrow [-\text{cons}] / \underline{\quad}$$

Rule (60) is postcyclic and hence it operates on the syllable structure of the word level. This is shown by the examples given earlier in (28), whose correct derivation depends on two assumptions: *v*-Gliding is postcyclic and the SSA applies continuously.

Incidentally, it may be noted that, with *v*-Gliding as a rule of Slovak, it is understandable why the feminine instr. sg. ending *-ou* does not shorten by the Rhythmic Law in words such as *krásn+ou* 'beautiful'. The *-ou* cited traditionally as an exception to the Rhythmic Law (for instance de Bray 1980) can now be interpreted as underlying //ov//, as discovered originally by Jakobson (1931). Our decision to assign *v*-Gliding to the class of postcyclic rules makes it absolutely clear why the Rhythmic Law, which is cyclic, does not affect *-ou*.

Let us now return to the other alternations in (56). We begin by observing that the problem which they highlight reduces to explaining the distribution of the approximant [v] and the voiced fricative [v]. The voiceless fricative [f] is clearly derivable from /v/ by Voice Assimilation (see 9.2):

(61) v+bit' [v] 'hammer in' *vs.* [f]: v+padnút' 'fall in', v+tiahnut' 'pull in'
     v blate [v] 'in the mud' *vs.* [f]: v práci 'at work', v chlebe 'in the bread'

---

[20] The [v] is an obstruent in this word, but the change /v/ → [v] is effected by a later rule. Thus, Isačenko's point holds, albeit for an earlier derivational stage.

[21] A later redundancy rule guarantees that the [−cons] *v* is interpreted as [u̯].

That is, if we are able to account for the occurrence of the voiced [v], we shall also be able to derive the voiceless [f]. In what follows we shall therefore ignore the distinction between [v] and [f] and concentrate on the general problem: the sonorant [v] versus the fricative [v/f].

Consider the words in (62):

(62) *a.* sonorant [v]:
      (i) voda 'water', v oku 'in the eye', v jame 'in the hole'
      (ii) vrana 'crow', v+rezat' 'cut into', v roku 'in the year', vláda 'government', v+lámat' 'break into', v lese 'in the forest'
  b. obstruent [v]:
      (i) vzor 'pattern', v+dýchat' 'breathe in', v doline 'in the valley'
      (ii) v+miešat' sa 'interfere', v mlyne 'in the mill', v meste 'in town'[22]

The distribution of [v] and [v] must be accounted for by rule, as is clearly indicated not only by the surface phonotactics but also by the alternations in (62). Thus, the prefix *v* as well as the preposition *v* surface either as [v] or as [v]. Similarly, *voš* 'louse' has [v] while the gen. sg. form *vš+i* has [f].

Given our earlier analysis it is clear that [v] is derived from //v// and not vice versa, but it is less clear how this change should be effected. Two options seem to be available:

  (i) we posit the rules of Obstruent Spreading for (62*b*(i)) and Prenasal Obstruentization for (62*b*(ii));
  (ii) alternatively, we introduce a general rule of obstruentization changing //v// into [v] context-freely and a later rule restoring [v] before non-nasal sonorants.

While both alternatives are comparably complex, (ii) is clearly preferable on typological grounds. On the one hand, the Obstruent Spreading (that is, spreading of [−sonor]) required by (i) would be unprecedented as a rule because it is generally believed that [sonor] as a feature does not spread. On the other hand, the context-free obstruentization required by (ii) is certainly nothing surprising in Slavic languages. This is exactly what has happened historically in Polish. In sum, we propose that Slovak has rule (63):

(63) Obstruentization $v \rightarrow$ [−sonor]

A decisive argument in favour of alternative (ii), and hence rule (63), comes from the consideration of Vowel Vocalization in prepositions and prefixes. This rule is discussed in detail in 9.1. For the moment it is enough to note that extrasyllabic *v* is spelled out as *vo*. Thus, /v vode/ surfaces as *vo vode* 'in the water', because the cluster /vv-/ is not well-formed and hence the initial *v* is extrasyllabic. Returning now to the data in (62),

---

[22] Before coronal nasals [v] and [v] are in free variation, for instance *vnuk* 'grandson'; see Král' (1988).

we observe that the *v* does not surface as *vo* in *v doline* 'in the valley', *v meste* 'in town', *v lese* 'in the forest', etc. This means that *v* cannot be extrasyllabic at the stage when the rule *v* → *vo* applies. Alternative (i) could handle *v doline* 'in the valley' and *v meste* 'in town' by ordering Obstruent Spreading and Prenasal Obstruentization before the *v* → *vo* rule. However, this would not explain *v lese* 'in the forest', in which *v* is phonetically a sonorant. Needless to say, /v/ and /l/ do not constitute a well-formed onset from the point of view of sonority, because they both belong to the class of approximants. One could, of course, manipulate the sonority hierarchy and claim that for a language-specific purpose *v* is stronger than *r* and *l*. Such a step is unacceptable, however, from the descriptive point of view (we address this problem below). These difficulties disappear if we assume that Slovak has rule (63). Phrases such as *v lese* 'in the forest' are syllabified at the stage when *v* has been changed into an obstruent. The SSG is not then violated. A later rule, which alternative (ii) requires anyway, restores [+sonor] in a subset of contexts enumerated in (62):

(64) Sonorization $v \rightarrow [+\text{sonor}] / - \begin{bmatrix} +\text{sonor} \\ -\text{labial} \end{bmatrix}$

The success of this analysis rests upon the assumption that the SSA applies continuously (here, after rule (63) and before (64)); but given our earlier evidence this is exactly what we would expect. Attention should also be drawn to the fact that Obstruentization (63) is a new type of 'rescue strategy' for extrasyllabic consonants. Our previous examples are all cases of insertion or deletion. Obstruentization is different in that it alters the feature content of the extrasyllabic segment and thereby makes this segment syllabifiable. In some ways this case is reminiscent of the Polish *r'* → *ž* rule discussed by Rubach and Booij (1990*a*).

An interplay between *v*-Gliding and Obstruentization[23] explains what in purely linear terms seems to be a paradox. In the environment of obstruents, //v// is realized sometimes as [u̯] and sometimes as [v]: compare *hláv+k+a* [u̯] 'head' (dimin.) vs. *v+kopat'* [f] 'dig in'. This paradox does not arise in the non-linear syllable-oriented statement of *v*-Gliding: only the *v* of *hláv+k+a* undergoes the rule because only this *v* is in the coda. We assume that Obstruentization is ordered after *v*-Gliding so that *hláv+k+a* has [u̯] at the stage when Obstruentization applies and hence is not an input. Given that *v*-Gliding is postcyclic, Obstruentization is best regarded as postlexical. Then the ordering relation need not be stipulated.

---

[23] This interplay might lead one to suggest that //v// is actually underspecified for the feature [sonor] at the underlying level. While such a step is possible, it is not particularly enlightening. The point is that the missing value for [sonor] would have to be supplied as the first step in the derivation, because, on the one hand, the SSA refers to it in a crucial way and, on the other hand, it is essential for the operation of early cyclic rules such as Liquid Syllabification.

We are now in a position to address the problem of why manipulating the sonority hierarchy for the sake of distinguishing v from the liquids is not desirable. Evidence comes from the variation between [u̯] and [v] in words such as the following:

(65) serv 'serve', nerv 'nerve', nerv+stv+o 'nervous system', konzerv 'tin' (gen. pl.), sálv 'salute' (gen. pl.), vúlv 'clitoris' (gen. pl.)

Let us add that Pauliny *et al.* (1955) observe that the [v] pronunciation is prevailing.[24] The variation in (65) is understandable only if codas composed of a liquid followed by v are not permitted. This effect is derived automatically by the SSG on the condition that v, r, and l are in the same sonority class of approximants. In that case, v cannot be in the coda in (65) and hence it escapes v-Gliding. A later adjunction rule fulfils the requirement of prosodic licensing. Let us look at the details more closely.

The dialects that have [u̯] in (65) are straightforward in the sense that v is adjoined to the syllable coda. In the case of the [v] dialects, which prevail, it is unclear whether v should be adjoined to the syllable node or to the phonological word node (abbreviated as m:[25] m for *mot*, Selkirk's (1984) term). However, one thing is clear: the rule is postcyclic and not cyclic because we do not know whether v can be syllabified or not until the word level. In *nerv* 'nerve' and *nerv+stv+o* 'nervous system' it cannot be syllabified, while in *nerv+u* 'nerve' (gen. sg.) it can. Words such as *nerv+stv+o* provide evidence in favour of (66b) over (66a), since the former but not the latter leads to a unique analysis. This is due to the fact that in the case of polysyllabic words (66a) would place *C either in the preceding or in the following syllable, as in (67a). On the other hand, if

---

[24] According to Král' (1988) the variation between [u̯] and [v] is found not only in the contexts enumerated in (65) but also word-medially before nasals and liquids, for instance in *sláv+n+y* 'famous' and *havran* 'raven'. Speakers who use the [v] variant must have a resyllabification rule which links //v// to the phonological word node and thus permits it to escape v-Gliding, a rule which applies in the coda.

[25] It is not clear at which point in the derivation syllables are grouped into a common constituent designated as the phonological word. The relevant rule—let us call it m-Placement—is most probably cyclic:

m-Placement

$$\sigma \rightarrow \sigma\,/\,[\,—$$

with m above σ (linked).

The node m is assigned to the first syllable preceded by the bracket [. The remaining syllables are then adjoined to m by convention. This adjunction process is governed by the Prosodification Constraint (30), that is, it is blocked by the bracket [. This predicts that morphological compounds are also phonological compounds, that is, they consist of two *mots*. Furthermore, it becomes clear that in compounds such as [[[*krátk*]*o*[*zrak*]]*ý*] 'short-sighted' the linking phoneme *o* is prosodified with the preceding and not with the following constituent. Similarly, -*ý*, which morphologically speaking is an inflectional ending of the whole compound, counts prosodically as a member of the second constituent, that is, it forms a syllable with *k* (*zra-ký*) and it belongs to the phonological word *zraký*.

(66) Postcyclic Adjunction   *a.*

$$*C \rightarrow C \,/\, \left\{ \begin{matrix} r \\ l \end{matrix} \right\} \overset{\displaystyle N''}{\underset{\displaystyle |}{}} \underline{}$$

       b.

$$*C \rightarrow C \,/\, \left\{ \begin{matrix} r \\ l \end{matrix} \right\} \overset{\displaystyle m}{\underset{\displaystyle |}{}} \underline{}$$

(66*b*) is accepted, then the placement of *C is entirely unambiguous, as in (67*b*).

(67)

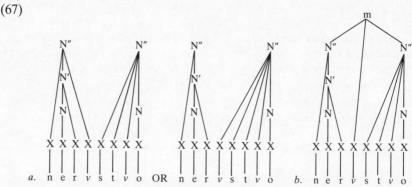

a. n e r *v* s t *v* o   OR   n e r *v* s t *v* o   *b.* n e r *v* s t *v* o

An ability to arrive at a unique solution becomes an asset when we attempt to state a rule which restores the feature [+sonor] in the /v/ of (65). Notice that this //v// is turned into /v/ by Obstruentization (63). The environment of Sonorization (64) is not met, hence we need an additional rule. This rule must be able to distinguish words such as *vzor* 'pattern' (in which an obstruent [v] appears phonetically) from words such as *nerv* 'nerve' and *nervstvo* 'nervous system' (which have a sonorant [v]). All of these words have an underlying //v//. Notice that the //v// in *vzor* is subject to Initial Adjunction (49), which is cyclic and hence applies at the stage at which //v// is still a sonorant. To restate the problem: it is crucial that the effect of Initial Adjunction in *vzor* should not coincide with that of Postcyclic Adjunction in *nerv* and *nervstvo*. The desired result is achieved by assuming that Initial Adjunction links consonants to the syllable node while Postcyclic Adjunction links them to the *mot* node.[26] A rule of

---

[26] The opposite assumption—that Initial Adjunction links consonants to the *mot* and Postcyclic Adjunction links them to the syllable node—is not an option. One reason why this cannot be the case is Vowel Vocalization, which we discuss in 9.1. This rule spells out, amongst other things, the preposition *k* as *ku* if it cannot syllabify, for example *ku každému* 'to every'. In phrases such as *k vzoru* 'to the pattern' the *k* can syllabify, as indicated clearly

sonorization for the *v* in words such as *nerv* and *nervstvo* is now stated as follows:

(68) Sonorization

$$v \rightarrow [+\text{sonor}] / \overset{\displaystyle m}{\underset{\rule{0pt}{1.2em}}{\big|}} \underline{}$$

The consequence of (68) is that Postcyclic Adjunction must be rule (66*b*) rather than (66*a*). The ambiguity as to the statement of Postcyclic Adjunction has thus been resolved.

Finally, let us point out that the distinct adjunctions in *vzor* 'pattern' (Initial Adjunction) vs. *nervstvo* 'nervous system' and *nerv* 'nerve' (Postcyclic Adjunction) are an instance of an asymmetry between the word-initial position versus the word-medial and the word-final positions. It is the same asymmetry that we found in the case of syllabic liquids and that exists independently in Polish and Czech (cf. Rubach and Booij, 1990*b*).

by the fact that it does not appear as *ku*. The syllabification of *k* into the onset in *k vzoru* would have been blocked if Initial Adjunction had been interpreted as a rule linking consonants to the *mot* node. The adjoined *v* would then have stood in the way of syllabifying *k* into the onset. On the other hand, if Initial Adjunction links consonants to the syllable node, an addition of *k* to the onset proceeds with no difficulty. Notice that the *v* in *vzor* is in fact part of the onset since, within the syllable theory adopted here, the onset node and the syllable node are both represented as N″.

PART III

Non-cyclic Rules

8

POSTCYCLIC RULES

In this part we look at non-cyclic rules. Following Booij and Rubach (1987) a claim is made that non-cyclic rules are of two types: postcyclic and postlexical. The former are lexical; that is, they apply in the lexicon. It follows therefore that they apply only within the domain of words. The latter are outside the lexicon and hence they may apply to strings larger than words.

8.1. DIAGNOSTICS FOR POSTCYCLIC RULES

Postcyclic rules as a class should be kept distinct, on the one hand, from the cyclic rules and, on the other hand, from the postlexical rules. The relevant distinctions are made on the basis of the following diagnostics:

(1) *a.* Interface: cyclic–postcyclic
          (i) derived vs. non-derived environment application
          (ii) cyclic vs. non-cyclic application
      b. Interface: postcyclic–postlexical
          (i) lexical information vs. no lexical information
          (ii) only word level vs. word and phrase level
          (iii) inputs arise in the lexicon vs. inputs arise in the syntax

We shall illustrate these criteria inasmuch as they refer to postcyclic rules. The discussion of postlexical rules is postponed till Chapter 9.

The properties of cyclic rules were discussed in Chapter 6. Therefore, we shall consider only the characteristics of postcyclic rules. Non-derived environments are those that arise inside morphemes and have not been produced by a feeding application of an earlier rule. That is, the input exists already at the underlying level. This type of situation is well illustrated by *ä*-Backing, rule (14) in Chapter 2. We repeat this rule here using the traditional notation in order to save space:

(2) *ä*-Backing   [+low] → [+back] / [–labial] —

The presence of *ä* in the underlying representation can be discovered by looking at the lengthening contexts. If the underlying vowel is //ä//, then a lengthening rule and Diphthongization produce /iä/, which is further changed into [ia] by rule (2). On the other hand, underlying //a// gives [á] under lengthening. Compare:

(3) *a.* žab+a //žäb+a// 'frog'—žiab (gen. pl.)
   šat+y //šät+i// 'clothes'—šiat (gen. pl.)
   okad+i+t' //okäd+i+t'// 'incense'—okiadz+a+t' (DI)
   b. šant+a //šant+a// 'prank'—šánt (gen. pl.)
   šacht+a //šaxt+a// 'pit'—šácht (gen. pl.)
   val+i+t' //val+i+t'// 'destroy'—vál+a+t' (DI)

The rule of *ä*-Backing applies to a non-derived //ä// in the words on the left in (3*a*).

The requirement that a rule must apply non-cyclically is best illustrated by the interaction of Glide Shortening and the Rhythmic Law. As we explain in 8.2 below, Slovak has a rule that shortens vowels after glides. This rule accounts for the alternation in, for instance, the dat. pl. of feminine nouns: *vod+ám* 'water' vs. *šij+am* 'neck'. The non-cyclic nature of Glide Shortening is illustrated by length contrasts in the present participle (cf. Dvonč *et al.* 1966). Recall that the present participle is //ác// and it is followed by an inflectional ending of the adjectival declension (see 3.1.7).

(4) *a.* vis+iac+i kabát 'hanging jacket' *vs.* stoj+ac+i vlak 'standing train'
   pros+iac+a žena 'wife who is asking' *vs.* hoj+ac+a sa rana 'healing wound'
   krič+iac+e deti 'shouting children' *vs.* boj+ac+e sa deti 'children who are afraid'
   b. cudz+í 'foreign' (masc. nom. sg.), cudz+ia (fem. nom. sg.), cudz+ie (non-virile nom. pl.)

The adjectives in (4*b*) show that the inflectional endings are underlyingly long. The short *-i*, *-a*, and *-e* in (4*a*) are derived by the Rhythmic Law, which is triggered by the long nucleus of the present participle //ác//.[1] The crucial examples are those with *j* in (4*a*). In order to derive them, Glide Shortening must be postcyclic. Compare the incorrect derivation of *stoj+ac+i* 'standing' in (5*a*) with the correct one in (5*b*). In the former, Glide Shortening applies cyclically, while in the latter it is interpreted as a postcyclic rule. The present participle //ác// must serve as an environment for shortening the inflectional ending in cycle 3. This can only be achieved if Glide Shortening is postcyclic and hence //ác// does not shorten in cycle 2.

The diagnostics which distinguish postcyclic from postlexical rules in (1*b*) are largely self-explanatory. Postcyclic rules may refer to lexical information. Thus, they may have exceptions. For example, Glide Shortening does not apply to the agentive suffix *-ár*: *lej+ár* 'moulder', *stroj+ár* 'builder'. By definition, postcyclic rules cannot refer to structures that first

---

[1] The present participle //ác// should be kept distinct from the adjectival //ac//.

(5) *a.* Cycle 2   stoj+äc   WFR: present participle
            —   Rhythmic Law
            stoj+äc   Glide Shortening

(5) *a.* Cycle 2	stoj+ä́c	WFR: present participle	
	—	Rhythmic Law	
	stoj+äc	Glide Shortening	
Cycle 3	stoj+äc+í	WFR: nom. sg. inflection	
	—	Rhythmic Law	
	—	Glide Shortening	
Postcyclic	stoj+ac+í	*ä*-Backing	
	*[stoj+ac+í]		
b. Cycle 2	stoj+ä́c	WFR: present participle	
	—	Rhythmic Law	
Cycle 3	stoj+ä́c+í	WFR: nom. sg. inflection	
	stoj+ä́c+i	Rhythmic Law	
Postcyclic	stoj+äc+i	Glide Shortening	
	stoj+ac+i	*ä*-Backing	

arise in the syntax. Thus, a rule that applies to prepositional phrases at the juncture between the preposition and the noun cannot be postcyclic. This follows from the fact that postcyclic rules are lexical, that is, they apply in the lexicon, hence to words and not to larger structures. They are therefore word-level rules. Let us illustrate this point.

In 8.2 below we show that Glide Shortening shortens *ô* [uo] to [o], for instance in the gen. pl. *fajok* 'pipe'. The rule does not apply if the sequence 'glide–*ô*' arises in the syntax: *daj ôsmu knižku* 'give the eighth book'. Similarly, Anterior Depalatalization, a postcyclic rule that we discuss in 8.3, applies inside words but not across word boundaries (voicing distinctions are ignored):

(6) t′ → t / — n
    kost' 'bone'—kost+n+ý [t] (Adj.) *vs.* kost' noh+y 'the bone of the leg'
    t′ → t / — l′
    závist' 'envy'—závist+liv+ý [t] 'envious' *vs.* závist' Ladislava Nováka
    'Ladislav Novák's envy'

This generalization is readily captured by assuming that Anterior Depalatalization is a postcyclic but not a postlexical rule.

In the sections that follow we analyse in detail the postcyclic rules of Slovak. However, some of these rules have already been discussed, for instance Prepalatal Spell-out (4/18) and Diphthong Spell-out (6/66), and they will not be repeated.

8.2. GLIDE SHORTENING

The facts are well known. D'urovič (1973: 35) quotes Štúr's statement made in 1852 that '*ja* must always be short' (my translation: J.R.). Isačenko (1966) postulates a rule that shortens all long vowels except /í, ú/ after *j*. Kenstowicz (1972) introduces a rule of *j*-Deletion after *j*. The position taken in this book is as follows. We develop Kenstowicz's idea and show that indeed only diphthongs undergo Glide Shortening, but we extend the rule to all diphthongs and include *ô* /uo/ along with the previously analysed /ie, ia/. Invoking the Obligatory Contour Principle we claim that the exclusion of /í, ú/ from Glide Shortening is systematic. Finally, we account for the surface exceptions to Glide Shortening by appealing to the rule of Fronting. The data are drawn from the standard descriptions of Slovak such as those by Dvonč *et al.* (1966) and Kráľ (1988), as well as from dictionaries and questionnaires that were administered to native speakers. We begin by discussing the input to Glide Shortening.

Compare the following contrasts in length:

(7) *a.* bij+em 'I beat' *vs.* nes+iem 'I carry'
   Likewise: pij+em 'I drink', šij+em 'I sew', žuj+em 'I chew', myj+em 'I wash', pracuj+em 'I work'

   b. vajc+e 'egg'—vajec (gen. pl.) *vs.* krídel+c+e 'wing'—krídel+iec (gen. pl.)
   Likewise: voj+n+a 'war'—voj+en (gen. pl.)
   lajn+o 'dung'—lajen (gen. pl.)

   c. fajk+a 'pipe'—fajok (gen. pl.) *vs.* kvapk+a 'drop'—kvapôk (gen. pl.)
   Likewise: spoj+k+a 'link'—spoj+ok (gen. pl.)
   čajk+a 'sea-gull'—čajok (gen. pl.)

   d. zmij+a 'viper'—zmij+am (dat. pl.), zmij+ach (loc. pl.) *vs.* ryb+a 'fish'—ryb+ám (dat. pl.), ryb+ách (loc. pl.)
   Likewise: šij+a 'neck'—šij+am (dat. pl.) šij+ach (loc. pl.)
   oj+e 'shaft'—oj+am (dat. pl.), oj+ach (loc. pl.)
   alej+a 'avenue'—alej+am (dat. pl.), alej+ach (loc. pl.)

   e. pij+ak 'drunk' (N) *vs.* let+ák 'flier'
   Likewise: za+bij+ak 'killer', voj+ak 'soldier'

The generalization is clear: the diphthongs *ie* and *ô* as well as the long vowel *á* are shortened after *j*. We look at the diphthongs first. A sample derivation of the gen. pl. *vajec* 'egg' and *fajok* 'pipe' is given in (8) (the yer *U* is the gen. pl. ending). In the postcyclic part of the derivation we give two versions: (8*a*) and (8*b*). Irrelevant information is omitted.

(8)

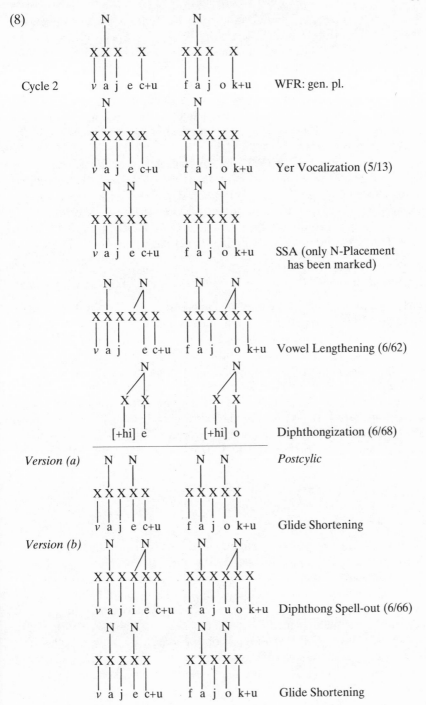

Cycle 2		WFR: gen. pl.
		Yer Vocalization (5/13)
		SSA (only N-Placement has been marked)
		Vowel Lengthening (6/62)
		Diphthongization (6/68)
Version (a)		Postcylic
		Glide Shortening
Version (b)		Diphthong Spell-out (6/66)
		Glide Shortening

Recall that cyclic Diphthongization adds the feature [+high] under the empty nuclear slot. A postcyclic rule of Diphthong Spell-out spreads the features from the head of the nucleus and thus derives [ie] and [uo]. The question is whether Glide Shortening should apply before or after Diphthong Spell-out, that is, whether it should delete a partially specified onglide as in (8a) or a fully specified onglide as in (8b).

To resolve this problem we return briefly to the denominal adjectives which we discussed in 6.4 (see the examples in (76) in Chapter 6). These adjectives are formed by adding the suffix /i/ to the base. The /i/ is subsequently contracted with the inflectional ending of the adjective and hence we find long vowels or diphthongs on the surface: *had+í* 'reptile' (Adj., masc. nom. sg.), *had+ia* (fem. nom. sg.). Relevant to our discussion are nominal bases such as *zmij*, of *zmij+a* 'viper'. If Glide Shortening can affect fully specified diphthongs, then adjectives derived from these bases should undergo the rule. The examples in (9) show that they indeed do:

(9) zmij+í //zmij+i+í// 'viper' (Adj., nom. sg.)—zmij+eho (gen. sg.) *versus*
     had+í //had+i+í// 'reptile' (Adj., nom. sg.)—had+i+eho (gen. sg.)

The adjectivizing //i// is deleted in *zmij+eho* by Glide Shortening. The input to Glide Shortening is /zmij+ieho/, an intermediate form derived from //zmij+i+ého// by Contraction (6/73).[2] In sum, Glide Shortening deletes a fully specified onglide of the diphthong.

There is an advantage in viewing Glide Shortening as a rule that acts on diphthongs rather than on long vowels as an input. Words such as *jód* 'iodine' and *rajón* 'region' with an underlying long //ó// are not then exceptions. Given this statement the shortening of long *á* in (7d–e) looks like a problem. The problem becomes even more serious when we discover that the lengthened *á* in (10) below is never subject to Glide Shortening:

(10) jam+a 'pit'—jám (gen. pl.)
      jazd+a 'travel'—jázd (gen. pl.)
      fujar+a 'pipe'—fujár (gen. pl.)

There are also non-derived sequences of *j* and *á*, for example *lojáln+y* 'loyal', *Ján* 'John' (cf. Pauliny *et al.* 1955).

Our dilemma can be solved in a straightforward way by assuming that the long /á/ which undergoes Glide Shortening is in fact the diphthong /iä/ at the relevant stage. This interpretation covers adequately the data in (7d–e) and excludes correctly those in (10). The relevant observation here is that the data in (7d–e) undergo Fronting (6/81), a rule that changes /á/ into /ä/ after stem-final segments which end in, amongst others, /j/ (recall the discussion in 6.5). The fronted /ä/ undergoes Diphthongization (6/68).

_____

[2] The gen. sg. ending *-ého* is //ɣho//. Contraction derives /iɣho/ and Round / Back Redundancy (6/84) produces /ieho/. Recall the discussion of Fronting in 6.6.

Diphthong Spell-out (6/66) produces /iä/. Glide Shortening and *ä*-Backing complete the derivation. In (11) we look at *pij+ak* 'drunk', an example from (7e). Irrelevant information is omitted.

(11)

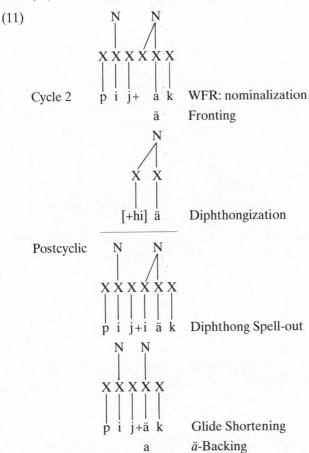

Cycle 2   p i j+   a k   WFR: nominalization

                    ä   Fronting

             [+hi] ä   Diphthongization

Postcyclic

           p i j+i ä k   Diphthong Spell-out

           p i j+ä k   Glide Shortening

               a   *ä*-Backing

We are now in a position to express Glide Shortening formally: see (12).

(12) Glide Shortening

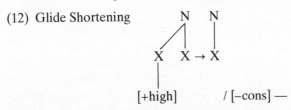

The rule affects diphthongs. Words such as *štúdi+ám* 'study' (dat. pl.) and *ide+ám* 'idea' (dat. pl.; see the data in (79) in Chapter 6) are not inputs to Glide Shortening since they do not have diphthongs. Recall that Fronting does not apply after vowels. Consequently, the *á* is back in these examples and hence it does not undergo Diphthongization.

As pointed out originally by Isačenko (1966), Glide Shortening fails to apply to the long /í, ú/:

(13) zmij+í 'viper' (N, gen. sg., or Adj., nom. sg.), kraj+ík 'country' (dimin.), pij+ú 'they drink', pij+úc 'drinking'

How can we account for this fact? Recall that, according to our interpretation, long /í, ú/ undergo Diphthongization (see 6.3). The derivation of [í] is as shown in (14).

(14)

The final step is the effect of the Obligatory Contour Principle that prohibits two adjacent identical segments at the melody tier (see 6.3). Given this principle the failure of Glide Shortening to apply in (13) is explained. It is not necessary to specify, as Isačenko (1966) did, that the inputs to Glide Shortening cannot be the high vowels /í, ú/. By collapsing the representation derived by Diphthong Spell-out in (14) into a long vowel, the OCP makes Glide Shortening inapplicable, because the rule affects diphthongs and not long vowels.

Now we turn to the discussion of the environment in which Glide Shortening applies. As stated in (12) it includes not only /j/ but also the glide /u̯/ (diphthongs do not appear directly after vowels). The back glide as an environment for shortening is necessary for those speakers of Slovak who have a chain of short [av] suffixes in verbs formed by adding the derived imperfective morpheme //aj//. These formations have become famous in the generative literature on Slovak. They were first cited by Browne (1970) in the context of the debate about simultaneous application of phonological rules. Browne's analysis was carried over into the discussion of the multiple application problem by Anderson (1974) and Kenstowicz and Kisseberth (1977). The facts are as follows.

To enhance the meaning of iterativeness it is possible to repeat several times the DI suffix //aj//. Forms such as nadáv+a+t' 'scold' (DI) and nadáv+av+a+t' (double DI) are standard (cf. Dvonč et al. 1966). However, for emphatic reasons they may be extended further, and thus we obtain chains of -avs such as those in nadáv+av+av+a+t' (triple DI). For many speakers the chain of -av suffixes is consistently short (D'urovič, personal communication). The Rhythmic Law alone would have derived an alternating pattern of long and short -avs but not a chain of short -avs. Recall that in 3.1.12 we postulated the rules of aj-Lengthening and Glide Backing. For convenience we repeat them below:

(15) aj-Lengthening   V →V́ / — aj]$_{DI}$

(16) Glide Backing   j → [+back] / — aj]$_{DI}$

A triple derived imperfective has the following underlying representation:

(17) a. Infinitive: *nada+t'* 'scold', UR //nadaj+t'//; the root is //nadaj// and
          not //nada// since the [aj] surfaces in the 3rd pl. present: *nadaj+ú*
          'they scold'. The *j* is deleted in the infinitive by Postvocalic
          j-Deletion (3/4): j → ∅ / — C
      b. Derived imperfective: *nadáv+a+t'* //nadaj+aj+t'//. Recall that the
          DI suffix is //aj//: the [j] surfaces before vowels, for instance
          nadáv+aj+ú 'they scold' (DI)
      c. Double derived imperfective: *nadáv+av+a+t'* //nadaj+aj+aj+t'//
      d. Triple derived imperfective: *nadáv+av+av+a+t'*
          //nadaj+aj+aj+aj+t'//

In the cyclic component the derivation of the form in (17*d*) proceeds as in
(18). We bypass cycle 5, in which the only relevant change is the deletion
of *j* by Postvocalic *j*-Deletion (3/4). As usual, the derivation is simplified
by omitting irrelevant information.

(18) Cycle 2   nadaj+aj   WFR: derived imperfective
                 nadau̯+aj   Glide Backing (16)
                 nadáu̯+aj   *aj*-Lengthening (15)
                 —   Fronting (6/81)
                 —   Rhythmic Law (6/51)
                 —   Diphthongization (6/68)

      Cycle 3   nadáu̯+aj+aj   WFR: derived imperfective
                 nadáu̯+au̯+aj   Glide Backing
                 nadáu̯+áu̯+aj   *aj*-Lengthening
                 nadáu̯+ä́u̯+aj   Fronting[3]
                 nadáu̯+äu̯+aj   Rhythmic Law
                 —   Diphthongization

      Cycle 4   nadáu̯+äu̯+aj+aj   WFR: derived imperfective
                 nadáu̯+äu̯+au̯+aj   Glide Backing
                 nadáu̯+äu̯+áu̯+aj   *aj*-Lengthening
                 nadáu̯+äu̯+áu̯+aj   Fronting
                 —   Rhythmic Law

                      N
                     /|
                    X X
                    | |
                 [+hi] ä   Diphthongization

---

[3] The fact that /j/ has been changed to /u̯/ on the previous cycle is of no relevance for
Fronting. Recall that the rule is sensitive to the diacritic SOFT and diacritics cannot be

We have now arrived at the relevant stage of derivation. Cyclic Diphthongization is complemented by postcyclic Diphthong Spell-out (6/66), which derives /nadáu̯+äu̯+iäu̯+a+t'/. At this point Glide Shortening takes effect and simplifies the diphthong /iä/ to /ä/. The rule of ä-Backing produces /nadáu̯+au̯+au̯+a+t'/. The derivation is completed by the rule which changes /u̯/ to [v] that we discuss below: [nadáv+av+av+a+t']. Without Glide Shortening the final output in (18) would have been *nadáv+av+áv+a+t'*, which indeed is true for some speakers (Wayles Browne, personal communication, and my own observations). In order to account for this dialect it suffices to assume that Glide Shortening is restricted to the environment of /j/ and that the glide /u̯/ does not trigger the rule. Evidence that /u̯/, surface [v], can function as an environment for Glide Shortening is scanty, to say the least. Outside derived imperfectives it is found only irregularly in a few nouns and pronouns:

(19) *a.* vojsk+o 'army'—vojsk (gen. pl.)
      stvor+a 'creature'—stvor (gen. pl.)
   b. môj 'my', náš 'our', váš 'your'
   c. tvoj 'your', svoj 'one's own'

The forms on the right in (19*a*) can be explained as an effect of Glide Shortening, since normally the vowel is long in the gen. pl. owing to Vowel Lengthening. The pronouns in (19*b*) have short vowels in the underlying representation: compare the feminine forms *moj+a* 'my', *naš+a* 'our', and *vaš+a* 'your'. The surface representations in (19*b*) must therefore be derived by Vowel Lengthening (and Diphthongization), which applies before the yer of the masc. nom. sg. The pronouns in (19*c*) are parallel to those in (19*b*) with the significant difference that the lengthened vowels are subsequently shortened by Glide Shortening.

Shortening after *v* is irregular rather than regular. In the typical situation there is no prohibition against diphthongs after *v*. Compare:

(20) *a.* underlying: vôl 'ox', vôbec 'not at all', hviezd+a 'star', sviež+i
           'fresh', viac 'more'
   b. derived in the gen. pl.: vod+a 'water'—vôd, dver+e 'door'—dvier

The contradiction between the data in (19) and in (20) has a historical explanation. Originally all instances of [v] in Slavic come from [u̯]. In synchronic terms we must assume that the historical glide /u̯/ has restructured to /v/, a labiodental approximant. The /u̯/ has survived in a few nouns, as exemplified in (19*a*), and in the pronouns in (19*c*). It also exists as a derivational stage in derived imperfectives. In these instances surface [v] is derived by Glide Strengthening, a rule that applies in the syllable onset:

erased by changes in phonetic-feature composition of segments that take place in the derivation. Note also that Fronting is permitted to return to cycle 2 because only now has *aj*-Lengthening produced a feeding change. (Recall that Fronting applies to long vowels.)

(21) Glide Strengthening

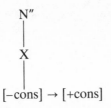

Rule (21) covers not only /u̯/ but also /j/. According to Stanislav (1953) and Král' (1988) Slovak *j* is a fricative [j] in the syllable onset and a glide [i̯] in the syllable coda. We thus have the following alternations:

(22) kraj [i̯] 'country'—kraj+e [j] 'countries'
    kuj [i̯] 'forge' (imper.)—kuj+em [j] 'I forge'

Glide Strengthening changes glides into consonants. Later redundancy rules spell out the consonantal /u̯/ and /j/ as a labiodental sonorant [v] and a palatal obstruent [j], respectively.

Finally, let us look at the interaction of Glide Shortening with other phonological rules. The derivation given in (8) and the data in (9) earlier in this section show that Glide Shortening is fed by Yer Vocalization, Vowel Lengthening, Diphthongization, and Contraction. The interaction illustrated in (5) in 8.1 makes it clear that Glide Shortening must follow the Rhythmic Law. The example in (23) below establishes the ordering of Yer Hiatus (see 5.7) *vis-à-vis* Glide Shortening:

(23) Ázi+a 'Asia'—Ázi+jk+a 'Asian' (N, fem.)—Ázi+jok (gen. pl.), UR //ázi+Ok+U//

The /j/ is inserted by Yer Hiatus. The vocalized yer /o/ of //Ok// is lengthened by Vowel Lengthening and further diphthongized by Diphthongization. The surface [o] in [ok] is derived by Glide Shortening.

All the ordering relationships that we have mentioned so far are predictable from our theory, since Glide Shortening is postcyclic while the remaining rules are cyclic. With our assumption that the block of cyclic rules precedes the block of postcyclic rules it follows that Glide Shortening is the last rule. What remains unpredictable is how Glide Shortening is ordered with respect to other postcyclic rules. We know from the derivation of the frequentative form in (18) that it must precede Glide Strengthening in order to be able to apply. Further, it must precede *j*-Simplification, a rule that deletes /j/ in contour segments (discussed in 4.6).

(24) *j*-Simplification

This rule deletes the /j/ inserted in the conjugational forms of *a*-stem verbs; compare derivation (31) in Chapter 4. Below we adduce some more examples. The extension vowel //é//, as in *nes+iem* 'I carry', is shortened to [e] after /j/:

(25) rez+a+t' 'cut'—rež+em 'I cut'
      maz+a+t' 'smear'—maž+em 'I smear'
      kop+a+t' 'dig'—kop+em 'I dig'
      syp+a+t' 'pour'—syp+em 'I pour'

Taking up the derivation at the postcyclic level we obtain (26), using *rež+em* 'I cut' as our example. As usual, we omit irrelevant information.

(26)

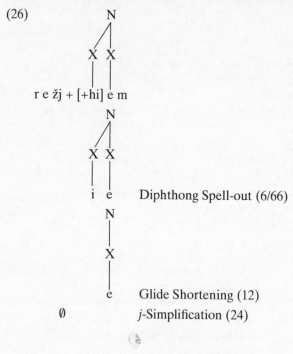

        Diphthong Spell-out (6/66)

        Glide Shortening (12)
    ∅   *j*-Simplification (24)

8.3. DEPALATALIZATION

Standard descriptions of Slovak such as Pauliny (1968) and D'urovič (1975) state that prepalatals do not appear before coronal consonants. This gives rise to the following alternations:

(27) t' → t   kost' 'bone'   kost+n+ý (Adj.)
              pút' 'travel'   pút+nik [pút+n'ik] 'traveller'
              závist' 'envy'   závist+liv+ý [závist+l'iv+í] (Adj.)
              otec [t'] 'father'   otc+a (gen. sg.)
     d' → d   čel'ad' 'group'   čel'ad+n+ý (Adj.)
              žalud' 'acorn'   žalud+n+ý (Adj.)
              deň [d'en'] 'day'   dň+a [dn'+a] (gen. sg.)

n′ → n kôň 'horse' kon+sk+ý (Adj.)
Viedeň 'Vienna' vieden+sk+ý (Adj.)
kameň 'stone' kamen+n+ý (Adj.)
koniec 'end' konc+a (gen. sg.)
sviň+a 'pig' svin+sk+ý (Adj.), svin+stv+o 'dirty trick'

Depalatalization does not take place before vowels or before non-coronals. Thus, alongside *žalud+n+ý* 'acorn' (Adj.) and *kon+sk+ý* 'horse' (Adj.) in (27) we have *žalud'+ov+ý* (Adj.) and *koň+mo* 'on horseback'. However, whether the coronal consonant in the environment is itself non-palatalized or palatalized is of no relevance: compare *pút+nik* 'traveller' in (27).

There is no doubt that Slovak must have a depalatalization rule: all the examples in (27) are instances of underlying //t′, d′, n′//.

(28) Anterior Depalatalization

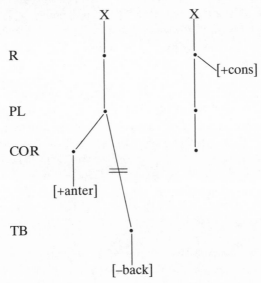

Anterior Depalatalization (28) acts not only on underlying but also on derived /t′, d′, n′/. In the case of derived palatalized consonants it undoes the effect of Coronal Palatalization whenever Coronal Palatalization has applied before a yer-initial suffix containing a coronal consonant and the yer has not been vocalized. Recall, for example, that the adjectivizing suffixes *-sk* and *-n* and the nominalizing *-ec* are //Isk//, //En//, and //Ec// at the underlying level (see 3.3). In sum, Anterior Depalatalization operates also in (29):

(29) pán 'sir'—pán+sk+y //pán+Isk-//
let+o 'summer'—let+n+ý //let+En-//
vod+a 'water'—vod+n+ý //vod+En-//
chod 'walk'—chod+ec [d'] 'passer-by'—chod+c+a (gen. sg.)
//xod+Ec+a//

Let us establish the status of Anterior Depalatalization: is it a cyclic or a postcyclic or a postlexical rule? The latter possibility can be excluded immediately since Anterior Depalatalization does not apply across word boundaries (Král' 1988; L'ubomir D'urovič and Martin Votruba, personal communication). Thus, for example, we have [n'] and [t'] rather than [n] and [t] in *kôň toho človeka* 'this man's horse', *kôň Ladislava Nováka* 'Ladislav Novák's horse', *čast' nosa* 'part of the nose', *čast' lode* 'part of the boat', etc. It is also clear that Anterior Depalatalization cannot be cyclic, because it applies morpheme-internally to non-derived—that is, underlyingly palatalized—consonants. Relevant here are examples such as *koniec* 'end'—*konc+a* (gen. sg.) and *deň* 'day'—*dň+a* (gen. sg.).

Given the statement of Anterior Depalatalization in (28), we would expect that the rule should also affect /l'/. This expectation is borne out only in part. The generalization is that a derived /l'/ undergoes depalatalization but an underlying //l'// does not:

(30) *a.* derived /l'/:
škol+a 'school'—škol+sk+ý [l], UR //škol+Isk-// (Adj.)
—škol+stv+o [l], UR //škol+IstEv+o// 'school system'
strel+a 'shot'—strel+ec [l'], UR //strel+Ec-// 'shooter'—strel+c+a
[l] (gen. sg.)—strel+n+ý [l], UR //strel+En-// 'shot' (Adj.)
pekl+o 'hell'—pekel+n+ý [l], UR //pekEl+En-// (Adj.)
b. underlying //l'//:
učitel' 'teacher'—učitel'+sk+ý (Adj.), učitel'+stv+o 'teaching staff'
topol' 'poplar'—topol+ec [l'], UR //topol'+Ec-// (dimin.)
—topol'+c+a (gen. sg.)
žial' 'regret'—žial'+n+y 'regretful'
Also morpheme-internally: l'stiv+ý 'crafty', bol'ševik 'Bolshevik'

Particularly telling is the minimal pair *uhol* 'angle'—*uhol+n+ý* //uhol+En+í// 'angular' vs. *uhol'* 'coal'—*uhol'+n+ý* //uhol'+En+í// (Adj.). Underlying //l'// resists undergoing depalatalization: not only Anterior Depalatalization but also, as we show below, Morphological Depalatalization. Marking all the instances of underlying //l'// as exceptions would thus miss the point. We propose to solve the problem by assuming that //l'// is underlyingly [−anter]. It thus contrasts with underlying and derived /t', d', n'/ as well as with derived /l'/, which are all [+anter] prior to the application of Prepalatal Spell-out (4/18), a rule that we discussed in 4.3. Recall that the function of Prepalatal Spell-out is to complete the derivation initiated by Coronal Palatalization and to supply underlying //t', d', n'// with the redundant features [–anter, +high]. Evidently, Anterior Depalatalization (as well as Morphological Depalatalization, which we discuss below) must be ordered prior to Prepalatal Spell-out. This ordering makes Prepalatal Spell-out postcyclic.

In addition to the phonologically conditioned Anterior Depalatalization there are also morphologically conditioned depalatalizations. They take place before the diminutive morphemes -Ek/Ok and the nominalizing -Eb:[4] see (31).

(31) Nom. sg.   Diminutive

	Nom. sg.	Gen. pl.

a. Underlying //t', d', n'// before -*Ok*
(all examples fem. except the last)

čast' 'part'	čiast+k+a	čiast+ok
pamät' 'remembrance'	pamiat+k+a	pamiat+ok
sukň+a 'dress'	sukien+k+a	sukien+ok
žrd' 'pole'	žŕd+k+a	žŕd+ok
kost' 'bone'	kôst+k+a	kôst+ok
koreň 'root'	korien+ok	

b. Underlying //t', d', n'// before -*Ek*
(all examples fem.)

smrt' 'death'	smrt+k+a	smrt+iek
mat' 'mother'	mat+k+a	mat+iek
sviň+a 'pig'	svin+k+a	svin+iek
skriň+a 'box'	skrin+k+a	skrin+iek

c. Derived /t', d', n', l'/ before -*Ek*
(neuter and fem. nouns)

sit+o 'sieve'	sit+k+o	sit+iek
hrud+a 'piece of land'	hrud+k+a	hrud+iek
dutin+a 'cavity'	dutin+k+a	dutin+iek
sardel+a 'anchovy'	sardel+k+a	sardel+iek

[4] Marginally, //n'// depalatalizes before the agentive -*ár* in three words, and //t'// depalatalizes before the collective numeral suffix -*oro*: *hrebeň* 'comb'—*hrebn+ár* 'comb-maker', *remeň* 'strap'—*remen+ár* 'saddler', *kameň* 'stone'—*kamen+ár* 'stonemason'; *pät'* 'five'—*pät+oro*, *šest'* 'six'—*šest+oro*, *devät'* 'nine'—*devät+oro*, and a few other numerals.

There is no doubt that depalatalization is conditioned morphologically and not phonologically by -*k* as the environment. On the one hand, this is documented by the fact that prepalatals may occur before *k*, for instance *red'kev* 'radish', *hned'+ky* 'at once'. On the other hand, it follows from the observation that depalatalization is also found before a vowel in the gen. pl. /nom. sg. in (31*a*). We hasten to add that the gen. pl. forms in (31*b*–*c*) —that is, those in which the diminutive suffix surfaces as [iek]—do have [t', d', n', l'] in their phonetic representations. The contradiction is only apparent. We address this problem in the following section.

Notice that there are no examples for //l'// in (31*a*). This is not an omission. As in the case of Anterior Depalatalization, an underlying //l'// does not depalatalize, for example *košeľ+a* 'shirt'—*košieľ+k+a* (dimin.), *chvíľ+a* 'moment'—*chvíľ+k+a*. This is not unexpected since, as we argued earlier, underlying //l'// is [–anter]. Depalatalization affects [+anter] consonants, which includes derived /l'/ as well as derived or underlying /t', d', n'/: see (32).

(32) Diminutive Depalatalization

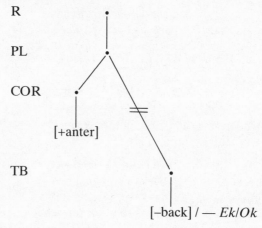

As noted by D'urovič (1975), Diminutive Depalatalization has a few exceptions, for instance *lod'+k+a*[5] 'boat' (dimin.), *siet'+k+a* 'net' (dimin.).

Another morphological depalatalization rule turns /t', d', n'/ into [t, d, n] before the nominalizing morpheme -*Eb*. This rule is different from Diminutive Depalatalization since it never affects /l'/, regardless of whether it is underlying or derived. The middle column in (33) below contains derived nouns in the nom. sg., while the last column lists the same nouns in the gen. pl.

---

[5] It should be noted, however, that the same morpheme *lod'* 'boat' undergoes Anterior Depalatalization: *lod+n+ý* (Adj.). This confirms the fact that Anterior Depalatalization and Diminutive Depalatalization are two different rules.

(33) plat+i+t' 'pay'   plat+b+a 'paying'   plat+ieb
     chod+i+t' 'walk'   chod+b+a 'walking'   chod+ieb
     klenú+t' 'bow'   klen+b+a 'vault'   klen+ieb

versus

mal'+ova+t' 'paint'   mal'+b+a 'painting'   mal+ieb
strel+a 'shot'   strel'+b+a 'shooting'   strel+ieb

The relevant rule here is (34). I assume with Halle (1992) that [later] hangs off the Root node, but this assumption is not essential (cf. Steriade 1987 and Sagey 1986, where it is argued that [later] hangs off CORONAL).

(34) *Eb*-Depalatalization

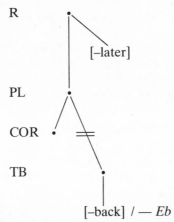

As regards the status of morphological depalatalizations (32) and (34), it seems most natural to assume that the rules are cyclic, since they apply before specified morphemes. They are ordered after Coronal Palatalization.

Finally, we should point out that the generalization given earlier for the gen. pl. forms in (31*b–c*) extends also to the data in (33): consonants are palatalized before *-ie*. We discuss this problem in the following section.

8.4. POSTCYCLIC PALATALIZATION

Given the facts of morphological depalatalization discussed in the preceding section, the question arises how the palatalization of the gen. pl. forms in (31*b–c*) and (33) can be accounted for. Coronal Palatalization is of no help. It must apply before both Diminutive Depalatalization and *Eb*-Depalatalization, since otherwise palatals would be derived not only in the gen. pl.—that is, before the surface diphthong [ie] in *sit+iek* 'sieve' and *plat+ieb* 'paying'—but also in the remaining forms, such as the nom. sg. *sit+k+o* //sit+Ek+o// and *plat+b+a* //plat+Eb+a//. We could not assume that Coronal Palatalization is restricted somewhat arbitrarily so as not to apply before unvocalized yers. Such an assumption would be incorrect, because in the case of /l/ the effect of Coronal Palatalization is seen in all forms, including those in which the yer has not vocalized: *strel+a* 'shot'—*strel'+b+a* //strel+Eb+a// 'shooting'. Also, we know that Coronal Palatalization is triggered by the yer of the imperative, which, being the last morpheme of a word, can never vocalize; compare *plet+ú* 'they weave'—*plet'* //plet+I// 'weave' (imper.).

We propose to solve this dilemma by assuming that Slovak has a rule of Postcyclic Palatalization which repalatalizes the consonant before [ie], or rather before any front-vowel diphthong. In addition to the evidence just discussed, there are three further arguments that support this interpretation: (i) surface generalizations, (ii) the operation of the Strict Cyclicity Constraint, and (iii) avoidance of allomorphy at the underlying level. We begin with the last and the least important argument.

Without Postcyclic Palatalization, alternations such as *tm+a* [t] 'moth'— *tiem* [t'] (gen. pl.) cannot be accounted for at all, short of listing the allomorphs: one with //t// for all the forms except the gen. pl. and the other with //t'// for the gen. pl. We are dealing here with a yer stem, which is shown by the zero–vowel alternation (actually, a diphthong, as predicted by Vowel Lengthening and Diphthongization). A reasonable analysis would assume that the [t'] is underlying, which is natural considering that Coronal Palatalization became cyclic in the course of historical development and hence stopped applying morpheme-internally. While this analysis is appropriate for the gen. pl. *tiem* //t'Em+U//, it fails to yield the correct output in all the remaining inflectional forms, such as *tm+a* (nom. sg.). The putative //t'Em+a// could not depalatalize, since Anterior Depalatalization does not apply before labials, for instance *det'+mi* 'children' (instr. pl.). With Postcyclic Palatalization as a rule of Slovak the problem can be solved very easily. The root *tm+a* has a hard consonant at the underlying level //tEm//. Coronal Palatalization as a cyclic rule does not apply morpheme-internally. After the loss of the yer we obtain the required [tm+a]. On the other hand, the gen. pl. *tiem* //tEm+U// has undergone Yer Vocalization, Vowel Lengthening, and Diphthongization, and consequently it is /tiem/ in the postcyclic component. Postcyclic Palatalization derives [t'iem] in the environment before the diphthong /ie/.

A different argument for Postcyclic Palatalization can be constructed given the following data:

(35) *Nom. sg.*   *Gen. pl.*
    liter+a [t] 'letter'   litier [t']
    kotlet+a [l] 'chop'   kotliet [l']
    toalet+a [l] 'toilet'   toaliet [l']
    katedr+a [katedr+a] 'pulpit'   katedier [kated'ier]

The consonants are palatalized before *ie* but not before *e*. At first glance it seems that we have a classic example where Coronal Palatalization applies in a derived environment in the sense 'derived by an earlier rule': Vowel Lengthening, Diphthongization, and, in the last example, also Yer Vocalization. However, this interpretation is untenable on both formal and theoretical grounds. From the formal point of view, Coronal Palatalization is not applicable to the forms on the right since Diphthongization (6/68) inserts merely the feature [+high] when the vowel has been lengthened. The feature [−back] is supplied by Diphthong Spell-out (6/66), a straightforward spreading rule. A contradiction in the analysis comes to light when we recall that Diphthong Spell-out is a postcyclic rule whereas Coronal Palatalization is crucially cyclic (see 4.5). Thus, the former applies after and not before the latter. In sum, the segment which is adjacent to /t, l, d/ in the gen. pl. forms in (35) is [+high] but not [−back] at the relevant stage of derivation. Consequently, [t′, l′, d′] cannot be derived.

A purely theoretical objection to this analysis can be made on the basis of the Strict Cyclicity Constraint. Notice that it is only apparent that the environment in the gen. pl. forms in (35) is derived. In fact, the front vowel or yer is already present at the underlying level, because the root of, for instance, *liter+a* 'letter' is //liter//. The application of Vowel Lengthening and Diphthongization produces a non-feeding change and, as we explained in Chapter 1, the Strict Cyclicity Constraint makes the morpheme-internal position open to cyclic rules only when an earlier rule has introduced a feeding change. That this is true can also be seen in Slovak. Thus, whether the yer of *sveter* 'sweater' (compare the gen. sg. *svetr+a*) has been vocalized or not is irrelevant for the purposes of Coronal Palatalization. The *t* should not be palatalized since the phonetic representation is [sveter].

We can avoid both the formal and the theoretical difficulties just outlined if we admit Postcyclic Palatalization as a rule of Slovak. The consonants are palatalized before the diphthong *ie* after its onglide has been specified as [−back] by Diphthong Spell-out. Palatalization is effected postcyclically, hence the Strict Cyclicity Constraint does not come into play.

The final argument for Postcyclic Palatalization refers to surface representations. It is a generalization that /t, d, n, l/ are always palatalized (including in morpheme-internal position) before the front-vowel diphthongs *ie* and *ia*. To put it differently, morpheme-internal palatalization is not predictable before *i* and *e* alone (see 4.5) but it is predictable before *ie* and *ia*. We stress that the *ie* and *ia* must be diphthongs and not sequences of vowels. We summarize these facts in (36), taking *d* as an example:

(36) *a.* Palatalization before diphthongs:
     dier+a 'hole', diel+o 'work', dial' 'distance', diabol 'devil'

   b. No palatalization before vowel sequences (we divide them with a
     dot):
       di.etetick+ý 'diet' (Adj.), di.ecéz+a 'diocese', di.amant
       'diamond', di.alóg 'dialogue'[6]
   c. Unpredictable palatalization before *i* and *e*:
       div+ák [d'] 'onlooker'—diván [d] 'sofa'
       del+o [d'] 'cannon'—delfín [d] 'dolphin'

The facts in (36*b–c*) follow naturally from the assumption that Coronal
Palatalization is cyclic, while those in (36*a*) are accounted for by Postcyclic Palatalization. The rule spreads the TB node of the diphthongal
onglide, as shown in (37). (The TB node is inserted by convention.)

(37) Postcyclic Palatalization

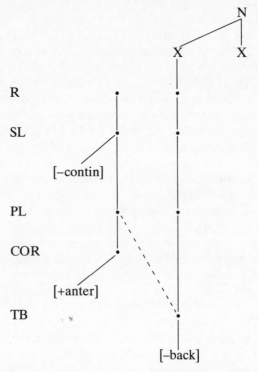

The fact that (37) is postcyclic has the advantage of simplifying underlying representations for non-continuants before diphthongs morpheme-
internally. Thus, *tiah+nu+ť* 'pull', *dier+a* 'hole', *nie* 'no', *lieh* 'alcohol' have

---

[6] An etymological fact that these words are borrowings is of no interest from the point of
view of synchronic description (see our discussion of Coronal Palatalization in 4.5). Incidentally, the word *diabol* 'devil' in (36*a*) is also a borrowing, and yet the *ia* is a diphthong and
the *d* is palatalized. The same applies to some other etymologically foreign words, such as
mušketier 'musketeer'.

//t, d, n, l// at the underlying level, and the phonetic palatals are derived by Postcyclic Palatalization.

We summarize our analysis by presenting in (38) the derivation of *sit+k+o—sit+iek* (gen. pl.), the diminutives of *sit+o* 'sieve', as well as *kost+n+á* and *let+n+á*, the fem. nom. sg. adjectives from *kost'* 'bone' and *let+o* 'summer'. Note that in *kost+n+á* the //t'// is underlying, and that the relevant adjacency for Anterior Depalatalization is established at the X-tier (hence unvocalized yers are bypassed; for discussion see Rubach, forthcoming). We may add that the final rule of the postcyclic derivation is Prepalatal Spell-out (4/18), which applies to the /t'/ of *sit+iek*, adding the redundant features [−anter, +high].

(38)

Cycle 2	sit+Ek	sit+Ek	kost'+En	let+En	WFRs: dim./adj.
	—	—	—	—	Yer Voc. (5/13)
	—	—	—	—	V-Length. (6/62)
	sit'+Ek	sit'+Ek	—	let'+En	Cor. Pal. (4/17)
	sit+Ek	sit+Ek	—	—	Dimin. Dep. (32)
	—	—	—	—	Diph. (6/68)

Cycle 3	sit+Ek+o	sit+Ek+U	kost'+En+á	let'+En+á	WFRs: inflection
	—	sit+ek+U	—	—	Yer Vocalization
	—	sit+ék+U	—	—	V-Lengthening
		(BLOCKED by Strict Cyclicity Constraint)			Coronal Palataliz.
	—	—	—	—	Diminutive Depal.

```
         N
        /|
       X X
       \ |
      [+hi] e
```

	—	[+hi] e	—	—	Diphthongization

Postcyclic	—	—	kost+En+á	let+En+á	Anter. Dep. (28)
	—	sit+iek+U	—	—	D. Spell-out (6/66)
	—	sit'+iek+U	—	—	P-cyclic Pal. (37)

	sit+k+o	sit'+iek	kost+n+á	let+n+á	Stray Erasure

The derivation of the examples for *Eb*-Depalatalization is parallel to that in (38). The only difference is that *strel'+b+a* 'shooting', in contrast to *plat+b+a*, would not depalatalize, since *Eb*-Depalatalization does not apply to laterals.

8.5. POSTCYCLIC RULES: SUMMARY

In (39) we summarize the diagnostic properties of the most important postcyclic rules discussed in this chapter. The typology of these properties was presented in 8.1.

(39)

	Non-derived application	Non-cyclic application	Lexical information	Word level
Glide Shortening	—	yes	yes	yes
Anterior Depal.	yes	—	—	yes
Postcyclic Pal.	yes	—	—	—
ä-Backing	yes	—	—	—

While it is clear that none of the rules in (39) could be cyclic, it is not certain that all of them must necessarily be postcyclic rather than post-lexical. In particular, the last two rules could be postlexical since, for independent reasons, it is not possible to establish that they are limited to the domain of words. The relevant environments are simply not found at word junctures. The status of these rules must therefore be regarded as unclear. With regard to the first two rules in (39) such doubts do not arise. Even though none of the rules checks positively for all the diagnostics, the number of 'yes' answers is more than sufficient to assume that the rules are postcyclic. The point is that the 'yes' answers are found under the diagnostics that contrast the classes of postcyclic and postlexical rules.

9

POSTLEXICAL RULES

In this chapter we look at rules which apply in domains larger than words and which are hence postlexical. In particular, we consider Vowel Vocalization, Voice Assimilation, and Voicing. The first two rules apply both inside words and across word boundaries. On the other hand, Voicing applies exclusively at word edges and is thus a classic instance of a rule whose inputs arise first in the syntax.

9.1. VOWEL VOCALIZATION

The prepositions for 'in', 'with/from', and 'to' appear either as simple consonants or as consonant–vowel sequences (most examples are from Zauner 1966):

(1) *a. v—vo*: v Bratislave 'in Bratislava' *versus*
   vo vode 'in the water', vo vláde 'in power', vo foteli 'in the armchair', vo fľaši 'in the bottle'
   b. s—so [zo]: s bratom 'with the brother' *versus*
   so ziskom 'with profit', so sestrou 'with the sister'
   c. z—zo: z domu 'from the house' *versus*
   zo zápasu 'from the fight', zo strachu 'from fear'
   d. k—ku [gu]: k rieke 'to the river' *versus*
   ku gazdovi 'to the farmer', ku garbiarovi 'to the tanner', ku kuchyni 'to the kitchen', ku koňovi 'to the horse'[1]

The generalization is that the vocalic allomorphs of the prepositions appear if the next consonant is either identical or very similar to that of the preposition. Characteristically, voice distinction is irrelevant. Thus, *v* is realized as *vo* not only before *v* but also before *f*, for example *vo forme* 'in the form'. That the occurrence of the vowel in the preposition is conditioned syllabically rather than purely segmentally is shown by the fact that no vowel is found in phrases such as *bez seba* 'without consciousness', *bez sestri* 'without the sister', *pod dozorom* 'under supervision'. The consecutive identical consonants belong to different syllables in these phrases, and hence the vocalic allomorphs of the prepositions are

---

[1] In the context of fricatives there is variation between the vocalic form *ku* and the consonantal form *k*, for example *k(u) chlapovi* 'to the man'.

not used. We conclude that the surfacing of the vowel in the prepositions in (1) is due to constraints on permissible onsets.[2] These constraints prohibit sequences of identical or near-identical consonants. If such sequences arise as a result of syntactic concatenation, then the consonant of the preposition remains extrasyllabic. This situation is remedied by inserting a vowel:

$$(2) \quad \emptyset \rightarrow \begin{Bmatrix} o \\ u \end{Bmatrix} / *C \text{—}$$

The problem with the statement in (2) is that the distribution of [o] and [u] in the prepositions is not readily predictable. Needless to say, there is no general constraint against having [o] after velars and [u] after coronals and labials. Thus, (2) seems to call for a complex statement: insert [u] after extrasyllabic /g/ and [o] after extrasyllabic /v, z/. It is hard to imagine how such a statement would look when expressed in terms of phonetic features. To solve this problem we argue that the prepositions are in fact represented as sequences of consonants and yers at the melodic level: //vO, zO, gU//. Now (2) must be rewritten as a rule of vowel vocalization that inserts an X slot over the yer, that is, over a floating melody segment (see Chapter 5). Evidence for the yers in the prepositions comes from two sources. First, *vo*, *so*, and *zo* appear not only as prepositions but also as prefixes, and these can clearly be shown to contain yers. Second, postulating yers in the prepositions is necessary independently in order to account for the form of the prepositions in lexicalized phrases.

The behaviour of prefixes in (3) below parallels that of the prepositions in (1):

(3) *a.* pliest' 'weave'—v+pliest' 'weave in' *versus*
       viest' 'bring'—vo+viest' 'bring to'
       valit' 'push'—vo+valit' 'push into'
    b. padnút' 'fall'—s+padnút' 'fall down' *versus*
       sadit' 'plant'—so+sadit' 'plant into'
       strelit' 'shoot'—so+strelit' 'shoot down'
    c. mrznút' 'freeze'—z+mrznút' 'freeze through' *versus*
       systematizovat' 'systematize'—zo+systematizovat' 'make systematic'

---

[2] Interestingly, Zauner (1966) gives a vocalic form of the preposition in phrases such as *vo Zvolene* 'in Zvoleň' and *ku školníkovi* 'to the janitor'. In some other phrases he notes variation, for example *vo svetle ~ v svetle* 'in the light', *vo Švédsku ~ v Švédsku* 'in Sweden'. Notice that coronal fricatives *s*, *z*, and *š* are transparent with regard to the constraints on permissible sequences of labials and velars. For example, we have the vocalic allomorph *ku* not only when the adjacency is direct in the linear sense, as in *ku koňovi* 'to the horse', but also when *š* intervenes, as in *ku školníkovi* 'to the janitor' just given. The transparency effect is obtained if the constraints are sensitive to the minimal scansion in the sense of Archangeli and Pulleyblank (1987) and Steriade (1987). In that case, they check the adjacency of the particular nodes that are dependent on PLACE. In the cluster /g šk-/ velar stops are adjacent at the DORSAL node.

We know independently of (3) that prefixes have yers at the underlying level. This follows from the fact that the yers surface as [o] via Yer Vocalization (5/13) if the stem has a yer. Compare the vowel–zero alternations in (4):

(4) zo+dr+at' sa //zO+dEr+t'// 'wear out' (perfective) *versus*
    zo+dier+a+t' //zO+dEr+aj+t'// (DI)
    so+br+at' //zO+bEr+t'// 'collect' (perfective) *versus*
    so+bier+a+t' //zO+bEr+aj+t'// (DI)

However, in (3) above there is no environment for Yer Vocalization, since the stems have no yers. Consequently, the appearance of [o] in *vo+viest'* 'bring into' etc. must be due to the same constraints on permissible onsets as was the case with the prepositions in (1). The alternations in (4) throw new light on our analysis, however. They indicate that the prefixes have yers in the underlying representation.

The other type of evidence for underlying yers, this time in the prepositions directly, comes from lexicalized phrases, for instance *zo dňa na deň* 'from day to day', *ku cti* 'in honour'. The surfacing of the vowel in the preposition is due to Yer Vocalization since the following noun has a yer: compare *deň* 'day'—*dň+a* (gen. sg.), *čest'* 'honour'—*ct+i* (gen. sg.). These phrases are idiomatic. They are listed in the lexicon and hence they are subject to Yer Vocalization, which is lexical.[3] The discovery that such lexicalized phrases exist is not particularly surprising. An exactly parallel situation obtains in Polish, as discussed in detail by Rubach (1985).

To summarize, we have shown that the prepositions/prefixes *vo, so, zo,* and *ku* have yers at the underlying level. Therefore it is not necessary to assume a vowel insertion rule such as (2) in order to account for the vocalic form of the prepositions/prefixes in (1) and (3). Rather, we have a rule of vowel vocalization that applies after an extrasyllabic consonant:

(5) Vowel Vocalization

$$\text{\textcircled{V}} \rightarrow V \,/\, {}^{*}C —$$

The derivation of *zo zem+e* 'from the earth' is now as shown in (6). Incidentally, (6) shows that Stray Erasure, which deletes unvocalized yers, must take place at the end of the postlexical and not at the end of the lexical derivation. Thus, the yers in //vO, zO, gU// are still present when

---

[3] The contrast between *vo dne* 'at the bottom' and *v dnešnom svete* 'in the present-day world' makes the point even clearer. Disregarding Yer Vocalization for the moment, the segmental context is the same in both instances: /v dn'-/. Yer Vocalization applies to the lexicalized phrase *vo dne* but not to the syntactic concatenation *v dnešnom*, even though in both instances //vO// is followed by a stem that has a yer: compare *dn+o* 'bottom'—*dien* (gen. pl.) and *deň* 'day'—*dň+a* (gen. sg.). The root *deň* 'day' is found in the adjective *dn+ešn+ý* 'present-day'. Yer Vocalization is a lexical and not a postlexical rule.

(6) Lexical derivation

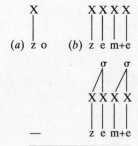

—   z e m+e   SSA: N-Placement, CV Rule

Syntax   *z zeme*

Postlexical derivation

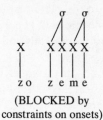

(BLOCKED by   SSA
constraints on onsets)

z o   z e m e   Vowel Vocalization (5)

z o   z e m e   SSA: N-Placement, CV Rule

---

prepositional phrases are concatenated by the syntax. Vowel Vocalization (5) is an example of a postlexical rule that applies in the domain of both words and phrases; compare (3) and (1), respectively. Had the rule been lexical, it would have applied only to the data in (3), since the phrases in (1) would not yet have been derived. The rule of Voice Assimilation that we discuss in the next section is of exactly the same type.

9.2. VOICE ASSIMILATION

Slovak requires that sequences of obstruents should agree in the value for voicing. This means that voiceless obstruents become voiced and voiced obstruents become voiceless before voiced and voiceless obstruents, respectively (examples from Kochik 1971, Zauner 1966, and Král' 1988):

(7) *a.* Voicing
    (i) inside words:
        pros+i+t' 'ask'—pros+b+a [-zb-] 'request'
        cvič+eb+n+ý 'exercise' (Adj.)—cvič+b+a [-ǯb-] 'exercise'
        mlat+ieb 'threshing' (gen. pl.)—mlat+b+a [-db-] (nom. sg.)
    (ii) across word boundaries:
        chlap+i 'men'—chlap [-b] zavolal 'the man called'
        golf+u 'golf' (gen. sg.)—golf [-v] budeme hrat' 'we shall play
          golf'
        ps+a 'dog' (gen. sg.)—pes [-z] breše 'the dog barks'
  b. Devoicing
    (i) inside words:
        srdeč+n+ý 'cordial'—srdc+e [-t-] 'heart'
        Srb+iek 'Serbian' (fem., gen. pl.)—Srb+k+a [-p-] (nom. sg.)
        muž+a 'man' (gen. sg.)—muž+stv+o [-š-] 'team'
    (ii) across word boundaries:
        muž+a 'man' (gen. sg.)—muž [-š] cestuje 'the man travels'
        plod+u 'fruit' (gen. sg.)—plod [-t] práce 'the fruit of work'
        dub+y 'oak' (nom. pl.)—dub [-p] padol 'the oak fell'

If we assume that Sonorant Default has not applied yet—that is, obstruents are specified for [voice] but sonorants are not—then the rule can be stated as in (8).

(8) Voice Assimilation

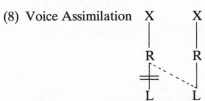

The value for voicing is spread from the laryngeal node of the following obstruent onto the preceding obstruent. Reference to the X-tier guarantees that unvocalized yers cannot block the rule.[4] Voice Assimilation is a classic example of a postlexical rule in the sense that it applies in both word and phrase phonology. A different type of a postlexical rule is exemplified by Voicing, to which we now turn.

D'urovič (1978) notes that West Slavic is cut by an isogloss which divides it into two areas with respect to Voicing. In East Moravian

---

[4] In all of our examples a yer intervenes between the obstruents, since, for instance, the nominalizing -b is //Eb// at the underlying level (compare the vowel–zero alternations in (7a) above).

dialects of Czech, in Slovak, and in Southern Polish, obstruents are voiced before sonorants if they occur at word edges. This rule is unknown in the remaining part of the West Slavic territory: Bohemian Czech, Sorbian, and North-East Polish. On the contrary, the presence of a sonorant across a word boundary serves as a devoicing context there.

Slovak Voicing is illustrated in (9). The examples in (9a) contrast with those in (9b) and demonstrate that the presence of a word boundary is an essential condition:

(9) *a.* pot+i+t' sa [-t-] 'to sweat', chlap+mi [-p-] 'man' (instr. pl.),
         št'ast+liv+ý [-st-] 'happy', hlas+n+ý [-s-] 'loud'
    b. brat [-d] i sestra 'brother and sister', chlap [-b] môže 'the man can',
         dost' [-zd'] lenivý 'quite lazy', hlas [-z] národa 'the voice of the
         people'

Voicing must apply after Sonorant Default has specified sonorants as [+voiced]. The limitation to the edge of the phonological word[5] (*mot*) brings out the difference between (9a) and (9b): see (10).

(10) Voicing

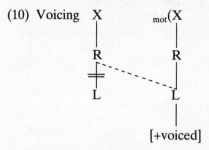

To complete our study of voicing effects let us note that obstruents are devoiced not only before voiceless obstruents but also before a pause:

(11) dub+y 'oak' (nom. pl.)—dub [dup] (nom. sg.)
      glg+u 'gulp' (gen. sg.)—glg [glk] (nom. sg.)
      zväz+u 'union' (gen. sg.)—zväz [zväs] (nom. sg.)

Thus Slovak has a rule of Final Devoicing that is familiar from the study of several other languages, for instance Polish (cf. Booij and Rubach 1987) and German (cf. Rubach 1990). The question is whether the proper context of the rule is the end of a morphological or a phonological word. For most data, such as those in (11), this is not relevant because the two coincide. A decisive argument comes from the study of prepositions that are made up of a voiced obstruent followed by a yer. These are the prepositions that we discussed in 9.1: *z/zo*[6] 'from' and *k/ku* 'to', which are

---

[5] The imperative clitic -*me* has the status of a phonological word since it causes voicing: compare *kúp+i+t'* 'buy'—*kúp+me* [-b-] 'let's buy', *kos+i+t'* 'mow'—*kos+me* [-z-] 'let's mow'.

[6] The preposition *s/so* 'with' behaves phonologically exactly like *z/zo* 'from'. The vocalic form *so* is pronounced [zo].

represented as underlying //zO// and //gU//, respectively. The voicing facts
are as follows:[7]

(12) *a.* voiceless [s] and [k]: z kina 'from the cinema', k tebe 'to you'
    b. voiced [z] and [g]: z domu 'from the house', k domu 'to the house'
    c. voiced [zo] and [gu]: zo sadu 'from the orchard', ku kapuste 'to
        the cabbage'

The crucial examples are those in (12*c*). They show that Vowel Vocalization (5) must precede Voice Assimilation (8) so that the latter can
be correctly blocked in (12*c*). In addition we must explain why Final
Devoicing does not apply in (12*c*). Two different paths of reasoning are
possible.

First, we might assume that Final Devoicing is sensitive to the end of
the word in the morphological sense. It is then rule (13):

(13) Final Devoicing (morphological)   [–sonor] → [–voiced] / —]

Since unvocalized yers, for example the nom. sg. yer in (11), cannot block
Final Devoicing (the rule applies in (11)), we must additionally assume
that (13) is extrinsically ordered after Vowel Vocalization (5) so that
the voiced forms can surface phonetically in (12*c*). Vowel Vocalization
counterfeeds Final Devoicing. In this interpretation Final Devoicing is
postlexical, because it is ordered after postlexical Vowel Vocalization.

Second, we might assume that Final Devoicing is rule (14):

(14) Final Devoicing (phonological)   [–sonor] → [–voiced] / —)$_{mot}$

Given this statement Final Devoicing need not be ordered after Vowel
Vocalization. Consequently, it may be interpreted as a postcyclic rather
than a postlexical rule. This interpretation seems natural, because Final
Devoicing is a classic word-level rule. The application of Final Devoicing
to the underlying //zO, gU// is now made impossible by the fact that
unvocalized yers are floating matrices. That is, they have no X slots and
hence cannot erect a syllable. It follows then that //zO// and //gU// are not
mots (phonological words) either, as the erection of the *mot* node requires
the prior existence of the syllable node. The derivation of *dub* 'oak', z [s]
kina 'from the cinema', and *zo sadu* 'from the orchard' is now as given in
(15). As a final step Stray Erasure deletes unvocalized yers: [dup], [s kina].
Note that the /zO/ in /zO sadu/ cannot syllabify into the onset of the *sa*-
syllable owing to the constraints on permissible onsets (see 9.1).

---

[7] In combination with personal pronouns beginning with a sonorant, *s* 'with' and *k* 'to'
should be pronounced as voiceless, for instance [s] *nim* 'with him', [k] *nemu* 'to him'. The
pronunciation [z] and [g] in these phrases is regarded by Král' (1988: 118) as non-standard.
To accommodate the standard pronunciation we must assume the existence of an allomorphy
rule that generates the voiceless variants.

(15)

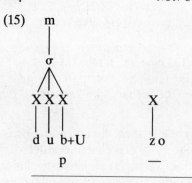

| | d u b+U | z o | *Postcyclic* |
| | p | — | Final Devoicing (14) |

| | *z kina* | *zo sadu* | *Syntax* |

Postlexical

— z o   k i n a   z o   s a d u   SSA

—   z o   Vowel Vocalization
                                           (5) and SSA

s   k i n a   —   Voice Assimilation
                                           (8) and Stray Erasure

9.3. EXCURSUS: THE STATUS OF *h*

In our presentation of the voice assimilation facts we avoided examples containing *h* since the representation of *h* requires some discussion. In this section we shall argue that the voiced laryngeal [ɦ], spelled *h*, must be interpreted as derivable from the velar obstruent //ɣ//, a voiced counterpart of the fricative //x//, spelled *ch*.

Before we proceed let us note that the distinction between *ch* and *h* is phonemic:

(16) chlad 'cold'—hlad 'hunger'
chodit' 'go'—hodit' 'throw'
slucha 'temple'—sluha 'servant'

We observe further that the distinction between *h* and *ch* is neutralized in devoicing contexts:

(17) *a.* Final Devoicing:
Boh [-x] 'God'—Boh+a (gen. sg.)
vrh [-x] 'throwing'—vrh+u (gen. sg.)
b. Voice Assimilation:
dlh+ý 'long'—dlh+š+í [-x-] 'longer'
roh+u 'corner' (gen. sg.)—roh [-x] stola 'the corner of table'

To account for these facts we can assume either of the following interpretations:

Interpretation (i): laryngeal //ɦ// is underlying and [x] is derived.

With this assumption devoicing rules produce a voiceless laryngeal /h/. To obtain [x] we need a rule that would add a supralaryngeal node plus the appropriate specifications for a velar fricative. Schematically:

(18) Supralaryngealization h → x

Recall that the feature theory presented in Chapter 2 characterizes [ɦ] and [h] as segments which are specified for the laryngeal node only. The change into [x] is thus an addition of the SL node.

Interpretation (ii): //ɣ// is underlying while both [x] and [ɦ] are derived.

On this account the devoicing facts in (17) are trivial. However, to derive the voiced [ɦ] in the related forms in (17) we need a rule with the opposite effect from (18): the supralaryngeal node of //ɣ// must be eliminated. Schematically:

(19) Laryngealization ɣ → ɦ

Three types of argument can be adduced in support of interpretation (ii), an underlying //ɣ//. They are: symmetry, palatalization, and free variation between [ɦ] and [ɣ]. We present them in this order.

Depending on which interpretation is selected, we obtain either the inventory in (20*a*) or that in (20*b*) in the class of non-labial and non-coronal sounds:

(20) *a.* k x —   *b.* k x
        g — ɦ   g ɣ

The one in (20*b*) is symmetrical, which speaks for the recognition of an underlying //ɣ//, as symmetrical systems are generally favoured over non-symmetrical systems. Preference for an underlying //ɣ// is further strengthened by the alternations subsumed under 1st Velar Palatalization (4/7):

(21) [k] → [č]: človek 'man'—človieč+ik (dimin.)
    [g] → [ž]: cveng 'chink' (N)—cvendž+a+t' //cveng+ä+t'// (V)
    [x] → [š]: tich+ý 'silent'—tiš+in+a 'silence'
    [ɦ] → [ž]: Boh 'God'—Bož+e (voc.)

First Velar Palatalization, as a rule turning velars into postalveolars, is understandable if [ɦ] has //ɣ// as its underlying source. Otherwise the pattern is deficient and the rule becomes practically impossible to state.

The last argument for an underlying //ɣ// comes from the consideration of the voicing facts. Král' (1988: 124) states that the distinction between *ch* and *h* is neutralized in voicing contexts in the sense that [ɣ] and [ɦ] are in free variation there, regardless of whether the input is *ch* or *h*:

(22) *a.* vzduch vel'komesta 'the air of a large city'
       nech berie 'let him take'
    b. prah domu 'the threshold of the house'
       vrh gul'ou 'shot-putting'

There is no doubt that we have an underlying //x// in (22*a*). It appears phonetically as [x] in, for example, *vzduch+u* 'air' (gen. sg.). Voicing rules turn //x// into [ɣ]. To obtain the free variant [ɦ] we need Laryngealization (19). In other words, this rule is necessary regardless of whether we assume interpretation (i) or (ii) for the underlying source of [ɦ]. Given that Slovak must have Laryngealization (19) as a rule anyway, interpretation (i)—that //ɦ// is underlying—becomes untenable.

In sum, Slovak has an underlying voiced velar fricative //ɣ// in its inventory and a rule of Laryngealization that we now state formally as (23). In accordance with the standard assumptions (cf. for instance Clements 1985), Laryngealization is a delinking of the SL node. The features hanging directly off the ROOT are delinked later by convention. (A segment that has no SL node must be a laryngeal.)

In (24) we give a few sample derivations. Our examples are *roh* 'corner', *roh+u* (gen. sg.), and *roh stola* 'the corner of the table' in (24*a*), and *drah+š+í* 'more expensive', *prah domu* 'the threshold of the house',

(23) Laryngealization

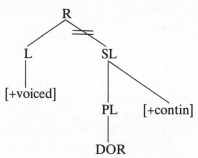

Condition: if word-final then optional

---

and *nech berie* 'let him take' in (24*b*). They illustrate the interaction between Final Devoicing, Voice Assimilation, and Laryngealization.

(24) *a.*

| roɣ | roɣ+u | roɣ stola | *Postcyclic* |
| rox | — | rox — | Final Devoicing (14) |

| | | rox stola | *Syntax* |

			Postlexical
—	—	—	Voice Assimilation (8)
—	rofi+u	—	Laryngealization (19)

b.

| draɣ+š+í | praɣ domu | n'ex berie | *Postcyclic* |
| — | prax — | — — | Final Devoicing |

| | prax domu | n'ex berie | *Syntax* |

			Postlexical
drax+š+í	praɣ domu	n'eɣ berie	Voice Assimilation
—	prafi domu	n'efi berie	Laryngealization

9.4. POSTLEXICAL RULES: SUMMARY

We shall now summarize the diagnostic properties of the postlexical rules discussed in this chapter. These properties include phrase-level application, that is, application in the domain of words and phrases, and syntax-dependent application. In the case of our data the latter means a restriction to word edges.

(25)   *Phrase-level application*   *Word-edge application*

Vowel Vocalization   yes   —
Voice Assimilation   yes   —
Voicing   —   yes

Laryngealization does not fit into this picture in any obvious way. As a context-free rule it applies of necessity in the domain of words, yet it must be postlexical owing to its ordering after postlexical Voice Assimilation and Voicing. Recall that Laryngealization is in part an optional rule. Thus, perhaps we should add optionality as a diagnostic property of postlexical rules.

10

CONCLUSION

The aim of this book has been, on the one hand, to provide a comprehensive description of Slovak phonology in generative terms and, on the other hand, to investigate how Slovak can contribute to the theory of Lexical Phonology and the associated theory of autosegmental representations. In conclusion we wish to draw attention to some of the most salient results which are of significance for theoretical studies.

Lexical Phonology, which is a theory about the organization of phonology, is best viewed in terms of a model that consists of three components: cyclic, postcyclic, and postlexical (Booij and Rubach 1987).

Only the cyclic component is permitted to interact with word-formation rules. These apply in tandem with cyclic phonological rules, as assumed in the classic version of Lexical Phonology (Kiparsky 1982). However, unlike the classic version, the model presented in this book does not envisage the possibility of having several strata that can interact with word-formation rules, at least not in the unmarked case. Slovak fully complies with this prediction: all word-formation rules are cyclic.

The postcyclic component contains word-level phonological rules which apply across the board—that is, morpheme-internally and across morpheme boundaries—because neither they nor postlexical rules are constrained by the Strict Cyclicity Constraint. The postlexical component has phrase-level rules which apply inside morphemes and words as well as across morpheme and word boundaries. However, there are also postlexical rules such as Voicing (9/10) which are restricted to edges of constituents. Characteristically, these constituents are prosodic rather than morphological. In the case of Voicing the environment is the edge of a phonological word.

A significant result of this study is the fact that no phonological rule of Slovak ever needs to apply in more than one component. This permits us to claim that rules belong to components rather than have components as their domains. What emerges is a much more restrictive theory than that proposed by other researchers such as Mohanan (1986): a rule is either cyclic or postcyclic or postlexical. This is the normal situation. If in some languages there must be rules that need to be both cyclic and postcyclic (or, even worse, cyclic, postcyclic, and postlexical), then such rules are exceptional.

With the result that rules belong to components rather than have components as their lexically assigned domains, it is possible to claim that we have ordered blocks of rules. This means not only that cyclic rules must always precede postcyclic rules and postcyclic rules must all apply before postlexical rules, but also that the status of a rule can be determined from its ordering. That is, if rule X is known to be ordered before rule Y and rule Y is cyclic, then X must also be cyclic. The significance of such predictions is demonstrated convincingly by the facts of Slovak (for example, see 6.7).

Slovak gives strong support to the two fundamental assumptions of Lexical Phonology: (i) that cyclic rules are subject to the Strict Cyclicity Constraint, and (ii) that derivations are organized according to the principle of the phonological cycle.

Strict Cyclicity is seen as a restriction to derived environments for rules that effect contrastive changes. Significantly, the environment counts as derived not only when a word-formation rule has taken effect but also when a structure has been derived by a phonological rule applying on the current cycle. This is a classic understanding of the derived environment and it goes back in its spirit to Kiparsky (1973). Derived-environment rules abound in Slovak. They effect all kinds of changes: from palatalization to diphthongization. There is also evidence that, in the course of history, rules may become subject to Strict Cyclicity, that is, they can change their status from non-cyclic to cyclic. A different status of rules at different periods of time is documented by the way in which borrowings are assimilated: early borrowings show the application of a given rule in both derived and underived environments, while later borrowings restrict the same rule to derived environments only. This is exactly how Coronal Palatalization (4/17) and Diphthongization (6/68) have operated.

The cycle as a concept is separate from Strict Cyclicity. Slovak demonstrates that it plays a significant role in derivation in three different ways. First, whether a rule applies cyclically or not has clear empirical consequences. Thus, in the class of shortening rules the Rhythmic Law (shortening after a complex nucleus) is cyclic, while Glide Shortening (shortening after a glide) is postcyclic. The effects of the two rules are different: the former produces an alternating pattern of short and long nuclei while the latter yields a sequence of uniformly short nuclei. Second, the cycle resolves ordering paradoxes of the type: rule A is ordered before rule B for one set of examples but after rule B for another set of examples (see 6.8 and 7.6). Third, the cycle explains a change in the directionality of application in rules which have moved from a non-cyclic to a cyclic component in the course of history. Yer Vocalization (5/13) is an instance of such a rule. At the time when it was non-cyclic it applied from right to left. Now, as a cyclic rule, it applies from left to right (from the root to the suffixes), exactly as predicted by the cycle.

Finally, the various types of rule—cyclic, postcyclic, and postlexical— exhibit different properties. In particular, they are differentiated according to the following parameters: cyclicity, derived-environment application, lexical information (morphological conditioning, diacritic features, exceptionality markings), word-level application, phrase-level application, and word-edge application (see 6.8, 8.5, and 9.4).

As mentioned earlier, the second area in which Slovak provides a contribution to a general theory of phonology is the paradigm of autosegmental representations. The least significant is the observation based on the operation of ä-Backing (2/13) and concerning the structure of the melodic tier. There is evidence that coronals and dorsals need to be able to form a class. This can be achieved if LABIAL is interpreted as a binary feature rather than as a node. A geometric layout of phonetic features finds support particularly in our study of palatalization rules in Chapter 4. It turns out that different palatalization rules must spread different features or nodes, for instance Coronal Palatalization (4/17) spreads [–back] while 1st Velar Palatalization (4/7) spreads the node CORONAL.

The contribution of Slovak to the study of the skeletal tier is much more significant than to the study of the melodic tier. The role of skeletal representation comes to light at both the interface between the melody and the skeleton and the interface between the skeleton and the syllable. The former is illustrated by the yers, and the latter by shortening and lengthening rules. Representing yers as floating matrices, that is, melody segments without associated X slots, provides a unified explanation for several different facts. Most importantly, it accounts for the visibility and invisibility effects: yers are visible to rules acting on the melodic tier, such as palatalization, but invisible to the rules of shortening and lengthening which act on the skeletal tier. Given that the property of being a yer is now geometric (absence of an X slot) rather than phonetic (laxness), it is predicted that any vowel can be a yer, and this is exactly what the facts of Slovak require. It becomes clear how it was possible to develop yers where they had never existed. A new interpretation of the yers simplifies the segmental inventory of Slovak because the distinctiveness has in part been transferred to the area of tier geometry. In addition, we have an explanation why yers have always occupied a special place in Slovak in that they, unlike all the other vowels, never contrasted in length. Such a contrast cannot be made for floating melody segments since length relations are expressed at the skeletal tier. The significance of the latter as a generalization has been made particularly clear by shortening and lengthening rules, which abound in Slovak. In a theory of autosegmental representations these rules are defined as operations on the skeleton: deletion or addition of X slots. It is thus predicted that distinctions holding at the melodic tier, such as those between long vowels, diphthongs, and (syllabic) consonants, should not play any role, which is borne out. The only relevant part of the representation for these rules is the relation between the skeletal and the syllabic tiers. It is now understandable how it was possible for Slovak to develop an opposition between long vowels and diphthongs such as *é* versus *ie* without affecting any of the quantity-sensitive rules: the opposition exists at the melodic tier only.

Investigation of the interface between the skeletal and the syllabic tiers has unveiled the existence of near-minimal pairs such as diphthongs versus vowel sequences, on the one hand, and glide-plus-vowel versus vowel-plus-vowel sequences, on the other hand. The relevant distinctions are then made at the syllabic tier, which has now gained significance because its structure cannot always be predicted from syllable-building rules (see Chapter 6). The nature of these rules was a subject of independent investigation in Chapter 7. Syllable-structure rules, both universal and language-specific, apply as a block and they reapply at every step in the derivation. These rules form the Syllable Structure Algorithm, which is characterized by its property of continuous application from the cyclic component to the postlexical component. In its application the Syllable Structure Algorithm is directed by the universal Sonority Sequencing Generalization and the heterosyllabicity of geminate clusters. It is also governed by the language-specific Obstruent Sequencing Principle, *j*-Constraint, and Prosodification Principle (the latter is perhaps universal).

The prominent role that syllable structure plays in Slovak is also seen in the fact that the identification of extrasyllabic consonants is crucial to the statement of a number of disparate rules. These rules are unified in their function of rescuing unsyllabified segments from Stray Erasure by providing prosodic licensing. The way in which the rescue operation is implemented is different with different rules. It ranges from vowel insertion (see 7.7) via vocalization of yers (see 7.2 and 9.1) and the syllabification of consonants (see 7.6) to changing the feature content of a segment in a way that makes the extrasyllabic segment syllabifiable (see 7.8). There are also extreme situations in which segments are forcefully adjoined to the syllable node (Initial Adjunction in 7.6) or to the phonological word node (Postcyclic Adjunction in 7.8). The significance of these operations is documented by the evidence showing that prosodically unlicensed segments are indeed deleted (or phonetically unrealized), as is the case in East Slovak (see 7.7).

This book has demonstrated at length that Lexical Phonology cannot be construed as an adequate framework without the associated theory of autosegmental representations. The opposite is also true, as shown throughout this study. Let us recall merely one example which illustrates this point clearly. Word-finally, extrasyllabic liquids are either syllabified or they trigger vowel insertion. These two extrasyllabicity effects are contradictory in that one precludes the other. The contradiction disappears in the framework of Lexical Phonology because, for independent reasons, Liquid Syllabification is cyclic while *o*-Insertion is postcyclic (see 7.7). Lexical Phonology and the autosegmental theory complement each other: the former determines how and where the rules apply, the latter controls representations on which these rules operate.

SUMMARY OF RULES

Below we summarize the most important rules discussed in this book. The list is incomplete with regard to the allomorphy statements discussed in Chapter 3. The rules fall into three groups: cyclic, postcyclic, and post-lexical. Only the rules subsumed under the Syllable Structure Algorithm apply in more than one component. In fact, they apply continuously throughout the whole derivation. Note that the suggested ordering of the rules is sometimes approximate. This is the case if the rules are mutually non-affecting. We follow the convention adopted in the book that the first number refers to the chapter and the second number to the rule itself. Thus, for instance, (3/20) means 'rule (20) in Chapter 3'.

I. CYCLIC RULES

1. SSA (7/34)

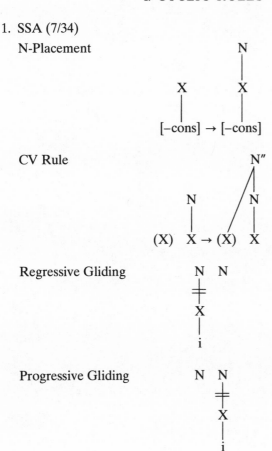

Coda Rule

Onset Rule

Complex Coda Rule

2. *j*-Insertion (4/40)

$$C \rightarrow C\, j\, /\!-\, [\text{-cons, } \alpha\,\text{back}]_{\text{VERB}}\, [\text{-cons, -}\alpha\,\text{back}]$$

3. CORONAL Specification (4/2)

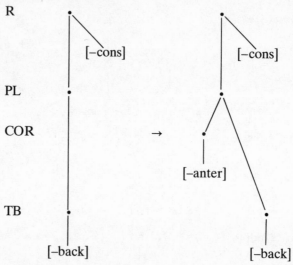

4. Glide Backing (3/56) $j \rightarrow [\text{+back}]\, /\!-\, aj\,]_{\text{DI}}$

5. First Velar Palatalization (4/7)

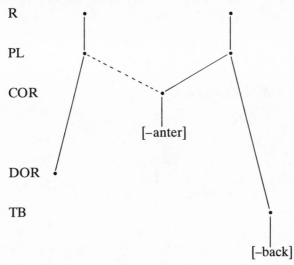

R

PL

COR

[−anter]

DOR

TB

[−back]

6. Vowel Deletion (3/8) $V \rightarrow \emptyset / - V]_{VERB}$

7. Imperative Vocalization (7/22)

X
|
$(i) \rightarrow i / *C -$

8. DI Raising (5/33)

X
|
$(V) \rightarrow \begin{bmatrix} +high \\ -back \end{bmatrix} / - C \text{ aj}]_{DI}$

9. Liquid Lowering (5/35)

$$V$$
$$[-back] \rightarrow [-high] / - \begin{bmatrix} +cons \\ +sonor \\ -nas \end{bmatrix}$$

10. Yer Vocalization (5/13)

X
|
$(V) \rightarrow V / - C \ (V)$

11. Vowel Lengthening (6/62)

$$X \rightarrow X \quad X / - C \ (V)$$

12. Nasal Deletion (5/39) $[+nasal] \rightarrow \emptyset / - C$

13. Liquid Syllabification (7/40)

$$*L \rightarrow L$$

14. *ova*-Shortening (3/61) $\acute{V} \rightarrow V / — ova]_{DI}$

15. Affricate Palatalization (4/16)

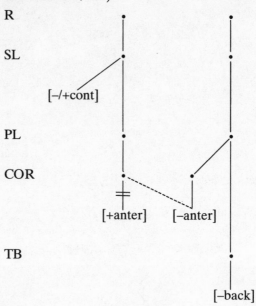

16. *aj*-Lengthening (3/53) $V \rightarrow \acute{V} / — aj]_{DI}$

17. *ík*-Lengthening (6/10) $V \rightarrow \acute{V} / — ík$

18. Numeral Lengthening (6/8) $V \rightarrow \acute{V} / —]_{ORDINAL\ NUMERAL}$

19. Fronting (6/81)

$$[+back] \rightarrow [-back] / SOFT —$$

20. *u*-Lengthening (3/36) $u \rightarrow \acute{u} / — t']_{INF.}$

21. Prefix Lengthening (6/14) $V \rightarrow \acute{V} / — [$
                          Condition: nouns

22. Fricative Assimilation (4/9)

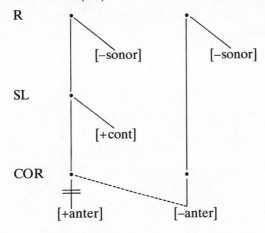

23. *o*-Lowering (3/55)   o → a / — C aj]$_{DI}$

24. Stop Dissimilation (4/10)

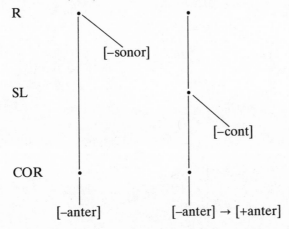

25. Coronal Palatalization (4/17)

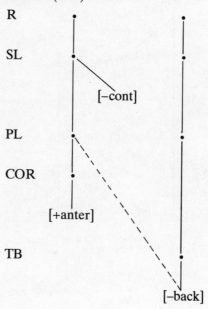

26. Iotation (4/41)

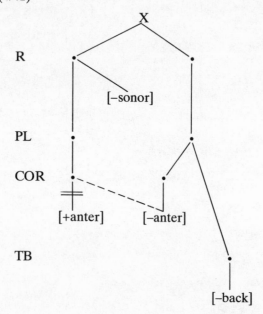

27. Affrication (4/3)

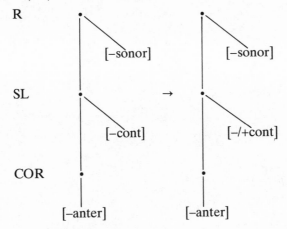

28. Second Velar Palatalization (4/13)

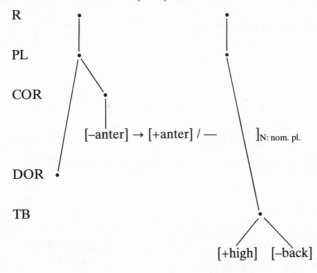

[−anter] → [+anter] / —   ]N: nom. pl.

29. Rhythmic Law (6/51)

$$\text{N} \quad \text{N} \qquad \text{N}$$
$$\text{X} \quad \text{X} \rightarrow \text{X} / \text{X} \quad \text{X} —$$

30. Postvocalic *j*-Deletion (3/4)   j → ∅ / — C

31. Yer Hiatus (5/52)   ∅ → j / V — Ⓥ

32. Closed Syllable Lengthening (6/28)   V → V́ / — C)σ]CLASS 1 VERBS

33. Diminutive Depalatalization (8/32)

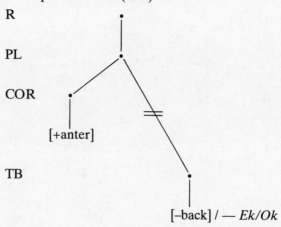

34. Initial Adjunction (7/49)   adjoin initial *C to the syllable node

35. *Eb*-Depalatalization (8/34)

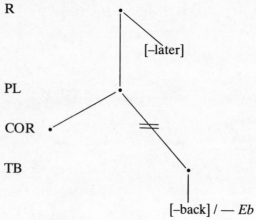

36. Contraction (6/73) $N_1 N_2$ $N_1 N_2$

$$X \rightarrow X$$

$$i \qquad\quad i$$

37. Diphthongization (6/68)

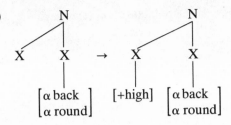

$$\begin{bmatrix} \alpha\,\text{back} \\ \alpha\,\text{round} \end{bmatrix} \qquad [+\text{high}] \quad \begin{bmatrix} \alpha\,\text{back} \\ \alpha\,\text{round} \end{bmatrix}$$

38. *CiV*-Lengthening (6/17) $V \rightarrow \acute{V} / — C\,i\,V$

II. POSTCYCLIC RULES

1. Dentalization (4/44)

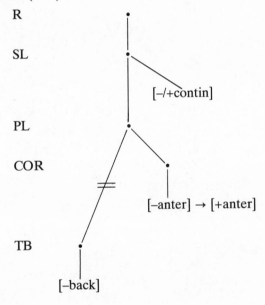

R

SL

$[-/+\text{contin}]$

PL

COR

$[-\text{anter}] \rightarrow [+\text{anter}]$

TB

$[-\text{back}]$

2. Anterior Depalatalization (8/28)

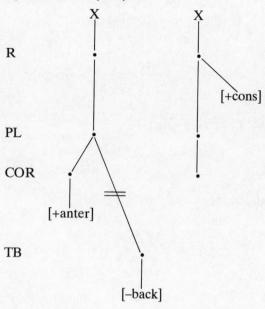

3. Diphthong Spell-out (6/66)

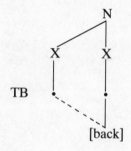

4. Postcyclic Palatalization (8/37)

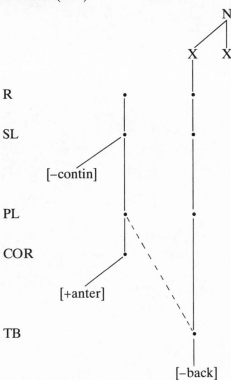

R

SL

[–contin]

PL

COR

[+anter]

TB

[–back]

5. Prepalatal Spell-out (4/18) $\begin{bmatrix} -\text{contin} \\ -\text{back} \end{bmatrix} \rightarrow \begin{bmatrix} -\text{anter} \\ +\text{high} \end{bmatrix}$

6. *o*-Insertion (7/53)

$$\emptyset \rightarrow \overset{\overset{\text{X}}{\mid}}{\text{o}} \; / - \; \text{*L}$$

7. Glide Shortening (8/12)

$$\emptyset \rightarrow \overset{\text{N} \quad \text{N}}{\underset{\text{X} \quad \text{X} \rightarrow \text{X}}{}} \; / \; [-\text{cons}] \; -$$

[+high]

8. *j*-Simplification (8/24)

C   j

9. Glide Strengthening (8/21)

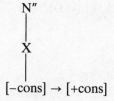

N″
|
X
|
[−cons] → [+cons]

10. ä-Backing (2/13)

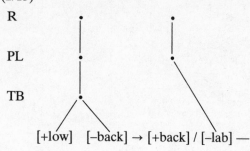

R

PL

TB

[+low]   [−back] → [+back] / [−lab] —

11. ü-Spreading (6/83)

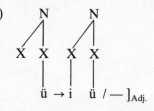

N   N
X X   X X
| | |
ü → i   ü / —]_Adj.

12. Round/Back Redundancy (6/84) $\begin{bmatrix} -cons \\ -low \end{bmatrix} \rightarrow \begin{bmatrix} \alpha\,round \\ \alpha\,back \end{bmatrix}$

13. Final Devoicing (9/14)   [−sonor] → [−voiced] / —)_mot

14. Änt-Allomorphy (5/47)   t → ∅ / —]

15. v-Gliding (7/60)

N′
|
v → [−cons] / —

16. Postcyclic Adjunction (7/66)

m
|
*C → C / $\left\{\begin{matrix} r \\ l \end{matrix}\right\}$ —

III. POSTLEXICAL RULES

1. Vowel Vocalization (9/5)

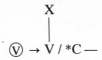

2. Voice Assimilation (9/8)

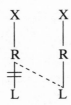

3. Obstruentization (7/63) $v \rightarrow$ [–sonor]

4. Voicing (9/10)

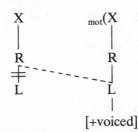

5. Laryngealization (9/23)

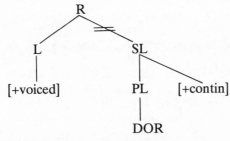

Condition: if word-final then optional

6. Sonorization (7/68)

$$v \rightarrow \text{[+sonor]} / \underline{}^{\displaystyle m}$$

REFERENCES

Anderson, S. R. (1974), *The Organization of Phonology* (New York: Academic Press).
—— (1982), 'The Analysis of French Shwa', *Language* 58, 534–73.
Archangeli, D. (1984), 'Underspecification in Yawelmani Phonology', MIT Ph.D. dissertation.
—— and Pulleyblank, D. (1987), 'Maximal and Minimal Rules: Effects on Tier Scansion', *NELS* 17, 16–35.
—— —— (forthcoming), *The Content and Structure of Phonological Representations* (Cambridge, Mass.: MIT Press).
Aronoff, M. (1976), *Word Formation in Generative Grammar* (Cambridge, Mass.: MIT Press).
—— and Sridhar, S. N. (1987), 'Morphological Levels in English and Kannada', in E. Gussmann (ed.), *Rules and the Lexicon* (Lublin: Catholic University Press), 10–22.
Bernolák, A. (1787), *Dissertatio philologica critica de letris Slavorum* (Posonii [Bratislava]).
Bethin, Ch. Y. (1992), *Polish Syllables: The Role of Prosody in Phonology and Morphology* (Columbus, Ohio: Slavica Publishers, Inc.).
Birnbaum, D. (1981), 'Rising Diphthongs and the Slovak Rhythmic Law', in G. N. Clements (ed.), *Harvard Studies in Phonology* 2, 1–16.
Booij, G. E., and Lieber, R. (1989), 'On the Simultaneity of Morphological and Prosodic Structure', Vrije Universiteit, Amsterdam MS.
—— and Rubach, J. (1984), 'Morphological and Prosodic Domains in Lexical Phonology', *Phonology Yearbook* 1, 1–27.
—— —— (1987), 'Postcyclic versus Postlexical Rules in Lexical Phonology', *Linguistic Inquiry* 18, 1–44.
Borowsky, T. J. (1986), 'Topics in Lexical Phonology of English', University of Massachusetts Ph.D. dissertation.
Browne, W. (1970), 'The Slovak Rhythmic Law and Phonological Theory', *Slavica Slovaca* 5, 253–6.
—— (1971), 'Some Questions of Slovak Morphology', *Jazykovedný časopis* 22, 49–57.
Chomsky, N. (1970), 'Remarks on Nominalization', in R. A. Jacobs and P. S. Rosenbaum (eds.), *Readings in English Transformational Grammar* (Waltham, Mass.: Ginn & Company), 184–221.
—— and Halle, M. (1968), *The Sound Pattern of English* (New York: Harper & Row).
—— —— and Lukoff, F. (1956), 'On Accent and Juncture in English', in *For Roman Jakobson* (The Hague: Mouton), 65–80.
Christdas, P. (1988), 'The Phonology and Morphology of Tamil', Cornell University Ph.D. dissertation.
Clements, G. N. (1976), 'Palatalization: Linking or Assimilation?', *Papers from the Chicago Linguistic Society* 12, 96–109.

—— (1985), 'The Geometry of Phonological Features', *Phonology Yearbook* 2, 225–52.

—— (1988), 'The Nature of Feature Representation in Phonology', a lecture given at the University of Bielefeld.

—— (1991), 'Place of Articulation in Consonants and Vowels: A Unified Theory', *Working Papers of the Cornell Phonetic Laboratory* 5, 77–123.

—— and Keyser, S. J. (1983), *CV Phonology: A Generative Theory of the Syllable* (Cambridge, Mass.: MIT Press).

Czaykowska-Higgins, E. (1988), 'Investigations into Polish Phonology and Morphology', MIT Ph.D. dissertation.

de Bray, R. G. A. (1980), *Guide to the West Slavonic Languages* (Columbus, Ohio: Slavica Publishers, Inc.).

Dogil, G., and Luschützky, H. Ch. (1990), 'Notes on Sonority and Segmental Strength', *Rivista di linguistica* 2, 1–54.

D'urovič, L'. (1973), 'Vokalický systém slovenčiny', *International Journal of Slavic Linguistics and Poetics* 16, 22–41.

—— (1975), 'Konsonantický systém slovenčiny', *International Journal of Slavic Linguistics and Poetics* 19, 7–29.

—— (1978), 'Morpheme Boundaries and Grammatical Meaning', in *Studia Linguistica Alexandro Vasilii Filio Issatschenko a Collegis Amicisque Oblata* (Lisse: Peter de Ridder Press), 87–93.

Dvonč, L. (1955), *Rytmický zákon v spisovej slovenčine* (Bratislava: Vydavateľstvo Slovenskej Akadémie Vied).

—— (1963), 'K jednému prípadu porušovania rytmického zákona', *Slovenská reč* 28, 224–30.

—— (1966), 'K otázke spoluhlásky l' v spisovej slovenčine', *Jazykovedný časopis* 17, 75–84.

—— Horák, G., Miko, F., Oravec, J., Ružicka, J., and Urbančok, M. (1966), *Morfológia slovenského jazyka* (Bratislava: Vydavateľstvo Slovenskej Akadémie Vied).

Dvončová, J., Jenča, G., and Kráľ, A. (1969), *Atlas slovenských hlások* (Bratislava: Vydavateľstvo Slovenskej Akadémie Vied).

Fabb, N. (1988), 'English Suffixation is Constrained by Selectional Restrictions', *Natural Language and Linguistic Theory* 6, 527–39.

Flier, M. (1972), 'On the Source of Derived Imperfectives in Russian', in D. Worth (ed.), *The Slavic Word* (The Hague: Mouton), 236–60.

Halle, M. (1959), *The Sound Pattern of Russian* (The Hague: Mouton).

—— (1963), 'O pravilach russkogo sprjaženija', in *American Contributions to the 5th International Congress of Slavists* 1 (The Hague), 363–82.

—— (1978), 'Formal vs. Functional Considerations in Phonology', in B. Kachru (ed.), *Linguistics in the Seventies: Directions and Prospects* (Studies in the Linguistic Sciences 8.2.; Department of Linguistics, University of Illinois, Urbana).

—— (1987), 'Why Phonological Strata Should not Include Affixation', MIT MS.

—— (1992), 'Phonological Features', in W. Bright (ed.), *International Encyclopedia of Linguistics* (Oxford and New York: Oxford University Press), 207–12.

Halle, M., and Mohanan, K. P. (1985), 'Segmental Phonology of Modern English', *Linguistic Inquiry* 16, 57–116.

—— and Vergnaud, J.-R. (1980), 'Three-Dimensional Phonology', *Journal of Linguistic Research* 1, 83–105.

—— —— (1987), *An Essay on Stress* (Cambridge, Mass.: MIT Press).

Havlík, A. (1889), 'K otázce jerové v staré čestiné', *Listy filologické* 16.

Hayes, B. (1982), 'Extrametricality and English Stress', *Linguistic Inquiry* 13, 227–76.

—— (1989), 'Compensatory Lengthening in Moraic Phonology', *Linguistic Inquiry* 20, 253–305.

Horecký, J. (1975), 'Generatívny opis fonologického systému spisovej slovenčiny', *Jazykovedný zborník* 4, 5–41.

Hyman, L. (1985), *A Theory of Phonological Weight* (Dordrecht: Foris Publications).

Isačenko, A. (1966), 'The Morphology of the Slovak Verb', *Travaux linguistique de Prague* 1, 183–201.

—— (1968), *Spektrografická analyza slovenských hlások* (Bratislava: Vydavateľstvo Slovenskej Akadémie Vied).

Itô, J. (1986), 'Syllable Theory in Prosodic Phonology', University of Massachusetts Ph.D. dissertation.

—— and Mester, R. A. (1989), 'Feature Predictability and Underspecification: Palatal Prosody in Japanese Mimetics', *Language* 65, 258–93.

Jakobson, R. (1931), 'Phonemic Notes on Standard Slovak', in *Studies Presented to Albert Prazák* (Bratislava: Slovenská Miscellanea). [Reprinted in *Selected Writings* 1, The Hague: Mouton, 221–30.]

—— (1948), 'Russian Conjugation', *Word* 4, 155–67.

—— Fant, C. G., and Halle, M. (1952), *Preliminaries to Speech Analysis* (4th edn., 1963) (Cambridge, Mass.: MIT Press).

Jespersen, O. (1904), *Lehrbuch der Phonetik* (Leipzig: Teubner).

Kaisse, E. M. (1985), *Connected Speech: The Interaction of Syntax and Phonology* (New York: Academic Press).

—— and Shaw, P. A. (1985), 'On the Theory of Lexical Phonology', *Phonology Yearbook* 2, 1–30.

Kenstowicz, M. (1972), 'The Morphophonemics of the Slovak Noun', *Papers in Linguistics* 5, 550–67.

—— and Kisseberth, Ch. (1977), *Topics in Phonological Theory* (New York: Academic Press).

—— —— (1979), *Generative Phonology* (New York: Academic Press).

—— and Rubach, J. (1987), 'The Phonology of Syllabic Nuclei in Slovak', *Language* 63, 463–97.

Kiparsky, P. (1968), 'How Abstract is Phonology?', MIT MS. Published in O. Fujimura (ed.), *Three Dimensions in Phonological Theory* (Tokyo: TEC Company), 5–56.

—— (1973), 'Abstractness, Opacity and Global Rules', in O. Fujimura (ed.), *Three Dimensions in Phonological Theory* (Tokyo: TEC Company), 57–86.

—— (1982), 'From Cyclic to Lexical Phonology', in H. v. d. Hulst and N. Smith (eds.), *The Structure of Phonological Representations* 1 (Dordrecht: Foris), 131–75.

—— (1985), 'Some Consequences of Lexical Phonology', *Phonology Yearbook* 2, 85–138.

Kochik, J. M. (1971), 'The Inflectional Morphology of Standard Slovak: A Descriptive Analysis', University of Pittsburgh Ph.D. dissertation.

Král', A. (1988), *Pravidlá slovenskej výslovnosti* (Bratislava: Slovenské Pedagogické Nakladateľstvo).

Kuryłowicz, J. (1947), 'Contribution à la théorie de la syllabe', *Biuletyn Polskiego Towarzystwa Językoznawczego* 8, 80–113.

Leben, W. R. (1973), 'Suprasegmental Phonology', MIT Ph.D. dissertation.

Letz, B. (1950), *Gramatika slovenského jazyka* (Bratislava: Štátne Nakladateľstvo).

Levin, J. (1985), 'A Metrical Theory of Syllabicity', MIT Ph.D. dissertation.

Lightner, Th. M. (1965), 'Segmental Phonology of Contemporary Standard Russian', MIT Ph.D. dissertation.

—— (1972), *Problems in the Theory of Phonology*, 1. *Russian Phonology and Turkish Phonology* (Edmonton, Alberta: Linguistic Research Inc.).

McCarthy, J. (1979), 'Formal Problems in Semitic Phonology and Morphology', MIT Ph.D. dissertation.

—— (1986), 'OCP Effects: Gemination and Antigemination', *Linguistic Inquiry* 17, 207–63.

Mascaró, J. (1976), 'Catalan Phonology and the Phonological Cycle', MIT Ph.D. dissertation.

Mohanan, K. P. (1982), 'Lexical Phonology', MIT Ph.D. dissertation.

—— (1986), *The Theory of Lexical Phonology* (Dordrecht: D. Reidel).

Murray, R. W., and Vennemann, T. (1983), 'Sound Change and Syllable Structure in Germanic Phonology', *Language* 59, 514–28.

Pauliny, E. (1963), *Fonologický vývin slovenčiny* (Bratislava: Vydavateľstvo Slovenskej Akadémie Vied).

—— (1968), *Fonológia spisovej slovenčiny* (Bratislava: Slovenské Pedagogické Nakladateľstvo).

—— (1979), *Slovenská fonológia* (Bratislava: Slovenské Pedagogické Nakladateľstvo).

—— Ružicka, J., and Štolc, J. (1955), *Slovenská gramatika* (Bratislava: Vydvateľstvo Osveta).

Peciar, S. (1946), 'Slovenská kvantita a rytmický zákon', *Slovenská reč* 12, 221.

Pesetsky, D. (1979), 'Russian Morphology and Lexical Theory', MIT MS.

Rubach, J. (1981), *Cyclic Phonology and Palatalization in Polish and English* (Warsaw: Wydawnictwa Uniwersytetu Warszawskiego).

—— (1984), *Cyclic and Lexical Phonology: The Structure of Polish* (Dordrecht: Foris Publications).

—— (1985), 'Lexical Phonology: Lexical and Postlexical Derivations', *Phonology Yearbook* 2, 157–72.

—— (1986), 'Abstract Vowels in Three-Dimensional Phonology: The Yers', *The Linguistic Review* 5, 247–80.

—— (1990), 'Final Devoicing and Cyclic Syllabification in German', *Linguistic Inquiry* 21, 79–94.

—— (forthcoming), 'Skeletal versus Moraic Representations in Slovak'. To appear in *Natural Language and Linguistic Theory*.

Rubach, J., and Booij, G. E. (1985), 'A Grid Theory of Stress in Polish', *Lingua* 66, 281–319.

—— —— (1990a), 'Syllable Structure Assignment in Polish', *Phonology* 7, 121–58.

—— —— (1990b), 'Edge of Constituent Effects in Polish', *Natural Language and Linguistic Theory* 8, 427–63.

—— —— (1992), 'Resolutions of Extrasyllabicity in Slovak', *Linguistics* 30, 699–729.

Sabol, J. (1964), 'O výslovnosti spoluhlásky *v*', *Slovenská reč* 29, 342–8.

—— (1989), *Syntetická fonológia slovenského jazyka* (Bratislava: Slovenská Akadémia Vied).

Sagey, E. (1986), 'The Representation of Features and Relations in Nonlinear Phonology', MIT Ph.D. dissertation.

Selkirk, E. O. (1984), 'On the Major Class Features and Syllable Theory', in M. Aronoff and R. Oehrle (eds.), *Language Sound Structure* (Cambridge, Mass.: MIT Press), 107–36.

Sezer, E., and Wetzels, L. (eds.) (1986), *Studies in Compensatory Lengthening* (Dordrecht: Foris Publications).

Siegel, D. (1974), 'Topics in English Morphology', MIT Ph.D. dissertation.

Sproat, R. (1985), 'On Deriving the Lexicon', MIT Ph.D. dissertation.

Stanislav, J. (1953), *Slovenská výslovnosť* (Bratislava: Štátne Nakladateľstvo).

—— (1977), *Slowakische Grammatik* (Bratislava: Slowakischer Pädagogischer Verlag).

Steriade, D. (1982), 'Greek Prosodies and the Nature of Syllabification', MIT Ph.D. dissertation.

—— (1987), 'Redundant Features', *Papers from the Chicago Linguistic Society* 23, part 2 (*Parasession on Autosegmental and Metrical Phonology*), 339–62.

Štúr, Ľ. (1846), *Nauka reči slovenskej* (Bratislava).

Whitney, W. D. (1865), 'The Relation of Vowel and Consonant', *Journal of the American Oriental Society* 8, 357–73.

Williams, E. (1981), 'On the Notions "Lexically Related" and "Head of a Word" ', *Linguistic Inquiry* 12, 245–74.

Zauner, A. (1966), *Praktická príručka slovenského pravopisu* (Bratislava: Obzor).

INDEX